Totally
FRANK

Totally
FRANK
MY AUTOBIOGRAPHY

FRANK LAMPARD
with IAN McGARRY

HarperSport
An Imprint of HarperCollins*Publishers*

This edition produced for The Book People Ltd,
Hall Wood Avenue, Haydock, St Helens WA11 9UL

First published in the UK in 2006 by
HarperSport
an imprint of HarperCollins
London

1

A CIP catalogue record for this book
is available from the British Library

ISBN-13 978-0-00-777839-3
ISBN-10 0-00-777839-2

Printed and bound in Great Britain by
Clays Ltd, St Ives plc

The HarperCollins website address is
www.harpercollins.co.uk

For the ones I love
Elen & Luna, Mum, Dad
Natalie and Claire

CONTENTS

ACKNOWLEDGMENTS

My Special People:
Grandad Bill Harris
Nanny Hilda
Millie, Mia, Stanley
Harry, Sandra, Jamie, Louise, Mark
Brian, Barbara and family
Gwen and family
Uncle George and family
Uncle Ken and family

My special thanks go to:
Ian McGarry for hard work, great writing
and becoming a good friend.
Steve Kutner for always giving me good advice,
always answering his phone, and being a special friend.

Thanks also to The Boys Tel, Billy, Alex, Finney and Hodgey;
Billy 'Blood' McCulloch, JT, Eidur, Jody and all my Chelsea

team-mates; all the Chelsea fans and everyone behind the scenes, Jose Mourinho, Roman Abramovich and Eugene Tenenbaum, Peter Kenyon, Claudio Ranieri, Ken Bates and Susannah, Sven Goran Eriksson, Laura Pollard and Claire Gilmour, Terry Venables, Tony Carr, Frank Burrows, Johnny Edwards, Mark Risley, Chris Boukley, Roso Khan, Colin Quy, and Terry Creasey. Sorry if I missed anyone out but thanks to everyone who has helped me in life and my career.

FL

INTRODUCTION

NOT THE END OF THE WORLD

IT'S a long walk. Those who have done it say it can be a harrowing experience just making your way to the penalty spot in a shootout situation. I know how tortuous it is. The second you break from the arms of your team-mates and take the first step you are very much alone, wondering where the journey will end.

For a footballer, there can be few trips in life as significant as the 60-metre path towards a moment that will remain with you as long as you live – like the walk down the aisle to be married or a sombre march to say a final goodbye to a loved one who has died. In those circumstances, though, at least you know what to expect.

The long walk to take a penalty invokes a similar intensity of emotion but without a pre-determined outcome. It's the World Cup quarter-final and the hopes of your family, friends, and team-mates, never mind those of a nation, weigh on your shoulders as you propel yourself towards destiny.

I can hear the cheers of the England fans as they try to encourage me – doing their best to ignore the nerves which make their voices tremble slightly. I focus my gaze on the white rectangle ahead. Not such a hard target. Twenty-four hours earlier I practised for this moment in the Gelsenkirchen Arena. Bang, goal. Bang, goal. Bang, goal. Bang, goal. Four from four after training. I knew what to do.

Back at the hotel I watched a DVD of the Portugal keeper Ricardo in action to discover his method of dealing with a penalty. However, his actions were too chaotic to act as a guide so it was a case of choosing a corner and steering it in. I had done this for Chelsea and England many times before. Stamford Bridge, Old Trafford, Camp Nou. Kick taken, goal scored.

I had been in exactly the same position two years earlier, in the Estadio da Luz, Lisbon, and at the same stage of the competition in Euro 2004. Portugal again. Ricardo again. Same long walk to the penalty area and same pressure. Bang, goal. I knew what to do.

Despite popular opinion, there is no certainty about a penalty kick. There is no divine right which favours the kicker or keeper on every occasion. I know this from history and statistics. I also know from experience – joyful and bitter. I missed one against Hungary at Old Trafford in our first warm-up match three weeks previously. It was my first failed penalty for England – not a pleasant experience. Still, only a friendly, so better to get it out of the way.

Since then I had practised regularly. England teams have traditionally taken stick for not placing enough emphasis on penalty technique but we were very assiduous. Every member of the squad took spot-kicks in training. As the elected penalty taker in normal play, I practised more than anyone else. I always do.

Fifty to be precise. I like to keep track. Fifty kicks and only two saved. Forty-eight successful strikes from a possible fifty. It had become slightly embarrassing because Paul Robinson and David James had only managed one stop apiece. They are both great keepers but I was very sharp – and confident.

As a squad we even practised the walk from the halfway line: familiarized ourselves with the solitude, the silence inside your head, the pressure mounting with every step. The only thing I hadn't prepared for was being first up in the shootout. That honour belonged to Wayne Rooney before he was red-carded in the second half after a spat with Cristiano Ronaldo.

No time for 'what if', only what is. This is our chance to make the semi-final, to avenge the defeat in 2004. This is England's year. This is our time. I look at the referee who signals that I must wait for his whistle. Fine. I'm in no hurry. Ricardo tries to catch my eye but I've seen his tricks before. I place the ball on the mark and turn my back to measure the run-up.

I decide to strike low left. That'll do it. Left and true. Left and true. I see the shot fly into the bottom left corner in my mind. I approach the ball and open up my body slightly. The strike leaves my boot but it's not how I pictured it, not quite wide enough, not hard enough. The keeper dives across and gets behind it. It's blocked. It's gone. Gone.

I feel numb. I look up to the night sky and see the moon. Luna. In an instant all that has been bad in my career concentrates into a single drop of poison inside my head. Scoring an own goal in my first-ever game aged five. A defeat in the final of a schools cup. Abused and hounded at West Ham. Defeat in the FA Cup final by Arsenal. Elimination in the semi-final of the Champions League.

I'm gagging but there's no vomit – only sickness. I begin the walk all over again. I hear the jeers from the Portuguese. I look to my team-mates, still locked arm-in-arm but now heads bowed as I walk the desperate walk.

A few hours later I am at the bar in the team hotel in Baden-Baden. I order a beer. Everyone else has gone to dinner but I am too nauseous to eat. The lads filter in a few at a time. We have a drink and the conversations start. Adrenalin pumps through my veins still and even though I am exhausted I can't rest. Everyone who played is the same. We pore over every detail of the match, vent our frustration about events, the decisions, Ronaldo.

I turn on my phone and a flood of messages come through. It's not my fault, they say. Keep your chin up. You'll come back from this. They are meant in kindness but it's the last thing I want to hear. When I go to bed I'm still wide awake. I watch myself hit the penalty again. Bang, save. Bang, save. Bang, save. F***.

I return to England exhausted. As we drive through west London I count the flags in the houses and on the cars. The sun is shining but the streets are deserted. The deflation has hit hard and I know how they feel. I don't want to show my face either. We get home. I speak to my Mum and Dad. More commiseration. There's no need. I know I'm not a villain and there's no one harder on me than myself.

Mum tells me to be kind to myself. I fall into bed and hope that I can rest. I sleep but the moment I struck the penalty is never far from my mind. I look around the stadium and everywhere the red and white which blazed during the match is doused with gloom. John and Rio are sitting on the turf sobbing, inconsolable. I'm in a daze and though people come to speak to me I can't hear the words.

I feel someone touch my face. Softly at first and then harder. There's a weight pressing on my chest and then gentle slaps. I open my eyes to see if I'm awake or still dreaming. Luna is lying on top of me scrambling around. Elen stands beside the bed smiling.

'Daddy,' says my little girl. 'Daddy!'

I repeat the name to her: 'Daddy! Daddy! Daddy! Daddy!'

Luna smiles her broadest smile and laughs with excitement. She knows. I laugh. Elen laughs and Luna laughs some more. She has said her first word and her timing couldn't have been more perfect. If only I had taken after my daughter!

Thirty-six hours since the time of my darkest despair and now the light comes flowing back into my life. When I missed that penalty I thought it was over. When we missed the third I knew it was. I have never felt so low and I never want to know that depth again. There were moments after we lost to Portugal when it felt like the end of the world. It wasn't. It was the end of the World Cup.

With one word from my baby daughter I realized the true value of life and the blessings I can count in mine. I have a successful career – never more so than in the past two years when I have won the top honours the game can bestow. There is a new season to look forward to and the challenge of winning more with Chelsea as well as qualifying for Euro 2008. There is also my work with the Teenage Cancer Trust and most of all my good fortune to be surrounded and supported by my family, my fiancée and my little girl. Football will always be an important part of my life but my family *is* my life. In reading my story I think you will understand.

CHAPTER 1

LAMPARDS AND REDKNAPPS

EVER since I was a child I have tried to reach heights that seemed above me. One was a bird cage in the back garden of my Aunt Sandra's house in Bournemouth. It was perched about twenty feet above the lawn and had been lovingly made by my grandad. Grandad was good with his hands. He was a carpenter by trade and often turned to crafting bits and pieces for his daughters. It was a beautiful thing made from wood and while nothing was actually kept inside it Aunt Sandra was very fond of it – as well as being proud of her well-kept garden. I loved going to visit her and Uncle Harry because it was the perfect mix of the things which were most important to me – family and football. Harry was a very imposing character even then, though later he would become a major figure in my life as my manager when I signed as a professional with West Ham United.

My Dad, who became Harry's assistant at Upton Park, and my Mum, who's Sandra's sister, would pack me and my sisters into the car and we would head for the south coast.

1

Natalie is the same age as my cousin Mark and similar in nature, and those two get on really well. My other sister Claire is a little younger but we all enjoyed our trips to see the Redknapps.

For me, the best bit was playing football with my cousin Jamie. He's five years older than me and so as a child I was always looking up to him – literally. We would happily play out the back for hours on end without much interruption from the adults or our siblings.

Jamie and I played keep-ball and I would chase him around the garden trying to get it off him. I followed him all over the place but he would just shield the ball, shrug me off and then knock it past me. It didn't matter, I just loved to play. I would sometimes get a touch on it but Jamie would keep control and I kept coming back for more.

I was a determined little bugger. Always running hard and snapping at his heels. I wouldn't let it go or give up but when we got tired we moved on to Jamie's special game. He placed the ball on a particular spot at an angle to the bird cage and then would try and hit the target.

First it was his turn and then mine. I was hopeless, too small to even get the ball high enough to threaten the thing. Jamie, though, was becoming a real nuisance to it. Wherever he put the ball down, whichever spot I chose for him, he rattled the wooden frame to its core with every single kick.

The poor thing was battered to bits before we knew it and Aunt Sandra wasn't pleased but Jamie and I just kept playing.

I was in awe of him. He was always trying new tricks and flicks and worked hard on his 'keepy uppy' and juggling. He was quite obsessed with it and was always practising. I was never into that sort of thing and even now I don't bother with it, which at times has caused me a little embarrassment.

I turned up to shoot a television commercial for Pepsi in Barcelona where the director had the best players in the world at his disposal. He was American and I'm not sure he really knew his 'soccer'. Before I arrived to film my part, guys like Ronaldinho had mesmerized him with their footwork while Thierry Henry had flashed through a special routine.

The director was clearly impressed. I got stripped, walked on set and waited for instructions.

'Ok Frank,' he said. 'Do what you do.'

I just looked at him.

'Do what?' I asked.

'You know. Your signature move. What you're famous for.'

I thought about it for a second.

'I tackle. I shoot. I score goals from midfield.'

It wasn't the answer he was looking for but neither is football all about tricks and flicks. Ronaldinho and Henry are fantastic players who can do amazing things with a ball. I admired what Jamie could do when we were kids but I was already being taught the basics of my trade and they didn't include any fancy stuff. Dad had a very clear vision of what would make a successful modern footballer.

Mum insists that I was holding and kicking a ball as soon as I was able but Dad was busy making sure that I was going in the right direction. He played in the garden with me, teaching me how to kick properly, and encouraged me to be more confident.

At the time, I wasn't really aware of who my Dad was beyond the familiar surroundings of our house and family. Playing football with a West Ham and England defender is not everyone's experience as a toddler but to me it was just messing about with my Dad the same as any other boy my age.

I would always prefer to kick the ball back and forth with him or my sisters rather than join in with a group of other kids. I was a shy child and quite self-conscious. As a result, it took quite a bit of persuading on Dad's part, and a lot of courage on mine, to agree to take part in my first-ever game.

We walked to Gidea Park which is only five minutes from my parents' house in Romford. I thought we were just going for our usual kickabout in the open space and it's only in retrospect that I realize he had arranged the whole thing. There was a local team training and playing there and Dad spoke to the coach and asked if I could join in.

I was excited and very nervous. The kids who were playing five-a-side were bigger than me and looked about seven. I was just five. The coach's name was Chris Snowskill and his son, Daniel, was already playing. I was invited on to the pitch and made quite an impression.

It was silly but I was so enthusiastic I couldn't help myself. Someone gave me the ball and I just turned round, saw the goal and battered it in. It was instinct. Basic instinct. I was well pleased with it and looked at my team-mates for some recognition. I realized something was wrong. It took a few seconds. Then I twigged from the way they were looking at me that I had scored an own goal. I was so embarrassed. The other kids were asking, 'Who is this little kid who scores own goals?'

I played out the match but was upset afterwards at my mistake. I was just so excited to be there and humiliated that I had messed it up. That day is my first memory of playing football. My first and, even now, quite painful recollection. Even so, it could barely have been more important.

The team I had joined was called Heath Park and the club would become an integral and important part of my life for the next decade. I played the next week, even though, strictly speaking, I was too young. It didn't matter to me and as it turned out, I stayed a year behind because I stuck with the same group of lads. It was a great education and a lot of fun. At Heath Park we won the league almost every year and when we didn't it would be won by our great rivals in the area – Senrab.

Essex has proven to be a rich breeding ground for foot-ballers and my era was no different. Senrab were more from the East End of London and had a bit of a rough edge to them. They were mainly working-class boys who were desperate to make it as footballers while Heath Park was slightly different. We were Essex lads.

Heath Park and Senrab have become quite famous as the clubs where players who have gone on to be a success began their careers. Ashley Cole, Ledley King, Lee Bowyer and J. Lloyd Samuel all cut their teeth at Senrab while a talented lad by the name of John Terry also started out there. John was three years younger than me so we never actually played against each other but even back then I began to hear things about him: how good he was, how strong he was.

Where I grew up, football was in people's blood. It was part of their DNA and it was certainly in mine. People talked all the time about the game and were interested in it at all levels. Nowadays, kids under ten go to academies which are part of professional clubs to train and learn. Others attend courses run by clubs or the Football Association. When I was that age, Sunday football was the academy.

It seemed that more often than not when we played Senrab in

the league that they would beat us but if it was a cup game then we would win. Fortunately, we had a habit of winning most of our games and when we won the league it was usually because we were more consistent than them. Our strength was in our team spirit. They had a few more 'individuals' and enjoyed playing that way but the rivalry between us was intense. Players were loyal to each club and people would talk about who was the best and who might make a career in football.

There was always a buzz about who the next professional player was going to be and at Heath Park it wasn't Frank Lampard. Michael Black was a team-mate of mine and everyone was sure that one day he would be a famous footballer. Michael was skilful, good with the ball and hard to beat. He was the best of the bunch – the Essex Wayne Rooney of his day. Whenever we played a game the would score or be man-of-the-match. I looked at Michael and made a decision. I wanted to be that good. In fact, I wanted to be at least as good and hopefully get better. That was how I felt at that age and I realize that it's been a recurring theme in my life and career.

Between Heath Park and Senrab we dominated the area and most years we carved up the trophies between us. I enjoyed my share of the spoils even if being the youngest of three kids and the only boy meant I had the smallest room in the house. That didn't stop me from getting it kitted out with shelves all around and I had all my trophies and medals stockpiled above me as I lay in bed.

We trained during the week and played at weekends. Our coaches would work on our fitness and try to develop our understanding of the game. When we played matches, though, it was more than just the manager's voice I heard from the touchline.

Almost everyone's Dad (and Mum) would turn out. Each would have different and constant advice for the team, which they would shout at will. You might think my Dad would have been at the centre of this scrum of tactical wit. What with his background and knowledge, the others would be quiet and let him speak. Not a bit of it.

He would deliberately stand behind the other parents, collar up and stay deadly silent. He was aware of the reaction he would provoke if he were to hog the touchline and shout the odds. More important, he knew how self-conscious I would be if he were to do that. Just knowing he was watching was enough to make me nervous so he became quite adept at pretending he wasn't there.

There were times when he hid behind a tree or a fence so that I couldn't see him. He must have looked a bit odd traipsing around the shadows like some football Inspector Clouseau. He couldn't keep up his disguise for long though. When I got home he would ask me how I had played. I would say 'pretty good' only to have him disagree. He would mention something I could have done better or a chance I should have taken and I realized that he had been there after all.

Dad has always been my football touchstone, my coach and critic, an inspiration and aggravation. I have an awful lot to thank him for even if sometimes I hated him. I knew from that very early age that I wanted to be a footballer. It was all I wanted. Dad knew it too and I think he wanted it just as much, perhaps more in those days.

He introduced me to certain training regimes which he knew would build up my physical strength and also instil a mental discipline essential to becoming the very best you can. Some of it was fun, though not for Mum. Dad would put mats down in different positions on the floor of the lounge in our house, then he would get a ball and throw it low down where I had to catch it and get up immediately when he would already be throwing it again in another direction. We would keep at it for ages until I needed a break. Mum would storm through the door shouting at us.

'Keep the noise down,' she'd say. 'And stop messing the place up.'

We'd stay very still. And silent.

'Honestly, you two think this place gets clean by itself.'

When it was safe to speak, Dad would get in his retort.

'It's important for him to be as agile as possible,' he'd say in the hope that his reason would register against Mum's protest about the housework. Mum turned on her heel and closed the door, pretending to be annoyed. We'd smile knowingly at one another and start again but it wasn't all good fun.

When Dad was at West Ham as an apprentice he bought himself a pair of running spikes which he wore when he practised his sprinting after training with the rest of the squad. I didn't inherit his shoes but I did get the habit. I think I was about ten when I started my 'spikes'. I would go into the garden and run the length and back repeatedly. It was important to start the sprint with a burst because that's what helps you catch an opponent or allows you to get away from your marker.

Almost every day I would do spikes. Mum got very annoyed because she had grown a beautiful lawn of lush green grass and there I was ripping it to shreds. Sometimes I did it with Dad's supervision, sometimes not. If Dad had been out and he found me in my room doing homework or watching TV he would always ask me, 'Have you done your spikes?' I was quite proud when I could say yes. When I couldn't, he wouldn't be forceful. Instead, he had a great knack of suggesting that if I didn't do them then bad things would happen. Not punishment of any kind. Oh no, worse – I wouldn't get quicker, more agile or have more stamina. In other words, I might come up short when it came to making the grade as a player.

For me, that threat was enough. Out I went no matter the weather and did my spikes. I still did them even after I turned professional. I used to hide them at West Ham's Chadwell Heath training ground because I was embarrassed but after training, when all the other older pros had gone home, I would run up and down outside the gym. Dad would sometimes catch sight of me from his office across the way and I would see him smile or nod. I became quite superstitious about it. Of course, it didn't help having Dad ask me all the time – even when I was in the West Ham first team. That was the thing with Dad. He didn't want to have to tell me. He wanted me to do it of my own accord.

It wasn't just me he affected in that way though. When Rio Ferdinand and I were apprentices at West Ham he would take Rio after training and do an hour's practice on his heading. Rio is an incredibly talented footballer. He can do things with his feet that a lot of ball players would struggle to. But when it was decided that he should be a defender, he wasn't the best with his head. Dad coached him and after a while Rio took it upon himself to find someone else to help him practise. The most important lesson was mental discipline and all of the players at the very highest level have it.

Gianfranco Zola used to hit more than a hundred balls every day after training was finished at Chelsea. When everyone else headed for the showers Franco stood in front of the goal and concentrated for a while longer. Bang, bang, bang. He was like a metronome. Even he, one of the most sublimely talented footballers I have ever played with, knew he needed to practise. It's common among the elite and rare among the ordinary. Wayne Rooney does it when we are training with England. So do I.

Dad introduced me to that, was instrumental in instilling it, and it has been crucial to my development. Now I come across young kids who think because they have a contract with Chelsea they have made it. They drive nice cars and can't wait to get into them and speed off after training. There are some good ones who will hang around and do a bit extra. I often stay on and practise shooting or free-kicks and one or two of the academy lads want to learn. They've got a chance of making it. I did my spikes and my agility training. I also practised in the park with the ball for hours.

Even before I signed for West Ham my Dad would take me to Chadwell Heath when the players had a day off and he would work on different aspects of my game. He would smash balls off the wall of the gym and make me stand with my back to the wall. I had to turn when I heard the ball rebound and react to whatever came my way. Dad knew that agility was a big part of succeeding in the middle of the park and I had to bring the ball under control. At times it was the last thing I wanted to do. Especially when it was freezing in the wind and miserable with rain. I still went though. He was obsessed with that kind of thing and in turn he made me obsessed. I was only 14 at the time.

I remember Tony Cottee was the man at West Ham then and Dad told me that Tony's Dad had brought him to the ground and done the same thing that we were doing. It was his way of goading me into trying even harder, a sort of 'He did it and look where he is' kind of thing. I remember thinking that if Tony Cottee did it then I wanted to do it. It wasn't usual to do that kind of work with a 14-year-old and I realized even then that my life was different from other kids. Most boys that age would never take up that kind of training but I was fortunate that Dad saw weaknesses before they were even there.

He was ahead of the game for that reason. He had a vision of how football was going and where it would eventually end up. When he played in the seventies, the game was much slower and less technical, athletic and competitive. It was completely different. Teams are tactically more aware now as well as physically stronger and my Dad, unlike a lot of others, saw that coming. He told me I had to increase my pace and strength. He would go on and on at me and I got fed up and angry with the constant nagging. When I was eleven I played in a game which hadn't gone well. Dad was angry with me but I didn't know what I had done wrong. He sat me down and got a pen and paper and explained to me how important it was when you played in midfield to cover runners. Before then, if someone played a one-two around me I would try to intercept the ball and the guy running would get played in behind me.

It's the kind of thing that most kids don't get coached on until youth level and there I was having it drilled in to me aged eleven. Covering runners is not fun and was probably the last thing I wanted to do. I was like every other kid who just wanted to get the ball and play without thinking about the consequences of the guy running in behind me. As you get older though, you realize their importance defensively and it gave me a head start.

I was already a very competitive child. Hardly surprising given my Dad's career though my Mum was always the one who encouraged me to keep going and do better. Right from the start Dad was great at identifying the things I should work on and needed to improve but it was Mum who told me I should do it for myself. There is a photograph from that time which was taken at one of the summer schools. Even now Mum reminds me of it. I was not a good-looking child by any stretch and there's me with my chubby little face and geeky teeth. 'Who would have thought that you would be the one who ended up playing for Chelsea and England?' she likes to say.

I am not alone in our family in having the honour to have played for my country. Dad played for England as did my cousin Jamie. When we were growing up, I can't say that it felt unusual to be surrounded by people who were so immersed in football. How could it be? It was mostly all I had known and I just assumed that every family was like mine. I was wrong.

Bobby Moore used to come to our house to see Dad. I would walk into the lounge and the two of them would be there chatting about West Ham and football, with Mum fussing around with tea and biscuits. It never occurred to me that the man who had lifted the World Cup as captain of England was sitting on my couch.

Even when we went to Uncle Harry's it didn't really register that there was something very different, very special about my family. It was just us. I used to go to their house in Bournemouth on holiday every year and it was like going to the beach. My cousin Mark was also a very good footballer but his career was cut short by a bad knee injury. Whenever we all got together we talked about football. There were exceptions but not many.

Summer down at the Redknapps was a great season and they had a big party for Jamie's birthday. The whole thing was over two days and when I turned up I was star struck. A few of the Liverpool boys were there, including Robbie Fowler. Trevor Sinclair was there too, though there was no doubt who the stars of the day were. It was the time of the infamous 'spice boys' and the lads had turned out in force. Jamie was very trendy and always first with new fashions. Quite a few times I got back from Bournemouth and told Mum what she needed to be buying to make me look good. On this particular occasion the lads were in Ralph Lauren shirts and tailored jeans.

There was a big barbeque in the garden of the house and it was crazy. There were gorgeous girls everywhere and, of course, Jamie was the king, the one they all wanted to talk to. It was an incredible sight. Jamie was cruising around with his mates, talking to everyone. I, on the other hand, felt a bit self-conscious. I was a lot younger and would not have blamed Jamie if he hadn't even noticed that I'd turned up. Thing is, though, he always had time for me. I can't imagine that too many big cousins who were in his position and at that party would have but he was very much like a big brother. When you grow up with someone like that you are always looking to them to set the standard and example. I went on my first boys' holiday to Cyprus with Jamie, Don Hutchison and couple of Jamie's mates from Bournemouth. I'm not sure how I ended up going at 17 but I persuaded my Mum it would be okay.

I had already been to Bermuda with my parents that summer. Dad did some coaching out there with former West Ham striker

Clyde Best. I put some suntan oil on my face when I was there and came out in a big rash. I couldn't believe it. I was going on holiday with Liverpool's pin-up boy and his mates and I looked a real mess. They were brilliant though. He didn't need the responsibility of having his little cousin there but he looked after me despite my beetroot face. While we were there we went into the main square of the town and before we knew it there was a huge crowd of people asking for autographs and to have pictures taken with him.

He was being really nice to everyone who approached him. I know now that it can become a nuisance. After all, you are there with your mates and trying to relax. In fact, I have seen players in that situation react very differently. I've seen some be very rude and tell people to get lost and the like – especially after a couple of beers. But Jamie was polite and it set something going in me. I thought that if I ever got to that level then I wanted to be like him. I appreciated how he was dealing with everyone. It was a lesson I wanted to be able to emulate. There's no doubt that the more famous you become the harder it is to have time for everyone. Even now, you can be in a rush or have the baby in your arms and the last thing you want to do is sign an autograph but I think about Jamie in that square and what it taught me.

There was something about Jamie – he could cope with the demands and the pressure even though he was only 22 at the time. He just handled it and got on with things. We didn't get to spend too much time together because of the distance between us when he lived in Liverpool but he always had good advice for me on the phone and I could call him whenever I wanted. He always had time for me and wanted to know how I was doing.

Even when I was 18 I was still learning from him. He came to train at Chadwell Heath when he was recovering from an injury while he was at Liverpool. We had a goal painted on a wall in the gym and in the corners of the goal were circles no bigger than the size of a ball. Each circle had a different number attached so that the top right corner was 1 and bottom right 2 and so on. Jamie and I wandered in there after I had finished a session and started messing around. He lined up a shot and shouted a number.

'One.' And the ball flew dead on target.

'Four.' Different corner. Same result.

'Two.' And again. And so on.

It was my turn. I was lucky to hit the goal never mind a circle. Jamie didn't laugh or take the piss. He stopped me and started lining my body up and then gave me some advice. That was Jamie all over. Always wanting to help. I guess because of that it was quite weird when we came up against each other on the field.

I played against Liverpool with West Ham and we were head to head in midfield. He went in hard on me and it was a little bit over the ball on the knee. He got up straight away, panicked that he had hurt me. Like me, he is very family orientated and I would not have thought for a moment that he had tried to do me but he was concerned that I was okay.

The tables were turned a few years later when we faced each other again when he was at Spurs. I caught him with my studs and almost ruined his good looks with a scar. I remember feeling the same panic he must have felt all those years ago. He ended up with about thirty stitches in his mouth and had to have surgery. He reminds me of it sometimes. I cringe at the thought.

I love Jamie the person – our relationship as mates has really blossomed over the past few years. We speak all the time and one of the things which says a lot about his character is that despite all the difficulties he had with injuries and sheer bad luck there has never been a single shred of jealousy about him. He has been a positive influence and encouraging voice throughout for me.

Jamie is one of those people in life who genuinely wants to know about others, their thoughts and views on the game as well as on life. He makes people comfortable and that's why he is such a natural on television and why he will succeed in management if he chooses to go into it.

Jamie was as good a role model as I could have wished for and as I got older the competitive spirit which had emerged in football began to manifest itself in just about every sport I took part in. As well as football I played cricket and was good enough to play for Essex at Under-12 to Under-15 level.

By that time my week was crammed full of sport. On Monday nights I went to Chelmsford to do nets with Essex cricket team. Tuesday was West Ham training and Wednesday was school team match or training. Thursday was Arsenal training while Friday was Tottenham and then on Saturday there was a school team game and then back to Sunday playing for Heath Park.

There was a point when I liked cricket almost as much as I did football. I was about eleven or twelve and Dad had played cricket for England schoolboys and was very good – probably better than me. He pushed me a bit but was wary that it might become as important as football. I liked it because I went to a school where they paid a lot more attention to cricket than football. I enjoyed batting and bowling. I was happy doing them and was more of an all-rounder, and that was what made me love the game as a younger kid.

At 14 I was playing in the first XI at cricket a year before I was at football which made it appear that I was better at cricket than I was at football but that wasn't true. Maybe the cricket team wasn't quite so good. I was a very stubborn little batsmen. I wasn't strong enough to whack it everywhere but I was dogged. I would just block what I couldn't hit far and stay in as long as I could – the Geoffrey Boycott type.

When I got older I had to field and that's when I lost patience as well as interest. A lack of patience is one of my weaknesses. My Dad also started to slip into conversations the fact that professional footballers earned a lot more money than cricketers. That may sound odd but as you get older and money starts to mean something to you, it has an effect. Not just the money but the glory as well. Football is the national game and number one sport after all.

I'm not sure how far I would have gone in the game – I can't imagine I was going to be a Freddie Flintoff – but it got to a stage when it was getting on my nerves. Mum and Dad had to pick me up at school at Brentwood and we set off on the journey to Chelmsford which took about fifteen minutes. I had to get changed in the back of the car which was a nuisance and I remember having the hump about it and started to make excuses so I didn't have to go.

I glossed over the issue with my parents with some petty story but the the over-riding reason for quitting was my obsession with perfection. There were a few people who were better than me at cricket and I didn't think that I could bridge the gap and that frustrated me. It was fine with football where I was good and thought that I could be better than everyone else. Being honest, that was why cricket faded out of my life. I accepted my limitations but it didn't mean I wanted to remind myself of them every time I played.

I focused on football and at 14 went to Lilleshall for the annual trials. At the time, Lilleshall was the FA's school of excellence for young footballers. They provided a two-year residential course which consisted of schooling as well as expert coaching. It was exciting but I was also nervous. I had broken my arm a couple of months before and I had it in my head that I wasn't as fit as I should be. There were thirty-two kids trying out for sixteen places. We had two days of tests and training as well as playing games.

I got down to the last twenty-four which meant I was on the way. Then we did the bleep test where basically you run between two electronic markers until you drop. The highest level was around fourteen and I only managed to get to eleven. I wondered what they thought of me as a result but there was nothing I could do. I was absolutely exhausted.

The day ended and I went home to wait for the final selection process which was done by letter. Two weeks later the envelope dropped through the door. It was nerve wracking. I had tried to prepare myself for the disappointment by telling myself that my broken arm had handicapped my chances. Deep down, I knew that wasn't true.

I was right about not getting in though. I was gutted. It was hard to accept the rejection. I was at a stage where I was regarded as one of the best players in Essex and I wanted to be the very best. To be told that I wasn't even in the top sixteen in the country was a heavy blow. Lee Hodges, who

I later played with for West Ham youths, was accepted though he decided to turn it down.

I wondered what Dad would think. In the end, he wasn't that bothered. Lilleshall had a reputation for being very old school and the kind of coaching they utilized wasn't necessarily what I needed. Players who have graduated from there have good things to say about it. You can't argue with the talent of the likes of Joe Cole and Michael Owen who went there and have become top professionals. In retrospect, though, it may have been a lucky escape for me.

I had been exposed to very different methods and levels of coaching. After the age of ten I started attending academy football at West Ham, Tottenham and Arsenal. They each had their good points – and their bad.

West Ham were quite antiquated in their attitude. They didn't really encourage you to become part of the club. There was a kind of arrogance where they just assumed that because you were a local boy who supported them then you automatically wanted to be part of their set-up. It was very impersonal. Spurs were actually the best. I had my eyes opened when I turned up to train and came across kids who were technically superior in many ways. It was all about the ball and what you could and should do with it. Not tricks but ways of beating a man on the run, or from standing still. I came up against boys there and thought 'I want to be able to do that.' They also had a different way of dealing with you. There was a meal after the session and everyone was friendly and encouraging.

Arsenal were something of a mix of the two. I enjoyed the coaching there though it was more physical. The people were very well trained in the latest techniques and seemed to know what they were talking about. For a few years I flitted between all three though it was clear in Dad's mind where I would end up playing.

West Ham were in my heart, as they were in his, and I played my youth football there at the same time as I was playing for Heath Park and my school. It was hectic but I was doing what I loved. I never really stopped to think about much else though there were times when I had to.

I began to realize that after I joined a new team or club and got to know people, some kids developed a certain attitude towards me. It usually didn't take too long. It had nothing to do with how fast I was, how good I was at football or cricket or how I spoke or looked. It was because I was Frank Lampard's son.

The majority were fine and I made some very good friends. But some kids can be cruel and are easily made jealous and I was the son of a famous footballer. I never hid the fact of who my Dad was. Let's face it, with a name like mine it would have been quite an act to pull off. I took a bit stick for it though and there were occasions when kids were determined to beat me at this or that because of who my Dad was.

It wasn't just kids either. At Heath Park there was a lad called Danny who played centre-forward. He went on to play at youth level with West Ham as well and scored a lot of goals though he disappeared after a year or so. His Dad used to come along to games and would slag off everyone except his lad. He would always have a dig at me because I was 'Lampard'. It really got on my nerves. I remember one game his son scored seven and I got eight but all he could shout was 'Come on Lampard, pass the ball!'

Michael Black and I would just slag him off on the quiet. It was our way of dealing with it, though one day Michael had enough and told him to 'F*** off.' He was only 13 and this guy was silenced for the first time. I preferred to just stay quiet and get on with my football. To be honest, I didn't really mind most of the time. I got used to kids reacting in different ways. When I turned up for a football game or athletics meeting most people were absoluetly fine but there was the odd time when I sensed someone was looking at me a bit differently.

I was shy but I wasn't ashamed. Far from it. And in a way, it worked in my favour because it made me more determined to do well. Not to prove them wrong but to prove to myself that I was better – better than them and better than the cheap shots about my Dad.

I was already good at football but that wasn't enough for me. I wanted to be good at everything. I concede that it may not have been the most healthy attitude at times. On one occasion I remember I was due to do a cross-country run after school and was so obsessed with how well I would do that I got a stress headache. It got worse throughout the day and was really thumping by the time I was changed and ready to race. I should have told the teacher and just abandoned it. But no, I was determined. I did it and I won but at the end I was just hanging in there.

It wasn't all about winning all of the time. I dropped in and out of other sports with the fashion just like most kids of that age. I had fun doing other stuff and hanging out with my friends but I can't deny that the desire to win was something which burned fiercely within me. Like the time I scored the own goal, there are other episodes which stand out in memory which I realize instilled in me the competitive edge which has been so essential to my development as a footballer and as a person.

When I was about seven I was due to run a 200-metre race. There was a another lad there who was bigger than me and was expected to stroll through it. I looked at him and thought I could take him. I was determined to beat him. The race went off and I fell a bit behind and then disaster struck; I fell over half way through it from trying so hard to keep in touch. I was distraught and had to be picked up off the track.

It was hard to get over. I was still in tears when I got home, and spent the rest of the day upset and hiding in my room. No one could talk me out of it. I was embarrassed but worse still, I knew what it was to fail.

Sport was extremely important in my life and usually came first for me but I was aware that I needed more than just games to get on in life. I suppose for a lot of boys who go on to become professional footballers schooling gets tucked away with your old uniform. My experience was a bit different.

Dad earned a good wage as a player and he and Mum wanted me to have a better start in life. I was sent to a fee-paying school to get a good education that would help me decide for myself what I wanted to do. Going to Brentwood was a great opportunity and one I'm glad of.

It's quite a posh school which has a bit of a reputation for producing high achievers. Sir Robin Day, and the comedian and actor Griff Rhys Jones went there as did Noel Edmonds. It was quite daunting to arrive at a place where the motto is 'Virtue Learning Manners', especially when you're a footballer's son from Essex.

It was a lot less stiff than I expected and I adapted quite quickly. My childhood – especially my craving for football – was undiminished by the fact that I went to school with kids who had been brought up without the obsession with football which I knew as the dominant force in my life. There was a real mix of different kids – some had parents who worked in the City, others were well off because their Dad happened to have done well in the building trade. I brought a strong sense of my own identity along with my determination. I was still an Essex boy with working-class parents who loved nothing more than football.

It was a new and interesting environment. None of my neighbours went there and I had a different outfit to some of the other boys around my street – including shorts and a cap in summer. It was very traditional but after a while the embarrassment wore off. Well, almost.

My parents felt a bit uncomfortable with some of the others at my school and they weren't really the type to get involved in meetings or administration. It didn't bother me except for one particular instance when it would have been nice if they had been paying attention to what was going on.

Mum took me in the car to school as usual but as we drove through the gates I realized that something was very wrong. All the children were wearing a different uniform. Well, actually, they all had the same uniform on – neat black shorts and shirts. It was just me who was wearing something completely different. I ducked down in the car like some kind of criminal and told Mum to keep driving. Why was I still in tweed blazer and trousers? Apparently, the uniform had changed for spring term but no one in our house had noticed. I was mortified and had the day off school while Mum went out and bought the new outfit.

She still laughs about that and it's a silly story but there is a serious point to it – people took the piss out of me because of where I went to school. All my Heath Park mates certainly did – mainly because I went to school on Saturdays so when everyone else was going out to play football with their mates or heading off to a game I was sitting in a classroom learning French and algebra.

It was very annoying. Like most kids, at one stage I really had the hump with school but I am thankful for what I experienced there and I made a lot of friends. My view of the world is a lot more rounded than it might have been and I think Brentwood played a big part in that.

On the whole, I was a pretty good student. There were a few minor scrapes that every kid has, though bizarrely the only real problem I had was the fact that I made the football first XI when I was in fourth year. A few of the older boys resented me for it. I was still just a young kid but I was good enough to play and I think some of the others were hoping I would fall on my face.

I didn't. They let me know how they felt at the end-of-year school dance when a couple of the older lads sauntered up to me to ask what I was doing there. It was more of a threat than an invitation to explain so I ignored them. I had done nothing wrong except put a few noses out of joint by being good at football. I was punching above my weight – something I have done most of my life.

The teacher in charge of our school team was a nice guy from Oldham called Chris Boukley and he took me under his wing and encouraged me to play even when the older lads were trying to intimidate me. Some kids tried to make an issue of my background being different to theirs but I had my own group of friends and I wasn't the only kid from 'new money'. There were quite a lot of us at Brentwood, and at football we used to play away games at the really posh schools like Eton. It was a very different world to mine. There were children from very wealthy and privileged families at my school but it was nothing like Eton.

You find your own way and make your own society in those kind of situations and I didn't hang out much with that crowd. We talked about politics and history but we still played football at lunchtime. I enjoyed learning but football was still my main ambition in life. Having to attend lessons on Saturday was difficult for me as was the fact that I played for the school team but was also playing at youth level for West Ham. It was only a matter of time before the two would clash. When they did, it was spectacular and the fallout was excruciating.

Dad bunked me off school so I could play an FA Youth Cup tie for West Ham. I never really thought much of it at the time. I was desperate to play of course and presumed I could get away with it. Anyway, my Dad was taking me. I played, we won the match and had a good game. Perfect, I thought. Wrong. I went to school the next day and there was a horrible buzz going about that I had been found out. The school team had also had a game the day before – the quarter-final of a cup competition. They lost, turning my absence into a major scandal when it might have been a minor irritation.

I sat in class like a condemned man waiting to be sentenced. I was guilty all right and if anyone doubted it they only had to look at my face. I was hoping for the best but knew it was a real issue when the headmaster marched into the room and shouted 'Lampard! Come with me.'

I was taken to his office and sat there ashamed and silent. He fetched a copy of the local paper and spread it in front of me. I was puzzled. Then I noticed a photograph of me playing for West Ham in all my glory. There goes my excuse that I was sick then. They took truancy very seriously, as they did loyalty and responsibility to the school and your fellow pupils. He told me that I had let down the school, my teammates and myself. He didn't need to rub my face in it. I knew already. Worse was to come. He sent me to see Mr Boukley to apologize.

I really liked him. He had paid me a lot of attention when I first arrived and had made me feel like I could succeed even when I had doubted myself. I was dreading the meeting. Of all the people that the headmaster had pointed out that I had disappointed he was the one I felt worst about. The rebuke was pretty brief but I was upset with myself after I saw Mr Boukley.

I was also pissed off that I got two hours' detention on Saturday afternoon – the worst possible. They made me write an essay that might teach me a valuable lesson: 'How Loyalty is More Important than Self-Interest'. I thought about it for a while and decided that I could be clever too: 'It's true, loyalty is very important but sometimes you have to look after your own interests because no one will do it for you,' was my conclusion. I was quite pleased with myself. My teacher, however, didn't find it so entertaining and got the right hump.

As far as the academic side went, I studied pretty hard while I was there. I was no fool and I guess the desire to succeed came across in class as well. I got ten GCSEs – an A$^+$ in Latin, three As, five Bs and one C – grades I needed to go on and study for my A levels. The school tried to put a case to me that I should stay on and I was promised that I would captain the football first XI. Mr Boukley made the point that it would be good for me regardless of my football ambitions to get a sound academic base. I could get my A levels and still go on to play football afterwards.

I thought long and hard about it. I got good grades in my exams and enjoyed studying French and Spanish. I went home and spoke to Dad. I had known for a couple of months that there was an apprenticeship for me at West Ham and that seemed the obvious thing to do. More than anything I wanted to play football, to be a footballer. But, when it was put to me that I should continue learning, it did turn my head.

My Dad turned it back. He was adamant I should take up the offer at West Ham. I didn't need that much persuading. I think I might have got bored with school. I wanted to play football more and more. I entertained the idea of staying on just in case I didn't make it in football and ironically, that was partly because all my life my Dad had told me how hard it was to become a professional player. It was what I had always wanted. It's true that when the school offered me a different option I wavered a bit but not enough. Dad was very clear: if I didn't do my apprenticeship then I wouldn't learn the real basics of the game. You need to know the background in football even when it means scraping the mud off of other people's boots and scrubbing the dressing room floor. Hardly the glamour of the professional game but essential.

It's easy for me to say I have no regrets. I don't. A lot of my mates went to a rival school and they went on and did A levels and then on to university. I have more experience now and I can honestly say that I'm not a great believer in further education for subjects other than science and technical ones. The likes of medicine and law are essential and clear about what they aim to achieve. I don't mean to sound snobby or judgmental but I went and stayed with some mates when they were at university and I didn't like the way they were living. There seemed to be a lot of time spent doing very little and experimenting with smoking dope and stuff and I have to admit that on that basis I wouldn't necessarily send my kids to university.

A lot of them didn't know what they wanted to do when they went to university and changed their minds a few times in the process. I realize that higher education can be of great benefit and is quite a privilege but I also think it can be a bit of a waste of time unless you apply yourself. It can also give you bad habits in life. I have this argument, even now, with my mate Billy Jenkins who spent five years at Durham University. We have known each other since we were five – he is the son of the former West Ham physio Rob Jenkins and we've always been close.

School was definitely enough for me as far as that academy was concerned. It was a positive experience and it gave me confidence as a person. Now I have an interest in the front of the newspapers – in politics and world affairs – as well as the back pages and football.

When I was a young professional I looked at players who had more to offer than just the stereotypical image of someone who is not very bright but earns a lot of money. I realized that people respect you if you have a bit more substance, if you are more than just another football player. It's important to be aware of more than football but unfortunately in our profession life can be very sheltered and being ignorant of the world is easy.

You get some kids who can't handle those who speak in a different way from them and react badly. I like to hold my own in conversation about politics and have been up until five in the morning with some of my mates arguing the issues of the day like Tony Blair's policies or the war in Iraq. I enjoy that kind of banter as well as all the football kind and I make no apology to anyone about the fact that I have interests which extend beyond training and ninety minutes of football. When I speak in public I am confident and, I like to think, quite articulate. For a footballer, that can be quite unusual. There is an unfortunate image of footballers – particularly some of the younger ones – as people who can barely string a sentence together. That may work okay in the dressing room but football is an integral part of society and maybe the clubs and the FA could take more responsibility for their younger players and the way they present themselves.

The schooling I had made me more fortunate but I still had to apply myself. My parents were not so lucky, though just as I had Dad as my football role model, he had one also. His grandad was a player in the army and so was his Uncle George. Dad was brought up with football and even as a five-year-old was playing with boys who were nine. It was part of the culture. Where he came from there were only three career options for any lad making his way in the world. You could work in Tate and Lyle's sugar refinery in the docks at Silvertown, you could live off your wits making money where you could, or you could become a professional footballer. Those were the only ways to better yourself and he decided at a young age that he wanted to be a footballer. He, like me, was frightened that he might not make it. At 15 he signed for West Ham when all his mates went to work in the docks. He earned £5 per week which was the same as those who were carrying sacks for a living.

The single-mindedness and determination which I have developed in my life and career were there in Dad. Even when he was a youth and might have been able to get away with going out for a beer with his friends, he would stop himself from the temptation because football was too important.

I had a different upbringing but we both took the decision very early in our lives that we wanted to make a career in football. He has always impressed on me the importance of doing things right, of being dedicated to achieve success. A lot of professional players whose Dads were also pros would be lying if they said they were not hard done by as children in terms of the way they were pushed.

I was pushed and Dad has never denied that. I always responded to his demands of me, not always in the way he wanted but he has a knack of knowing how to get the best out of me. He has put me through some really rough times. He never shied away from criticizing my performances and there have been occasions when I think he went too far. He admits that too. There have been screaming matches after games – times when he has had to drop me home and then go off to walk around the park near the house to calm down because things got out of hand between us in the car.

The worst I remember was after a defeat when I was about 14. We had a furious argument about the game and how I had played. I don't recall the detail but when we got back I was in tears. He tried to calm me down and took me to Gidea Park and we walked for about twenty minutes. He could see I was inconsolable and knew my Mum would bollock him when she saw me in that state. I managed to breathe deeply and got rid of the tears and we went back to the house.

Of course, there was no point in trying to hide it. Mum could sense there was something wrong but I ran to the bathroom, locked the door and got in the bath. I couldn't contain myself and was crying my heart out. I was still sobbing half an hour later. Mum has always been very perceptive in how best to handle me in situations like that. She knew there had been an almighty row and left me to get it out of my system before coming to talk to me. Eventually I emerged and she calmed me down. It wasn't just about what had happened in that particular match. At that time I was plagued by the insecurity that I might not make it in football.

Being told by Dad that I had played crap was bad enough. But being told every single fault in your performance by someone who had made it and knew what it took was worse. Mum helped me a lot in that respect and however substantial the debt I have to my Dad in helping me in my career I owe just as much to her for picking me up when I was down. She knows what to say and when. When to leave me alone to figure things out for myself and the right moment to reassure me when situations seem impossible. I don't blame my Dad for what he did. I know it was for the right reasons: for me, to make sure that I achieved my potential and realized my ambitions.

I also think some of what drove him to push me so hard was the fact that his Dad was not around to motivate him in the same way. His father was killed when he was only two years old when the truck he was in was involved in an accident with a bus about half a mile from where they lived. His grandad replaced his Dad as the male figure in his life, aided by his Uncle Ken. The insecurity which he suffered about whether or not he would make the grade came from not having his father around. Ironically, some of mine came from my Dad always being there.

My Mum is the counterbalance. She has a way about her that makes her capable of coping with anything. She has seen me take all kinds of vile abuse from supporters as well as achieve a lot of success but she is very down to earth and calm and has maintained the same level through all of it. When it's been bad she has been there with the right kind of support. There have been times when I was younger when I would have a bad game and my Dad was too harsh on me – partly because he was such a strong character. Mum could provide balance with the right words and when things were going badly at West Ham she heard a lot and but never let on and always tried to shield me from it.

She is the ultimate proud Mum who is very protective of me and I can only imagine how hard it's been for her on occasions when people have been slagging me off around her and she has had to bite her tongue and remain dignified. I have needed that in my life as much as I have been lucky to have Dad to teach me and drive me on in my career.

Dad is very thick-skinned and you need that to be a professional footballer. I have a bit of that in me but I have my Mum's nature which makes me a bit more sensitive in certain circumstances. We have both learned to develop a stronger side to our personality especially through everything that happened at West Ham and that has made the bond between us stronger.

The fact that I have two sisters who have also enjoyed the same levels of support and affection that I have makes me wonder even more at just how Mum achieves it. My sisters Natalie and Claire and I are very close. We had our childhood skirmishes the same as every family but they are both older than me and were very protective towards me when we were teenagers. Despite winding me up and calling me Wurzel Gummidge when I first spiked my hair, they would look after me when I first started to socialize in Essex.

Only four years separate the three of us but that felt like a big gap when I was about 12 and hated everything about the female race. All I wanted was to kick a ball around which was very annoying for two girls who were becoming young women. And they let me know it.

We all lived at home for a long time and while we would get on each other's nerves at times my childhood was quite ordinary but also idyllic. We did everything together. Christmas is a very special time for everyone and in our house we always had my grandparents round and it just felt right. Actually, it felt like that on any given Sunday when Mum had all of us for dinner.

That was part of her secret. No matter the arguments or fall-outs, and no matter who they were between, Mum knew the importance of bringing us all together. Every night the Lampards would sit down and eat dinner at the same time. Every night. There were some exceptions but no excuses. It worked.

As I grew up I began to appreciate Natalie and Claire more. They were very understanding towards me even though I could often be the annoying little brother. Because of the football and, I suppose, because I was the only son, Dad had always paid me a lot of attention. He was great with them too but there must have been times when they felt a bit left out. Remarkably, Mum would mediate and negotiate through all of this.

I'm glad they persevered with me and I distinctly remember my feelings change towards them when I was 15. There is a time when most boys finally start to appreciate their sisters for who they are. I did and fell in love with them. After that, there hasn't been a moment when I have not felt their love and support. Not once.

As the youngest in the family, I looked up to them and respected them and I was lucky that I learned how much it meant to have them at quite a young age. Natalie can be quite combative and there were a few instances when she got involved with punters at West Ham when they were slagging me off. It's not just fans though. She loves football and has very strong opinions and it's not unusual for her to call me after an England game and say 'Why did Eriksson take you off when so and so was s***?'

We are lucky because we still spend a lot of time together with our partners and our children and the environment we grew up in has very much continued and grown bigger. Mum has been the central figure in our family life and still is now with the grandchildren whom she is very much involved with.

Life, however, can become quite heated at times in a family which is as competitive as ours but she is a very calming influence. If I have had a bad game then I would always call Mum whereas I don't want to speak to Dad. He will only tell me the things that I did wrong and I punish myself enough for them. Not with Mum. She might not even talk about football with me but having a conversation with her just helps me get some balance back. It's not that she doesn't have an opinion or isn't passionate about my football. I know that she has had arguments with Harry if I wasn't playing at West Ham. They wouldn't be straightforward 'Why's my boy not getting a game?' either. She was more subtle than that. She would just throw in a remark about some other midfielder who maybe wasn't playing so well and Harry would suddenly pick up what she was getting at. She wasn't alone. One evening her Dad – Pop to me – was at Harry's house for dinner at a time when I wasn't getting a game. Pop had been talking football with Harry and working his way towards the subject of me and why I wasn't in the team. Eventually, he ran out of patience and asked outright.

'So Harry, why's young Frank not getting a game at the moment?' Pop asked.

'Because I say so, that's why. He's not Maradona, your grandson,' Harry replied.

I quite liked Harry's comeback. Hearing those stories helps me better understand the emotion involved for every one of my family when it comes to football. I don't hold any grudges. Far from it. It makes me proud that I come from stock which is so passionate about football and is not afraid to express it. With Pop I can see where Mum got her sharp wit and she can be equally blunt as Pop when she chooses to be.

We were sitting at a table in the Royal Lancaster Hotel the night I was named Football Writers' Player of the Year in 2005 and a journalist who had been particularly nasty in print about me during my first year at Chelsea was sitting talking to her. He was saying how well I had done and so on. She listened politely, nodding her head in appreciation until he had finished and then just cut him down with one sentence: 'You didn't always say that about him though did you?'

It's not in my nature to be confrontational. It's not in her's either but when it comes to protecting her children she will do whatever she judges to be right. I have only ever had one row with Mum. We were in a shopping centre and I was being a little brat, wanting to do something that she didn't. We had words and fell out for about twenty minutes until I went crying to her saying that I didn't want to row with her anymore. And we haven't since, not even in the worst moments when I have done something stupid or am being stubborn. When the *News of the World* published the story of me and a few other players cavorting on video with some girls while on holiday in Ayia Napa my Mum didn't shout at me. Dad did. He came down on me like a ton of bricks though I couldn't tell you what he said. But I do remember very clearly what happened with Mum.

I was sitting in the bathroom of my flat feeling sick as a dog and sorry for myself. Mum phoned and said that footballers who get involved in stuff like this end up in the gutter with their career down the drain. She was very emotional, not crying but I could tell how upset she was from the tone of her voice. I can honestly say that her reaction had more effect on me than anything else about the whole business.

I am very proud of what I have inherited from my parents. My Mum's perception, humanity and sensitivity have helped me become the person I am whereas I would never have become a footballer had it not been for my Dad's ambition, hard work and vision. You need to find the middle ground.

I was always worried that I might not make it and it gives me extra pleasure now knowing what I have achieved. I knew I would never lose the tag of 'somebody's son, somebody's nephew' while I was at Upton Park. It's hard enough to emerge from the shadow of other people when it's just your team-mates and peers.

I was always measured against my own flesh and blood but I feel differently now. I know how proud my family are of me. And, just as important, how proud I am of them.

CHAPTER 2

THE ACADEMY OF FOOTBALL

ENTERING the 'Academy of Football' wasn't quite what I expected. West Ham United had prided themselves on producing some of England's finest and most successful footballers. They revelled in the rich history which had seen the graduation of players such as John Bond, Martin Peters, Geoff Hurst and of course, Bobby Moore. They still do.

Three of those players were at the very heart of England's World Cup winning team in 1966 and their achievements helped make the claret and blue shirt a symbol of all that was great about football. Dad and Uncle Harry played under Ron Greenwood in the same West Ham side as Moore and I was brought up on stories of the glory days.

My nan lived a mile away from Upton Park and used to go to games to watch my Dad before I was born. She is well known around the club and is looked on very fondly by people she once gave sweets out to as kids who still go there now. I was one of those children as were my sisters and cousins. When I was older, I would sometimes play a match and then take her some pie and mash. On other occasions I would pop round and she would make me a sandwich with big lumps of cheese and pickle. We'd talk about the football and catch up on family news. She was neighbours with West Ham and grew up with the club. So did Mum and her sister and when they chose their husbands they joined more than the institution of marriage – they got West Ham United as well.

None of this was strange. When you grow up in a community which reveres the local club the way West Ham is treated by a section of London's East End, family and football go together like man and wife. Me and my sisters inherited our allegiance and were staunch in our support.

Around our house were little bits of memorabilia which made the film footage of the old days more immediate to a boy born between the two famous FA Cup victories of 1975 and 1980. I have seen the photographs a thousand times and asked Dad to tell me again and again what it was like to play for our team. By day, I would work hard on my football and by night I dreamt of the moment I would follow in my father's footsteps and pull on a West Ham shirt. The dream was perfect but the reality was less than ideal.

Jamie had been put on schoolboy forms with the club before I joined. Uncle Harry had wanted him to go there because that was where he had learned his trade and with our family tradition, it seemed the natural thing to do. Blood, after all, is thicker than water.

Jamie, though, was not impressed with what he found at West Ham. Eddie Bailey was head of youth development at the club which was ironic given that you would have been hard pressed to find someone who was more old school. The coaching was below par and not aimed at developing and nurturing talent. The people who ran the team were older and it seemed they were still using the same methods which had brought through the likes of Dad, Trevor Brooking and Paul Allen. That was fine except football had moved on significantly in terms of physical fitness, muscle development and technical coaching. It was 1994.

Those aspects were very important and they might have gotten away with an inferior coaching regime had the feeling at the club reflected the community which turned out in their thousands to support them every week. People looked at West Ham as a family club. The East End ethos has always been that you looked after your own. However, that didn't happen with the apprentice professionals.

Jamie was perceptive and decided pretty quickly that he was not going to learn what he needed there. He was a very gifted footballer and wasn't afraid to work hard on his game but he left and joined the Tottenham academy before signing a Youth Training Scheme (YTS) form there. I was surprised by his decision at the time. I'm not sure Uncle Harry was shocked but he respected Jamie's wishes. I asked Jamie about his reasons and we talked a little. He picked up on a certain attitude within West Ham which I had an inkling about when the club first started talking to me about an apprenticeship. Whenever I asked questions about why I should commit to them instead of another club the answer always seemed to be a variation on the same theme. We have a long history of bringing through our own players. We give young players a chance more quickly. West Ham is the Academy of Football.

I wasn't convinced and clearly, Jamie had gone in the opposite direction. I had played youth football with West Ham for a few years and had trained there extensively. I had also gone to Tottenham and Arsenal where the training was much more skills based and I felt I was improving my technique. There were other reasons too which were important. Most 16-year-olds suffer bouts of insecurity about whether or not they are going to make it. You need to be told and encouraged, nurtured. At Arsenal, I got a lot of attention from people like Steve Rowley who is a very experienced guy and is still the chief scout. He would come and pick me up and take me over for games at Arsenal's training centre at London Colney and I remember feeling that I wanted to sign for Arsenal simply because of the treatment I got there. They were extremely professional but more than that, it was the personal touch that made the difference, that made me feel wanted.

They were little things. Steve would take me for some dinner after a game – usually sausage and chips – and talk through what had happened, what I had done well, where I might improve. Afterwards, he would come in and talk to Mum and Dad about how I was progressing. He had a way about him which was caring and which made me feel that Arsenal was a place where they wanted you to do well. He scouted me to start with and spent a lot of time with me. But it wasn't just me. He did it with a lot of other kids as well and that is why he has had such a successful career at Arsenal.

All of this was in stark contrast to my experience at West Ham and I started wondering if I was getting the support I needed there. In a way, it didn't take much to work out why great players like Tony Adams and Ray Parlour had ended up at Arsenal. Both of them were local boys from Essex. Ray is a Romford lad just like me. They were West Ham fans as were their families and both had played youth football for the club. Neither signed.

John Terry was a couple of years below me and lived and breathed West Ham the same as the rest of his family and friends. Dad remembers him playing and training at the club until he was 14 and then he went to Chelsea. There have been others. Some stay, some get away. That's a fact of life. I can't help thinking that it could have been different if the club's attitude had been less arrogant.

At the time, Billy Bonds was the manager, Uncle Harry was a coach and Dad was a part-time scout. None were directly involved in the youth team and when the time came and I had to decide who to sign for, I was in a dilemma.

I had serious thoughts about playing for Tottenham. The coaching was of a higher quality, they were the first team to scout me and I had links there through Jamie - even though in the end he went back to Bournemouth to do his apprenticeship because he was homesick. I had seen a lot of good players from my area go to Spurs. And they had a new training ground. I confess, I was very tempted. They even offered me more money. In fact, Arsenal offered a better contract as well though the difference between them and West Ham financially wasn't huge.

The real bottom line was that money would never be the most important factor. I was a fan and had supported the team all my life. Dad sensed my indecision and asked Jimmy Neighbour to come and talk to me. Jimmy was in charge of schoolboys at West Ham and had served the club well as a skilful winger. He arrived at the house and was brought in to talk to me. At the time, I had no idea that he was there at the request of Dad. He told me that the club knew I was in demand and that he wasn't surprised; that I was a promising young player who had the potential to become a very good professional.

It was nice to hear. Even if it had taken awhile, better late than never and in my case, just in time. Only now can I really see that I signed for West Ham out of emotion rather than good sense, or even football sense. Dad had a lot to do with it. He put pressure on me even though he tried to let me make my own decision as much as possible. He was funny that way. He would insist that it was my life, my career and I should do what I felt was right for me. And then, if he sensed I was straying from what he thought was the right thing he would intervene, like asking Jimmy Neighbour to have a chat with me. Typical really. He made the point that I would get into the first team earlier at West Ham because the standard wasn't as high there and there were all sorts of other emotional reasons why I should sign – all of which I felt the weight of.

The first YTS contract I signed paid me £30 a week with another £50 which went to Mum for my digs. At that time I was just starting to go out and so all my money could be gone in a single night. Thankfully Mum would slip me some of the other money back though it was still tight. She was good that way. That deal was signed with the proviso that if I did well then I would turn pro at 17. The difference was substantial. My first professional contract with West Ham was £500 a week which rose to £550 the next year and then £600 the following year. But for me, money didn't come into it. A few of the lads I had played youth football with had also signed forms: Lee Hodges, Danny Ship, and a couple of others. I was among friends and I felt at home.

Fortunately for West Ham, when Dad and Harry took over from Billy Bonds they knew where things had been going wrong in terms of recruiting young players and turned the whole thing round. Things were organized properly and they saw that the whole operation needed to have a more personal touch, one that had been missing. They are both good with people and caring is in their nature.

Almost immediately they went to see Joe Cole and his family to discuss his future. Joe was widely regarded as the most promising kid of his age in the area and was known to just about every club in the country. Unlike me, Joe is a not a West Ham boy – he's from Camden which has no real tie to the club – and Dad and Harry recognized that they could not depend on tribal ties with him even as a starting point. They were perceptive that way, and persuasive. West Ham was hardly the most glamorous of Joe's options but they made the right noises when they spoke to him and his parents about where he should sign up. They knew what it was to have their own sons coming through and the decisions which parents had to help their kids make when it was time to choose. Again, it was the little things. Joe was invited to travel to an away game on the first team coach. He was made part of the squad for a day which was a huge thing for a young kid but hardly a massive gesture by the club. It didn't matter. The signals were right and that was the most important thing.

They sold West Ham properly and brought in Tony Carr as youth team coach. A couple of years after I signed it was pointed out that myself and Rio were knocking on the door of the first team. At last, they could deliver on the promise that this was a club which cared about the next generation. They gave youth a chance. They returned West Ham to its roots and once again made it a family club. Somewhere along the line that had been lost. It may seem strange to those who see Upton Park as the breeding ground for some of the best young talent in the country but for a long time they didn't bring through any players. Under Dad and Harry all of that changed. Apart from myself, Rio, Joe Cole, Michael Carrick, Jermain Defoe, and later Glen Johnson, all came through the ranks and helped make West Ham a fantastic team.

Of that batch Rio and Joe were the two most naturally talented. Rio had the edge though because he also had the physique needed to succeed quickly. Joe had to work hard on that and has continued to do so. Carrick was probably the most technically gifted of the group while Defoe was a pure goalscorer. Rio and I were talking about this while on England duty and it made me wonder where I came. I guess it was somewhere in between. I had a bit of talent, some skill and I could score a few goals. Rio agreed and I suppose that has come to be the case given how my game has developed since then. For West Ham, it was a great position to be in, to have such a talented crop coming through, though later they would also benefit considerably from selling players who had cost them nothing. That, however, is another story.

Having signed my contract I could not have been happier. I was finally living the life which I had aimed for ever since I could remember. After years of eating, drinking, and sleeping football I was also being paid to do it. It was the best feeling I could imagine. First year youth is about as much fun as football gets. You have your own little community of team-mates and you are still way under the surface of the cut-throat world of the first team and making it as a real professional. It was a period where school met work and there were elements of both environments about it. We trained knowing that this was part of our job and our education. There were a lot of chores to do as well but I didn't care.

I was a footballer now, a West Ham player, though that sense of awe and privilege was soon knocked out of me in my first pre-season.

Billy Bonds was always very good with the young players. He knew your name, how you were getting on and would often have a joke with you. Unfortunately, he was also a very good long-distance runner. Actually, he was better than anyone else at the club. Running? He was the best and he liked to show it.

Every player accepts that plodding endless mile upon mile is the painful and tedious part of pre-season, consequently it's also the part that most of us hate. I was a decent runner at school and never minded that much though I know some lads who would rather clean the stadium toilets after matchday than go on one of Billy's marathons. We would plough our way through Hainault Forest, up hills, down hills, through streams. Then we would start on Epping Forest and all the time Billy would pick up the pace at the front and then run to the back of the pack and give them some 'encouragement'. He was remarkable – like Steve Ovett in football boots.

I would finish the thing but was completely knackered. My legs had turned to concrete. It was never like that at school. You could stop, tell the teacher that you just could not go on, and they listened. Not here. This was more like army training where there is no choice but to keep going. It would go on like that for between two and three weeks. It was relentless and I quickly realized that I had entered another world, one where there were no boys, only men. You got used to it but I couldn't help thinking that it was all a bit archaic.

Claudio Ranieri was a big fan of running though not like that. It was only when Jose Mourinho became Chelsea manager that I came across the idea that extreme running in pre-season is not a pre-requisite for a successful campaign. As Rui Faria, our fitness coach, eloquently put it: 'If I am working with a concert pianist why would I make him run round the piano until he drops? Will it make him a better pianist?' I am not sure how much better at football I became as a result of those cross-country runs but I gritted my teeth and got on with it. It also built up mental strength and created a threshold within me for that kind of exercise which is invaluable.

We moved on to sprinting and when the ball eventually came out, it was more drills than anything else. We practised heading and little volleys back and forth, running with the ball and passing and shooting. This was more like it. This was what I signed up for. Tony Carr was our coach and he was great with me. He set the tone just right as far as I was concerned. He never showed me any favouritism and when he needed to have a go at me he would. I appreciated that. It was a potentially difficult situation because of who my Dad and uncle were and he helped me a lot.

Tony was quite strict about our routine as YTS boys and always asked that we start our day an hour before the professionals arrived for training. On Mondays and Wednesdays we had to run the mile – which was measured by five laps of the pitch. We'd get in at 8.30 am and by nine we were out on the field. It could be quite a daunting prospect. We would have played on Saturday and had Sunday off so the idea of kicking off your working week by running as fast as you can for that distance was not exactly appealing. Neither was there any let-up.

We'd come straight back into the dressing room and we would prepare the training kit for the first team squad and make sure the boots were clean. Then we would set up the gear outside while the pros were getting changed. It was all part of the routine though one of the worst jobs was collecting the balls after they had finished training. That was mainly because Julian Dicks took particular pleasure in booting them as far as he could. Anyone who ever saw him play will know that Dicksy has a shot on him like an express train. He didn't slow it down when he was blasting the balls to all corners of the training ground either. He also had a wicked sense of humour. When we'd managed to collect most of them back into the bag he would sneak back and start smashing them all over again. If there was one missing then a search party was sent out to the fence which surrounded the area to find it.

I liked doing the jobs around the ground. Traditionally each trainee was assigned a couple of pros whose boots you were responsible for keeping spotless. I was given Dicksy and Lee Chapman. Dicksy was particularly pedantic about his footwear and if he spotted a smudge on one of his boots he would call you in and throw them at you. The big thing for us about that job was the Christmas bonus, when the pros – who were on big money – would bung us a few extra quid for doing the job all year. I was already on a promise. Dicksy had pulled me at the start of the season and told me that if I did a good job he would see me all right come bonus time. I gave him my word and he was as good as his. Just before Christmas he called me over and gave me a hundred quid. I was quite shocked – and made up. It was a lot of money but then Dicksy was a generous guy who respected people whom he thought had done the right thing.

Not for a moment did I think he would tip like that though. Expectations were raised and so was the ante. Lee

Chapman was one of the club's biggest earners and I had scrubbed, scraped and polished his boots until the skin on my fingertips was peeling off. He gave me twenty quid. Just my luck but I didn't complain. How could I? These were the guys I aspired to be and I was chuffed if they just called me by my name. It's something that I do now with the youth team players – try to learn their names, remember them and give them a bit of my time. I was that young player once and I haven't forgotten what it's like.

Dicksy could be nasty to me sometimes but he never meant any harm by it. I didn't mind because at least he was paying me some attention. Anyway, Dicksy was a legend. To say he had a beautiful left foot would be the equivalent of saying Paolo Maldini was a half decent defender. Before training, everyone else would dutifully do their warm-up. It was group stretching and loosening off before the real stuff started. Not Dicksy. He would go out with a bag of balls over his shoulder and set up in front of goal. While we were touching our toes he was smashing, volleying and bending vicious shots into the net.

On the pitch, he had the reputation of being a real hard man though he would likely have done more damage with one of his shots than his tackles. He was, however, a fantastic player. He could bring the ball down and beat men, and to the fans he was an absolute idol – the captain and main man. Maybe there were times when he went a bit too far. He did go right through people now and then. But as I got older I learned he was actually quite a sensitive guy. He had a certain way about him. He was a maverick and I liked that about him.

Certain senior players would behave around me in a specific way because of Dad and Harry. I would never know if they were being genuinely nice or whatever but Dicksy would tell me to 'F*** off' the same as he would anyone else. He couldn't care less if my Dad owned the club. I respected him for that.

Cleaning his and anyone else's boots was not the worst job by a long way. We had to clean the canteen, corridors, dressing rooms and scrape the gym floor once everyone else had gone. Then, at the end of the day, we would be made to sit in the canteen while Tony Carr would check all of the jobs to make sure they had been done properly. It was a nervous part of the day. We waited patiently because if there was a single bit of sloppiness then we all had to stay behind while it was corrected. It was a pain in the arse if someone hadn't pulled his weight properly but I could see the point. It was all about teamwork and not letting your mates down.

There was the odd occasion when we were made to stay on and more often than not it would be Rio's fault. A few years later Sven-Goran Eriksson apparently described Rio as 'a bit lazy', but he was wrong. Rio isn't 'a bit lazy'; he is a complete lazy bollocks – off the pitch that is. At training, during matches, and in his spare time there are few players I have come across who are as committed to their game as Rio. He's like that now and was the same then. He was very dedicated to his football but he also hated doing the chores and was always trying to duck out of cleaning the gym and stuff. Sometimes he would sneak off and other times just go into a big strop about the state of someone's boots or the mess in the showers. I found this quite amusing.

It didn't stop him claiming the credit for a job well done of course. I found it very funny and Rio is so loveable that you would end up doing most of his part as well while he made

you laugh. It was carefree and I loved it. There was a camaraderie then which was unique and which I haven't known
since. It was founded on the excitement of starting off on that
adventure but also on the fact that we were realizing every
boy's ambition.

We would lark around and dig each other out for things
that happened in training and that would carry over into our
daily jobs. Rio and I became mates right away as soon as he
joined West Ham. He was promoted to my team almost
immediately even though he was a year younger but he was
very good and made the grade.

We used to have a game called 'D's' where we played two
versus two in the gym hall. Me, Rio, Hodgey, and Joe Keith
were thick as thieves. The rules were simple enough: you had
just one touch to control and the other player had to knock
it back to the other team inside the D which was drawn on
the floor. It was good fun but we were very competitive. The
fact that one man could easily cock it up led to banter which
could drag on for days. We spent so much time together it
was best not to be on the receiving end.

Hodgey was always the stronger player between us in that
first year. He could play anywhere in the midfield or off the
main striker. He was strong and athletic, the talk of the town
then. He had played for England schoolboys and was head
and shoulders above the rest of us. He also had a real eye for
goal. Not just any old goal either. Hodgey had the Midas
touch – the golden bollocks of our team. Whatever he hit flew
in the top corner and usually from thirty yards, on the volley.
I'm sad to say that his career was ended prematurely by a bad
knee injury though glad that we are still good mates.

They were great times, for football as well as the social life I was discovering. We were 16 or 17 and we would play a game on Saturday mornings and then go for lunch at McDonald's. Not quite the perfect after-match nutrition but we loved a burger and fries. Stan, who used to drive our minibus, would take us there and wait while we got our food and we would eat it in the van while we drove to Upton Park. Those were the best days, when West Ham were at home and we would get to the ground a couple of hours before kick-off.

As trainees we got to stroll around behind the scenes and I loved soaking up the excitement around the dressing room and tunnel during the build-up to the match. There might be jobs to do: the kit-man might need a hand or a message would need running. All the time the ground would be filling up and three o'clock was getting closer. There was such a buzz around the place and I fed off it. Watching the players pull on the jersey and then walk out on to the pitch as the crowd cheered and sang 'I'm Forever Blowing Bubbles.' I would drift into a daydream, picturing what it would be like to be one of the eleven about to start the game. Just the thought gave me goosebumps and made me nervous in my stomach.

I was quickly brought back to earth. If the team were losing at half-time or worse – had lost the match – you had to be careful what you said. Harry would be in a temper and if he caught any of us laughing at each other's jokes as we hung around would shout 'What the f*** are you smiling about?' That usually had the desired effect of scaring us into silence. He would have the real hump but we were just young lads.

Harry doesn't just love football – he lives it. He takes defeat very seriously and is not two-faced about his reaction whether you are in the first team or the youth team. It was just his instinct, then and now. I remember he came into the gym when we were playing D's and having a laugh. He was in a foul mood about something and he banned us from our favourite game – picking on one of us in particular. 'You should be out practising your f***ing heading instead of in here playing.' We looked at our feet instinctively. He could be quite foreboding when he wanted to but in this case we knew he was right. D's had become too much of a jokey culture with us. True, it was good for our skill development but we were neglecting other parts of our game which weren't as much fun to improve.

Harry was very adept at calling situations like that. He has a sixth sense for certain things happening around his club which he develops through taking a keen interest in every level of how it operates. More important, he knows all of the people involved including the youth team. People say Harry is a players' man but he's also a man of the people. Whether you are first team, reserve, coaching staff or the laundry lady, Harry treats you the same and makes sure you know how important you are to the success of the club.

When he came down heavily on us we realized it was because he wanted the best for us, because he cared. He was very capable of taking the piss and having a laugh like he was one of us. As young lads we craved his attention, and even if that meant facing his wrath at least we were on his radar.

We didn't know the pressure of playing in the first team – or managing it. After everything was cleared up and we had successfully stayed out of Harry's way, we would all head home and get our best gear on to go out for the night. One of the good things about that youth team was we would all go out together. There were no cliques or splits. There was a spirit we shared, a bond that was quite unique. Only now do I realize that it was one of the happiest times of my career, a life without the constant pressure I would come to know later.

Rio was a year younger which meant he started YT in the year below me. For that, his antics around the training ground, and some of the outrageous gear he wore, he took a bit of stick. He deserved it. Never mind the fact that he was always the last to turn up on a Saturday night because he had to travel across town to Peckham and back.

It's easy to feel nostalgia for certain times in our lives. Everyone has memories which can conjure up a certain feeling inside that enhances the mental image. For me, those Saturdays were very special. They still are. Can you imagine what it felt like to wake up knowing that you will play football for the club you love, then go watch the club you love play, and round the whole thing off with a night out with your best mates in the company of some gorgeous girls? Living the dream, that's what I was doing, living the dream.

Our keeper was Neil Finn (Finny) and he, along with Hodgey and me, were the ringleaders. Finny and I are still close. He never quite broke into the first team but played one game. He was 17 and not ready for first team football. He travelled to Manchester City as back-up for Ludo Miklosko. Ludo pulled out the night before the match and Finny was thrown in. It was a great achievement to become the youngest player to appear in the Premier League at that time. I spoke to his Mum and Dad before the game and they were rightly very proud of their boy. I could understand how they felt, though I also wondered how nervous my goalie mate must have felt just before kick-off.

It was a fantastic moment for Finny and I was jealous, which means I still take the piss out of him even now because they lost 2–1 and Niall Quinn scored twice. Regrettably for Finny, he dived at his feet for the second but Niall just chipped it over his body. I reckon it was the only classy goal big Niall ever scored and I won't let Finny forget it. He plays non-league now with Romford and hasn't lost any of the cheek he had then. If I begin to cane him for his performance he just reminds me that at least he was there, in the first team.

I could give out a bit of stick but I was used to taking it as well, mostly behind my back, but it was probably inevitable given the fact that Dad and Harry were in positions of influence. I can't say I was overly aware of it, more like I sensed it going on around me – just little episodes or the undercurrent of friction with some people at the club. I never really let it get to me or hamper how I thought I should be getting on but there were a few players who I know were funny about it.

My reaction? I just tried to win their respect for playing the way I could. Dad's reaction was a bit different. He would have a few digs at me if the result hadn't gone well just to make sure I wasn't getting special treatment. I understood. And I was used to it.

My greatest concern was learning as much as I could and becoming a better player. Our youth team was good. Very good. We won the league and I scored twenty-five goals from midfield that first season. I felt comfortable. I have always played there even though it was commonplace for young players to try a few different positions. I was the exception to the rule though. I always played central midfield. Always. I remember Rio playing up front and in defence but I always stuck to what I knew and now I can feel the benefit of that early experience. Things were changing though.

Both physically and mentally I was becoming much more aware of football. I realized something very important at that time, that I wanted to be more than a little ball player who just got a hold of possession and then passed it on so someone else could do the next part. I wanted to dominate my position and get forward and score goals.

When I first joined as a trainee I found almost everything harder than I ever had before. The physical demands were greater and I needed to go to the gym to build a level of strength and stamina that would allow me to compete with my peers. Dad would drum into me all the time that I needed to do the basics of midfield as second nature. Learn the basics of your trade he would say, then add the rest. The beautiful side would come later. He was right. That's partly why I feel comfortable whenever I have the ball. The ugly side of midfield – tracking runners and blocking play as well as tackling – I learned during that time and it was a while before I actually concentrated on practising shooting and started scoring goals. The nasty side of commanding the middle of the park was the foundation on which everything else would be built. I needed to be strong and to be mentally tough.

Training with the youth team is much more tedious than with the first team. I supplemented that with training on my own. I had routines which I practised off my own back. I would spend a lot of time banging the ball against the wall and forcing myself to control it and do the same thing over and over to improve my reaction time. I would vary the exercise and let the ball run behind me and sprint after it. Then I would start again and put myself under pressure. Other kids would wander into the gym and do something that was fun – the way we did playing D's. There are things we could all do that were creative and not such hard work but it was harder to make yourself do exercises that were boring and strenuous.

West Ham were able to attract some of the best young players. I knew that. I was playing with some of them. One guy who came in at 17 though had not grown up with the likes of me and Hodgey. His name was Martin Mullins. He was a Scotland schoolboy cap and had been signed from under the noses of the Old Firm as well as a few English clubs. He was quite a big lad and arrived with an air of self-assurance which suggested he knew he was the real deal. I had heard he was a good player and he looked the part in training. On one occasion everyone else had finished up for the day but it was time for my spikes. It was wet and I went outside to do my sprints. The sodden grass was perfect for 'doggies' – short bursts between two fixed points. The rain meant I could slide to one end simulating a tackle before getting up and repeating it from side to side – nothing you would ever find in a coaching manual but Dad had told me to do it and I knew I had to. Mullins walked out dressed for the weather to find me darting around and sliding in the mud. 'What the f*** are you doin'?' he asked incredulously. I didn't say a word. I stopped very briefly and then just carried on. I felt very self-conscious about the extra training I undertook and even though I believed in what I was doing I was too shy to defend it to anyone else. Mullins was a flash kid who thought he had everything he needed to make the grade. He just looked down his nose at me and walked away shaking his head. I was nervous but it didn't stop me going out and doing it again because I knew where I wanted to get to.

Dad was responsible for a lot of the regime but inventing

new challenges was entirely my idea. I would start off to do eight box-to-box runs and as I was approaching the target number I would up it to ten. Then I would do it with the ball because that was harder. Later, when I got into the first team, I came in on my day off and would do the same drill. It could be slightly embarrassing. I was out there and Tony Carr was taking the youth team and all of a sudden I realized they were all watching me. It was nothing like the Mullins incident though. Tony was simply pointing out that it was my day off and there I was. Maybe they thought I was mad. I don't know. I just knew that I wanted to become a better player and to do that I had to train more and harder. It's a lot easier to think that you've got everything in your locker to make it than it is to go out and do what is required. It takes a lot of hard work.

Dad had always told me that it was a slog to make it as a professional footballer so I grew up not expecting anything less. From the time I arrived at West Ham I had some ground to make up. I knew that. The mile runs which we would do twice a week were a nightmare when I first started. I used to be sick trying to run it as fast as I could. Tony Carr and Frank Burrows – who was reserve team coach – helped me to build up my strength. I suffered because I hadn't developed physically the same as some of the others and my legs couldn't get the pace in training. Players like Hodgey were already men – I knew that because he would show off the hairs on his willy in the showers.

I played in the youth team when I was 16 and my first year YTS was split between the youth team and a few games in the reserves. That was a massive step up for me at that time – one I really felt. In the first year of YT we won the reserve League

Cup which was a two-leg tie for the final and it's significant for two reasons.

The first is because we played against Chelsea. The second is Rio. In the first leg we went a goal up – which I scored – but got beaten 4–1. In between the first match and the return, the first team went to Australia. It was the end of the season and they were going on a tour. The club had given up the ghost on the final after the hammering in the first leg and I suppose you couldn't blame them. As a result, a few of the older reserves went down under and some of the younger trainees came into the side for the second game at Stamford Bridge. Everyone, including Chelsea, assumed it was a formality.

We weren't expected to salvage it and as a result we played without pressure. You can't lose what you've already lost and so the coach put this young gangly kid in the hole behind the two strikers for the match – Rio. What happened was remarkable. Rio was just on fire. He was playing like Ronaldinho complete with the tricks and flicks. There were moments when I just stood back and watched in complete amazement. The rest of the team was playing well but Rio was having the match of his life. We were two up, then three before they pulled one back. It didn't matter. We were on a roll and wouldn't be denied.

We won 5–2 in normal time and the game went to extra-time and then to penalties. We held our nerve and scored our kicks. We won – a bunch of young lads who were left to do whatever we could in the name of the club after they opted to take the majority of the regular players away. It was my first taste of glory and it was special. That it came at the home of Chelsea made it even more so. Rio was ecstatic. So was I. It was an incredible experience, one of those which can really only happen in football and we had been right at the heart of it.

Dad was a bit shocked but not surprised. He had played a big part in bringing Rio to West Ham. Rio tells the story about when Dad turned up at his little flat in Peckham where he lived with his Mum and brother Anton. Rio was impressed right away. Dad had a big black Mercedes and the kids around his place had never seen a car like it. He was funny when he first came to our house as well. He thought it was some kind of mansion. We were quite well off and I realized that, but Rio's face was a picture when he came in the front room and looked around as if someone had dropped him on Mars.

Signing Rio was a big coup for West Ham. He was a real prospect. He struggled with his co-ordination as everyone does when they are growing up. I certainly did. I remember going to watch him and being amazed at how leggy he was. He was all height and pace but not quite as graceful as he is now. He was a good player, no doubt about that. At that stage he was playing in midfield but he was very insecure about his physique. I knew exactly what that was like because I had suffered from growth spurts and I knew how disorientating they could be.

'I'm not going to make it. I'm not going to make it,' Rio would say all the time. He was a bit clumsy and I remember worrying that he might be right. He overcame that insecurity and found his feet when he got into the youth team. And, for whatever reason he was played in the hole in that League Cup final second-leg, it doesn't matter – it was tactical genius.

After that, Rio developed quickly. His control was always great and he was a natural at bringing the ball down with his first touch. He improved further and the word came from

Harry that he wanted Rio moved back into defence. There was a bit of consternation. Rio and I gave each other puzzled looks but we were used to doing what we were told. Harry believed that with Rio's physique and ability there was the potential to make him a great ball-playing centre-half. West Ham had a history in that position and when Rio is mentioned in the same breath as the late, great Bobby Moore I often think of exactly that moment when the decision was made.

People can say a lot of things good and bad about Harry but he saw something in Rio that could be great for club and country. And he was right. Even then Rio played much the same way as he does now for Manchester United and England. He has always been able to dribble the ball out of defence and to be honest I can't remember a time when he didn't, from youth team right through the system and into the first team. There were a couple of times when he lost possession and, of course, he was given stick. It's the English way. Criticize, don't encourage him. Put him down and tell him he should have punted it long. Rio, though, was very single-minded. He knew what he was capable of and football for him is more than just defending. He probably improved his defending more when he left West Ham for Leeds United. David O'Leary was a man devoted to the art of defending and he was good for Rio. Maybe he needed to improve his focus during the game.

At the time before he left Upton Park he saw himself very much as an all-round footballer but all players need to learn and improve. I have and so has Rio. We have lost a bit of that closeness we used to have because he has moved up north but when we are together on England duty it feels like yesterday when we were playing at West Ham.

Back then everyone was talking about Rio being the one who would be a great player. I was jealous. I wanted to be the one everyone was talking about. Rio was already a great player – even in midfield. I was different from him. Where Rio was blessed with amazing football talent, I knew I had to work harder. We were also physically different. Though I was slightly embarrassed about it at the time I know I was a chubby kid. There's no getting away from it. I had good feet and a good touch so I could score a lot of goals through using my head and the talent that went with it. Things changed for me when I went to West Ham at first though. I struggled with my mobility and had trouble getting round the pitch. I realized quickly that it was harder to get in the box and score goals at that level and as that season passed and the next one started there was a difference again, moving from first year YT and into the second.

Fortunately, nature kicked in and helped me out. I was a bit of a late developer and through the age of 16 I grew up. I stretched a bit in height and as a result lost some of the weight. I was stronger and I remember thinking that I was all grown up but that season taught me I still had some way to go. To Swansea and back to be precise.

I remember vividly Harry telling me that he wanted me to go on loan. I was lying in bed chilling out in the afternoon after training at my Mum and Dad's house when the phone went. Mum answered and brought the handset to me.

'Listen Frank,' he said. 'An opportunity has come up for you to go on loan.'

'Where?' I asked nervously.

'Swansea. I know it's lower league but it'll be good for you. Build you up son.'

I was very unsure. It felt like I was being rejected. I had spent all of my life at and around West Ham and here I was being told that my best chance of staying for a long time was to leave in the short term. I was also confused. I didn't want to leave home. Not even for a few weeks. What if it went well? Maybe I would end up being there even longer? Home and my family had always been very important to me and I kind of wanted to make that point to Harry. He would understand. He was my uncle after all.

'I'm not sure Harry,' I replied. 'Maybe it would be better if I stayed with the club and did a bit more training, maybe a bit more in the gym and stuff. That'll build me up.'

I don't know if he was listening to me or not. I was so panicked that I wasn't able to sense a reaction one way or the other to my plea for leniency.

'You have to be there tomorrow,' he said bluntly. 'You'll be fine. It'll do you good.'

I didn't even know where Swansea was. I had just passed my driving test and had to get a map out. I was just getting to feel a permanent part of the set-up at Upton Park and Wales seemed a very long way away.

Dad – though he believes that I have gone on to a higher level than he played at – experienced similar things to me in terms of improving himself. The late Ron Greenwood was manager at West Ham and pulled him in when he was 18 to be told that he was going on loan to Torquay. At the time, going on loan was not the same as it is now for a young player – it was almost like being sold. He resisted though it must have been a very hard call for him to make; he thought the world of Ron Greenwood and respected him greatly as a manager and a man. To refuse his wishes was a big step. West

Ham was a successful club at the time and there seemed to be a conveyor belt of talent which spanned the youth and first team from which good players would simply fall into positions all over the pitch. Dad knew what he wanted though. He got his head down and grafted. He did his spikes and worked phenomenally hard and had to go through a very tough process to get where he wanted to be – at West Ham, nowhere else.

One of Dad's favourite sayings is something which Greenwood told him and Harry when they were youth players at the club. Occasionally he would turn up at their training session, and when he spoke to them he always said the same thing: 'Simplicity is genius.' Greenwood was widely seen as being ahead of his time technically and tactically and in my Dad he had a willing pupil. At the age of 17 he and Harry went back to their old school to coach fourteen year olds – something I did at the same age when I was at West Ham. Teaching kids helped me realize what I had learned – and how to apply it better. Maybe I was more talented but he wanted to instill the same work ethic in me. It was good for me. Though I understand Dad's decision to stick it out at West Ham he didn't give me any choice – he also told me I had to go.

I was full of trepidation about leaving home. I had only just got my Ford Fiesta Si and was worried about driving on the motorway. I was also worried about the football. I was 17 and saw myself as a ball-playing midfielder. My strength – because I didn't have much physically – was getting on the ball and playing a bit. How was I supposed to do that in the old Second Division? I wasn't even sure what kind of football they played on the pitches of the lower leagues. I wasn't disrespectful. I was ignorant. I genuinely didn't know. I am actually quite proud of it though. The experience made me stronger physically and mentally and I am grateful for it. It turned out to be the best thing that could have happened. I believe that I went there as a boy and came back a man.

I had to grow up in many ways. For a start, I was lodged in a hotel which was a bit traumatic in itself. I was used to being at home and having my family around for support. Just eating dinner with Mum and Dad or mucking around with Claire and Natalie helped take the pressure off. And I was separated from my mates.

Swansea's training ground was a bit grotty and I was shocked at the lack of facilities, never mind the difference in the way they played. There was an Irish lad there who was on loan from Wolves – Robbie Dennison. He was an old pro and had a cynical side to him which goes with years of experience at the less glamorous end of the game. I'm not sure what he thought of me at first but he ended up being a really good lad. We were in the same digs and had a couple of beers together on the odd night.

Though I was homesick I made the most of the time. I learned a lot from training and playing with guys who only ever knew football as a hard slog of a job, where making enough to pay the bills was the first priority. I learned respect for my fellow professionals – regardless of ability.

Everything was very different from West Ham and most of it was a surprise. When you got there in the morning the kit was all rolled up and if you were late in you might not get something you needed for training. We had to fight for everything. We walked a few hundred yards to the training pitch and it always seemed to be cold and raining. I was a bit of a novelty for most of them but they all turned out to be decent lads. It was old school though – training at the stadium before the games and then doing some weights. At West Ham we were pampered by comparison – your kit was always laid out nice and neat and everything was prepared for you. At Swansea, a different player would take the whole kit each week and clean it. I managed to avoid that chore as I was staying in a hotel and because I didn't stay long enough for anyone to notice I hadn't taken a turn.

In all, I stayed two months and played a few games. I even scored at Brighton and we won but there was neither room nor time for glory boys down there. I was clocking up the miles in my little dark-blue Fiesta at weekends, dashing back to Romford listening to a few dance tunes and wondering what Rio and Hodgey had been up to, knowing I would get the full story as soon as I arrived. The Swansea boys were a good bunch though and near the end of my time we had a couple of nights out in the town after games. We were in one particular pub with Robbie and few of the lads when this huge Welsh bloke squared up to me. I think he knew who I was. 'Why don't you f*** off back to London you cockney bastard,' he growled. I was small compared to this bloke and not really in the mood to lose most of my teeth. I didn't want to involve anyone else and just said 'All right, I'm leaving.' And I did leave.

For my second last game while I was there I was put on the bench because they knew I didn't want to extend the loan and stay another month. It was coming up to Christmas and I wanted to be back home. It was the right time to go back. We only won about two games and there were only a couple of thousand fans there at best watching us struggle to avoid relegation. But it was worth the pain. Rio agreed: he went to Bournemouth and came back much improved, as I had. I see kids at 17 now at Chelsea and I know they wouldn't last five minutes at that level of football. West Ham then was probably more than they could cope with but I went to Swansea and survived. I came back stronger. Though not that strong apparently.

I still had skinny legs and I knew I had to build up my muscles. Dad knew it too and he used to get me running from box to box after training. A real midfielder's run: get up, get back, get up, get back. I now had a better idea of what was needed to sustain myself in the competitive environment. I developed a lot after that and when I broke into the first team properly at West Ham the next season, at age 18, I was capable of scoring ten goals due to making those runs. I was a different player. I wouldn't get involved in play in the middle of the pitch the way I do now because I was trying to get on the end of those balls from a forward run.

That came from a lot of hard graft doing weights to build up my legs and upper body strength. I was helped by some killer sessions with Paul Hilton who was the reserve team coach. He would make us lap the pitch in sixty seconds at three-quarter speed and then the next group would go and sixty seconds later you had to go again. We used to hate him for it though he was actually a good lad. Not that he seemed very nice when a lot of us were throwing up by the end and he would just stand over us, shouting. I could do that pretty easily now. It only makes me realize how far I have come physically in my career. It was a level I had to achieve before I could even think about making the first team.

I see now that was what Dad had been aiming for through

all the years of training, exercise, and routine after routine. It was also what Harry knew when he packed me off to Swansea. I wasn't ready for West Ham then – not physically anyway, maybe not even mentally – and they recognized that. I didn't see it of course. I couldn't. As a young player you have a certain confidence about you that makes you think you are invincible. I wasn't absolutely sure that I could perform for the first team but it didn't stop me from believing I could.

It was probably just as well since my debut came unexpectedly and as a substitute against Coventry City at Upton Park. Gordon Strachan and I came on at the same time. He was about 38 at the time and there was I, twenty years his junior and coming on for my team for the first time. Harry could sense my nerves. He put his arm around both of us and made a joke about the age difference. 'Go easy on him!' he said to Strachan. Given that we both played central midfield we were actually going head to head. Strachan might have been at the end of his career but it doesn't stop you from thinking about what he had achieved. And there I was at the very start of mine and about to make my senior debut. I was excited – terrified actually. I watched my Dad play for West Ham, and Harry too. I had grown up listening to their memories of the good times and the bad. Both were there with me now: Dad in the dugout, smiling but looking just as nervous as me; Harry telling me what he wanted me to do when I got on there. I had dreamt of this moment so many times – as a child and a teenager. The numbers were held up indicating the players who were coming off and I heard the crowd roar as I crossed the white line for the first time.

It was a great reception from the fans and it's a good

memory. Even now, looking back over my career – the different stages with West Ham, Chelsea and England, and the success that I have worked hard to achieve – it was a great feeling. I didn't however do much in that game. Ran around for a few minutes and touched the ball a few times. The best thing was the applause I got and the feeling of excitement in the crowd about Frank Lampard's son coming on. I felt that I had arrived but I knew for sure that I hadn't made it.

As expected, I was back on the bench for the next game. Making my debut was part of my development, another step on the long way up. Some players make an incredible impact in their first game. Wayne Rooney did it for England against Turkey but I was no Rooney. Mine was more a rite of passage than a ticket to the first team. I knew it would take a bit longer before I would be pushing my way on to the team sheet.

The next time I played was against Stockport in the League Cup in the first leg at home. Someone got injured on the morning of the game – I think John Moncur had been sick – and I got a phone call from my Dad who was at the ground.

'Frank. Get yourself down here,' he said. 'You're playing.'

I was actually in the park over the road from my parents' house doing a warm-up, just some stretches and sprinting. It was still enough to panic me. I wondered if I had overdone it and how it might affect the way I would play in the match. I needn't have worried too much. I did okay but the thing I remember most was how hard it felt athletically. I felt like a boy playing against men. It was a really hard contest which we ended up drawing 1–1. I had a chance to score and missed. I felt gutted afterwards and came away from the game feeling nauseous.

The fans were turning on the team at that time. We had

drawn at home and then lost away to Stockport and were struggling to score goals. Even the lads were a bit fractious in the dressing room as a result of all the pressure. I was a young kid coming into all that. I didn't actually play a lot after that game. That season I made seven more appearances as sub and the Stockport game was the only one I started.

Next season came round more quickly than I had wished for, but physically I felt stronger than ever after a hard pre-season in Scotland. Rio and I were the only two young players who were taken. It was pretty intense – especially with guys like Iain Dowie and Ian Bishop around. I enjoyed the stint and felt more comfortable than ever when we played a couple of warm-up games.

We had a really tough opener away at Arsenal and I started but was taken off after seventy minutes. It was traditionally a hard place to go for West Ham, indeed for most teams. We lost 2–0. I was disappointed, for the team and myself. I really wanted to make an impact but it was Highbury and Arsenal were just beginning to look the part under Arsene Wenger who had taken charge the season before.

I always put myself under pressure to perform but there was even more significance now because my contract was up for renewal. Now it was even more important for to me to show what I was capable of but I didn't start any of the next seven games. Worse than that, I was beginning to take a bit of stick from the fans. I had been aware of it before then. Just a couple of games after my debut against Coventry there were a few instances when I heard fans shouting a bit of abuse at me. It turned really quickly and I couldn't understand why. It probably didn't help that I was on the bench because that was seen by some as a compromise. Being Frank Lampard's son brought with it different rules than those which applied to every other player. If someone else was on the bench it was simple – they were recovering fitness or form or were seen as being able to make a difference if called upon. With regard to me, a section of the support believed that I wasn't good enough for the starting line-up so I was put on the subs' bench as some kind of favour. And they let me know this every time I moved to do a warm-up.

Obviously, it subsided when I didn't play but that 96/97 season I came on twice more after Arsenal but didn't make much of an impression. I tried as hard as I could but once the New Year came in I was already looking towards the pre-season, devising ways of becoming a better player. I worked harder than ever before but apparently I still wasn't quite ready for the first game of the 97/98 season when we played Barnsley away. I knew that I would be on the bench. It was both exciting and disappointing. I wanted to start but had to bide my time. I knew the script and until you got a chance to play the part you had to stick at being understudy.

I'm not sure if that was an excuse for breaking the rules. I wasn't the first and I won't be the last but it was the first time for me. Dad always said never to go drinking on the Thursday night before a Saturday game. And, of course, I never did. Finny – who was youth team goalie and effectively number three – phoned me up and asked if I fancied going out for dinner. It was a Thursday night. We did, and we had a few beers. I turned up at training on Friday feeling very guilty. It got worse. I was told I would definitely be on the bench. It's hard enough to feel physically and mentally attuned for a pre-season match. My body felt fine but there was a voice in my head telling me that I must be below par because I had been out for a few hours two nights before. It was Dad's voice, and my own.

It didn't matter to me that it wasn't a competitive game. Everything I had trained so hard for in my life was aimed at being the best I could be. Not just some of the time. All of the time. There wasn't a lot I could do. I warmed up when told to and was soon wondering if I might get a chance to go on. On the pitch we were doing all right. The score was 1–1 and I wasn't sure that I would get the call when, of course, I did. By this time I had managed to convince myself that everything would be fine. I briefly thought back to the Thursday night but knew there was nothing to do but just get stuck in there.

So I did. Won a few tackles and when a chance came for me to shoot I let fly and saw the ball soar into the net. I had scored but I wasn't quite sure what to do. With all of the time I had spent worrying about what had happened before the game I didn't have time to wonder what might happen during it. I turned around and spotted Rio. He was way back in his natural home in the centre circle. We were on the attack after all. The natural thing to do was to run to him. We were mates and I wanted to share the moment. What happened next though was entirely unplanned and unexpected.

Rio was waiting for me – I didn't expect him to leave his comfort zone – and we just started dancing. It was very spontaneous. Afterwards, people thought we had prepared it. But we hadn't. We had been to Cyprus that summer and Rio was fond of doing this mad dance where he lifted one leg up, kind of like a demented flamingo. I stood in front of him and copied it. Actually, he still does that dance even now when he's on a night out. I couldn't have cared less if he had waltzed me round the pitch. I had just scored my first goal for the club.

We calmed down and as the ball came back to be kicked off I looked to the bench and saw the smile on my Dad's face. I think it was pride rather than amusement at the celebration, though there was probably a bit of both. It was an incredible high but unfortunately it was followed by the predictable low.

I was sub for the next few games and didn't get a look-in until there was an injury in midfield which meant I got a run of games. I was still just a young kid. I would come on and try to get involved. There were times when I might have been pushed off the ball or whatever but I was trying my best. Harry kept putting me in there and soon I started to score. I got a hat-trick against Walsall in the League Cup which was amazing in my first full season. I was 19 and happy as Larry. I finished with ten goals to my name and had established myself as a regular in the first team squad. To be honest I thought I had made it. I was wrong.

My Dad went to meet the chairman, Terence Brown, and Harry to talk about a new deal. The chairman had a habit of reading fanzines and listening to the views of more extreme supporters – some of whom had started to turn on me. I had been aware of it but tried to ignore it and just get my head down and play. There was a conspiracy theory among them that the manager had been putting me on late in games to get me appearance money because I was his nephew. The punters read these things and I think there was a small group who decided to make it their cause when the team was playing badly. It started with a few people from the local area who thought I was getting an easy run. Things like that spread around the ground like a cancer and other people jumped on the bandwagon, though to be honest, I never dreamed the chairman of the club would be among them.

Once again, I was wrong. Brown brought this nonsense up claiming that there had been allegations of nepotism. He asked Harry to explain it.

'What the f*** are you going on about?' Harry responded angrily. 'Do you think I bring a player on to get him five hundred quid? Frank is a very good player who we need to get on a long-term deal.'

When I was told about all of this I was pissed off and a bit shocked. I had been slogging my guts out for the club and was desperate to do well for West Ham. I was a West Ham boy, born and bred. I had come here to support the team as a child. I had signed for that reason.

For the first time I felt suspicious about the people running the club and from that moment I would never trust them again. I began to question the way they looked at me and the way they viewed Harry and Dad. I had thought Brown was a genuinely good guy but he wasn't a football man and we all called him 'Mr Dead' – a character on the *Harry Enfield* show at that time. Brown wore the same pinstripe suit and had a very serious demeanor when he came into the dressing room.

After he mentioned nepotism I was more sensitive about what was going on around me. A couple of times I heard murmurs from the punters behind the dugout when I was called to warm up or was about to go on. But it got worse. It had been getting worse from two seasons earlier when I made my debut. There was booing from a certain section of the crowd behind the dugout when I was told to leave the bench and stretch. That wasn't even the worst part of Upton Park.

That was on the other side at the 'chicken run'. I wasn't being paranoid. It was becoming an ordeal for me just to be a sub, to the point where I didn't want to be there. I still had my pride and my determination to succeed but I couldn't tell Harry how I felt. When you are playing away and the punters give you stick it's fine – it's different, it's what you expect. Not at home. I was extremely conscious of what was going on. It was very clear. Shouts of 'Sit down, you!' and 'Go sit down with your Daddy!' were common.

Sometimes it was worse than others. Sometimes it was so bad that I would rather have been sitting in the stand, or at home well away from it. Hodgey was on the bench with me for one game. Harry had told me to get stripped and it started almost immediately, the odd shout and rumble of discontent; I was expecting it. Hodgey grabbed my arm. 'You have to get out of here as quick as you can mate,' he said. 'You don't need this s***. You don't deserve it and you're better than this.'

I didn't say anything. He was right. I knew he was but you can't just wipe away your childhood supporting a club or the love you have for it. I am a loyal person by nature and I wanted to do well for West Ham and for my Dad and Harry who found their professional integrity being questioned. I didn't feel sorry for myself; I felt sorry for them. I thought about all the years they had been good players there, loyal servants. They had brought success and they were doing their best to bring success again. So was I. We were in this together whether we liked it or not and I felt reassured by the fact that I had people I could trust with my life fighting for me. I would never give anything less than everything for them and they knew that.

I understood that they were in an awkward position but

they are both strong and sometimes quite foreboding characters. When I was young I was quite wary of Harry. I was also in awe of him. Between the ages of 8 and 14 there was no real football relationship between us. Like most kids that age, I kept my distance from adults when the conversation turned to serious stuff. From my point of view, even as his nephew, he was exactly the same person that people outside of the family knew him to be. He was outspoken and a real character. Though desperate to learn about football I was scared to say anything in front of him in case I would embarrass myself even though as an uncle he was very loveable. That made what happened when I was older all the more difficult.

I never really lost that innate apprehension after he became my manager at West Ham. Somewhere deep inside me I was still that little boy and he was still Uncle Harry. There were times at the club when I would have the hump with him like every player has with their manager but of course everything was so much more complicated by our relationship.

There was a time when I wanted an explanation about why I wasn't playing. Instead of just knocking on the door and confronting him like anyone else I found myself outside his office pacing around. I was scared to go in and I know that stems from the days of being in his company as a child and feeling inhibited.

He and my Dad had their disagreements. There were times when I was dropped from the team and Dad would make a case for me playing. Maybe he was taking my side as a father, that's only human nature, while Harry was protective of his own position.

I understood that. I sensed when Harry was feeling uncomfortable about something to do with me. It became still more complicated though when the fans started to have a go as well. When I look back now I have a lot more sympathy for the situation Harry found himself in at that time. He protected me when he thought I needed protecting. He also stood up for me when it really mattered in situations with Terence Brown and the likes. It's part of our nature, our family. The culture of London's East End means looking after your own, which is fine. But when it's carried into professional football, where the environment is very cut-throat, it changes. You have to act differently. That was tough on the family at times, though they tried to hide it from me.

People just looked at the fact that my Dad and uncle were in charge and they thought the worst of it. That was where the agitation and aggravation came from. When they saw the unique situation which existed at West Ham they were not happy with it. I know what it's like from the other side. Jamie will speak to me after a game now and I know that he is talking from my point of view rather than an objective one. It's our point of view, the Lampard/Redknapp point of view.

There was no getting away from it and the situation was both strange and stressful. I understand just how fractious it was because when I speak to Harry now it's completely different. Now we speak on a much more equal basis. Until I left West Ham that wasn't possible but I feel I have earned his respect. There have been occasions – winning the Football Writers' Player of the Year in 2005 – when he called me up to say well done that I realized we were finally free of the difficulties which affected our relationship at West Ham. That was very liberating – not just for me but for all of us.

Harry was sitting with Aunt Sandra in front of me at the Player of the Year dinner and I could see she was quite emotional as I spoke about ways in which they had helped me. Sandra is very much like Mum. She gave support and encouragement to Mark and Jamie but when I was around she found just as much time for me. She was kind and understanding – even when I was helping Jamie obliterate her beloved bird cage in the back garden – and I realize now that it wasn't just my relationship with Harry which was affected. I could relate to Sandra in the way I did to Mum and I respect her for the way she would be the gel in her family during the highs and lows which a life in football brings. I regret that it became impossible for us to enjoy a normal family friendship during those times. I found myself being pushed a little farther away from someone who I had been very close to as a child. We are relaxed and we can talk more now. It's a shame we had all the years of pressure when we were so involved at West Ham.

My experience was different from Dad's and Harry's. During my childhood and development as a player it was quite hard to have a Dad who was a famous player. Dad is someone who is extremely well regarded in the history of West Ham and I was following on. I also had an uncle and cousin who I was, inevitably, compared with. But Jamie was a peer and gave me something to aim for and emulate. It was a huge motivating factor to have a cousin as good as him. I lived that moment with him and was desperate to get up there with him. The flip side, as I discovered, was being referred to as a poor man's Jamie Redknapp. I had hardly had a chance in the first team but already I was being compared unfavourably with my cousin. The thing with my Dad and Harry was only there when I was at West Ham but with Jamie it extended beyond that because he was the top man.

I wanted to reach that level and win the league and there was real pressure behind that. In some senses it took me quite a long time to overcome that pressure. I was nowhere near as confident. Jamie was seen as a player who exuded natural talent whereas I have been perceived as someone who had to graft. People still say that Jamie had more talent and that I work harder. I know why that's said but in all honesty I think it's a very lazy assessment. People who have raw talent can smack you in the face with it and by that I mean someone like Ronaldinho who is mesmerizing to play against.

On the other hand, is it fair to say that someone like Roy Keane doesn't have any talent, or John Terry, because it's not right there in your face? Talent isn't just the ability to do tricks and beat men. Yes, that is a fantastic skill, and maybe some people are born with that ability where others aren't. But there is also a different kind of talent which is about how much you drive yourself inside to be the very best. I am insulted when people say that I have worked hard because I am not the most talented. My talent is what I am now. It combines how hard I have worked, how much I have learned, how many goals I have scored and how many games I have played.

It's a generalization which I don't think is right. I may have agreed in the past because I was ignorant of what constitutes genuine talent. Keane has as much technical ability and talent as Ronaldinho and has proven that, when he has pushed himself in his career – through perseverance, application, and sheer desire to achieve. That, takes real talent.

I understand the argument when you look at someone like Wayne Rooney who exploded on to the football scene at 16.

It's easy to describe his as God-given talent. At 17, I wouldn't have had the strength or the mental maturity to play for England but there is no rule which says that everyone needs to peak at an early age. Very few do – especially for their country. Talent is what you make of it and it's not all about hard work.

I had to build myself up physically to make it as a professional. I recognized that but there are lots of people who don't and just go out of the game because they think they can make it on ability alone. I played with some great youth teams, players who had great feet, could score goals but never realized that you had to bridge the gap between having the potential to be a player and doing what was necessary to become one.

I had the ability. I used to run past people for fun at school and with my club team and youth team I was banging in twenty odd goals without difficulty. But then I realized that when I tried to make the step up I was struggling to make it round the pitch. I didn't have the physique to battle it out in tackles. I was a chubby kid and I needed to work on my speed and agility and I spent hours trying to improve myself. I would often just go to the park near the house and do stuff with Dad. We would practise shooting or running, just to sharpen me up. It was a useful exercise partly because it made me a very keen trainer from an early age but not all the sessions were positive.

Once when I was around 14, Dad was crossing balls for me to head or shoot into the empty goal. I couldn't hit a single ball. I don't know if I was having a growth spurt or if I was unwell but nothing I tried came off, not even the simplest thing. I was devoid of co-ordination and eventually got so upset that I ran off. I couldn't tolerate that I wasn't able to do it well and a massive fear overcame me that I wasn't good enough to be a footballer. I was beginning to wonder about the future and whether or not I would be offered a contract as a trainee professional. I got back to the house in tears. Dad asked me why I had given up but I was having a panic attack that I wasn't going to make the grade. Yet next day I went back and tried again, and it was better.

I learned that there are certain times when I knew that I had to improve a part of my game or my body to make sure that I could compete. I have always worked hard to overcome any obstacle. If that didn't work then I would work harder still. It's something which has been apparent in everything that I have done in my life and I am sure a lot of people will recognize it. For me it really hit home that in order to get a contract at West Ham, get into the reserves, make the first team, I had to work for it.

There have been moments when maybe I wasn't ready for the next step. I had to do a bit extra to get there. Maybe players like Rooney have it straight away but I didn't. I am lucky in some ways to have had that because it has made me respect the effort it takes to achieve your goals. Whatever I succeed in it is because of hard work. I can play football and score goals well enough but the minute I stop training or working hard I know that I won't be what I am. If I slack off in training I know that I won't score as many goals or be such an imposing figure in a match.

Now if I have a quiet game I ask myself a whole host of questions. Am I training to my optimum? Have I been making as many tackles in 'keep ball' or getting tight on my man in practice games? Have I been standing off the pace? I need answers and I will lose sleep until I am satisfied that I know why. At other times I will know that I am not at my best during a game and I try to up my tempo to make sure that I am competing. There are occasions when you might be able get away with it. Maybe you score a goal and get man-of-the-match. But I know if I haven't been putting myself through what I should, and I have to get my head down and start again.

Trying harder is a natural cycle for me. When I was in my first year as a pro at West Ham my Dad got Manny Omoyinmi to run at me one-on-one. Manny was lightning quick and skilful on the ball. He skinned me – ran at me and round me – ten times on the spin. Then on the eleventh I got a little touch and the next I knocked the ball away and by the end of the session he couldn't beat me. That was a great lesson and reminder to me that you can always work out how to deal with a situation. I still do it. Even now in pre-season I can sometimes have a shocker in five-a-side when I've had a few weeks off. Someone once said I'm a slow starter. I don't think that's the case. I do everything to make sure I come out of the blocks quicker than my opponents. I try to better myself. I am aware that I need to be put under pressure to get on the right level.

You learn what you need and I know what I need and one of the great things about working with Jose Mourinho is that he respects his top players and recognizes that they know best what they need. Claudio Ranieri would always try to tell me that I should do this or that even though I felt that I needed something else. Claudio had a thing about shooting practice. He would tell me that instead of hitting a hundred balls all I needed to do was imagine hitting one and picture it as it beat the keeper. I understand that this is quite a common exercise in sports psychology. But different players need different things. I would always opt for knowing that I had spent half an hour hitting the target with a ball than simply thinking about it. Doing it properly is my idea of positive thinking. It always has been. With younger players, Mourinho will be strict because they need to learn but he is very instinctive about what the senior players require and I never experienced that before working with him.

Working with Dad and Harry was becoming more complicated. Life was getting harder instead of easier. Having a Dad-and-uncle management team was a unique scenario in English football. There were advantages and disadvantages to having them in charge and I think that during my time at West Ham I saw and felt them all, more than I care to remember. On the positive side I got extra time in coaching and as far as my development was concerned, having that close proximity was fantastic. Dad and Harry saw every strength and weakness in my game and so I was never short of people who mattered to me telling me what I needed to do.

I was still young though and needed the off-the-pitch stuff like a hole in the head. Unfortunately I didn't have the courage or knowledge to deal with certain things directly and so had to depend on others. One of the worst experiences I had was when I went to a Fans Forum. I was sitting on the podium with Iain Dowie and Marc Rieper, Peter Storey and Harry. No one wanted to know about me. I was just the young kid on the end and as is normal with these things, the questions were mostly about the price of season tickets or directed to the senior players about how the team was playing. I wasn't even sure why I was there to be honest. They were handing out a bit of stick but I don't think anyone had even noticed me. Then, one guy stands up and addresses Harry.

'Frank Lampard isn't good enough for West Ham,' he announced.

'Uh oh, here we go,' I thought.

'Why are you playing him? Is it because he's your nephew?'

I sat there thinking, 'What the hell?' The guy was entitled to his opinion even if I thought he was out of order; what really pissed me off was that not one other fan who was there said a thing to counter him. I had become sceptical about what was thought of me but I was still a West Ham player and deep down I believed we were all in this together – all fans. Surely I deserved more of a chance than this guy was willing to give? I was just a kid but already I wasn't good enough. Strangely enough, it turned out that the guy asking the question was the uncle of another youth player who was older than me who hadn't got a chance in the team. Again, this wasn't my fault but somehow it had been turned into an issue because of who I was. I was devastated. It was a killer blow to my confidence, which was already fragile. I didn't speak but Harry did and was calm about it.

'Frank was one of only four young players to be called into the England squad under Terry Venables at Euro 96,' he began. 'Terry said that he is a great prospect and a future captain of his country. We are lucky to have a young player of Frank's ability at West Ham and it doesn't matter which family he comes from. He's a great young player who will become even better. Just you wait and see.'

I appreciated the support. I realized what Harry was doing. In short, it wasn't just my uncle and my Dad who thought I was any good. Afterwards they said they would get the guy banned from West Ham but I never saw him again.

I would love to see him now though. What a coward, standing up and attacking a kid in front of 300 people. That's when it really started going against me at West Ham. That's when I knew that Hodgey was right. I had to get out.

CHAPTER 3

MAGIC MOMENTS

MOVING out of Mum and Dad's house was like being given the keys to a new world. I decided that I should be more independent. I could afford to buy a flat and when I found the right place I took the plunge. It was more a case of doing what I thought I should than what I really wanted. I was very comfortable at home. I enjoyed having my family around. Some of my mates were in their own place though and it seemed like the right thing to do. It was. Well, I thought it was. I quickly found that instead of gaining freedom I had a lot more time on my hands. I could do whatever I wanted. I just wasn't sure what that was.

At first, I did what I knew best and went back to Mum and Dad's house. Ate there and hung out with my sisters. After a few weeks I actually moved back there for a few days because I was so lonely. Mum didn't say anything. She knew what was going on and that I needed to get it out of my system. I drove back to the flat in Woodford Green and decided to get my mates round. I was bored. I didn't really know why. Suddenly the restrictions which had governed my whole life didn't exist. No more 'Where 'you going and what 'you doing?' I was a bit lost without Dad's third degree every time I opened the door to go out.

A lot of my mates lived close by: Sam – who we call Tel – Billy Jenkins, Alan (Alex), Finny, Banger (Mike), and HK (Sam). Good lads. Most of them went to a rival school but we had got together when we were about 15 and bonded. I phoned them and would get them round to watch the football on a Sunday. It was the natural thing to do. There was no one else there, I wanted company, and the lads were up for watching the game. It didn't seem so bad then. We would have a laugh and muck around and for the first time in my life I was doing the things that most people my age were doing. I was having a life. A life outside of my job. Outside of football.

In the evening we would pop down the pub and have a couple of drinks. The place was heaving with people squeezing the last out of their weekend. If there was no midweek game I would be off on Monday. Now and again I would feel like my weekend was still in full flow. So we would go to a club and have a few more beers, talk to some girls and stay out late.

I never did it directly before a game. I was up for it but I wasn't stupid. It was always Saturday after a game, or Sunday, or maybe early in the week. I think most young players go through it. I wouldn't say it's good for you but it's necessary. It's not until you realize you're not training as well as you should be that the effect kicks in. You just can't train to the same level if your body is tired and still trying to get rid of the booze from the night before. I don't mind admitting it, I realize that it wasn't the best idea for my career but for me it was something I had never had experience of. My childhood and youth were not the same as most people's.

Some go out with their mates when they are 15. They hang around a shopping centre or the local park and get a can of beer from somewhere and experiment with drinking. There were a couple of occasions when I did that towards the end of my schooldays but they were very rare. Mum and Dad were strict. They always wanted to know where I was going and why, and point out that I had training. I didn't need the constant reminder. Some of my mates were going down the route of taking their social life seriously but I was already on the road to becoming a footballer and there was nothing I wanted more than that. That's partly why it was such a liberating feeling to get my own place. No one to stop me going out or having my mates around me whenever I wanted.

The lads could do whatever they pleased. As a footballer I couldn't. But there were times when I would drink on a Sunday to blank out what had happened at the game the day before. It was a release for me, especially at times when I was taking so much stick and would be very down about West Ham. When the lads came round and had a drink I would be at ease again. We'd talk about everything and anything other than the game and I relaxed, de-stressed. I had to go through it and realize for myself that there are right times to do it and times that you don't. I want to go out and I still do now. The difference is recognizing the right time to do it. You have to know your body.

People remark that I've played 164 games consecutively and that I don't rest for matches. How do I do it? I live well, I eat well, I rest well but I still like to go out for a few beers with the lads after a game or in a week when there's no match. It's about balance but sometimes to find the balance you have to overdo it and that's what I did when I moved away from home.

I went through the same thing as most at that age though the experience was slightly different as a footballer. I would get recognized. When Rio and I went out it was unavoidable but it was nice. We earned good money and we got attention. We got into clubs easy and we could get our mates in as well. It was a good feeling. We had the money to do it. We could go out every night if we wanted. I had my freedom and I wanted to explore. It was a whole new experience for me, something that I had been aware of through my mates without ever feeling a part of it. Maybe I threw myself into it too much. For a while, I was at the centre of it and was happy to be there. I had to learn and that was the only way.

On occasion I would overdo it. Just like anyone else, a few too many could lead to embarrassing incidents. I had a particularly late Saturday night/Sunday morning after a game. We had won and I was up for enjoying myself. I slept it off for a few hours but was still feeling pretty rough and decided to call my agent, Steve Kutner, for something.

I had known Kutner since I was 18. Dad dealt with him when West Ham were trying to buy Steve Bould from Arsenal. Kutner had represented Bouldy who was interested in making the move to Upton Park. Though the transfer never materialized, something about the way Kutner had handled himself impressed Dad. I didn't have an agent at the time and was looking to appoint one so Dad and I met Kutner at the Swallow Hotel near Chadwell Heath.

The three of us talked and I began to understand the

importance of having a really good agent to look after you. Kutner made a lot of sense. He wasn't pushy or flash. His company is very small and he specializes in dealing with his clients' every need. I see young players now signing up to agencies which have 200 other guys on the books because they think that's impressive. I have also seen players get terrible advice from their agents because the underlying motive was not to do what was best for the player's career. With Kutner, I don't just have the best agent in the business, I also have a very good and loyal friend. There is no conflict of interest either because we became mates after we had a business arrangement. Some players employ a friend as their agent, and this I think is asking for trouble. I would hate to feel I was getting bad advice from a mate, never mind a mate who also happened to be handling my business and career. I have disagreements with Kutner and he with me but I can be absolutely sure that the end result is what is best for me without either of us feeling compromised. I know where I stand with Kuts though and so does he – side by side. Some people find him a little odd when they first meet him. He is very individual, can dress embarrassingly, is quite eccentric, and is often disarmingly blunt. However, I felt that I could trust him and that was the most important thing for me.

At the time in question, he had a routine of playing tennis with George Graham every Sunday morning. George was manager of Spurs and at this particular time, I was playing well and Spurs were interested enough in me to have started talking to West Ham about a transfer fee. George had just upped his offer for me to over £5 million. I dialled Kutner's mobile number and started to recount the events of the night before. I must have sounded a bit hazy. And loud. Normally, he would shout back at me, slag me off or whatever but on this occasion he was very quiet. After a couple of minutes I realized that he had cut me off. I wasn't bothered. But I should have been.

Kutner called me back a few hours later.

'You sobered up yet?' he asked.

'Yeah. Why?'

'When you called me this morning George Graham was sitting in my car and you were on speakerphone. It didn't make for good listening to a manager who has just bid over five million quid for you.'

'Oh s***. Did he know it was me?'

'Thankfully I realized it was you and cut you off. George was all right. He just said "Stevie. Who the hell was that?" but I told him it was one of my music industry mates who'd obviously been on the lash.'

I came off the phone feeling sick. And a bit stupid. It was one of those things but it wasn't one of the things I wanted to be happening on a regular basis. To be a successful footballer means being in the right place at the right time. I hadn't even arrived yet. Kutner didn't give me a lecture. He didn't have to. I knew from his tone of voice he wasn't impressed. He still loves telling the story and I have even heard him tell it to George. Thankfully, George regrets not getting me for £5 million but the whole episode reminds me of the thin line between success and failure.

Sometimes you have to learn the hard way. Being a footballer means you have to live your life by a different rule book to most other people. There are things you can and can't do because of the demands of the job and others which you need to be aware of because of the rules of celebrity.

I have always been very conscious about my health and fitness but when I went on my first lads' holiday I was oblivious to the second. I went to Ayia Napa in Cyprus with Jamie when I was 17 and our group was pretty sensible – though I had to assure Mum that Stan Collymore wasn't with us!

Back in 1996 Ayia Napa was the place to go if you were young and wanted a laugh. I wasn't disappointed and went back five years on the trot. When I went with Jamie I was completely unknown. There was no pressure of people coming up and asking for autographs. I was just a kid and in complete awe of everything.

In the following years Tel, Billy and I went there together. Then it was just Rio and I, but we weren't big-hitters at the time. I had played Under-21s and we had both made our West Ham debuts by then but we were still well below the radar in terms of being hassled. We certainly weren't the target of any tabloids – just two young lads enjoying our holiday the same as anyone else.

Rio, Tel and Billy returned the year after and had a good week but I was shocked a few days after I got home when a girl I had met there sold a story to a newspaper. It was embarrassing. I was 19 and had gone on holiday and I had done what every lad my age was doing but it's not the kind of thing you want your Mum and Dad to be reading over Sunday breakfast.

It jolted me but I was naive and Ayia Napa was the place to go and the place I knew best. I should have gone somewhere else because it had very much become the destination of choice for young footballers. I'm not sure if the Premier League had started running package tours but you saw so many faces on the beach and in the main square it certainly felt like it.

Inevitably, anywhere the cream of England's young football talent go to let their hair down will also be infested by the dregs of the scandal sheets. Lads having a laugh, having a few beers in a venue where the girls are doing the same. In retrospect, it was the ultimate honey trap and therefore only a matter of time before there would be a sting.

For our next visit in 2000 I was on my toes a little and at the beginning of the week I was nervous when we were in bars and when people came up to our group because they recognized us. But of course I became more comfortable and more relaxed after a couple of drinks and joined in the holiday spirit. I was out one night with a couple of mates and another lad who was someone we had met as part of another group of friends.

We met some girls and worked our way from a bar to a club and then back to one of our hotel rooms. We were mucking around having a laugh getting carried away on the booze and the freedom of being on holiday. Clothes were discarded and we were fooling around. I didn't think much of it and in that kind of situation I think most people just go with the flow.

Then I realized that the guy who we knew less well had produced a camcorder and was doing a running commentary of jokes. Well, it seemed funny at the time. Though we were all tired and hung over the next day, by the time we got out in the sun we were winding each other up about the night before. There was no fear of any consequences, no worries because we hadn't done anything wrong.

We flew home a couple of days later having enjoyed ourselves and I went to the Punch and Judy pub in Covent Garden the following Saturday to meet with Tel and couple of the lads for some lunch. We had just finished eating when Dad called me. His voice seemed a bit panicked but I couldn't make out what he was saying for the noise. I went outside and what he told me was the last thing I wanted to hear.

He explained that a newspaper had a copy of the video from the night in Ayia Napa and were running a story the following day. Dad was angry and disappointed.

'How could you be so stupid?' he said. How could I.

My knees had buckled and I felt sick. I was shocked and didn't know what to make of the information. I called Kuts who explained that a video of the night we spent in Ayia Napa had been bought by the *News of the World* and that myself, Rio and Kieron Dyer – who had been filmed in different incidents – were the subject of a story due to break the next day.

I felt so stupid. And humiliated. I didn't have to ask how bad it might look. I was there in the room and I knew. Now the whole country was about to find out as well. It was a nightmare. I tried to prepare myself for the shame of putting myself and my family in such an awful position.

When the paper dropped next morning it was actually worse than I had expected. Not only had they described everything in detail (with pictures as well) but they had also taken a moral stance claiming that we had been 'disrespecting and degrading women'. That was absolute rubbish. No one had done anything they didn't want to. I hadn't done anything illegal. I was a single young lad who was the victim of someone else's greed for money and the public's appetite for salacious scandal.

It was all very predictable. Any story about footballers and their behaviour had to contain a negative and sinister slant. It was too much to expect even-handed treatment, though I found their tone a bit rich for a newspaper with their weekly content. Unfortunately, I was in no position to throw stones.

The rest of the press jumped on the bandwagon and for a week everyone had their say about me, about footballers, and about the disintegration of polite society. It all seemed wildly over the top to me but I had no voice to defend myself because I was there on tape and therefore open to accusation.

It was all very tacky and I have never felt so humiliated in all my life. I felt sick from the embarrassment, and experienced gut-wrenching, stomach-churning nausea for days. Dad was right. How could I have been so stupid? I didn't want to be tagged as an irresponsible young reprobate. It wasn't me. I wanted to be a decent person and for people to regard me as a young player with a good reputation and a bright future.

I wasn't brought up to be the person who had been vilified in newsprint. I'd made an error of judgement in a situation where I should have been more aware of the possible consequences. I was disappointed with myself and have never felt so low.

Facing Mum was the worst. The whole thing was the most mortifying combination of events I think any son could present to his mother. She wasn't angry, just very hurt.

'You've let us down, Frank, but more than anything you've let yourself down,' she said. 'This isn't you. It's not the way you behave and it's things like this that send the career of a young footballer into the gutter and down the drain.'

I was motionless. There were tears running down my face and even though there were a million things racing around my head I couldn't bring myself to speak. I knew she was right. She felt the brunt of the shame. I'd let her down badly – her and my sisters, my nan and grandad.

I knew from football that some of the best lessons are those you glean from mistakes and now I had to do the same in my life. I should never have put myself in such a compromising situation and in retrospect I should never even have been in Ayia Napa. Needless to say I haven't returned.

It was my first real taste of the damage the papers can do and how ruthless they can be. I'm pleased now that I can talk about it as being such a long time ago without the possibility of anything similar being thrown at me. My bad experience with the press didn't end there, however. Worse, it raised its ugly head again around one of the most infamous days in modern history, 11 September 2001.

Reports of the terrorist atrocities that were taking place in New York began to filter through just as we were preparing to start training that morning. There was no way of realizing what was actually happening at that moment and when we returned to the dressing room afterwards there was a tension about what we might discover.

Some of the staff were very upset and when I found out the extent of what had happened I left Harlington immediately and spent the rest of the day in a horrified trance watching the news channels and trying to comprehend what was going on. I got a call from the club telling me that our UEFA Cup game which was scheduled for later in the week was likely to be called off but that I should report for training as usual.

The world was still in shock and the roads were noticeably quieter when I made my way towards the training ground which is adjacent to Heathrow Airport. The sombre atmosphere was made worse when Ranieri told me that my blood test had shown a low iron count and that I was being given the day off. I hate not training, especially when I really needed to focus on something else to take my mind off other things.

I got in the car, called my mate Billy and drove east around the M25 to his house. We went for a run for an hour and when we got back I had a message from Eidur to say that everyone had been given Thursday off and some of the boys were going out for lunch.

Billy and I met them in the pub down the road from the training ground but by the time we got there, JT, Jody, Eidur, and Frank Sinclair were already finishing up their food. We stayed and had a couple of drinks before moving off to another pub. You don't have to travel far to find one around the village so we settled down at a table and ordered some beers.

There was nothing unusual about the place. There were some other people in there eating and having a drink and while the general atmosphere was still touched by tragedy, everything seemed normal enough. We were getting more in the mood and with each round I suppose the noise level was rising. I doubt very much that we were the only people in the country who were looking for an outlet that day even if we chose the wrong way.

The company got more boisterous and we were itching for a change of scene so we moved on. Perhaps we should have decided to call it a day – especially when one of the lads got a tip to say that we were being followed by someone from the press. Unfortunately, we had gone beyond the stage where good sense was the obvious choice.

We breezed through another bar before deciding to head

for the Holiday Inn just off the M4 exit for Heathrow. It was just after 5 o'clock and we had been at it for a few hours. They had Sky News on in the corner and some people were sat around waiting for answers the same as the rest of the world. I don't imagine our entrance was graceful but we found a table away from the main area where we could carry on with the banter without affecting anyone else. We ordered some food and drink and were in the mood to have a laugh.

It was the wrong decision, a stupid thing to do on the day after so many people had lost their lives in America. I look back now and I realize how naive it was to put ourselves in that situation. There is no excuse. As high-profile footballers it was a very bad idea to go out drinking at such a sensitive time.

However, I can honestly say that we did not at any point abuse any Americans who were in that bar. We didn't shout at them or moon at them. The most we were guilty of was being loud and a bit rowdy but we kept ourselves to ourselves. Of course, that was not how it appeared in the press.

Two days later we were called to a meeting in the gym at the training ground by the managing director of the club, Colin Hutchinson. The *News of the World* had taken details of the story, including 'witness' statements about us, to the club. Colin was waiting for us with a reporter and photographer from the paper and told us that we were being fined two weeks' wages for breaking club rules.

He also explained that the reporter was there to get our side of the story so that we would at least have the opportunity to defend ourselves in print. What a joke. We went through what happened in the knowledge that it didn't look good but in the hope that at least some of it might be printed.

Some of it was – anything which incriminated us and helped stand up their 'version' from their 'eyewitnesses'.

The pictures were even better. Each of those published had us looking like convicted criminals – I had been whacked in the eye at training earlier in the week and the bruise had coloured just nicely to make me look particularly guilty. The story was followed up by the inevitable wave of condemnation about footballers and the shame and disgrace of it all.

I knew, because no one felt more shame than I did. To compound my misery I received a call from Sven-Goran Eriksson a few days later to tell me that I would not be considered for the upcoming England squad for the World Cup qualifying matches. He explained that the FA had instructed him that I was not to be picked but that he would speak to me again after all the furore had blown over.

I was angry and upset that I had allowed myself to get into the position where my reputation had been damaged and now my career was suffering as well. I was very down but made a promise to myself that I would come back better and stronger for the experience. The world had painted a very negative picture of me and I was determined to show what I was really like.

Kutner has always been around to remind me when I have needed reminding. When he tells me something it's what he thinks – no bullshit, no flam. It's for my benefit and the good of my career. Over the years I have learned to know what's best for me whether it's to do with football or life but I have been greatly helped by the people around me. When I go out now I know instinctively if it's right. Part of the reason I play so many games is knowing when and how much to do it. Some players drink to excess and I have seen the results of that along my career. Others won't touch a drop and not eat food they're not supposed to. I eat well but I am not obsessive about food. I still eat what I want without being overly fussy.

Finding the balance is the crucial thing. That takes time and I was still learning where to draw the line back then. My football was not going as well as I would have liked. The 98/99 season was a good season, but not for scoring goals. Six was not a great return. The season before had gone well because I had established myself as a player. People always said the second would be harder – harder physically, mentally, harder just to get better.

It wasn't as exciting as my first. The goals wouldn't come and partly because of that I felt a bit deflated. There was a lot to be happy about around the club though. We had a very good team. Myself, Rio, John Hartson, Eyal Berkovic were all playing well. People still say to me that if West Ham had kept that team together then maybe the club would have won a trophy. Trevor Sinclair was doing well while Michael Carrick and Joe Cole were just coming through, but it was a strange campaign. We were middle to bottom of the table usually. Then that season we found ourselves climbing up and up. We drew confidence and we became something of a force to be reckoned with. Well, at home anyway.

There was a good blend in the team in that period and we had some good characters too. The older lads were still there – Lomy, John Moncur and the likes but Neil Ruddock came in as well and there was a strength about us which I hadn't known before. There was also a creative heart.

I am not Berkovic's biggest fan as a person but he was a good player and I enjoyed playing with him. You just had to give the ball to his feet and he would slip people in on goal. He was adept at it and he was in that sort of form that year. Paolo Di Canio had been shown the door at Sheffield Wednesday and when he turned it on we were exciting to watch. We ended up coming fifth and that was a huge achievement for West Ham. You only had to remember that it was as far back as 85/86 that the club had come third, long before any of us were on the scene. After that we were a bit of a yo-yo team: relegated, back up, relegated, back up.

Harry deserves credit. We were on the verge of another drop into the First Division but he had the vision to sign unusual players. Di Canio, Berkovic, Davor Suker. Not many people have the kind of eye for a player that Harry has. He's still doing it. Maybe it was a loan signing of a player who was getting on and no one else wanted – players who may have looked unconventional to others; too young or just too much trouble. Harry, though, had a way of harnessing all kinds of talent.

He got it wrong on a few occasions. Dmitri Raducioiu, Ilie Dumitrescu and Paolo Futre come to mind but Harry was in a position where he was taking chances on people and the law of averages dictated that not every one would be brilliant. The problem with those particular guys was they had made their name in the game already and their hunger and desire was gone. When some of them rented apartments in Chelsea Harbour, when we trained about an hour and half's drive in the opposite direction, you began to question exactly why they had come to play in London. I don't think they knew what they were signing up to at West Ham. We were more about spirit than silky soccer and there were a few characters around who were strong and liked to assert themselves. It couldn't have been comfortable to land at Chadwell Heath after a few years in the sunshine of Spain or Portugal.

To be fair to Harry, the chairman probably threw those guys in his face when he wanted to moan but the bottom line was that he got it right far more times than wrong. And, he didn't pay a fortune for players either. Slaven Bilic and Igor Stimac gave us experience at the back as did Neil Ruddock.

Razor Ruddock was important as much for his character as his football. He was our social secretary and was brilliant at getting the right place for a game of golf, followed by lunch and then a night out. He was also a great laugh.

Razor could mix with anyone – whether it was the older lads, me and Rio or the foreign boys. He was hilarious even when he didn't mean to be. At training we would do one-on-one and he would have Joe Cole running at him full pelt with the ball. He was slowing down so he would just back off. And off and off. Eventually, Joe was so close to goal that he would shoot from six yards and the rest of us were bent double laughing.

Ian Wright was another one. Wrighty had done his time, scored goals and broken the records when he arrived at West Ham. He didn't have anything to prove and didn't need to practise. He did anyway and I was glad of his professionalism. I would be heading out to hit a hundred balls and he would come with me and advise me on free-kicks and how to strike a ball best. He was 33 then and Roger Cross would clip balls in from wide areas for us to hit at goal. I have a lot of respect for Wrighty and I'm a lot sharper around the box partly thanks to his tips and watching his movement off the ball.

There were others whose careers had been thwarted by injury and Harry had faith in them. Trevor Sinclair was one.

Everyone remembered Trevor as a brilliant winger with Queens Park Rangers who was unlucky enough to sustain serious injury. He came to us and got fit again but there was something about Harry which instilled confidence in Trevor and very quickly he became a major influence on the right wing and as second striker. I got on great with him. He was quite laid back and there were also no airs and graces about him. With some players I could detect a reluctance to get too close to me because of my Dad and Harry. Trevor never bothered with that. We would come in after training and he'd say 'Tell your Dad he's put on a s*** session there, Lamps!'

I loved it. It was very refreshing. He treated everyone with the same boisterous banter and didn't care much how they reacted though I rarely found anyone who could resist his company. There was one year at the team Christmas party when we started off in a bar in Romford and were due to end the night in a club. On the way between the two Trevor decided we should stop off for a swift drink in another pub. I didn't see why not – even though we were in fancy dress. I'm not sure what we looked like when we burst into this place but I'm sure I could feel the proverbial tumbleweed follow us through the door. Trevor didn't give a monkey's. He ordered some drinks and invited everyone in the bar to join us in a song.

After twenty minutes, the whole place was in great voice being led by West Ham's right-winger who was decked from head to foot in 'neon pick' Seventies' gear, the likes of which Huggy Bear from *Starsky and Hutch* would have been proud. We crashed out of there, pissing ourselves with laughter, but that was Trevor – infectious and fun to be with. We needed people like that at West Ham to galvanize the team spirit. Harry knew that and he delivered. He also brought stars.

Paolo Di Canio was probably the biggest in terms of impact of all his West Ham signings and Upton Park was a place which any Premiership team would have worried about visiting that season.

The difference was we had never played without suffering before. We always seemed to be struggling with players some of whom may not have quite been up to standard. The quality was quite good enough and there were a lot of battlers in midfield – guys like Martin Allen and Paul Butler. Good players who were not always easy on the eye. Ian Bishop could get on the ball but the team were suffering and so did he. The fans were impatient and wanted a more direct style of play which Bish didn't subscribe to.

Lomas came in, I did, Berkovic and Sinclair. Lomy would hold, I would get up and down while Berkovic would link it together. There was a confidence about the team and the pattern we established. We could play. We were actually quite upset that we didn't do enough to qualify for UEFA Cup automatically and we went to the Intertoto instead.

I had proved a lot of people wrong in my first season and in the second season I put myself under a lot of pressure to do better. The team had improved but I found things quite difficult. It had been easy to see the difference the year before. I had looked and felt comfortable on the ball. Maybe it wasn't as discernible. The leap was not as obvious and from the outside I wondered if it looked as bad as it felt. There had been a freedom about running forward the season before, which had seen me score goals. My legs were light and at times I just knew I was going to get on the end of something.

It was different now. I felt heavier. Some of the joy had

gone. It was harder to defend and that year I realized that I couldn't always just run forward at will. I needed to be more disciplined about choosing when. It was the first time I had been conscious of the need to curb that part of my game for the good of the team, of getting results instead of glory. Things weren't dropping for me in the box and I have always been very aware of progress in my game. I found it harder to identify where I was improving and that worried me.

We were winning games 1–0 and it was a real learning curve for me that season. I played nearly every game. I became a seasoned pro. There was nothing better than playing. The contrast was amazing though because I had come into a struggling team when the fans were getting on top of Harry. The contrast to being part of a good team which was playing well was amazing. I could sense that training was sharper and more enjoyable. It just clicked. There was an element of good fortune. Harry had bought good players but there were good players who were coming through as well, players who were fresh, enthusiastic, hungry, and who wanted to do well for the club.

There was a transition taking place and I could feel it, see it. I have every respect for the lads who had served the club well when I was an apprentice, guys like Dowie, Dicks and Bishop who individually had been very good players for West Ham and had character in spades. But as a group maybe their time was over. It was very old school and they were quite set in their ways. The problem was that football was moving in a new direction and being up the back of the bus with bottles of beer and wine on the way back from games seemed less acceptable.

They all had great character and at that time West Ham

needed that kind of player to get them out of trouble. But it had had its day in terms of improving the club and there was a natural evolvement to the newer team with younger players. Harry and Dad realized that if they gave the younger lads more responsibility then they wouldn't have to rely on the more experienced ones as much. There were a few clever buys as well.

Igor Stimac was one. He was an intelligent man and I got on with him very well. He would pick me up for training and we would talk a lot about his experience as a player. Igor was a tough character as well who had seen and done a few things in his time. I knew right away I could learn from him.

He had fifty caps for Croatia and had played in his home country and in Spain as well as with Derby County. He was clever and could get on with anyone. He had the unusual knack of being able to sit with the older boys and hold a conversation on anything at the back of the coach, even have a drink of wine with them, and then mix just as easily with the younger generation. He even came for a drink with me and my mates once in the local bar. We might be mucking around playing pool and stuff but he would look very comfortable sitting there with a cup of coffee, chatting away. Even though we were only 19 or 20 and he was ten years older he was able to bridge the age gap with ease. And style.

Igor only stayed at West Ham for a couple of years but he was one of the new breed. Suker was another. Davor was very urbane. He too had been around a bit – including a spell at Real Madrid – and came to us from the much loftier climes of Highbury. He was soon made one of the lads. Moncs gave him the East End tag of 'Dave-or' and he loved it. He was a great player too – the ultimate goalscorer who had a deadly left foot. I took to him straight away. He was different and, like Igor, I knew I could learn from him. Davor was very self-confident – assured. He has enjoyed a successful career and was wealthy before he signed for us.

There were times when he chatted about how best to invest money. Property. Here and in Croatia. He favoured stocks and shares too and none more infamous than a company called Magic Moments. Davor obviously knew the markets and had good advisors. John Moncur was not quite so well versed and when he asked Davor for a tip it was Magic Moments which was the best buy. Moncs was impressed by the fact that Davor was sinking about five hundred grand into these shares. Brilliant, he thought, I'll have some of that. Buoyed up by Davor's track record and expensive car, he went in for £20,000. West Ham were not the best payers and so that was a substantial sum for Moncs.

It all went well for a couple of months. Each morning we would be getting changed for training and John would ask how the Magic Moments were doing.

'Great,' said Davor. 'Up two pence,' and so on.

This exchange became as common as any other in the dressing room until one day, it wasn't great. In fact, it was very bad. The price had gone through the floor and the stock was worth less than what they had paid for it.

'Magic Moments,' said Moncs. 'F***ing Tragic Moments more like.'

'I'm sorry, Moncs,' Davor replied.

'F*** me, Dave-or. It's all right for you but I can't feed my kids because of them shares.'

It wasn't Davor's fault. And he had lost a lot more money. He never complained though, unlike Moncs, who would go on about Tragic Moments every other day for months while the rest of us laughed. The banter was great, mainly due to the cast of unlikely characters whom Harry had introduced to the place.

Di Canio was another though there could never be another Paolo. He was very professional in his own particular way. I can't say that I agreed with everything he did. Everything had to be right for him even if it was wrong for everyone else. For instance, it would annoy me when he would go back to Italy for two weeks' rehabilitation when he was injured. But, there was no denying that he was doing for himself what he saw as being for the benefit of the team. There were times when we would be training at Chadwell Heath, usually when it was freezing cold and pissing down with rain, when I would wonder where Paolo was. He would often return on a Thursday with the news he was ready to play on Saturday.

He looked after himself but he was too selfish to be a great professional. It was tempting to think he was enjoying a bit of sunshine but I know Paolo and I learned that wherever he was it was because he was trying to recover and get back as quickly as possible. Paolo had different routines from the rest of us even when he was there. He would say he wanted to do some special stuff with the fitness coach and while the rest of us were running our nuts off with Harry, Paolo would be in a corner of the pitch doing some little jazzy exercises. He was such a special player he could get away with it. He knew it, we knew it and we accepted it. We needed the likes of him and Igor to move forward – away from the relegation zone and into the realms where we were winning games with the ambition of achieving better things.

Later in my career I began to understand that transition of mindset much better.

With Chelsea, under Mourinho, we are used to winning every game. We go into matches not expecting to lose. I felt that change in mental attitude through the years and, retrospectively, I can see that it happened with West Ham in that season. It was on a smaller scale than I know now but it was there.

I had been there a long time, all my life, but I had never been in a team where I looked around and saw quite so many good players: Paolo up front, Trevor Sinclair on the wing, Joe Cole beside me, and Rio and Igor behind me. There were players who made the transition with me. Steve Lomas and John Moncur were old school, players who you could rely on in a battle, especially if it was a fight for survival. John had a way with the young lads as well though. He encouraged us and I think he saw that we were a slightly different group of West Ham players to the ones he had been used to. I had a great respect for all of the lads who had played through the Nineties. I had watched them from the stands and in training before actually becoming part of their group as a young player.

As I got older I knew that I wanted to reach for greater things than just the odd victory over a big club or a decent cup run. I wasn't alone. Rio was ambitious and so was Joe. We were less cynical. At the start of your career you always look up and not down and that's maybe why we were much more comfortable with the new upwardly mobile West Ham. The club had become a bit set in its ways. They started each season expecting to battle relegation. We were different. We had aspirations to do better and if we were honest, perhaps we already had an idea that ultimately that would mean leaving Upton Park. We would talk about it and it's a natural progression for any young player who comes through at a club like West Ham. Loyalty in football has changed a lot since the Sixties and Seventies when it was likely that you could spend your whole career at one club.

Look at the case of Matt Le Tissier. He had his reasons and he deserves credit for the fact that he spent his whole career at Southampton. It doesn't stop a lot of people from wondering why he didn't move to a bigger club and a bigger stage – one that his talent certainly deserved. Maybe even he asks himself that same question now and again. I have always believed that the greatest strength in a person is to do everything possible to realize your full potential – get as close to the top as you possibly can. That is one of the reasons why Rio and I are where we are now. It's not arrogance or conceit. More like an inner determination to succeed. I have seen and heard some foreign players declaring themselves to be the best in the game, league – even the world. Even when they say that they are going to win a certain game I cringe.

Even if I believed it I would never say it in public. Foreign players are quite comfortable with it which is something we do not admit in our culture. It's not English to pronounce or appoint yourself to a lofty position. In England we always look on that kind of behaviour as arrogance.

Nonetheless, I think we are intrigued by it. When Muhammad Ali sung his own praises I think we all looked at him with a grudging admiration as well as affection. He did it with a smile not a sneer. In general, though, we tend to frown on that kind of behaviour from one of our own. I suppose Chris Eubank in his pomp is another boxing analogy. I think there is a breed of English player now who is in between the two extremes. If the old way was to never build yourself up, keep your head down, and work hard then the new way has moved on. But it's not quite reached the excesses of some foreign players who build themselves up too much.

I have learned that it's okay to be ambitious and why shouldn't I say that I am a good player but I want to be an even better player. There is a time and a place though. I can say that I want to be better and play in great teams and win trophies but the problem I had then was how that would be interpreted. The minute I say that I am an ambitious player and I want to go right to the top that is interpreted as 'Frank Lampard Wants to Leave West Ham.' Then you get in trouble. Accused of being disloyal because you have been a fan all your life, you are not allowed to want to do better for yourself – better than you could if you stayed.

My football education was still progressing with West Ham. There was a different buzz around the club after we came fifth and though we missed out on direct entry to the UEFA Cup the club took up the option of entering the Intertoto Cup and trying to qualify that way. This was my first taste of continental football! There was a certain irony about the fact we drew a team called FC Jokerit in the first round. Here we were embarking on West Ham's first European campaign in nearly twenty years and we're off to Finland. It was brilliant.

The Toolo Stadium was basic and small but that didn't matter to our fans. About 2000 of them had decided that this was a major event and I could barely believe my eyes when we went out to warm up. There they were with flags, banners and plenty of air in their lungs singing like it was the Champions League Final. It was quite a sight and it stirred a deep feeling of pride which still burned within me. Despite everything, West

Ham was my club and the people in the stadium were my people. To make it sweeter, I scored the equalizer from a free-kick in a 1–1 draw and we progressed to the next round having beaten them 1–0 at home in the first leg.

Even though the opposition were poor and we were still effectively in pre-season, I picked up on the subtle difference of playing in Europe. It was more technical, more patient. At that level it was harder to put your finger on and in years to come I would learn the hard way with Chelsea. The moment was sweet nevertheless. Before the Premiership even started we were playing the second round of Intertoto against the Dutch club, Heerenveen. At home first, I scored again – a goal which I regard as my best for West Ham. I still watch the mental replay. Twenty-five yards out. Boom. In off the upright. I ran to the fans. They were going mad. It was Europe; we were winning; I was scoring. Magic. They were better than Jokerit but we had them beaten. The away match was another 1–0 victory and though it may have only been a little step on the ladder of European football, for a club like West Ham it felt like winning the lottery.

The club needed the money. The players wanted the experience and the fans wanted the trips. Everyone was happy. I banged in my third of the season on the opening day of the league campaign when we beat Spurs – again – 1–0. It was a bit like the old Arsenal.

We were consistent with results and recorded another 1–0 in the final of the Intertoto against French club Metz. Unfortunately, the result was in their favour, and it was at Upton Park. And I missed a penalty. It was the first one I missed at the top level. I was very upset, though not at the time. You have to blank it out and get on with it. The crowd didn't give me too much stick either. They were already looking forward to the second leg and at least it was still alive. I walked towards the tunnel reliving the penalty and feeling miserable.

It was a terrible result to suffer in a European tie. I was desperate to get into the UEFA Cup and taste the real competition. We had played well in the other games and I was sure we would make it. If only I had taken the kick differently, better, just scored the bloody thing. We had to wait two weeks for the return. I don't know who was more impatient – the players or the fans. We were still unbeaten having drawn away at Aston Villa and beaten Leicester at home. There was a confidence within the dressing room that we could go to France and get a result.

The fans felt the same. At least, that was the feeling among those who left for Metz from Upton Park almost immediately after the Leicester game. They climbed on to buses in their hundreds, complete with packed lunches, dinners, and a few beers. Maybe it had been such a long time since West Ham were in Europe that our fans hadn't realized that there were new ways to get to the game: aeroplanes, trains, and so on. Not the Hammers. They were traditionalists to the last. I didn't see all of it all but Nan told me that it was like an evacuation of the East End – convoys of coaches full of supporters heading for the ports.

The team flew (thankfully) and I remember the build-up to that match having an extra edge to it. It was normal for us to stay in a hotel before away games. I can't say they were ever really top notch but I'm not complaining. They were good and I was used to it. Just that in Metz it was a step up even in accommodation.

RIGHT: Cousin Sam plays hold the baby with me in the back garden of my parents' house.

FAR RIGHT: Showing a keen sense of fashion for a 2-year-old while out in the local park.

LEFT: Natalie, Claire, Dad, Mum and me at the front with Dad's FA Cup winners' medal from the 1980 Final.

BELOW LEFT: Looking very stripey in my nursery school class photo, aged 4.

BELOW: Excited to be wearing my wellies inside nursery school because it was snowing that day.

Summer holiday fun at Bournemouth with Claire and cousin Mark Redknapp.

Class photo from Gidea Park College: sporting my first school uniform.

Sweeping my first girlfriend Kirsty off her feet with my performance in the school play as a soldier – uniform made by Mum.

The infamous 200 metres race at Brentwood, aged 7. Five metres later I fell over from trying too hard and cried all the way home.

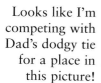

Looks like I'm competing with Dad's dodgy tie for a place in this picture!

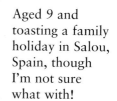

Aged 9 and toasting a family holiday in Salou, Spain, though I'm not sure what with!

Anyone for Mum's turkey? Christmas day with the family at home.

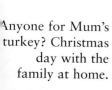

ABOVE: Another victorious Heath Park league winning team in 1980.

RIGHT: The worst school uniform ever and cause of much scorn. Brentwood School circa 1980.

LEFT: Asleep on the sofa with Dad after a hard day's training, aged 13.

LEFT: Christmas dinner with the family 1986. Left to right: Natalie, Nanny Hilda, Claire, Dad and me.

BELOW: Nicky Butt, Don Hutchison, Jamie Redknapp and me having a lads' laugh on holiday in Ayia Napa.

ABOVE: Dressed up to the nines for a day out with mates at Ascot races.

RIGHT: On the beach with the boys in Ayia Napa (Stan Collymore far right and Jamie front left)

LEFT: Father and Son take a moment out from training at West Ham's Chadwell Heath ground.

ABOVE: The apprentice practising shooting in the early days with West Ham.

LEFT: Uncle Harry telling 39-year-old Gordon Strachan to go easy on me in my debut for West Ham against Coventry City!

BELOW: Showing early signs of responsibility for taking penalties with West Ham.

FAR LEFT: Dad still cutting a fine figure of a player in his thirties for the Hammers.

LEFT: Looks like a near miss from Lampard in the early days with West Ham.

Clashing with Patrick Vieira
for the first time at Highbury –
possibly not the best thing
to be doing.

Pass the parcel. Paolo Di Canio
was desperate to take this
penalty against his old club
Sheffield Wednesday.

Chuckling at Rio's attempt
to hold me off on his return
to Upton Park as a Leeds
United player.

We arrived at a chateau outside of the city and it had a really nice feel to it. The club recognized the potential of overcoming this hurdle and had pushed the boat out. We appreciated the effort. When you are used to being mid-table and fighting for another place up or down, some games merge into others. It's not that they weren't important but there are some matches I played with West Ham that I simply can't remember. Metz isn't one of them. On the way to the stadium there seemed to be waves of claret and blue flooding the streets of the city, singing, drinking, expecting.

I thought we had taken a lot of people to Finland and Holland but this was on a different scale. By the time kick-off came round the reinforcements had arrived as well and there was a huge bank of West Ham fans in the ground. They were in good cheer and so was I after I scored the opener. We went on to win 3–1.

I took a moment to absorb the sight after the game. The lads had gone over to celebrate with the fans and I was headed to join them. Everywhere there was unadulterated joy. Football provides many moments of pleasure as a player and fan. Sometimes they coincide but rarely is the emotion of the stands replicated on the pitch. But it happened in Metz that night. We were all fans, delirious that we had shared a little bit of history for West Ham. I had atoned for my penalty miss. We were going to play in one of Europe's big competitions. It was a special feeling.

Igor Stimac was pleased with the draw for the first round. He was going home to Croatia and we would play Osijek. Once again we played home first. I scored and we won convincingly. Whether or not that cushion gave big Igor reason to believe the return would be a formality I am not sure. I would like to think that it was a sense of security about the result rather than a security risk that saw him arrange a gun club for the lads. It has to be one of the most bizarre pre-match activities I have ever come across. Imagine the scene after lunch.

'What you doing now then?'

'Gonna have a sleep. You?'

'Watch a bit of telly probably. What about you, Moncs?'

'Going to a field with Igor to fire some rifles.'

They fired at targets but all of a sudden the bullet holes which riddled the walls of houses around the country took on a more sinister appearance. Croatia had suffered a war and this was my first experience of travelling in the Balkans. Our hotel was basic and was more like a hostel. There was a hard single bed in the corner of the room and the sheets were the scratchy, starchy kind which never quite feel right. So much for the pampered life of the professional footballer. Despite the distractions, we managed to keep focused and won our way safely through to the next round. We were on a roll and it was exciting. It turned out to be my best season at the club. I scored fourteen goals and even though the European run didn't last that long there was still a feeling among the players that we had achieved something. Taking the next step was the hard part.

It was hard to see West Ham continuing to progress where they would break into the top four. Football was changing rapidly and unless you had the funds then it was going to be very difficult to make much more significant progress. The money just wasn't there.

I understood the team's potential and also the tradition of the club. We had players who played in the right way and the fans were right to expect that. That was one of the reasons that football fans outside of London wanted West Ham to do well. It goes back to the 1966 World Cup when there were three West Ham players involved but I could understand why a lot of people had a soft spot for the club. There was a lot of romance attached to it. Unfortunately when you come fifth the fans automatically expect you to better that.

That was a false expectation in West Ham's case. The fans expected to win the league even though the club had never achieved that feat. Even back in the days of Moore and Hurst they still didn't win the championship. Harry often jokes that the team he played in had six or seven great players yet they always finished mid-table showing how bad he and the other four were.

You can get caught up with playing really glamorous and entertaining football and not win anything and perhaps West Ham fell into that trap. People respected the ideal but practical aspects such as the playing staff and the budget dictate that it's just not possible. To be fair, this is not just an issue for West Ham. Football fans everywhere naturally aspire to the glories of the past. I was the same when I was a kid. They hope and pray that one day they will witness something similar. There is a problem though with inflated expectation and we had that at West Ham the year after we finished fifth.

Despite the fact that we had achieved something special – and done it with quite a few kids in the team – there was a large section of the support who automatically set their sights on fourth. Again, fine. Nothing wrong with wanting to do better and being optimistic.

I felt the same way. Well, I had the same dream. Reality rarely matches up though and that brought out the negative feeling in the crowd. It didn't take much. A few dodgy results in the league and we were getting hammered by the punters. Sometimes you have to take a step back to go forward. At West Ham that wasn't allowed. Dad and Harry were doing everything they could to improve on the previous season. Europe was a big adventure for everyone at the club and the fact that I had been scoring regularly had not gone unnoticed in other quarters.

There had been some talk of me being called up for England. As ever, it started in the newspapers and spread around the media. I didn't take that much notice. Jamie was the established mainstay of the midfield for England and there were guys like Paul Scholes and Nicky Butt who had already played for the national team. Kevin Keegan had been asked about me ahead of a friendly against Belgium which was to be the warm-up match for the Euro 2000 play-off with Scotland. He had been kind in public but you never know where you stand with a manager until he actually picks you and you can work with him first hand.

I wasn't a stranger to the international set-up. Far from it. I had played for the Under-21s though my first taste of what it was like to be involved with the senior team was under Terry Venables. They were preparing for Euro 96 and had gathered at their training base at Burnham Beeches. The idea was to give some younger lads experience of what it was like to live and train with the senior squad as they got ready for the most important games to be played in this country since the World Cup Final thirty years previously. It certainly had an effect on me.

I turned up at the hotel beside myself with nerves. Things had not gone as smoothly as the manager would have liked up to that point. High spirits on a night in Hong Kong during a pre-tournament trip followed by high jinks on a plane on the way back had left the press baying for blood. And that was before the tournament started. I can't say I noticed too much panic among the players. If anything, there was a tangible sense of unity. Terry Venables had answered the criticism by closing ranks and refusing to slaughter any of those who were involved in the incidents.

The siege mentality tactic is one I have since seen deployed a few times. It can be an effective tool and even though I was a young lad coming into a group of men I could sense a bond of solidarity which was going to be difficult to breech. Thankfully, Jamie was there and was very much one of the lads. As a result, I was accepted by them much more easily than I could have expected.

That was quite difficult given that I wandered around the place like star-struck teenager. I was only 16 and Chadwell Heath wasn't quite populated with the same calibre of player. Every time I turned a corner in the hotel there was Steve McManaman or Robbie Fowler. I had met those lads before with Jamie so I felt relatively comfortable in their company. It wasn't until I walked out on to the lawn in front of the hotel that I almost fell over. There was Gazza playing table tennis – playing table tennis with all of the enthusiasm and venom that he played his football.

To one side of him was an area which had been set up for the lads to play head tennis. There was a game going on but I didn't even notice who was taking part. I was transfixed. Actually, I was completely in awe and I wasn't the only one. Hotel staff had parked themselves at a safe distance to observe the whirlwind at play. Gazza had that attraction. He would suck anyone within a hundred-yard radius towards him without trying. He was magnetic. Even a talented group of experienced professionals could not escape his gravitational pull. The likes of Alan Shearer and Tony Adams were stuck in his orbit the same as me. Those who saw him as a singular force on the pitch knew nothing about how much that extended to everything which happened beyond the kick of a football. It was remarkable.

His presence was so powerful that he was noticed just as much when he wasn't around. Just knowing he was somewhere in the building generated a sense of wonder and curiosity. The first morning the entire squad had gathered for breakfast in the team dining room. It was normal practice before the day's training regime and we were kitted up in our tracksuits and trainers. The tournament was still a couple of weeks away but the place was already buzzing with expectation. The talk was of what was happening that day, what might happen that month. Everyone was there, even the kit man and physios. Everyone, that is, except Gazza.

I sat with Jamie and Robbie and ate my cereal. Terry Venables made a point of coming over to say hello as he went to the buffet. I was chuffed by the greeting but I could sense a degree of distraction elsewhere in the room. Only later, after experiencing it at first hand, did I realize what was causing the discomfort.

The Gazza veterans in the squad – and there were a few – knew that trouble was only moments away when the great man wasn't where he was supposed to be. Usually that could be funny – for some – other times not. Hence the nervous tension as each minute passed and still no show. He eventually turned up and didn't let anyone down with his entrance.

He was cloaked in his dressing gown cradling half a water melon under his arm. In between guzzling spoonfuls of the fruit, he christened all of the hotel staff serving breakfast with hilarious nicknames. I wasn't sure how to react. I had never seen anything like it but I found out that it was just the way he was. Gazza ruled the place, could do what he liked and was a popular king. I had, of course, heard stories – everyone had – in the dressing room or talking with older pros from other clubs. There was always somebody with a weird and wacky tale about Gazza.

My only previous experience was from afar. I had seen him play at Upton Park when I was a boy. He was just a teenage lad in a Newcastle United shirt – all wiry and unpredictable but somehow he managed to run a man's game against West Ham. That was as close as I had got to the Gazza phenomenon in the past. Now here I was staring it in the face.

He was mad as a lorry – no doubt about it – but any excess in his behaviour always had the edge taken off it by the fact that it is impossible not to love Gazza. Everyone did and with good reason. He had a heart to match his larger-than-life personality along with a mischievous and very infectious sense of fun. There were pranks galore which led to laughs and apprehension. 'Where's Gazza?' was a common question, he being all the more conspicuous by his absence. As the new lad, I expected to become a victim and I didn't have to wait long. I was sound asleep in my room when the phone rang.

'Hallo!' bellowed the voice on the line. 'I dinna suppose ye can tell me what's on Channel 4 at quarter past three, can ya Frankie lad?'

Semi-conscious, I scrambled around for the light switch and a newspaper. I found the TV listings and told Gazza that there was a documentary on the changing climate of the Antarctic.

'Really!' he said enthusiastically. 'Thanks for that.'

I put the phone down and closed my eyes as it dawned on me that I had been had. I wondered how much stick I would take at breakfast. Bring it on. I was one of the lads now that Gazza had done me in cold. Unfortunately, it wasn't over yet. By morning I was still sleeping when a loud knock on the door had me jumping out of bed. It was him, in his robe again. He didn't say a word, well, not to me anyway. He just brushed past me counting to himself: 'Eighty-one, eighty-two, eighty-three', and so on. I realized he was measuring his paces. The way a referee moves back a defensive wall at a free-kick.

'Gazza,' I said. 'What are you doing?'

'Eighty-nine, ninety, ninety-one.'

He had already circled my room and was heading for the door when he turned round and raised a finger to his lips, motioning me not to speak, like it might break his concentration, or his stride. I watched him leave – still counting as he made his way down the corridor. It was an experience all right. Slightly surreal but invaluable.

The rest of the time wasn't all cleaning boots and moving kit either. I got to train with the squad up until the opening game against Switzerland before I returned to my more ordinary life – one with no Gazza. I had seen enough though, enough to make me realize that I had a lot of work to do before I would be ready to play for my country at the highest level. I was grateful for the insight. I felt comfortable in the environment and enjoyed it immensely. It gave me an appetite for making that step up.

In the interim, I served a three-year apprenticeship with the Under-21 team and was made captain by Peter Taylor at the age of 19. It was useful preparation for the senior side because tactically and technically the levels are quite similar. But in every other respect – physical, mental, awareness, competitiveness, for example – the difference is as night from day. I scored regularly for the Under-21s and found Taylor a very able coach and likeable man. He was a progressive thinker unlike his successor Howard Wilkinson whose old school approach and attitude I couldn't see working with the younger players. But with every game I played I was focusing more and more on breaking into the senior side. I had an idea of what I needed to do but I had to wait – three more years to be precise.

The landscape of international football in England changed dramatically during that time. Venables had taken the team to the verge of the final at Euro 96 and was then told he no longer had a job. Glenn Hoddle was appointed his successor and managed through France 98 before Keegan took over. My form had been good from the beginning of the 1999/2000 season. The goals were flowing as well – five in my first twelve games but it was still a surprise when I got the call-up to the full England squad in October. We were playing Belgium, in a warm-up for the Euro 2000 play-off against Scotland, at Sunderland's Stadium of Light.

One of the first calls I got after the squad was announced was from Jamie. He had been selected as well, though, unlike mine, there was no surprise that his name was included. Jamie was excited at the prospect of playing together. It was something we had joked about as kids though back then we had envisaged it being with a club, not our country. As we got older maybe we dared to mention it now and again. Then when I was training with the full squad before Euro 96 a couple of other lads joked that one day I would join Jamie in the team. I laughed it off as banter. In my head though I had dreamt of the scenario. It's every boy's dream to play for his country. But to share that with your cousin who is one of your best mates, that was a fantasy.

Jamie was there when I joined up with the rest of the squad. His presence made the whole thing easier for me, just as it had three years before. Once we got out on the training pitch I felt less awkward and self-conscious. Football is a natural leveller and rarely have I come across a player in an England squad who looked out of his depth. Jamie was in great form in and out of training and I relaxed. I began to realize what it might have felt like for Gary and Phil Neville to be brothers. Brothers in family and family in football. Jamie and I were cousins and very much a football family. I looked up to him at that moment in the same way as I always had. He was bigger than me, older, wiser, and more confident. Better at football and better looking. But as far as Jamie was concerned, only one thing was important and that was helping me be the best I could be. Well, that and England winning.

As always, I was grateful for his guidance. I became more nervous as the game got closer and while I felt I had trained well I didn't expect to start. Not for my country. Not when I had only just been called up. That Friday before the game, Arthur Cox, who was Keegan's assistant manager, pulled me to one side and said I should tell my family that I was starting. I didn't know what to say. I blurted out a thanks. Seeing I was slightly shocked he offered an explanation as a way of making it more real. Paul Scholes (who had scored a hat-trick against Poland in the qualifiers) would be on the bench – he was already established – and so the manager wanted to give me a run and see what happened. Fine. Scholesy out and Lampard in. Good. No pressure then. It took a few moments to sink in during which time I rehearsed all of the best and worst things that might happen. Then I went to look for Jamie to tell him that the dream we had as kids of playing for the same team was about to come true.

I barely slept that night for excitement. Being told that you're twenty-four hours away from something that you have dreamt of all of your days is an odd experience to say the least. At some point in life, everyone imagines what it must be like to win the lottery. Can you imagine, though, what it would be like to be told that you were going to win the lottery at 3 pm the next day? Unfortunately it didn't turn out to be the jackpot I would have wanted.

We won – which was important. In fact, Jamie scored the winner with a typically gorgeous left-foot shot. I ran to him to celebrate but the image I have in my head doesn't match the feeling in my gut. We're both laughing yet there's something missing. It still upsets me now. I don't have any amazing memories of it. I have tried hard to recover some lost sense of exultation but it's just not there. It never was. People say that the day you make your international debut is such a big occasion – and it was – but I feel very strangely about it. I was only 21 and I was so focused on doing well and so scared of failing that I didn't really take it in. I didn't allow myself to enjoy the experience.

I can hear the national anthem and recall feeling the pride swelling in my throat and chest but I don't have a particularly vivid memory of the game. All of the technical stuff is there: Paul Ince played in the holding role behind me and Jamie with two wing-backs – Kieron Dyer and Steve Guppy. Alan Shearer was up front with Kevin Phillips. Changed days indeed! Jamie was a huge help during the game. He had been playing at the top level for a few years and he gently helped me through every step and pass. When the game allowed, I gave a fleeting thought to those days in his back garden and my grandad's birdcage all battered and falling apart. Now we were playing for England, surreal as that was. On the other hand, when you're young you imagine that playing for your country is the ultimate game yet when you do it suddenly feels very normal.

At the best of times I am guilty of blocking out any emotion during an occasion where I want to retain control and focus. I only realize later what has happened and by that time it's too late to actually feel it. In retrospect, one of the reasons I don't have great memories of that day is that it became absolutely separated from the rest of my England career.

Hoddle hadn't even mentioned my name after I went training with the Euro 96 squad and my next cap after Keegan resigned was for Sven-Goran Eriksson in his first match against Spain at Villa Park in February of 2001. Dad met Claudio Ranieri at the game and we only found out a year after I signed that Chelsea were scouting that night. As far as England went though, there was nothing after that game and I had to wait two years to get my next cap. It was still a great day. The fact that it was with Jamie and that my Mum and Dad were in the crowd along with Harry and Sandra made it a very proud moment. I went out with a few close mates after the game and they were all pleased for me but I still didn't really feel any great sense of achievement. What soured it the most though was still to come.

I got up the next morning more eager than normal to see the papers. The day itself had passed so quickly that I almost needed to see my name in black and white just to confirm the whole thing actually happened. It was true all right. I was there and so was Jamie but the headlines were all about what Keegan had supposedly said to both of us at half-time.

According to the papers, the manager said he dished out a bit of stick to the midfield at the break which was what had got us going. The truth is, however, he didn't say a word to us. Not directly. And certainly not in the terms made out in the press. It was completely crazy. I didn't recognize any of what was printed. Apparently he told us that we weren't getting the ball enough and hadn't used our possession well. If he had said that then fair enough. We did though play a lot better as a team in the second half and so I can only think that he wanted to take the credit for it.

I was surprised at what Keegan was supposed to have said after the match. If he had given me a bollocking at the break I would not have expected him to make it public, given that it was my debut and I was only 21. I would have been upset by that but it's worse when something is reported that never happened. Jamie rang me up when he saw it, puzzled. It annoyed me. I wondered why Keegan needed to take the credit. I knew that I'd had an average game but it was a reasonable international debut.

My Mum spoke to me and said it was another obstacle I would overcome but it had really spoiled things. The repercussions were immediate and I thought it was all unnecessary. I decided to put the whole experience behind me. I had to. I returned to West Ham where we were facing one of the most important games in the club's recent history – a UEFA Cup second round tie against Steaua Bucharest. The game was pretty forgettable as we lost 2–0 but my memory of it is clear for other reasons. First, it was a horrible night when the rain came down in sheets and the pitch was almost waterlogged. Second, Larry Hagman greeted us as we lined up on the pitch before the game. But why JR Ewing of *Dallas* fame was shaking our hands on a wet October night in Romania was never explained. Given Moncs new liking for guns I asked him if he'd shot JR? He didn't laugh. To say it was surreal is an understatement but then again there was something slightly unusual about the whole campaign.

There was a great support again and it was a proper introduction to the harsh reality of European football. We were under the impression that we could play quite open football and we were putting a few passes together. They were allowing us to because that's the way they wanted to play. Then, just as we were beginning to get comfortable, they scored. And then scored again. After that they just ran hard at us, closed us down and locked the whole game up. It was a lesson for all of us. Since then I have encountered that kind of scenario repeatedly.

You suffer from a dodgy result but think that you still have the second leg to make up the difference. When we played Steaua at Upton Park we threw everything at them. We actually played quite well but couldn't break them down. That pattern became quite a familiar one after I left West Ham. The first couple of years at Chelsea we encountered the same thing. European teams can be very 'cute' in the manner in which they draw you in and then punish you. In fact, it wasn't until I started playing Champions League regularly that I felt comfortable and able to really read and react with confidence in that situation. It was a learning curve for me and for West Ham. The days of playing in continental competition with an English style of play – the old school of getting right into them – are over and you have to be smarter than that.

The fallout from our exit was hardly spectacular – at least, not in the first instance. We weren't expected to go as far as we did and it was fantastic while it lasted. The team – with Harry and Dad in charge – had given West Ham a taste of something which the club had craved for many, many years. For some older fans it rekindled memories of the days when some of Europe's biggest names would roll up in the East End and they got to see them at close quarters. For the rest it was a flavour of the exotic. They thrived on it at the time, celebrated it and spent their hard-earned money on following the team for as long as it lasted. The players really appreciated that support. I certainly did. Those trips introduced me to a kind of camaraderie which I hadn't really felt since I was in the stands supporting my West Ham heroes as a child.

Inevitably, there was also a down side, though not straight away. Our results at home were up and down in the immediate aftermath but it was the fact that we didn't qualify for another European adventure which began to cause some problems with the fans. They are entitled to raise their expectations when the team raises their game and look like achieving better things. It's only human nature. They loved the trips and they saw that we were a young team with promising players who could deliver exciting football and get results.

We were going places and that could have been the start of a whole new journey for the club but the powers that be were not willing to speculate to accumulate.

The chairman and the board at the club were happy to bask in the reflected glory of what Harry, Dad and the players had managed to pull off on the pitch. I'm sure they enjoyed the hotels, hospitality, and sampled a few good restaurants as we skirted the fringes of European competition. And why not? Problem was that they should have backed that team – the coaches and players – to improve, grow, and go on to do even more. But they chose not to and I will never understand why. The club had not spent heavily in the transfer market. The best players who'd come in had come through the youth system or been signed for next to nothing.

West Ham had reached a crossroads and they had to choose which direction they wanted the club to move in. I felt it, Rio felt it and I know that Dad and Harry were keen to know how they could take the next step. Rio and I spoke about it and wondered if we would be able to continue to develop our game there. There were other young players like Joe, Michael and Jermain coming through while some of the older lads were either just past their peak or ready to move on. Di Canio did continue for a couple of seasons before moving to Charlton but for guys like him a signal from the club was not as important. It was the ones who had grown up with the club who needed to know what plans there were for the future. The core already existed. Loyalty and enthusiasm were already in harness and what was needed was some strong leadership, a willingness to invest in the present so that the club might build on the solid foundation.

All we got was silence. By the time we reached the end of

that season the enthusiasm and drive which had followed on from the league position the previous season and the subsequent venture into European football had all but evaporated. We limped out of the campaign with a painful home defeat by Middlesbrough. I could sense the break-up of the team then. Players often speak of the spirit within a team which bonds it together. I have known that spirit to come in different volumes. It rises and falls in line with results, circumstance and atmosphere but the spirit is only as strong as the vessel which holds it. At West Ham, it was fragile for a lot of reasons.

Harry's knack for signing players was defined by his ability to spot, recruit, and then blend all sorts of varied nationalities and talents into a functioning unit. Some of the constituent parts were not ones which would naturally mix. For instance, Berkovic is a good footballer whose passing is very valuable when he is on form. At the same time, he wouldn't win any medals for bravery. Guys like Lomy and John Moncur were the flipside of that coin – men's men who would fight with every breath for you but in Lomy's case, lacked the finesse on the ball which can mark you out as a player at the top level.

There were other opposites in the dressing room but the common denominator was Harry. He had the character and personality to embrace everyone and turn them into a cohesive team. When so much is dependent on one person to hold things together, the fabric may not need to be torn too much before it starts to come undone. That is what happened at West Ham when Leeds United opened their bid to sign Rio. As ever, it started with a story here and there in the papers. The club denied that there was anything in it. The year before

I had signed a new contract and was absolutely assured that Rio would not be sold. Nevertheless, it was a story which did not and would not go away.

At one point, there seemed to be a rebuttal from someone every time the prospect of Rio moving was mentioned. I tried to remove myself from the frontline. People knew that Rio and I were good mates so all I ever got were questions I couldn't always answer: 'Was he going?'; 'Did he want to leave?'; 'How would I feel if he did?' Like everyone else I listened to the TV and radio and read the newspapers but with every assurance that Rio would not be sold I felt more angry, more annoyed. I knew that there had been meetings. Whatever they told me or the fans publicly, I was aware of exactly what was going on. I knew he was leaving.

I wonder now if people like Terence Brown and Paul Aldridge – who was managing director – thought that I believed what they were telling me. I knew I was being bull-shitted when they said Rio was staying. They obviously realized that selling Rio was not the right message to send to either the fans or other players at the club. Even though he was still only 21, every man and his dog who had an idea about football could see what a player he was already, never mind how good he would become. To sell Rio was worse than flogging the family silver – it was tearing part of the soul from West Ham United. Whatever the reason – and in the end there were eighteen million of them – that decision had been taken. It would not have been my choice but then Rio was one of my best mates apart from his obvious value to the team. I knew I would lose out twice when he left.

I don't dispute that a part of Rio wanted to go, to discover a new challenge away from London. We'd talked about it many times and neither of us could see ourselves as old pros looking back over a lifetime career at Upton Park. But that didn't matter, the timing did, and the manner in which the whole situation was handled.

I understand that people in football lie, some more than others. And in some situations people feel that they have to lie. What I object to is the fact that I was being lied to right up until five minutes before the deal went through – lied to my face. I couldn't believe that they thought I should be treated that way, that I was so gullible. If the people at the club had been more truthful with me then I might at least have been more sympathetic to their way of thinking. As it was, someone decided that it would be lies, lies, and more lies. They clearly suspected that I would react badly if I knew the truth. They were right.

On 18 November 2000, we travelled to Elland Road to play Leeds United in the Premiership. We won 1–0 thanks to a goal by Nigel Winterburn. Rio played and so did I. It was the last time we lined up together for West Ham. Eight days later, Rio became the most expensive defender in world football when he signed for Leeds United for £18 million. Strange that, given that the papers had been saying it would happen for weeks; that Terence Brown had met with Rio's agent; that a fee had been agreed. But all along I was told the same thing. 'He's not going.' What kind of a mug did they take me for? Did they think that I would accept the deceit, that I would just keep ticking over and take it on the chin because I was Frank Lampard's son? I was West Ham through and through after all. I was Frank junior. I would make a fuss and stay anyway. I was used to it.

I thought about the time I missed out on Young Player of the

Year. I had been playing in the first team all season and it seemed 'stuck on' that I would pick up the award. It wasn't voted for as such – the decision was taken in-house by the coaches but there was no competition. When the award was announced Manny Omoyinmi won it. He had played in the youth team and played well. It wasn't the same thing though. I never did discover how that decision had come about. I believe it was political. After all, Harry had been taking stick for putting me in the first team. Perhaps that was seen as enough reward. No point in giving me an accolade to confirm how well I had done into the bargain. Different year, same scenario. Give it to Manny. Frank won't mind. I didn't mind it going to Manny because he was my mate. But I also cared about the reasons why I had been excluded from the reckoning.

It was assumed I wouldn't complain to anyone about it. That was true. It hurt though. I wanted to win the award. It meant a lot to me because I was a West Ham fan. I didn't let on to Dad that I was upset by the whole thing though Mum knew just by looking at me when I got home after finding out. She felt that the politics of my situation regarding Dad and Harry made it impossible for me to receive the recognition I deserved. Mum was very upset about it. Maybe I expected too much. What I craved was a bit of recognition that I had done well. Instead I got a kick in the teeth. Worse than that, it made me suspicious about the way the club saw me.

It was another episode of what went on behind the scenes that forced me to confront the fact that I was fighting a losing battle. Everyone on the outside wanted to dig me out because they believed that the only reason I got ahead at the club was because of my Dad and my uncle. Meanwhile, people inside the club were afraid to admit that I had done well in case they were accused of favouritism.

And just in case I hadn't got the message that I couldn't win – if I ever dared broach the idea that maybe I should leave, then I was called a dirty traitor. I have found the strangest thing about football is that people can make it into something which it is not. I understand that they are passionate about it. I am passionate about it. However, just because we feel emotional about it doesn't mean to say that football has its own set of rules – rules which apply only to it and not in real life. For instance, people would abuse me on the pitch, call me s***, insult me and Dad.

When it comes to making decisions about my life though, they expect me to remain loyal to West Ham. To stick with the club because I supported them as a boy and ignore all of the other stuff, as they do. There is a big difference though. The people who go to games and spend time shouting at me, the coaches or any other member of the team go home afterwards to their wife and family and forget about what has happened at the game. They return to real life. Football for them is a pastime albeit a consuming one.

I don't think they ever stop to wonder how their actions during those ninety minutes might affect the people they are having a go at. There wasn't a single time that I left Upton Park after being slagged off or jeered by some of the supporters that I didn't take their anger home with me. People say that you have to be pretty thick skinned to be a footballer. I am actually quite sensitive, that's how I am. I'm not ashamed of it and it's part of what makes me the person I am. It doesn't mean I feel angry about the treatment I got all of the time. I didn't mope around wishing I could answer my critics. On occasions,

I actually passed up the opportunity. There was one teenage boy who sat behind the home dugout at every game. If I was on the bench he would be first on his feet when I went out to warm up. 'Sit down, Lampard!' or the old faithful 'You're only wearing that strip because of your Dad and uncle!' At first I tried to keep my head down and ignore it but now and again I would look over. There he was, face contorted with rage. I wondered what I had done to him to deserve that kind of treatment, apart from the fact he was only about 14 or so.

Bizarrely, I used a local bank quite frequently and one of the tellers was a lovely woman who was a West Ham fan. She was always very friendly and polite and made a point of saying hello. She usually mentioned her son who was also a big fan and in my mind I formed an image of an innocent young lad as keen on West Ham as I was at his age. Coincidentally, I met her outside Upton Park one day. I said hello as I always would and there beside her was the same little bastard from behind the dugout. She was very friendly and made a big deal of introducing me to her son – who was also a fan and who loved me. Apparently.

I felt like saying 'Oh yeah, he has a funny way of showing it. And did you know he smokes?' He just stayed quiet and looked very sheepish. For a split second I thought about telling her that her little boy was actually a foul-mouthed prize pain in the arse. But I bit my tongue. What was the point? I knew that her son was more important to her than me and rightly so. Why bother giving her something which would upset her about her family? That was my point. Mum had got it in the neck from fans who sat around her in the directors' box. My sisters had to endure it at games and in the street. When they went out at night there would often be some bloke or other come up to them and make a comment about West Ham and your bloody Dad and your brother. They were just expected to take it on the chin. Why?

What's it got to do with them? Just because members of their family happened to work for West Ham somehow that gives people the right to interrupt their evening with a few choice words slagging us off. They are my family and they are entitled to my support just as they give me theirs – unequivocally. Mum sums it up perfectly. When people ask her who does she support, West Ham or Chelsea, she always replies Chelsea. The question is thrown back at her. How can you change your colours? 'Because he is my son, my family, and my blood.' She has been criticized for changing allegiance. So has Dad, my sisters and some of my mates. It's the people asking the questions who don't understand. If I were to ask them were West Ham more important than their family then I am sure I know what the answer would be.

The Lampards are no different in that respect. We back each other. I remember it being a problem and causing pressure, the fact that the three of us were so involved. Harry would take it home more than Dad. If we had a bad game on Saturday then he couldn't let it go. It would sit heavy in his mind and needle him: what he did, what he didn't do, what he might have done. I guess it's quite normal for any football manager but he would keep poring over it for the whole weekend. Dad was different. Since he stopped playing he had developed his own businesses and had broadened his horizons. He has always been able to see a bigger picture and didn't allow football to override everything else.

Maybe because he was assistant manager rather than manager it was slightly easier for him to detach himself and our family from it. When I was playing it became harder for everyone because we were both at the centre of it, but it works both ways: if things were going well then we had double the joy.

With Dad the pressures were usually kept at arm's length. Harry bore the full brunt. When the punters were calling for his head he knew all about it while Dad could have been getting the same stick but he was still a step behind Harry. Dad took a conscious decision not to involve Mum, me or my sisters as much as possible. I know he did that for our benefit and it was very unselfish of him. There were a lot of times when I wished nothing more than to disappear after a game which had gone badly and then found myself walking into a discussion from hell in the living room just because Dad was home. Generally, though, he would try to keep work out of the house as much as he could. He recognized that I was under a different pressure from him and the last thing I needed was to share the burden he was carrying with my uncle. All those years he had devoted to teaching, guiding, encouraging and pushing me to become a professional had paid off.

I was in a position then where the only person who could really make me succeed was me. Dad didn't want me to suffer from his problems as well. I had enough on my plate with getting in the team and trying to make myself a better player. I didn't need to know that there had been a board meeting or that the transfer budget had been frozen. That's not to say I didn't want to know. I found out stuff here and there from other people and when it was relevant Dad would tell me what he thought I should know. He was a good judge of what was important and what was not and he filtered the information on that basis. I knew a lot of things that other players were not privy to, sometimes about the politics of the club and about the squad.

We would talk about football all of the time. It wasn't about a ban on chat. He preferred to keep some things to himself which he thought were unhelpful. There were a few senior players who thought nothing of barging into his office and demanding to know why they were not playing or on the bench and whatever. Everyone likes to be nosy about their work and know what's going on and I am no different. If I knew a player had been in shouting the odds at Harry for something I would keep it to myself. That doesn't mean that when I next saw him in the dressing room I could look at him without thinking about the scenario which had been described to me. But none of it ever affected me or my relations with team-mates. I was able to distance myself partly because I was used to inserting a psychological barrier between myself and the fact that Dad and Harry were in charge. I had to. There were certain older players who thought little of being offensive or abusive to Harry and Dad. I realized it was part of football culture and in most cases it was just people letting off steam. Sometimes that could be hard. I was still young and it all felt very raw.

Looking back now I'm glad I bit my tongue because it really wasn't my place to get involved. I would have the hump with it because I would take it as a personal affront to my family. I felt that way about a lot of things I experienced but there are times when I forced myself to look at situations from a wider context. If a player isn't in the team and he believes he should be he has the right to ask for an explanation. The irony for me was that I remembered how I felt on those occasions when I was pacing up and down outside of Harry's office because I was afraid to go in and confront him about exactly the same situation.

Some things got Dad so worked up that he couldn't help himself. Di Canio stormed into Harry's office one day demanding that he be allowed to leave for Chelsea. Gianluca Vialli had expressed an interest in signing him and Paolo being the way he was couldn't help himself. I got the whole picture and knowing Paolo it sounded bang on. There had been raised voices and much flapping of arms – all of them Paolo's. Fair enough, I thought, except I then had to listen to him bleating on about how West Ham are his second skin and how if you cut him he would bleed claret and blue. I was annoyed, partly because that was actually true of me and my upbringing but I never played that card. I am more relaxed about it now because as you get older it's easier to recognize when a player is being cute, and let's face it, there's a lot of bollocks talked in football anyway.

It was a strange position. I took all of it in. I stored a lot of it away – some of which became useful and some which still rankles. In general it was a time of learning. I learned some of the most harsh and useful lessons which I realised I had to confront and move on from. I carried a lot of responsibility during my time at West Ham. I signed for the club with great expectations and left it with an awful lot of baggage. Much of the weight was not of my making. I understand precisely the unique pressure and antagonism associated with a father/son manager/player relationship.

I have seen this situation elsewhere – Brian and Nigel Clough, Steve and Alex Bruce – and only those who have been involved can know its intensity. It's catch-22. Is a Dad supposed to ignore his son even though he is the best option just in case he is accused of nepotism? Or should he do what is best for the team and therefore himself as a manager regardless? It seems that nothing divides people like family which is not the way it should be. Nor is it how I was brought up. I grew up in an area which was full of West Ham fans where the motto in life was: always look after your family.

I saw it in the harshest way possible. I was a part of the West Ham family, literally: my nan, my Dad and Mum, my uncle and my sisters. But I didn't get looked after. I didn't receive any backing. That is a complete contradiction of the local ethic. When I go back there now people still blame me for leaving. I am accused of being disloyal. Where was their loyalty to me? Or my Dad? Or Harry? Harry and Dad dug West Ham out of the mire when they were in real danger of being relegated and losing further ground.

Then with the help of players like Paul Kitson, John Hartson and the likes they managed to push the club further up the Premiership than they have ever been. They introduced a new kind of player to the club which provided the fans with the brand of exciting, entertaining football that they craved. On top of all of that, they nurtured young talent, encouraged it and then gave players a platform on which to develop and help make West Ham a real force to be reckoned with. In doing so, other parents whose kids were coming through trusted the club to help their sons make the grade the way it once did.

Under Harry and Dad West Ham could once again lay claim to being the Academy of Football. How were they repaid for their efforts, for the years of hard work making the club credible? Harry was sacked one day and Dad the next. I was shown no loyalty as a player by the fans who booed me.

Considering what Dad and Harry had achieved, my family was not shown any loyalty by the board when they were sacked.

It was Mum who took the phone call. I was in her house when she came into the room and told me that Harry had been fired. She was very calm. I was surprised – by her reaction, and by the news. Harry and the chairman had been having rows ever since Rio was sold six months before. It was nothing new. He was desperate to take the club forward and wanted to reshape the squad. Instead of money he got excuses. The club were in debt. The stadium needed to be modernized. Maybe we should have seen it coming but when your entire life has revolved around one entity it's impossible to see things from the outside.

West Ham were that influence for us. I never really envisaged a life outside of them – whatever my grievances. Mum called Sandra straight away to make sure she was okay. Sandra was upset but she was worried about Harry. I asked how Dad sounded on the phone and was told he was fine. He is a strong character but for him there was also a sense of inevitability about the situation. Only Harry had actually been sacked and in typical West Ham style they had left him and the other coaches hanging on, wondering what would happen to them. It was never an issue for Dad. He was loyal and if he wasn't asked to leave he would tell them he was going.

I never saw him that upset about it. He got angry, but more from his inherent sense of pride that he had somehow failed than anything else. He was also upset for Harry. More than anyone he knew what Harry had gone through in the job. He had seen everything that was hidden to the rest of the world, behind the boardroom door and in the manager's office after everyone else had gone.

Harry was much more intense about the whole thing while Dad was more laid back. He was disappointed by the way it had ended but there was an element of relief for him as well. People say that all managers know with certainty that one day they will get the sack. Maybe they prefer not to think about it too much and who can blame them?

I called Harry to see how he was.

'I'm all right, Frank,' he said in his usual gruff voice. 'How are you?' A typically robust answer.

'I'm sorry, Harry.'

'Sorry for what, son? There's no need for sorry. What's done is done. I'm fine. I will be fine. You wait and see.'

Even then I found the conversation difficult. Family ties had always got in the way of football conversations and here it felt like the reverse was happening. He appreciated my sympathy. He was my uncle and I wanted to look up to him the same as I always had. He wanted that too. I could tell he was hurt but he didn't want to admit how much.

'Look after yourself,' I said as the conversation drew to a natural end.

'Thanks son. But you look after yourself. All right, Frank?'

I knew what he was saying. And he was right. I knew it and so did Dad. Very quickly Dad concerned himself with my future. It was his natural instinct. He accepted what had happened to him and he wanted to protect me from the fallout in whatever way he could. My gut feeling was simple: get out, get out as quickly as possible. This wasn't even about football anymore; this was family.

Had I had a brilliant relationship with the fans then maybe it would have been different. Had Rio stayed, maybe so would I. Had they not lied to me about that, then who knows? Nevertheless, I was intrigued when I was called to meet the chairman, Terence Brown, a week after Dad and Harry had left.

I had undergone a hernia operation and was out of the team. My last game had been a home defeat by Leeds at the end of April. A week earlier I had scored at Newcastle with ten minutes to go when we were two down. It was a penalty.

I met Kutner and asked him what he thought.

'Let's just go and listen,' he said. 'It will be interesting if nothing else.'

We walked into Brown's office and he greeted me with as much warmth as he could muster. There was a certain amount of trepidation as well and I wondered what he thought I might say. He was nervous but he pretty much got straight to the point. The club wanted me to stay. I was surprised. It wasn't the impression they had given me. Brown said that he understood that it had been a tough time. I looked at him as he spoke. I heard the words but the whole thing seemed slightly unreal.

Did he understand? Really? Did he know what it was like to be barracked by thousands of people when you are trying your best to do well for them? Did he have any idea how much I had tried to ignore the abuse in the hope that I could win over my own people? Could he comprehend the hurt, embarrassment and disappointment West Ham had caused my family over the way they had treated my Dad and uncle? I didn't think so. I couldn't hear anything in his words which even began to demonstrate any empathy for what I had been through.

And yet, he had the nerve to sit there and tell me that the club wanted me to sign a new contract and help build a brave new future. I looked into his eyes. I suppose I was hoping to see some trace of emotion, even a little bit of acknowledgement of what I was feeling. Nothing. Not even a hint of sorry.

I tried to rationalize what was going on. Did they really want me to stay to play in the team or was there something else going on? After all, if I signed a new deal then my price in the market would automatically increase. From what I had heard, they were already telling interested clubs that I would cost £14 million. Apart from that, I was due to be paid loyalty bonuses on my contract if they chose to sell me – money I lost if I formally requested a move. Was the plan to push me into asking for a transfer so they could recoup even more money? It seemed likely but I wasn't for biting. Brown could sense that he was not getting through to me. I gave them my time, my attention, my loyalty. In return, I felt they were trying to cash in on me.

Kutner said that, in the circumstances, it was better that I leave West Ham. He was sure they understood. I stood up and made to leave Brown's office. I was desperate to get out of there. I had felt nervous before going in and the conversation had turned my stomach further. Unexpectedly, the chairman made a last effort to try and persuade me.

'Would knowing who the new manager is change your mind Frank?' he asked.

I stopped to consider the proposition. Would it make any difference if I knew who would replace my flesh and blood? It only took a second.

'I don't give a f*** if you get Fabio Capello. I'm leaving.'

I walked out of his office for the last time. Kutner put his hand on my back to reassure me. I felt lighter – like some of the weight that I had carried for so many years had slipped from my shoulders and as I walked out of West Ham for the last time I felt relieved. It was over. Finally over.

I didn't leave West Ham only because of what they did to my Dad. It's true that I had ambitions to better myself as a player. But the simple truth is that if Dad and Harry had stayed then so too would I. I am grateful for the experience I had there because it has helped shape me and make me the player, and the man, that I am today. I am pleased to say that I still carry some of the East End family ethos in me now. In fact, it's stronger than ever. That is my loyalty to my family.

I will always look after those who are closest to me. First, last, and always.

CHAPTER 4

END OF THE AFFAIR

WEST Ham continue to provoke very strong feelings in me. Sometimes – for instance when I go back to play there with Chelsea – the bile that spills out against me from the stands at Upton Park has a resonance which incites an anger and resentment which I tried to leave behind when I left the club. And, though there are times when I like to think I could cut West Ham out of my life completely, I realize that will never happen. It's impossible to discard the best part of twenty years of your life – ridiculous to think I can cast off the club I loved more than any other.

Now, however, I mix with very few people who are loyal to West Ham, which is a strange situation given that I grew up in a house and community which was touched in every way by the club. It's also one I am more comfortable with. The reason? The treatment I was subjected to by a large section of the West Ham fans.

There were certain people who were good to me, people who stuck by me and supported me even when the fashion was to do the opposite. I have not and will never forget them. They are the real soul of West Ham in my eyes: fans who appreciate the commitment I showed to the club while I was there and the effort I made to be the very best I could. Unfortunately, they are in the minority, and when I think and speak about West Ham in such a negative way it makes me very uncomfortable. I don't want to insult those people at the club who have only ever offered me support and affection – they are exempt from any criticism. However, I cannot ignore the feelings I have nor can I forget what I have suffered.

When I return to Upton Park some people say that they don't agree with the things that were said and done against me – ordinary people, people in the streets of London, in restaurants and wherever I go and am recognized.

I get letters as well from people telling me that they are proud of what I have achieved as a West Ham lad who came through the system. This has happened more during the years at Chelsea under Jose Mourinho when success has been tangible in the shape of trophies and medals. On the surface, there seems to be a genuine source of affection and admiration among such people, and they also apologize for the way I am treated when I go back to West Ham now.

That's all very well and good, but I don't see anyone standing up and protesting about the cauldron of hate which stirs around them when I run out in the blue of Chelsea. I don't expect people to be on my side – I'm not asking for allies – but I don't understand how anyone can claim to have sympathy for what I have been through and then stay silent while the abuse pours down from every corner of Upton Park. If they're not brave enough to speak their mind when they are in the company of the people they disagree with, then why tell me differently? After all, I am not the first to be treated in this way at West Ham.

Paul Ince was a legend there, a player whom the fans adored and revered because of his commitment and drive. I was a fan of his too. I looked up to Incey when I was a kid and I wanted to be like him – to be as dynamic as he was; to get to the edge of the box and score important goals. He was exactly the kind of player I hoped to become. Incey called himself 'The Guv'nor' and no one would argue with that title. However, after he left West Ham he became the arch-traitor.

I was there with a few youth team colleagues when he came back to play at Upton Park for the first time after his transfer to Manchester United. He got absolutely murdered. They used to have public executions in the East End but this was a football lynching. Right from kick-off he was jeered and booed and it got worse as the game went on. There was a disturbing edge to the chanting which was born of extreme anger. Incey had his moment though and with typical pathos he scored the equalizer in the last minute and the place went even wilder. The abuse he got was actually quite frightening.

I have tried to understand how people can become so anti-Paul Ince or anti-Frank Lampard. Football is a very passionate game and fans pride themselves on their love of their team and the depth of their commitment to a club. I am sure of this because I feel the same way. There is a difference though, when the attention is wholly transferred to one individual. That's what happens when I return to play at Upton Park. I'm not sure how or why but somehow the whole occasion is turned into a Frank Lampard hate-fest. It's audible when the ground is still filling up and the teams are read out. There's a rumble of dissent at my name, a bit like the old days when

I was playing for the home side. It gets worse, and from the first whistle they lose themselves in trying to have a go at me: 'F*** off, Lampard!' 'F*** off back to Chelsea, Daddy's boy!' 'You Judas!' and, of course, the most charming of all, 'F*** off, you fat c***!'

What is supposed to be a football game is transformed into some kind of mass protest about Frank Lampard's return. I'm not being big headed, or paranoid. Anyone who has been to a West Ham versus Chelsea game has heard the abuse and most likely become bored of it – if they are not a season ticket holder.

I have heard and read West Ham fans justifying their atti- tude towards me on account of the fact that they 'have long memories'. I would laugh but it's not funny. In fact they have very short memories. If their recollections were as vivid as they claim then perhaps they would have seen a five-year-old boy wearing a West Ham top and draped in a scarf that was too big for him heading to Upton Park to watch a game with his Dad and sisters, excited by the prospect of cheering for his team. If they were diehard fans they might even have turned up at the odd youth team game and seen the son of a West Ham legend trying his best to emerge from the shadow of his Dad, or working his bollocks off in training and in reserve games so that he might one day be good enough to get a game for the club he loved.

It seems those who claim to have the recollection of an elephant are no better equipped in that department than a goldfish. People wonder why I still bother about the bad times at West Ham given how my career has progressed since leaving. The main reason those memories endure is because it lasted such a long time. I was criticized to the hilt when I was there for being Frank Lampard's son and for not being a good enough player. Now that I have come runner-up to Ronaldinho in the vote for World and European Footballer of the Year and won the Premiership with Chelsea, it has become harder for my critics to handle.

They said I wasn't good enough for West Ham, but now I am good enough to play for the Premiership champions and England. They have been proven wrong. So what's their response? To admit the mistake? To accept the error and keep their own counsel when it comes to me? No, oh no. They go completely the other way. In their cock-eyed world view they know they've been shown up but instead of letting it go they lose all sense of proportion and castigate me even more for having succeeded. They stick their heads in the sand, swear allegiance to West Ham, and decide that they still feel the same way, regardless. They're West Ham fans and they hate Frank Lampard. How sad.

Had I left and failed to improve, had I frittered away what talent I had at Chelsea and never made an impact, then when I return to Upton Park and get the usual 'You wanker, Lampard' and 'What a waste of money', it wouldn't be such a crusade against me. It's become a crusade because of what I have become – better and more successful than I was as a West Ham player and they hate to have been proved wrong.

When I was about 18 I went through a spell when I used the internet to look at the fans' sites. There are hundreds of chat-rooms and the like devoted to West Ham which are visited by supporters who would express varying degrees of resentment towards me: from the casual slag off to the lunatic rant. In these schools of football critique I was generally referred to as 'son of', something I was well used to. They called me that to my back, when I was running on to the pitch or warming up on the touchline, so at least they were consistent. So was I – consistently hard working, and trying to do my best. If a fan says that I have had a bad game then that is his opinion, one which he is entitled to if he has been at the match, and something we can agree with or not. As a player you can be hurt or pissed off by criticism about your performance but what winds me up is being accused of something of which I am clearly not guilty – one such accusation was that of being lazy. This was a particular obsession of West Ham fans on the internet when I was, in fact, the hardest worker at the club.

I was always in on days off, always stayed behind after training to do extra work, and always tried to improve myself. I am a lot of things but lazy is not one of them. Another laughable jibe was that I only ever scored goals in cup games, and against crap teams. The phone-ins were great fun for that one. These punters had so many hang-ups about me that I began to wonder if the torrents of abuse I received were actually some amateur attempt at collective therapy.

If I was playing well and there were no problems, they would invent one. A favourite was the claim that I never got subbed, or dropped, because my Dad and Harry were in charge. Now here I have to hold up my hands. My Dad and Harry *were* in charge. And, on the issue of never being a player to get dropped from the starting line-up, I have something to declare. After I joined Chelsea, I played the first four games and was suspended for one, having been sent off. Subsequently, I started 164 Premiership matches to set a new record in English football. It was achieved over five seasons and under two different managers. So to all those West Ham fans who complained that I was always on the pitch I take off my cap. You were right about that but wrong about the reason why. It had nothing to do with who was picking the team, as proven by events since I left West Ham.

There were other incidents when I was at West Ham when people would regularly approach me after games if I had gone out for a drink. 'Look at you. You played s*** today. You have some nerve showing your face after this afternoon.' So it went on. One particular evening I had gone out with Moncs and a few of his mates who were hard core Hammers' fans. The bar we went to was full of burly blokes with very little hair and even less time for me. 'Oi, Steve,' someone shouted. 'There's that Frank Lampard. You've been caning him all afternoon.' We had won 2–1 and played well but it still wasn't good enough. I was still a kid. I was surrounded by ten men and I couldn't wait to get out. I left a few minutes later feeling utterly deflated.

It got to the stage where I didn't have to be among them to feel their anger. It seemed to follow me around: at home, in the street. I was aware of it when I closed my eyes to go to sleep at night and it was still there when I woke in the morning. It got so bad that I would dread driving to and from the ground on matchdays. The nerves would begin to kick in the day before and get gradually worse. I couldn't quite grasp what was wrong at first. I thought it was just the normal nervousness about playing: what the result would be and whether I would play well, badly or even at all. It was only when I left the stadium after a match and was still carrying the same dull ache in the pit of my stomach that I realized something more was going on.

Years later Mum brought the subject up. She told me that she had been very worried about me. I looked pale and pensive on Saturday mornings and would withdraw into myself as time wore on and the game got nearer. She put it down to matchday nerves at first but knew quickly that it ran more deeply than that. I was sad. I didn't want to leave the house because of what I was walking in to. Mum realized that highlighting it would only make me more conscious and that I would try to pretend it wasn't happening so she left me alone. I didn't feel this way every week. There were times when I was playing well and knew it, times when I felt more confident and robust. I didn't get much praise for it though – just less stick. Still, I was grateful for any small relief.

It didn't take much for it to change, though – a couple of misplaced passes or getting run off a ball. I would hear it on the 'chicken run' first – the central area of the stand opposite the dugouts where the hard-core fans gathered. Given the volume of noise a crowd of 30,000 people can generate, you could say it started with a murmur. Once those few made their voices heard, it soon gathered momentum. Shouts and jeers followed before it spread around the ground like a cancer. I knew the signs and it got so bad that I became nervous about receiving the ball. It was ridiculous. I have always been able to take possession from a full-back or centre-half and spread the play. I have been doing it since I was a kid. I do it all day long still. It's the most natural thing in the world for me. But back then I became very conscious of what would happen if I messed up. I would see the angle to take the ball from a team-mate and think twice. Maybe there was an opponent tracking me tight from behind and I would be under pressure and I wouldn't make the run because I was scared it would result in more abuse from the fans.

Ian Bishop was one of the most gifted ball players at the club. He was the generation before me but he suffered a similar kind of criticism when things were not going right for him. It was weird. There were other, more workmanlike, players at the club who were revered because they made the odd tackle. Michael Carrick came after I left and he took the same stick. Why? Because he liked to play the game the right way. It's confusing. West Ham pride themselves on a history of teams who played football in the great spirit of the game yet players who tried to ignite that spirit were slated. As a young player attempting to go about things in the correct manner there will be times when you give the ball away. You never learn properly without making mistakes. Nobody is perfect. I have chatted to Michael about this since he left West Ham and there was some similarity in the way we were treated.

It was, however, a lot more vitriolic for me. That was partly down to the situation with Dad and Harry, but I think that any club will always have one or two players whom the fans like to get at even when the team is playing well and winning. It's human nature, or rather the nature of football clubs.

Paulo Wanchope got slaughtered at West Ham and it got worse when the team was struggling. Paulo was very unorthodox. He could be brilliant one day and not so brilliant the next. It happens to everyone! It was just how he was, something that is not unusual for talented players. But when it becomes a real problem is when you see it affect a player's confidence. There are occasions when you look into a team-mate's eyes and you can tell there's nothing behind them but fear and loathing – no mental strength, no desire, the only thing occupying their thoughts being apprehension about what might happen next. That isn't good for football. I saw it happen at West Ham. Now, I am pretty thick skinned. If I give the ball away I can get through it and won't shirk going back for the next pass but back then there were very dark moments – days, weeks, even the odd month.

Every time I got off the bench to warm up, a particular section of the stand would give me stick. I'd go into a sprint to get past them quickly and into the safety of the corner. I'd do the same on the way back. That's how childish it had become. There were times when I didn't even want to play; times when I was on the bench and already getting stick and found myself hoping that Harry wouldn't put me on so I wouldn't have to face more; times when I wanted to just walk away and leave it all behind.

I didn't have the energy or the will to keep going. I became morose and very depressed about the situation. Dad knew. He watched me play and saw me off the pitch, at training, and around the family. You can hide in a football match. It's actually quite easy to do. I have seen it done. Players give the ball away a couple of times and get uptight about doing it a third time so they shout to you for a pass but they're already running in the opposite direction. I was guilty of the same during the worst moments. Dad would have seen it but he never dug me out. Instead, he encouraged me to keep getting on the ball, stick to the basic football values, face my fear and conquer it. There were occasions when I could have gone under but Dad was always there to drag me back to the surface.

I spent a lot of time considering my options, wondering if I should drop down a level and play lower league. It got to the stage where I thought about jacking in football altogether. I would rather be working nine to five with my mates than taking abuse from 30,000 people every other week. I tried to get out of West Ham a couple of times. I went to see Harry and told him but he said he wouldn't let me go, that Rio and I had a future at West Ham, that we *were* the future. Despite my reservations I could see his point, and, stupidly or otherwise, believed there would be light at the end of the tunnel.

I knuckled down and worked harder. I thought and fought my way out of the trough of depression – told myself that I would succeed. The mental strength I developed as a result has been a major factor in my progress since. I realize now that the one benefit that I have accrued from the whole situation is psychological toughness. That is important because I can still get wound up by the past. One of the things that annoys me is a tendency in West Ham fans to say that I have really come on a lot since I left. I don't deny that I have improved dramatically since I joined Chelsea – that's evident – but I cannot accept that they couldn't see my potential at West Ham. Of course I have developed since I was aged 18–21, but whether through ignorance or otherwise, these fans refuse to acknowledge that there were signs of what I could be even then. If they had given me a chance then maybe I would have stayed there longer or at least departed on amicable terms.

I don't enjoy the fact that there is so much animosity between myself and the club I grew up with and loved for so long. They could have given me more of a chance. They might have looked at me all those years ago and seen a young boy who was trying his heart out to do well, a player who was the son of one of the club's most loyal servants and part of one of their most successful sides. They could have thought of that when I made a mistake, and encouraged me to do better next time. They could have given me a chance.

155

I see Rio return to Upton Park and he has no problems at all. I used to wish that was me. I used to think that I would like to be able to go back, get a decent reception, and be done with it but it's all gone too far now. I won't change my mind about West Ham. I can't. There have been too many incidents which have produced too much bad blood. If I were to run out at Upton Park now and get cheered I would throw it back in their face. I don't want it now.

When I left the club was in financial difficulty and had to sell players. They got £11 million for me – not bad when you consider they signed me for nothing; not bad either for a player who the fans didn't think was worth a place in their team, never mind Chelsea's. It upsets me that I feel no warmth for my time at West Ham. It should have a very special place in my life and my career. I never felt anything but fortunate to be born into a family with such strong ties and staunch loyalty to the club. It was my boyhood ambition to play for my club and when I finally realized that dream I wondered if anything else in life would ever make me feel so proud and so happy. Those feelings changed and I am genuinely sorry that they had to.

It's important to me that people understand just how deeply I feel about what happened. Most players who support a club or have enjoyed a spell with one will always look out for that club's results after they move on. I remember when Joe Cole first came to Chelsea he would react that way to West Ham. After a match, one of the Chelsea backroom staff would come round the dressing room and recite the day's scores and Joe would ask about the Hammers. If they had been beaten, he would turn away in disappointment. My wounds from my West Ham days were still very much open then and I would greet the news with a wry smile. That's how deeply I felt. I wanted West Ham to lose. Now I don't have that same enthusiasm. I don't even look for their results.

That may sound strange, vindictive even, but I defy anyone to be put through the ordeal that I faced and come out any differently. To those who would revel in the abuse which was directed at me I will not apologize. Why should I? Am I supposed to suffer this kind of thing for ninety minutes from thousands of people and then just forget about it as soon as the final whistle blows? That's not how life works. What fans can forget too easily is that what happens to players in a game is a big part of our lives. I was badly affected by the experience I had at West Ham. Most of the suffering happened when there was no audience around, after they called me 's***', 'fat', 'crap', 'a c***' during a game. Am I supposed to retain a place in my heart for West Ham after this? So too my Mum and Dad and my family? I don't think so.

The truth is that my family have no feelings for West Ham now. What happened was an attack on all of us. It went beyond football and invaded our lives without consideration or mercy. At Chelsea it's different. There were a lot of West Ham fans who mocked the fact that the club had paid a lot of money for me. At the start it didn't really go well and the Chelsea fans could have turned against me. They didn't. I was given the opportunity to show what I could do, and when I started to play well and settle in they immediately recognized it. They sang my name and cheered when I touched the ball. I remember being on the pitch at Stamford Bridge and knocking a long diagonal ball behind the defence to Jesper Gronkjaer. He got on the end though the move ended in a corner. As soon as he picked up the pass there was a huge roar of appreciation and when I walked over to take the corner-kick there was a chorus of *'One Frank Lampard...'*. I thought, 'F***ing hell, that's never happened before.' This came from fans of a club to which I no previous allegiance. It made me realize what it is to be given a fair crack of the whip, to be given time to show what you are really capable of. My affinity for the club has grown, and I know that whatever happens in the future – if Chelsea want to sell me or the manager doesn't want me – there will always be a place in my heart for them. I will always look for their result and want them to win.

I wouldn't swap the time I have had at Chelsea for anything. They have shown me a respect I never knew at West Ham, nor did my Dad. If you talk about West Ham greats then he is in the first XI. He was there twenty years and played more than 700 games for the club. He broke his leg when he was 18 and fought his way back and played on before working for them and becoming assistant manager. When people talk about Bobby Moore, Geoff Hurst and Billy Bonds, Dad deserves to be mentioned in the same breath. I am not comparing myself to Dad, but I feel that given the level of loyalty he showed I might have been treated differently. I wasn't and now, neither is he.

It's very sad and upsetting that when Dad goes now to watch a game at West Ham that he is treated badly because of me. Instead of seeing the legend who devoted his life to the cause there are some who prefer to tar him with the brush of who he has for a son. 'Tell your son he is a f***ing Judas c****!' was one message he was asked to pass on to me. Dad did well not to react, though the guy did well to move away quickly or he might have been in trouble. But it shouldn't be like that. What kind of way is that to treat him? What kind of 'fan' would be so disrespectful? I hate that. They can call me whatever they like but should leave Dad out of it. Whatever gripe they have with me doesn't justify the treatment he receives. Dad stuck around all of his career, won the FA Cup twice, and gave the West Ham fans some of their greatest memories. The least they can do is show him some loyalty in return, but I don't expect anything of the kind, just as they should not expect anything from me.

I have tried not to think too much about what happened on 15 March 1997 but in light of everything that has gone on since, it's hard not to. We were away at Aston Villa and I had started a match which was scrappy and very competitive. After about half an hour I went to challenge for a ball and caught my studs in the turf. Pain shot through my leg and I knew straight away that it was broken.

The physio ran on to the pitch, saw the agony in my face, and the state of my leg. He called for the doctor and stretcher bearers. My memory of the following minutes is clouded by the searing pain and my body's reaction to it. I can, however, recall some cheering and applause as I was carried off around the visitor's end at Villa Park before being taken to hospital for treatment.

I spent the next four months in plaster and rehab but was fortunate that I could regain fitness during the summer and was back and ready for the start of the following season. During that time I focused on recovering and put everything else to the back of my mind. It was only when I was relaxing with a few mates that I discovered what had actually happened that day in Birmingham.

A couple of the lads I was out with were at the Villa match a few months before. We had a couple of beers and started to chat about the injury and the game (it was a 0–0 draw). They had been afraid to bring the subject up with me before but admitted that a section of the West Ham support had cheered the fact that I was being taken off – even though I was on a stretcher and in severe pain. My mates apologized, embarrassed that they had even shared a stand with people who could be so vindictive and nasty. I could barely believe what I was hearing. I knew all about the element in the crowd that didn't like me but I never thought they would be pleased that I was badly injured. It made me feel sick to the stomach. I was only 18. What kind of coward treats an 18 year old like that? They were grown men – but men whom I have looked in the eye and seen only hatred.

I tried not to let on how much it had affected me. I kept the conversation going. Most of my mates – closest and otherwise – were all regulars at West Ham so I asked them about their impression of the fans when it came to me. 'Be honest' I said, 'I want to know.' It turned out that each of them had at least one guy who sat beside them or near them who spent every home match dishing out stick to me – for the whole game. Some had more than one, and others, most of a section. I wasn't surprised. Mum and Aunt Sandra used to sit in the directors' box and even they had one geezer who sat a few rows behind them who would launch into tirades of abuse. Mum and Sandra are easy to recognize so he knew what he was doing. Mum would occasionally stand up and glare at him to try and make him feel uncomfortable but still he ranted.

Mum never stopped going to games even though she was sick of the abuse I was getting and I went looking for that bloke a couple of times after matches but he was always long gone. I haven't forgotten though, nor has Dad. He doesn't usually show any emotion when I score goals. He has learned over the years to remain passive – especially as he will often sit among fans of the opposing team at Chelsea away games and such. Mum told me that the only time she ever saw him celebrate a goal was when I half volleyed one in at Upton Park in January 2006. They were back in the directors' box and Dad jumped to his feet with fists clenched and slowly turned around to make sure that everyone whom he wanted to be seen by had had a good view. I suppose he was looking for that same bloke who used to get at Mum and Sandra but it didn't matter if he was there. Dad was making a bigger statement about his allegiance: family first.

Of course, I had received the now customary welcome that day – jeered, booed, and abused from the moment the Chelsea coach pulled up outside the Boleyn Ground: 'Fat Frank!' 'Judas c****!', 'Waste of money!', and so on. I find it amusing that West Ham fans attempt to justify their hatred of me on the basis that I left the club for Chelsea. So many times I have heard them plead that they only boo me because I am a traitor. I laugh when I see it written that 'I am an ex-West Ham favourite who the fans have now turned against.' Bollocks. I was never a favourite. They booed me almost every week when I was there – for years. Now they are creating a myth that the way I am treated is a direct result of my own actions. Had it been that simple then I would have an understanding of their feelings. In fact my moving was a direct result of their actions. They can and they do deny it but I know what happened and so do others.

I was having dinner with Ian Wright after he had compered the World Player of the Year Award in Geneva in 2005. We reminisced about West Ham days and he brought up the subject of the stick I would get from the fans when we played together there. It's strange. Sometimes I look back with a sense of disbelief that it had really been as bad as I seem to remember. And then someone like Wrighty recounts his memories and I realize just how grim it was.

I have become a stronger person for it. I know that I deal with disappointment better and that I have a determination to succeed which is even more driven because of what I experienced in the past. Others have seen that in me. Rio has spoken privately and publicly of what I had to endure and how it made me a better player and a stronger person. I think I earned the respect of people who worked closely with me at that time for the way I conducted myself. They didn't think I would make it and I did.

Even now I am at a bit of a loss to trace the root of all of this: why it started, why it got worse, and how it has reached the rampaging level it runs to now. I came into a team that was struggling to stay in the Premier League. We were fighting for survival and no struggle looks pretty. I was up for the challenge but I was not physically or mentally mature enough to cope with that pressure. It was different for Rio. He had a natural elegance to his game which had already seen him dubbed 'the new Bobby Moore'. Rio worked just as hard as me at his football but I think he was more easily accepted by the fans because his talent was more obvious. I had ability but I knew there wasn't much about me that would smack people in the face and make them shout 'Now that's talent.'

People said I was too slow to be a player. I am quicker now at 28 than I was at 18 and that's through working on my sprinting and fitness, but it's a lie to say I lacked pace. I'm no sprinter and I have an unusual gait which means I will never look like Thierry Henry on the run. I have a different way. Zinedine Zidane has his own way. He is not fast but his speed is deceptive because he is busy with the ball and always looking up for an option rather than bearing down on goal. I am not comparing myself to Zidane. I wish I could. In my opinion, he is one of the greatest players to grace the game. But I know that I am quicker than people gave me credit for.

I was certainly faster than some of our lads at the time but pace isn't everything. And neither, it seemed, was playing good football. There was a bit of confusion about how West Ham actually played and how people claim they played at that time. It's a fallacy to assert that we were a good football unit because that's not the team I remember most of the time. We were direct and high tempo. We had to be. When you are in a relegation battle there is no time for fancy football and free-flowing moves. I tried to get the ball down and play but I wasn't over-elaborate. At the same time, I was more concerned with constructing moves than maybe some of our more senior players, and when things don't go your way that can become a target for the supporters.

There was an environment of contrasting appreciation at Upton Park at the time. At one end of the spectrum, they would cheer a thumping tackle and make heroes of their hard men. At the other, a little trick or flick which beat a man but didn't necessarily gain advantage was greeted with great reverence. I didn't do much of either, if any at all. Mine was a very simple way of playing football, simplicity being genius, as Ron Greenwood always told Dad. Unfortunately, the purity of that style escaped certain people who were only interested in the very basic pleasures which football can offer up.

I'm not saying that I was a paragon of everything great and good in football. What I was doing was trying my best to do what I thought was correct, and booing me for that was out of order. Even after I scored ten goals in my first full season I was still getting it in the neck. Instead of giving me a chance to do even better, I got criticized for not being good enough.

And no matter how much crap I have had to take from West Ham fans, they always make up a new and ingenious angle to try and put me down more. After winning the Premiership twice and playing at the highest level for England, West Ham fans will still have you believe that I only got this far because I had an easy run into the team because my Dad was the assistant manager. I can only imagine that these are people who are uneducated about football. If you have any idea about how to treat a young player who is trying to do his best then you would realize that the only way to screw him up more is to boo him. The only way to help him improve is to allow him time and be constructive. I never got any constructive criticism from West Ham fans. They wanted the opposite – to destroy me. They were willing me to fail, and they still do.

As a result of my selection in the team, maybe the fans who saw older and more proven players slip out of the line-up started to ask themselves why I was in it. They had a ready-made and convenient answer sitting on the bench: Dad and Uncle Harry. It wasn't just me who was getting it at that time. We lost a couple of games to teams below us in the table and the team was barracked, and Harry would have season tickets thrown at him along with the request to 'F*** off.' Generally speaking, he would return the compliment and the season book with a swift flick of the right arm. There was a belief among the supporters that I had been given a shirt without having to work for it or prove myself. Had I been brought in having made my name at another club as a promising young player maybe it would have been easier. Had my name not been Lampard it certainly would have been.

People insist in all other walks of life that you can only play with the cards that you've been dealt. I am no different. I was the victim of circumstance in a lot of ways and I couldn't help who my Dad was and I wouldn't change that; or the fact that I was pushing to break through into the team at the age of 17. I have no regrets because it made me strong – strong enough to deal with anything.

By the time I reached 21 I realized that I was fighting a losing battle. I would never cast off the 'daddy's boy' tag at West Ham and I started to see myself at other clubs and playing in different colours. At first I was a bit shocked. All of my life I had dreamt of pulling on the West Ham shirt and if you'd offered me any club in the world I would have turned them down for my club – West Ham United.

And then, after years of constant and debilitating abuse it turned. I would have done anything to get out. I would have dropped a division or gone abroad; I would have gone anywhere. Now I am at Chelsea I feel fulfilled in every possible way with my career, and I find it laughable that I am still such a target for abuse.

After my relationship with Elen and our daughter Luna the thing that gives me most satisfaction in life is having left Upton Park and gone on to achieve what I have. The fans who booed me and called me for everything can take credit for helping to drive me on to achieve greater things. To a certain extent, they still do. My family and I know that even if I won the World Cup single-handedly for England there would still be West Ham fans who would say that I missed an easy chance or misplaced a pass. We have a good laugh about it because that's what it is – laughable; laughable that people could hold a grudge for no good reason.

If the best revenge is to live well then I am glad to say that life is very sweet for me, very sweet indeed – better than it ever was at West Ham even though they were the club I had always wanted to play for. Now, I know I will never play for West Ham again.

CHAPTER 5

BLUE IS THE COLOUR

I LIKED Claudio Ranieri from the moment we met. I was excited as we drove to his house in Parsons Green and not only because I was about to meet the Chelsea manager with a view to signing for the club. Kutner picked me up in a taxi and there was a sense of adventure as we drove through the streets of west London. There was something about the drive that gave me a good feeling about what the future held. The area around Knightsbridge, Chelsea and Fulham Road was almost completely alien to me but I felt an immediate attraction to it. It was a new world, exotic and challenging. I'd lived in Essex all my life and didn't know much more than travelling from home to Chadwell Heath for training and to Upton Park on matchdays.

The air was warm and the sun bathed row upon row of white houses which gleamed in the light. Kuts was busy talking tactics about how the meeting might go. I listened but didn't feel nervous. I felt optimistic. Good about the move, myself, and the direction I was going in.

When we arrived, Ranieri's housekeeper answered the door. It was the first time I had come across a housekeeper and was a little taken aback. The house was very elegant – the kind of place which I supposed was used to having staff around. We were shown into a room where the Chelsea manager was waiting for us.

I found him to be very friendly and open. He greeted us politely but with the same warm humanity he showed everyone who came into contact with him. He was well dressed – sports jacket, trousers and shirt, smart but effortlessly Italian – classic Claudio as I would learn over the following years. His dress sense was very much a reflection of his personality. Ranieri was of another generation to the players he coached and nurtured. He came from an era and culture which felt the need to retain a certain formality, hence the jacket. At the same time, he had a keen sense of the football environment – how the way you dress and the car you drive are an inherent part of the impression you make at a club. I think he struggled sometimes with his leaning towards old school but then again he had a black Ferrari he had bought in Italy and driven over which was very nice – very nice indeed. Even beside the impressive line-up of cars at our Harlington training ground the boss's motor drew some admiring looks. He liked that.

Unfortunately, it was a little difficult to talk freely at that first meeting because his English wasn't great and almost the whole conversation had to be translated by Gary Staker. People probably first became aware of Gary as the guy who interpreted for Gianluca Vialli when he arrived at the club. He became an assistant under Luca and has been a fixture at the club ever since. Ranieri also relied on him quite heavily when he came to London.

I can't imagine he'd had much time for English lessons in his first few months. Having replaced Vialli after four games of the 2000/01 season the culture of Chelsea was very much to achieve results first and figure everything else out along the way. This had led to an image of Ranieri among the fans and media which was distorted by his inability to express himself exactly as he would have wanted.

I discovered the real man straight away. There was nothing vague about Ranieri. We got the pleasantries over with quickly. He laughed about the weather. I laughed. I'm not sure why but it seemed appropriate. Then it was down to business – not money, football. He went to great lengths to explain his philosophy and ideas. He viewed me as someone who cared about the technical side of the game. Who was keen to study and learn. He got that one right. He is an intuitive man in that sense – a good judge of character. Even though I was hearing almost everything through an interpreter I already began to understand him.

There was an instantaneous respect, mutual respect. I liked the fact that he was also very blunt. I appreciate people who are straight with me and didn't flinch when he said he wanted to improve the defensive side of my game. There was nothing wrong with the attacking part. He had watched me play, studied me closely on video, and reckoned there was a split of 70/30 in favour of getting forward. I can't say that I disagreed too much with his assessment. I loved getting forward into goalscoring positions but was intrigued by his explanation of how I could be more effective. The plan was simple: he wanted to balance my play to 50/50 by coaching me to be more aware of when to make runs forward, how to time them better while picking up more on play while I was in the middle of the pitch.

He wanted me for my energy and potential. Ranieri believed he could harness both and help me to become a better player. I was impressed. I had hardly said a word but already he'd tapped into my desire to want to improve.

He outlined his vision for the team. There were to be other signings – major ones to complement me. He planned to bring in another midfielder and I was intrigued when he mentioned Emmanuel Petit. He had left Arsenal for Barcelona but had not settled as well as his ability should have allowed. Alongside Patrick Vieira, Petit had been the fulcrum of the Arsenal side which had steamrollered their way to the League and FA Cup double in 1998. He had also won the World Cup and European Championship with France and now he was coming to Chelsea to play beside me. Good. No pressure then.

There would be other arrivals but my mind was already racing over a hundred different things. What could we expect to achieve in the season? Would Petit be the sitting player, as he was at Highbury, and allow me to run? What squad number would I get? I had to stop myself. Ranieri was still talking but he sensed he had got through to me. More than anything else, though, I picked up on his over-riding urge to succeed at Chelsea.

He began to explain his planning for the pre-season. I was used to the traditional methods of Harry and Dad at West Ham. We were creatures of habit. We went back in the first week of July and would go running for a week over at Hainault Forest. It was simple and it worked and I enjoyed the slog as well as the camaraderie after the summer break. We would do physical training and then start on five-a-sides. It suited the mix we had – some good young players as well as the older characters who were comfortable doing what they had been used to all of their career. Harry knew there was no point trying to teach old dogs new tricks and the thought of someone like Razor Ruddock being put through a complex fitness test by Roberto Sassi – Chelsea's fitness coach – was not easy to visualize. I remember Dad had tried to make Razor run in spikes once, though I'm not sure why. He was, after all, about 33 years old and 16 stone at the time. Maybe Dad was being a bit over-enthusiastic and thought he could improve Razor's speed. Within about five minutes he had got a result but not the one he envisaged as Razor limped off to see the physio after pulling his calf muscle.

We actually had an Italian fitness specialist at West Ham for a while. Arnoldo Longaretti – we called him 'Arnie' – had worked in Serie A, and Harry's openness to new ideas led him to bring him to the club after a recommendation. It was an interesting experiment but it was a bit too intense for some of the older lads. Ian Wright, Razor and even Moncs were getting on a bit and Harry ended up having to tell Arnie he needed to stop. Paolo Di Canio loved him. Of course he did. He would do extra work with him, jumping over cones and burst sprinting. It opened my eyes to different methods but it was really just a taster of what was to come for me at Chelsea. I had acquired as much character as I had muscle development during my training at West Ham and I was thankful for it but I had changed and was ready for something new. Dad had seen that in me and encouraged me to go and find what I needed to take me to the next level.

As we sat in his lounge that afternoon Ranieri already knew every detail of how he would prepare the players for the season. My mind is naturally very organized and this appealed to me. Ranieri is similar despite a public perception of him as someone who would bumble his way through, amusing and infuriating people in his dealings with the media. There were times when he would try to translate Italian sayings into English or use English phrases in the wrong context in his efforts to get his thoughts across. That kind of incident happened only occasionally with the players and could be amusing to us as well. Ranieri, however, was very precise when it came to matters concerning the team.

There was a lull in the conversation which until then had been pretty much full on. His housekeeper brought in some drinks. Ranieri was very proud of his roots and recommended the coffee as it was Italian. I liked his style. I felt comfortable with him and sat there for a moment while he spoke, considering my options.

Aston Villa had expressed an interest in buying me though I hadn't really given the idea of moving to Birmingham a lot of thought up to that point. Leeds United had been the first to come in for me and I was very tempted by the aura which the club had built up around themselves in a relatively short space of time. They were very much the up-and-coming team in England and had the reputation of being 'the next big thing'. They were already doing well – they were beaten by Valencia in the Champions League semi-final the previous season – and were now expected to kick on and challenge Manchester United and Arsenal for the Premiership.

I went up to meet David O'Leary who was widely regarded as the best young manager in the country. I had done my homework. After all, Rio had moved there for a record transfer fee the previous season so it was an easy call to make. He explained that there was a great team spirit. The majority of the lads were young and shared a hunger and ambition to win things. Alan Smith, Robbie Keane, Dom Matteo and the like were good players and the team was a tight-knit group which liked to work hard and relax together. Rio reckoned the change of scene from London had done him a world of good. It was something I had considered seriously. After everything I had been through at West Ham the idea of cutting loose from the area was very appealing. Leeds was far away – far away from the taunts of 'daddy's boy' and accusations of nepotism. I could be myself in Leeds and also learn to stand on my own when it came to getting things done. I was desperate to put some distance between myself and my past. Leeds could be the answer. The area around the training ground at Thorpe Arch is beautiful and there was a distinctly different feel to life there from what I had been used to.

In purely football terms, when I knew I would be moving I had asked myself the hypothetical question of where I would prefer to go, and Leeds were the first club which sprung to mind. As it turned out, they were also the first team to make an offer for me – an extremely attractive one at that. In retrospect, given their reputation as the high rollers, that was hardly surprising. But at the time they had results on the pitch to match the spending.

All of this created a real buzz about the club but I was perturbed by the way it came across in my meeting with O'Leary. I was aware that Leeds were a club which knew where they wanted to be. There also seemed to be determination to stop at nothing to get there – no price was too high, whether in terms of transfer fees or otherwise. I felt it was all a bit too much. I wondered where I fitted into this grand scheme of things and O'Leary wasted no time in telling me. He was polite enough in his manner and said Leeds wanted to buy me but after that I would have to fight for my place. Lee Bowyer, Olivier Dacourt, David Batty, Eirik Bakke, and Stephen McPhail were already at the club and battling it out for the central midfield berths. I have to say I was a bit shocked, not by the fact that I wouldn't be guaranteed a start – I was happy to prove myself and expected it – but by the lack of forethought.

Given that Leeds had indicated a seriousness to match West Ham's valuation of £14 million for me, I had expected them to have a plan on how best to use me – which position I would play and who with; what would be expected of me. This was pretty basic stuff and the kind of thing I would have thought essential when weighing up spending that kind of money. Not a bit of it. Even though the whole experiment at Elland Road turned out to be as flimsy as the cheques which financed it, I thought the manager would at least have a vision of where I slotted into his plans. O'Leary, though, didn't seem to feel as strongly about it as I did. He knew about the rival offer from Chelsea and changed strategy. In his opinion, Chelsea were still throwing money at old pros whose hunger for success had long been sated or never amounted to anything more than a big salary in the first place. It was hardly a new slant on the Stamford Bridge recruitment policy of that time. Gus Poyet, Gianfranco Zola, Petit and even Vialli were all players who had signed in their thirties. Each had performed with differing degrees of effect. Leeds, on the other hand, were young and ambitious and would go to the top whether I joined them or not.

This was quite a risky tactic in front of me. Leeds carried themselves with an attitude that some considered arrogant and which in some ways I quite admired. I wanted to get to the top and wasn't ashamed to admit it. The difference between Leeds and me though was that I would never be as blatant as they could be; nor, at that time, did I have their self-confidence. Overall, I was unimpressed. O'Leary said that if I wanted more money then I should stay at West Ham. I found that offensive, a complete misjudgment on his part. Money had never been mentioned. The only reason I had driven all the way up the M1 was to talk football with him. Contract details, salary and everything else financial were things I did not get involved with. I cared about what I was being paid the same as anyone, but the manner in which he raised the subject implied that I was just toying with the idea of moving. This annoyed me as well. By suggesting I should stay at West Ham where I was comfortable and playing every week he was telling me something I didn't need to be told. I wasn't there to waste his time or my own.

By the end of the conversation O'Leary had talked a lot but I still didn't feel that I knew much more in terms of which part I was supposed to become in the Leeds machine. I had been very hopeful about the prospect of moving to the club. More than anything else I was desperate to better myself and become part of an ambitious team which was going places but the experience had left me a bit disorientated. With Ranieri, I knew exactly where I stood, and where he wanted me to be. That was the big difference between him and O'Leary. After that I never really gave Leeds another thought.

Ranieri made it clear I was a player who he valued greatly as well as someone he thought could benefit from playing for him. I mulled it over, thinking about what it would be like to sign for Chelsea. I had never supported them though neither did I hate them. I was a West Ham fan. West Ham fans had a healthy dislike for Chelsea fans, fired by the normal city rivalry. There was a bit of history but since it had been a while since either club had been considered the dominant force there wasn't that much to get excited about. Apart from the geographical difference and the fact that Chelsea had recently been seen as one of the biggest spenders in England, West Ham fans seemed quite content to target more traditional rivals like Tottenham. None the less, it was still a big decision for me. I had been brought up with West Ham who consider themselves a big London club, and the thought of playing for another club in the city was one I hadn't previously confronted. Why should I? I had been immersed in West Ham all of my life and naively believed for most of that time that I would never play anywhere else. Well, certainly not in London. My background and history was well documented and I wondered how Chelsea fans would react to me. I was, after all, a fan of another club who would be playing for them.

There was no history between West Ham and Leeds. I was leaving a club where I was getting it in the neck for being who I was. I didn't need to sign for a different one where I might risk similar treatment for the same thing. The last thing I wanted was to jump out of the frying pan and into the fire as far as the fans were concerned. I just didn't know if I would be accepted.

I sought the opinion of a couple of other players I was close to – Steve Lomas and Jon Moncur – and confided in them. My dilemma was that Chelsea were notorious for having a lot of players, most of whom were considered stars, and if I signed for them I would obviously have a fight on my hands to get into the team. On the other hand, just being in that environment would give me the chance to better myself. Moncs and Lomy were adamant. They knew I wanted to better myself and told me that I needed to put the issue of the fans to one side. I should put my football first and at Chelsea I had the chance to become a better player because I would have better players around me. Coming from seasoned pros whose opinion I respected, this assessment was important. Then again, maybe they just wanted me out because it meant one less midfielder!

When it came, the bid which was accepted from Chelsea was relatively late but everything moved very quickly once I had met with Ranieri and seen the stadium. They had paid £11.1 million for me. I tried to comprehend what that meant but in all honesty there was so much happening that I found it difficult to gather my thoughts. I didn't even sign on the day I was supposed to. I had to go for my medical which was routine though I had had a hernia operation earlier that summer. Word was out but the announcement itself was postponed until the following day and Colin Hutchinson – who was managing director of the club – sat at the press conference and talked about how I had been signed to replace Gus Poyet and Dennis Wise who had just left the club. I listened to him speak and realized this was quite a daunting prospect. Poyet was a legend at Chelsea who had a record of scoring goals, although I arrived with a history of doing the same for West Ham. I was given Poyet's number 8 shirt which really pleased me. It was my lucky number and when you move to a new club there is no guarantee you will be that fortunate. I answered a few questions but found the whole thing slightly startling, weird even. We walked out on to the pitch at Stamford Bridge to have photographs taken. I looked around the stadium, which I found familiar enough having played there on several occasions.

Colin gave me my new shirt and the snappers shouted this way and that; I looked at the blue against my skin and just for a moment realized how much my life had changed – I had set a new course for the future. West Ham were behind me, far away to the east. It was all a bit surreal, dream-like, though at the same time it was entirely natural, even liberating. My gut feeling was good. I had dreaded standing there and feeling completely out of place. Instead, I felt at home. I breathed in the air and caught a glimpse of myself in the all-blue kit. My back straightened up and I lifted my head. I felt something I hadn't experienced in quite some time: I was proud to be a footballer again.

We finished with the photo call but there was still one formality I had to complete. I had yet to meet the chairman. People saw Ken Bates as 'Mr Chelsea'. He was, but he left the football side of things to his managers and Colin. I didn't know him before, though from his high profile in the papers most people probably reckoned they had a handle on him. He was infamous for his strong opinions and for that reason I was quite apprehensive when Colin told me we had been invited to have lunch with him at Fishnets restaurant in Chelsea Village.

Though he is rather small, Ken Bates is quite an imposing individual, very much the larger-than-life character which he plays so well. I was a bit self-conscious. It's not every day you come face to face with someone who has just paid eleven million quid for you, but he couldn't have been nicer and I ended up becoming quite close to him. Bizarrely, I feel I owe him a lot because he was prepared to pay so much money for me. I wasn't responsible for the state of the transfer market – that was the going rate – but when the money being paid involves you, it's natural to feel a little anxious. I had no doubts about myself but it was still a huge act of faith on Ken Bates's part, and a very expensive one.

But something between us clicked and he took a special interest in me right from the start. He wasn't particularly intrusive but sometimes you would get little snippets of feedback in the dressing room about what Ken was and wasn't happy with. If there was a problem then he wouldn't be slow in letting you know about it. Thankfully I managed to stay on his good side – most of the time.

It wasn't until the night before the final game of that first season which was against Middlesbrough away that I found myself in trouble. We were in the team hotel when he saw me walking through and invited me to sit down. Straight away I realized that it was no coincidence. He asked me if I had gone to a nightclub in London the previous Saturday. His tone was, as ever, quiet. I admitted the charge but I was confused and a bit apprehensive about where the conversation was headed.

'You were drinking in a club,' he said.

'Yes. I went out and had a few drinks,' I replied.

'Well, I know the bouncer there and he said you were drinking too much.'

I was on the back foot and not really sure what to say.

'Mister chairman. I wasn't that drunk. I was out with a couple of mates and had a few drinks,' I said, but he cut me off.

'Listen. I paid eleven point one million pounds for you and I don't want you letting me down.'

That was his way – to be really straight without getting too heavy. I look back and I respect him a lot. He wanted me to know that he knew what was going on but he also wanted me to take responsibility for my own actions. It was the same when I did an interview for a men's magazine. It was the first one I'd done and will be the last. I had been asked a few questions about the dressing room, the banter and it had come out badly. There were some sexual references and one of the tabloids seized on it and made it into something else completely. It was my own fault but word reached me that the chairman had the hump about it. I hadn't been summoned to see him but I was walking through Stamford Bridge one day and heard his unmistakable voice.

'Frank! Come here please.'

'S***,' I thought, 'I'm cornered.'

I felt a bit like a guilty school kid. I knew what it was about and before he even spoke I let him know that I was sorry and that it wouldn't happen again. He didn't want to have a row, though. Instead, he was quite emotional. He told me that I had more class than to do interviews like that. I should think first before speaking – think about how it might be interpreted. He was right but I wasn't sure how to respond. I had been given a telling off of sorts. I felt that he was disappointed rather than angry with me. He had taken me under his wing and I had been caught out and that had hurt him.

He was genuinely interested in the players and without being disrespectful to the many foreign players who have served Chelsea magnificently, he seemed to have a particular concern for the welfare of the English boys. When Jody Morris and JT (John Terry) got into trouble outside the Wellington nightclub a year later, he defended them in public, supported them and was the first to herald them when they were acquitted.

Ken was a very loyal person and expected the same loyalty in return. He ran the club like an extended family and his partner, Susannah, added the maternal influence. She was very interested in the wives and girlfriends of the players and she was a real help to me when I joined. Susannah had a very gentle way about her which was in stark contrast to Ken. Her personality is very caring and she reminded me a lot of my Mum in that sense.

At the end of the first season after I signed I started dating Elen Rivas. Elen is Spanish and while her English is perfect she can sometimes find it difficult to adjust to certain conversations, especially with people she has just met. Ken and Susannah knew we were serious about each other and invited us out for dinner at La Famiglia, an Italian restaurant near Stamford Bridge. I was nervous about going. We turned up at the Chelsea Village hotel and were told to go up to his apartment. He was charming and showed us around before we headed out and climbed into a cab. Ken was talking to the cabbie in that arrogant kind of manner he could have, asking him if he was a Chelsea fan. The poor guy replied that he was a Tottenham supporter – wrong answer, and Ken gave him stick until we arrived. We were seated at a good table – of course – and the waiter poured some drinks. I had a glass of red wine with my dinner which I was quite keen to taste but at the same time afraid to touch in case Ken disapproved. I think he noticed and I had literally had one sip from the glass when about halfway through the dinner he simply left me out of the round when he was topping up the drinks. I thought it was hilarious. Ken is great company, a real raconteur. Unfortunately, he was chatting away about football but speaking so quickly that Elen was finding it difficult to follow the conversation and panicked a little bit. Susanah could see what was happening and brought the conversation back round to make Elen comfortable.

I think he did the same thing with JT – it was his way of saying that we were the English core of the team, the heart and soul of the Chelsea which he had envisaged. Without his decision to fork out the fee for me I might not have been at the club or achieved what I have in my career, and I am very grateful for that. I thought it was a lot of money though not too much, in the way others seemed to believe.

In fact, I was actually quite proud of the fee. I wanted it to be a lot simply because it meant that I was a valuable player to the team who paid it. I didn't feel any great pressure from it. There were probably a lot of Chelsea fans who thought it was too much at the time and even more West Ham fans who were rubbing their hands at the thought of it but I believed in myself more than anyone else did. Franny Jeffers went to Arsenal from Everton on the same day for just a little less so it was all relative and down to the market at the time. The only person I really spoke to about it was Dad. He told me not to worry, that I would be worth double in a few years time. I laughed at him. I knew he was trying to make it easier for me though he likes to remind me now that he was right. In any event, there was nothing I could do about the fee – it simply had to be put to one side.

There was a pre-season trip to Roccaporena in Italy in early July but before then I had a little bit of holiday time and moved from Essex into a flat above a shop in Walton Street in Chelsea which the club had rented for me. It was a big deal for me and I spent a few weeks preparing myself for it. I know I was only moving across London, so to speak, but I had spent my whole life around where I had grown up – it was familiar and safe. Kutner had Mark Bosnich as a client at the time and he was already at the club and lived locally.

That was a help because he showed me around and filled me in on a few things about the club.

Bozo was a real character. He took me to training on my first day and I realized he was very much cut from the cloth with which they make goalkeepers' gloves. He projected his voice so it would boom in front of him and when he laughed the volume rose accordingly. This was no act. That's what he was like almost all of the time – larger than life and always full of mischief.

We would go out to dinner locally together. He lived nearby and my flat was great simply because of its location. Walton Street is a real little pocket of shops and restaurants and my place was just above Scalini. It didn't take me long to depend on it and just a little longer before I had the waiters doing takeaway on just about anything from the menu. It was funny because when I was with West Ham eating out at Scalini was very much a big occasion, and there I was, living two doors away phoning in my order and one of the lads would knock on my door a few minutes later. It's still my favourite restaurant in London to this day.

While I was settling in just fine to the area, it was a bit of a culture shock arriving at the club. Everything was very different from West Ham. For instance, at Chadwell Heath we had our cook, Shirley, who, God bless her, was lovely but who had a limited repertoire: chicken and mushroom pie with pastry on top, shepherd's pie, and occasionally spaghetti bolognese. It really was a case of Sunday roast on a Monday and heavy meals all the way through the week. It was food that I loved though not necessarily food that loved training and football. The best way to describe the West Ham canteen was that it resembled a little café or burger bar. There were no real facilities there. At

Chelsea's old training ground at Harlington it was not much better in terms of the environment. The facilities were crap and upstairs we had a big open kitchen but the food was very different. There was a choice of different pasta and salads and I realized very quickly that my diet was going to change pretty dramatically from the first day.

Apart from the culture shock of the canteen, Ranieri was also very keen on keeping track of his players' fitness levels through blood tests. I had one on my first day and was quite shocked when they took about ten small containers of blood for examination and testing to learn about my metabolism and general health. Strangely enough, on that first day they found that my blood iron level was low – not quite anaemic but bordering on it. I was very sceptical of this routine at first. At West Ham this kind of thing didn't happen it at all. If a doctor took a blood test from some our lads at Chadwell Heath he might have found ten pints of lager and a couple of glasses of wine on a bad day and I don't think we wanted to know that! Harry knew it wouldn't have worked for us and was cute enough not to push it. Seriously though, during that first year at Chelsea Ranieri would give me a day off training or rest me now and again without telling me exactly why. It turned out to be so that my body could restore the iron level in my blood.

Personally I thought he relied on this practice too much. I had no problem with the process but I am a great believer in players knowing their own body ahead of any doctor when it comes to general health. Ranieri wanted to inject me with iron at one point but I wasn't too keen. It wasn't explained to me why. As far as I was concerned, I was fit and I didn't need it. In the end I started taking iron tablets, and have continued to do so pretty frequently, but it occurred to me that I had spent four years at West Ham and not once had this problem been diagnosed. Until that point I was very much dependent on reading my own body. If you feel good you play and if not then you tell the manager and see what happens. Modern football needs much more thought and Ranieri was used to working with sports science as a way of everyday coaching.

The most we ever had at West Ham was a cholesterol test but at Chelsea we even had our ability to jump tested. Roberto Sassi was the fitness coach and he measured the spring we had during pre-season – mine was pretty poor. I had never worked on specifics like that before but Ranieri loved it and would sometimes leave a whole day to Sassi to work with us. We used sprint training and then running with five different kind of jumps during the exercise, and at first I wondered 'What the hell is this?' Now looking back and seeing how my physique has changed since I have been at Chelsea, I realize how beneficial it's been. The first two years were arduous but I recognize how much my muscle structure has developed.

There were some things I was asked to do that I couldn't do well, or even grasp properly. I was actually quite embarrassed about it. I had been bought at a cost of £11 million and must have looked a bit of an idiot because I just wasn't used to this kind of training. I'm not sure if Sassi had too much rein to do what he wanted but I appreciate that it helped me.

About six or seven of the big players didn't return for pre-season right away because they had been playing World Cup qualifiers and international matches. The likes of Jimmy Floyd Hasselbaink, Eidur Gudjohnsen, and Marcel Desailly

had all been given a bit of extra time off. I was quite pleased
– especially as I was struggling a bit to find my feet.

Ranieri had a habit of taking his teams to a little village in
the mountains of Italy for pre-season and that summer I got on
a plane with a group of lads I hardly knew, many of them
younger players I didn't recognize. I sat next to Joe Keenan
who was another English lad and a midfielder, which made it
more comfortable, and two seats away from me was Billy
McCulloch. Billy had just joined as masseur and was a lot
quieter then than he is now. I remember thinking at the time,
'Who is this geezer?' which is a bit strange when I think about
it now since Bill reckons he's more famous than the players! He
was very much in a similar position to me at the time. We were
both new boys trying to feel our way into the company without
making too much fuss or making a fool of ourselves. To be fair,
Billy worked his nuts off on that trip and showed just how
good he is at his job. Jody Morris noticed it quite quickly and
Bill has never shied away from doing anything he can to make
sure a player is in the best possible condition. I benefited a lot.
JT and I wind him up about his 'magic hands' but we're not
kidding – there is no way I could play so many games if it
wasn't for Billy's expertise and commitment. We bonded on
that first trip. I said to him that if he looked after me then I
would do the same for him and that was it. We were mates.

Jody Morris and John Terry were there and I had a natural
affinity with them because they were English lads and my age.
We had a three-hour bus ride to the hotel which actually was
more like a hostel. It was quite a nice setting but it was
remote. I roomed with Jody who I knew from going out in
London with Rio, and against whom I had played in the
youth team.

We had sixteen days there which was very intense – and boring. The facilities were spartan. The beds were small and we had a little TV in the room which had only foreign language stations. It was hard work but it made me focus on why we were there in the first place. At West Ham there were always other activities to entertain us – a bit of golf in the afternoon or whatever – but this was all about training. I found myself trying to stay afloat every day. It was a level up from what I had been used to, sharper and more physical. I was struggling to impress, and some days I'd finish feeling quite down because I knew I hadn't done well. Even the simplest things seemed a little bit more difficult.

After a session had finished we would stand about forty or fifty yards from each other, JT, Jody, and me and ping long passes to each other. Jody was a good player and had already played Champions League and was a Premiership regular. He had come through the ranks at Chelsea which was no mean achievement given the way the club had been importing players at the time he was maturing. I'm not sure he received the credit he deserved either. Jody is a very skilful player, a player's player. He will never leave you struggling for an outball – when you are being closed down and need a team-mate to pass to. He has a great football brain and makes space for himself and others on and off the ball. When you play with Jody you can be sure of two things: that he will pass and receive the ball without endangering possession; and that he will stand firm beside you no matter the opposition. Jody is one of a dying breed in modern football – a man's man. He is exactly the same on the pitch as he is off it and you can be sure that he will always tell you how it is – no bullshit. I appreciate him for that and know he and I will always be mates.

Some teams will have a premeditated plan to try and intimidate you. Chelsea have traditionally been seen by some teams as a softer touch. It hadn't happened a lot in my time, but when it did and Jody was in beside me, I knew I could count on him. We didn't take any nonsense and whatever people say about the physical side of the game, I would always like to have Jody beside me if a team is cutting up rough. He can play as well though, but his contribution to Chelsea has been slightly eclipsed by the abrupt manner in which the contract he was offered to stay was withdrawn for financial reasons.

John has many similar qualities but was still a young player, though he was doing the same as Jody on the training pitch in terms of passing. I had been a regular starter for West Ham and they had just paid a lot of money for me. Even so, I realized that Jody and JT could hit long balls with two feet better than I could. I had just had an operation and had lost a bit of strength in my left leg: my passes were falling short and I knew it. I was a bit embarrassed. At times I found myself in awe of Zola or Desailly which was a failing on my part.

At West Ham I had been used to sharing a laugh if one of us messed up but at Chelsea the culture was very different. I made a mistake during one early session of keep-ball and looked up to find one of the experienced pros looking down his nose at me – not quite sneering, more a look of incredulity that I had managed to fluff something which he clearly believed everyone should be capable of pulling off. I was a little surprised. Thankfully, I benefited from one of Dad's anecdotes about Bobby Moore. Apparently, if you mishit a pass to him, he wouldn't fly off the handle at you – it wasn't his style. Instead, he would just give you a look, a little reminder, as if to say, 'Come on. That's not the standard we are playing to here.' Moore was the greatest player West Ham ever had and I realized that I had made a significant step up coming to Chelsea.

As the new lad I had to follow tradition and sing a song at our training camp, an event scheduled for about a week in. In the days leading up I became progressively more nervous, so much so that I don't think I cared about training because I was just s***ting myself about singing the song. And it got worse. All the star players started turning up so I knew I would have the privilege of making a fool of myself in front of all the top boys as well. I couldn't even have a glass of wine or anything for a bit of Dutch courage. I was beside myself. Some others had chosen to sing Sinatra and the like. 'Good for them,' I thought but there was no point in taking unnecessary risks. I decided to play safe and belted out 'Maybe It's Because I'm a Londoner'. It was the easy way out but I didn't care.

There were a few who had to sing, like Bolo Zenden and Petit. When it was Billy's turn he was quite shy and said he couldn't sing a note. Instead, he volunteered to tell a few jokes. There was a strange silence. Football is a very ordered society which is run on pretty much the same hierarchy as a school playground. It's not the place of the new boys to change the rules. Neither is it the kind of audience you want to bomb in front of. People will judge you harshly in that environment and a bad first impression can make or break you. Either Billy was extremely confident or very stupid. He was given a chance and got a few laughs – and then a few more until he had the whole place in stitches. That was the start of Billy the comedian. After that he got up every night and made us laugh. He's still doing it.

JT was really quite young then, at 18, and was a bit quieter, though you could see his personality coming through and I had heard he was developing into a really good player. When we started training I realized just how good he was. He had just won the club's Player of the Year award, quite an achievement when you consider the older stars of that team, but even then there was an aura about John which suggested he was the future, the captain-in-waiting. There was something about the way he trained. You could see in his eyes the determination to get better and to succeed and I could relate to that. Although quieter, he had a strong sense of identity which was detectable beneath the surface.

The trip itself was an insight into how intense training was going to be under Ranieri and Sassi. We did 1000-metre runs at altitude and lots of sprints. I had just had the hernia op and felt a few twinges in my groin during shooting practice but I didn't want to say anything. I was new and wanted to make the right impression and I ended up doing some extra work to show how enthusiastic I was. When everyone else was finished I would do shooting practice with Angelo but I wasn't connecting. I could feel a bit of pain and it was made worse by the feeling of nervousness rising in my stomach. It was like the first day at a new school and when I think about how comfortable I am now at Chelsea it seems like a lifetime away, but I was just so desperate to do well.

We played some pre-season games and for the one at Leyton Orient – where their fans gave me some stick – I had been assigned a role in the centre of midfield because of the players who had left. Also, Roberto Di Matteo was injured and there were doubts that he would return. Zenden had come in on the left and Jesper Gronkjaer had arrived part of the way through the previous season, and there was Jokanovic and Sam Dalla Bona and Mario Stanic.

Myself and Petit were supposed to be the mainstay in the centre and I was looking forward to playing with him. I was excited about the balance in the midfield four with two wingers and Petit as a holding player. He was naturally left-sided and I liked to get forward. Ranieri flirted with pushing me out wide a couple of times during pre-season matches and I began to get a bit nervous as to how well I would start the season.

The concern was not unfounded. Ranieri sent me both left and right of midfield and now I wish I had been more assertive in expressing my feelings about that right from the start. Position wasn't the only teething problem, though, as Petit was no longer the player he had been at Arsenal in terms of consistency and we never really got the chance to gel in those early weeks. There were matches, though, when he was really on his game and was class. He had a lot of injury problems though, and my partnership with him didn't quite go to plan, partly because of the tinkering.

Apart from that, Manu was a difficult character to figure out. He wasn't one of the boys and when it came to banter and hanging out he didn't join in, making it even harder to get to know him at any level. After a while I realized that it was just how he was. We were never going to be best mates. He was a bit moody and withdrawn and whatever he thought of me, he kept it to himself. I accepted it, though you need a certain amount of camaraderie with a guy you are playing beside if it's really going to work.

Before my debut some of the negative stuff that I had suffered at West Ham briefly raised itself in my mind. You never really know how you will be received by a different set of supporters, and I had come from a rival London club. I listened as the stadium announcer ran through the team. He got to my name and there was a hearty cheer. Thank God for that. We played Newcastle in that first match of the season in a 1–1 draw. Zenden scored but Clarence Acuna equalized. The result wasn't what I had wished for but the most disappointing thing was the fact that I got a sign of things to come. I started in the middle of the park and did all right but ended up on the left. That happened a lot that season.

I was pissed off, not because I felt it was my divine right to play in central midfield but because I was feeling my way in and had been shunted out to the right or left for the first few games because of injuries. It wasn't anyone's fault, not really. The second outing was better when we won at Southampton and I got man-of-the-match in a couple of papers but I was still getting moved around the midfield and was becoming restless about it.

We were away at Tottenham the following week and I was obsessing a bit about my performances and position. Games between Chelsea and Spurs have always had a certain edge to them and unfortunately for me the league match at White Hart Lane became something of a landmark event. Up until that point, I had never known what it was like to be sent off.

I found out that afternoon and did not find it a pleasant experience. I was hardly a villain – two bookable offences, the second of which was extremely disappointing. I fouled Simon Davies for the first which was fair enough. But the game had then got a bit heated and was tied at 2–2 after Jimmy had scored with a penalty. I had already set Jimmy up for the opener but we had been pulled back twice when I was sent through on the keeper and was brought down. It was a clear enough incident. Ledley King had caught my foot and over I went but the referee waved play on and as I got up Neil Sullivan and Chris Perry were in my face accusing me of diving. I hate that. I am no cheat and anyone who knows me knows I don't go down without reason. There was a bit of a shoving match but play was still going on until the ball ran out for a throw and I saw the ref coming towards me. I knew what was coming. I walked off, feeling angry and frustrated.

Afterwards, Ranieri came and spoke to me. 'Frank, on the pitch you have to be an iceman. Cool down.' I was calm by that point. The red card didn't bother me that much because it was down to the referee's interpretation of what happened. It was the fact that they had called me a cheat which had really got to me. If I had dived then I would have taken the stick but I had been fouled and the accusations just made the whole thing worse.

I was very upset. Marcel scored in the last minute of the game and we won which took the edge off it a bit but I couldn't see past the fact that I was ordered off. I hate being sent off and putting the team under pressure like that. If it had been a situation where I felt I had no choice but to bring someone down then it would not have felt as bad. This was just pointless though, and unlucky.

I had only been at the club five minutes and was already getting sent off – not a good start. Ranieri knew I was upset and he knew when to give breaks. He gave me that week off training. I was puzzled though. It was only two weeks into the season and I was fine and wanted to train but he insisted that I should rest because my body would respond better.

I scored my first goal for the club in the next match which was a UEFA Cup game against Levski Sofia. Things appeared to be looking up but the game after kind of summed up our season when we were at home to Middlesbrough and were cruising at 2–0 ahead at half-time but ended up drawing the match 2–2. I thought I had played well that day and Ranieri substituted me with half an hour to go at 2–1 up. They got a dodgy penalty late on but that game showed up our fragility in that kind of contest – one where we were totally in control but still blew it.

It wasn't just domestic competition where we struggled, though no one could have predicted the controversy and furore which dogged our second-round UEFA Cup tie. The events of September 11 in New York had already affected European competitions and when we gathered round to listen to the draw a few of the boys were already a bit edgy about the prospect of playing a team from Israel.

As seems to be the case when you wonder about things like that, we drew Hapoel Tel Aviv and immediately most of us assumed the away game would not be played in Israel because of the obvious security risk. There was so much hostility and nervousness around the world at that time that it seemed inconceivable that we would have to go there to compete.

We were convinced that we would end up playing in Cyprus or another suitable neutral venue and couldn't believe it when we found out that we would, after all, be playing in Tel Aviv. There was a lot of unrest in the squad. The club had got wind of it and called a meeting of the players and manager in the gym at the training ground where a security officer from Special Branch had been invited along to speak to us and answer any questions. Chelsea were desperate to send the top team out to play and this guy did his best to reassure us that we would be well looked after. We would have an armed escort at all times and our flight would be secured in the air and on the ground. Not everyone was convinced. There was a lot of chatting between members of the group, and a few worried faces. Ranieri could be quite astute at sensing those things and his reaction was a good one. He was under pressure from the club but he made it clear that no one would be forced to travel and that he would not penalize any player who opted out. He was very much on our side.

I think Ken Bates wanted everyone to go but it was a difficult one to call. At one point we discussed whether or not we should just take a collective decision not to go but the club warned us that if that were the case then they would send the youth team. We knew the club needed the money from a decent run in Europe, and because of the possible sanctions by UEFA they would rather send someone to play. Even if they got beaten 10–0 it was better than a hefty fine and ban from future competitions.

The manager left the room so that we could talk it over. Crisis meetings were not unusual that season. If we lost a game then we would get together and thrash out what had gone wrong and clear the air. This was a bit different, though, and it was also a bit awkward. In those meetings it was normally the captain – Marcel or Graeme Le Saux – who would lead the debate. In the end, neither of them made the trip, so it was up to the rest of us. As a group we considered the position. A straw poll was taken of which lads were prepared to go and it ended up that only six of our senior players opted out. The younger lads who were unmarried were more at ease whereas the older guys with kids were the ones who were more concerned: Desailly, Le Saux, Petit, William Gallas, Chappy Ferrer, and Eidur Gudjohnsen.

I don't blame them. I was nervous about going and I didn't have a family of my own at that time. But anyone getting on a plane in the aftermath of the atrocities in New York will remember that it was not a comfortable or normal experience. The press made it worse, labelling the players cowards and traitors. That was really harsh given that we were being asked to travel to one of the potential flashpoints in the post-9/11 world. Graeme is a guy who would play his heart out for the team, no matter what the opposition, and Marcel will go down as one of the greatest defenders in the world, a very strong character who lived by his principles. He also was very family orientated and strong in what he believed to be right. Oddly enough, I remember that most of the media guys were given the same option and some didn't travel either. The press made a lot more of it than was necessary and I don't think they really considered all of the factors involved. They just wrote what they wanted because it was fashionable to have a bit of a dig at Chelsea.

I had complete sympathy with the lads who opted out but I had worries of my own and at one point didn't want to go either, but in the end I felt under pressure to do so. I saw the criticism in the media and expected it would get worse. I was also very conscious that I hadn't been at Chelsea that long and was still trying to find my way at the club while guys like Marcel and Manu were older and had done everything in their careers. I had just signed and was supposed to have the English toughness and spirit about me and I didn't want that questioned. People think that there must have been friction between those who went and those who didn't but the reality is a lot simpler. The guys who got on the plane didn't want to go either.

Looking back – now that I have Elen and my daughter Luna – if the situation arose again then I might not get on the plane. I asked Mum and Dad what they thought at the time. Mum didn't want me to go while Dad pointed out people would question my commitment to the club if I pulled out – the £11 million price tag, again.

In the end I didn't have the courage to say no and got pushed along by the crowd. The fault really lay with UEFA because Chelsea should not have been put in that position. A couple of seasons later Manchester United were told not travel to Israel and played in Cyprus instead. There was a feeling that because we were not major players in the politics of football it was easier for the authorities to make the decision they did. If it had been AC Milan or Real Madrid in our position I wonder if the outcome would have been different.

These were just a few of the thoughts I was having when we made our way to the plane to take off. It was all a bit surreal though the flight was fine. Pretty normal except for the fact that we had armed guards in the cabin with us and then the coach ride to the hotel was surrounded by an army and police escort. It was the same at the team hotel where every floor was secured by guards who would patrol the entrance and exit areas. All of this was supposed to calm us down but it made me more on edge.

I couldn't wait for the game to be played partly because I wanted to get back home as quickly as possible. After the savaging the lads who didn't travel received, we could barely have suffered a worse result, beaten 2–0. We had the players to do better and the only young lad who started was in central defence – Joel Kitamirike. We conceded both goals in the last minute of the game which was a disaster. In the circumstances, a draw would have been respectable and reasonable, especially as we were missing six of our best players.

The atmosphere was hostile but not so much against us as in support of their own team. Ranieri had a real go at us at half-time when it was 0–0 and I thought we were doing okay, all things considered. He shouted about what the hell was the matter with us. Maybe the pressure of the whole thing had got to him, though he would quite often employ reverse psychology so that if we thought we were playing well he would cane us. You could be two up and in control and he would question us because he wanted to make sure we would stay on the ball in the second half. Mourinho doesn't do it but that was Ranieri's way.

I was used to that. He would often lose the rag with us when we were a goal or more up and leave us a bit dumbfounded – looking at each other, everyone thinking the same thing: that we were doing all right. It was his way of keeping us on our toes. I respected his opinion on what was the best way to handle that situation but I'm not convinced it always had the right effect. It ignored the fact that he was dealing with grown men and experienced professionals. We knew if we were playing well or not and even though I realized he was simply employing a method to try and motivate us further, it was unconvincing.

It wasn't until Mourinho arrived that I saw the other side. The first time we were winning he came into the dressing room with a grin on his face, waited until we were all ready and told us how fantastic we had been. He pointed to all of the positives and then said there was no reason why we shouldn't go on and win by five or six. It was a real vote of confidence, and trust. It also made us feel good and had the desired effect. For Mourinho, it's more important to treat his players like men, especially when things are going well.

That's not to say he won't tell us if we are playing rubbish. Equally, he has no qualms about spelling out exactly what we are doing wrong but again, he does it in an adult way. There's not even a hint of trying to kid us on. For whatever reason, he calls it how he sees it and more often than not that's the same way we see it. Even when a game is too close to call from the outside, the players will often know if they are going to go on and win. So does Mourinho.

The message was a little more confused with Ranieri and so was I. It was hard to imagine that things could get much worse in the wake of the Tel Aviv game but they did. We hoped to banish the memory of the whole fiasco by going through to the next round and in a show of unity and strength, five of the six who didn't travel to Israel started the home leg two weeks later. We went a goal down in the first half and then pulled it back level but we just couldn't do any more and we lost 3–1 on aggregate.

It was slightly weird. I had no experience of it but I knew Chelsea had lost to St Gallen the year before and it was beginning to feel like the club had acquired a reputation for this kind of thing. It shouldn't have done, given how well they had played in getting to the quarter-final of the Champions League a couple of seasons earlier. Probably the worst fallout from the whole mess was the effect it had on those who were made the scapegoat for the defeat, people like Graeme Le Saux. Graeme is a good pro and a good family man who did what he thought was right for him and those closest to him and got pilloried for it. That must have had an effect on him and to me that was unfair.

My problems were of a different kind. When I wasn't being taken off I was still playing outside of central midfield on a regular basis and I was beginning to get more and more annoyed. Even when I started in the middle, Ranieri would make a change and Jokanovic would be coming on and it was: 'Lamps go wide.' 'What the f*** is this?' was my usual reaction at those moments. It got so bad that JT and Billy would stop me on the morning of matchdays and say 'Where you playin' this week, Giggsy?' Despite the nickname, I'm no Ryan Giggs and while I was trying to cut in as much as I could it just wasn't comfortable. I have a lot of admiration and respect for Ranieri and will always say good things about him but the tinkering and moving players around so much made a lot of us feel uncomfortable.

I ended up playing fifteen games on the right before Christmas and I hated it. I tried to tell the manager and he just said it was for the good of the team. There were injuries and he didn't think that others could play there whereas I had the legs to do it. I sat down with Ranieri a few times and we talked about it. I knew I was a victim of circumstance and not some cruel joke. I was also prepared to do what I had to.

It wasn't helping me to progress, though. I had moved to Chelsea to further my development and become a better player but I felt trapped in the wrong position and frustrated that I wasn't able to be as involved on the ball or get into positions where I would score. It was worse for me as I had never played anywhere outside of central midfield my whole career – only on the rare occasion for West Ham but never for a stretch like this. I let it go for a while because whenever I brought it up with Ranieri he said it was his only choice. I was still new and didn't want to push my luck. I was conscious though that while he said he was happy, the fans and press were asking why he had paid so much money for a central midfielder just to play me on the wing. Dad came to the games and, typically, he would tell me that I had to have a word with the manager about my position.

I knew what he was saying. I was in danger of being cast as an average right-winger when I wanted to excel in the middle of the park. I was worried that I wasn't performing to my potential but I never heard any real discontent from the Chelsea fans through those first few months, unlike the West Ham fans who would jump on you in a second.

The pleasure of making my return to Upton Park was almost upon me. I knew what to expect but, as it turned out, my granddad found out before me. He lived in Chelmsford and had a habit of going to the local butcher to get his shopping. The day before we were due to play West Ham he was standing in line, minding his own business, when he heard the woman in front talking to her mate.

One asked the other if she was going to Upton Park for the match. The reply, apparently, was as sharp as the butcher's knife.

'The only reason I'm going is I want to give that Frank Lampard some stick,' she said.

Granddad didn't hesitate: 'What did you say love?'

'That Lampard. I'm going to give him what for after the way he walked out on us,' she said.

'That's my grandson you're talking about,' he butted in. 'And before you go slagging him off you should think for a minute what he was put through when he was at West Ham doing his best, doing his best for the likes of you.'

She bowed her head in embarrassment and ducked out of the shop quickly. When he told me about the incident I was very proud of the way he had stuck up for me, and our family. Pop has since passed away but it was typical of his desire to defend his own.

At the same time as he told me, though, I felt a little sick that I would be walking back into that same environment. They were relishing the opportunity to have a go again and were even making it a reason for turning up. True to form, I got the anticipated reception.

I was desperate to go and get a result and had high expectations. We stayed in a hotel the night before and as we drew up in the team bus I was nervous and excited. I knew I was going to get caned and it started as soon as I stepped off the coach. 'Traitor', 'Judas', and 'F*** off, fat Frank' were among the more polite remarks. I tried to ignore it and just looked straight ahead as we went towards the dressing room. Whatever the problems with the fans, though, as soon as I got inside the ground I was made to feel at home. Everyone, from the security guys to the Eddie the kit-man and the woman who made the tea, welcomed me. They are all genuine West Ham fans and genuine people. They saw what happened to me when I was there and told me how pleased they were that I was doing well. They still do. To them I was a local lad whom they had seen growing up. There was no agenda or vendetta. Even now they apologize for the way the fans treat me when I am there and I appreciate it.

Unfortunately, Ranieri decided I was Giggsy again and I started the game in left midfield. I was gutted because I wanted to do well and boss the game from the middle but there I was on the flank. Apart from anything else it put me right up against the chicken run and the abuse started from the moment the whistle went. It all felt uncomfortably familiar and it got worse.

Michael Carrick scored and so did Freddie Kanouté and I got switched to the right. It was a nightmare. Jimmy got us back in it and then a cross came in from the left and I caught it well but Shaka Hislop stopped it with his feet and no matter what we did we couldn't get back. I tried everything and thought there was a chance I might sneak one at some point before I was aware we were making a change and looked with horror as my number flashed up on the board. I had to look twice to believe it and felt the dread harden in my gut as I moved towards the touchline.

I don't think Ranieri was sensitive to the situation – his decision was tactical and oblivious to the impact it would have on me. I sat on the bench and had to endure the mocking and gloating going on behind me from the fans: 'What a waste of money,' 'You're still not good enough for West Ham, Lampard,' and so on. I was devastated. I got escorted from the ground by security to a car which was waiting for me. Predictably, there was a gauntlet to run and the usual torrent of vitriol showered me as I climbed in.

The next day I rang my Mum who intentionally stayed away because she knew what the atmosphere would be like. She was very disappointed: she had listened to the game on the radio and heard Tony Gale talking before the match. Perceptively, Gale said that I would get stick during the match that day and that in his opinion I fully deserved it for the way I had left West Ham. Mum was very angry about it. Quite rightly she reckoned that any Hammers' fans on the way to the match listening to the radio might make more of a point of giving me a hard time now that my name had been brought up again. Basically, he had wound up the situation needlessly. Gale was a West Ham player for many years and knew me and my Dad and I couldn't understand his comments.

Apart from anything else, my Dad and uncle had been sacked and I had decided to move on for reasons of family pride as well as to better myself so I'm not sure which circumstances he thought would justify my leaving the club. It was the right thing for me to do and yet he felt it was all right to criticise me without taking anything else into account. He doesn't know me well as a person and I don't remember him saying that about anyone else who had left, so I wondered why he had a go at me.

There are certain ex-footballers who for one reason or another like to have a go at current players. Gale was at West Ham after my Dad finished a very successful and popular spell with the club and then left before he became assistant to Harry and I came through the ranks. He was never one to make himself known to me the way other former club pros did. A hearty hello and reference to my Dad were normal when I met people who used to play for the club but Gale was not among them.

I had gone out after the game and had a few beers and when my Mum told me all of this I was raging. She was really sick about it and I rang Kutner and asked him to get me Gale's number. I called him.

'Is that Tony Gale?' I asked.

He replied, 'Who wants to know?'

I thought, 'Who answers their phone like that?' Flash bastard.

'It's Frank Lampard.'

'Nah. You're jokin', ain't ya?'

'No. It's Frank Lampard and I've got a problem with what you said about me on the radio yesterday.'

'What? I was quite complimentary about you.'

'Don't bulls*** me,' I said. 'I know what you said and you have upset my family. Don't you know better than that? As an ex-player you can't say things like that to fans.'

I explained to him that I had moved to better myself and because the club had sacked my Dad he had no right to go saying what he had. I asked him if he had a son and he said yes.

'How would you feel if your son was put in my situation then?'

He clammed up and cited a family situation of his own as a reason for saying what he did. For the following fifteen minutes I had a go at him again but he displayed a very arrogant attitude and kept insisting that he hadn't done anything wrong.

'Those same fans who you were inviting to cane me have been having a go since I was 17,' I said. 'You went to West Ham then and you know that.'

'Rubbish,' he said.

This made me angrier. I didn't understand why he had been so aggressive, not at that moment but on the radio. I imagine he thought I was just a young kid who had no right to phone him up and dig him out. What really pissed me off was the fact that he didn't know me – me or my situation. Gale is one of those ex-players who hears whispers about this and that coming out of his old club. For that reason alone he must have known there were things going on with Dad and Harry.

Despite that, I felt in this instance that he never offered any kind of balance to his comments. Had he taken the time to call me or Dad and ask the circumstances then we would have been happy to let him know. Instead, he chose to make his own interpretation and that's what annoyed me so much. It doesn't take a genius to work out that things are not going well when my Dad and uncle are sacked.

He had no excuse. One of his peers, Alvin Martin, has a similar position in the media and makes the effort to find out first what has actually happened before voicing his opinion and I respect him for that. It's obvious that he realizes that some balance is needed in what can be delicate situations. With Gale the whole situation has just rumbled on and on. It still does. He had a decent career so I didn't understand his apparent need to slag me off.

I had pushed myself to the verge of a starting spot before Euro 2004 and, sure enough, before the tournament started Gale was writing that I was a million miles away from being picked and others should be. There have been many other examples of this.

When reports broke in the summer of 2005 that Real Madrid had offered Michael Owen to Chelsea plus £20 million I knew what was really going on because Kutner had taken a call from Spain explaining the situation. It came from a conduit in the deal who was acting for Real and they wanted to know if I would consider moving to Madrid. It was the same time as Steven Gerrard was mulling over his future and like clockwork, Gale waded in with his weighty opinion: 'Steven Gerrard is the world's best midfielder and that is why Real Madrid are so keen to make him a galactico. The Spanish giants, backed by a staggering £110 million transfer kitty, have also been linked with a cheeky move for Chelsea's Frank Lampard. I'm sure Real would rather have Gerrard at the Bernebeu next season.'

Kutner called him and asked him reasonably why he always wanted to put me down. Stevie is the calibre of player who would interest any club in the world, but that wasn't the point. My problem was with Gale. Even when the subject didn't concern me he still found a way of dragging me into it. He denies it but it's simple enough to trace – to my original call of that Sunday morning. I can't understand why it's lasted this long. He could have called me and buried the hatchet. We were both West Ham lads and I don't want any bad blood but such instances make that very difficult.

It doesn't stop with me either. There was an incident when Harry was considering returning to Portsmouth from Southampton and Gale tore him to shreds on the radio. Jamie was listening and immediately called Gale's mobile and let him know what he thought in a long and very angry message. Funnily enough, he's still waiting for a call back.

It's got to the stage now where it has become a standing joke between me and my family and mates. I don't care what he's made of his career, I just wish he wouldn't feel the need to have a go at other players in the papers or on TV.

I rang Dad to tell him that I had spoken to Gale and he was pleased I had stood up for myself though reckoned I would have put his back up even more. Dad has a habit of trying to calm me down by saying that even Bobby Moore got stick at West Ham and he was the best defender there ever was. He was very much taken under Bobby Moore's wing at West Ham as a player and a person and he often says he sees a lot of him in me – the way I move and play, the fact that I never react to a tackle or get the needle – which is very flattering.

I wasn't the only one dodging bullets at that point, though.

As a team we were beginning to get a bit of stick in the media for being inconsistent and, unfortunately, the ensuing run of games showed it was justified. Chelsea have a habit of playing well at Old Trafford and when we went there at the start of December we thrashed them 3–0 and played them off the park. It was the kind of display which we were easily capable of but it followed two depressing draws against Everton and Blackburn which once again exposed our fatal weakness with regard to pushing on and doing great things, which required consistency.

I reflected on the first few months of my time there. There is no doubt that I made the move with the intention of challenging for the league but once we started the season I quickly realized that we were not on championship form and in retrospect we just didn't have the capability. The consistency was missing and we didn't have the all-round quality in the squad. A few of us had just signed, including William Gallas and myself, and you could tell a natural pattern of play was failing to evolve, but the team was changing every week and you can't win the title when the team is different from match to match.

We would play against teams which were mid-table or lower down and get beaten or draw. It didn't need much analysis to conclude that we weren't going to be at the very top come the end of the season. It was even worse when it happened at home. We lost 4–2 to Southampton and were outplayed during the Christmas period and results like that just don't add up to a title.

What made it worse was that we had good players but there were just too many games when we were poor. I felt that I was the epitome of that. I was still finding my feet and

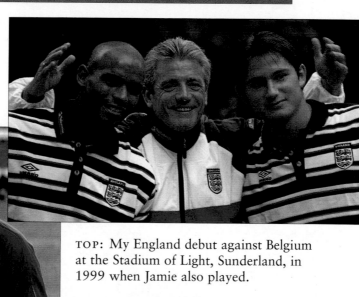

TOP: My England debut against Belgium at the Stadium of Light, Sunderland, in 1999 when Jamie also played.

ABOVE: Thanks Kev! England manager Keegan with two new lads to the squad – me and Trevor Sinclair.

LEFT: Looks like someone stole the pitch at Stamford Bridge on the day I signed for Chelsea.

LEFT: My Chelsea
debut against
Newcastle United
– quite a day.

LEFT: Looking a bit nervous as I face the press after my move to Chelsea in 2001.

RIGHT: Midfield battle of the cousins as Jamie and I square up to each other in a Chelsea vs Tottenham match.

RIGHT: Luke Perry of Tottenham accused me of diving. A second yellow card was to follow.

BELOW: Graeme Le Saux (far right) and Eidur cannot believe I have been sent off for the one and only time of my career – so far.

Early Chelsea days
practising my headers.

LEFT: Eidur cracks a rare joke and, even more unusual, makes me and Claudio Ranieri laugh!

RIGHT: I scored the opening goal against France at Euro 2004. Not bad for a player who can't head!

ABOVE: Smashing in the extra-time equaliser against Portugal in the quarter-finals of Euro 2004. One of the best feelings I've had in football.

RIGHT: Saluting the fans after scoring for my country – you can't beat that feeling.

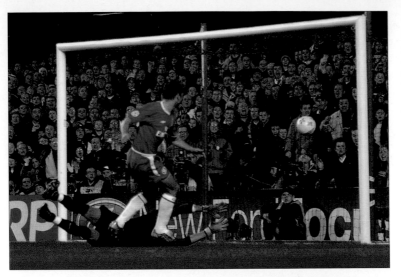

LEFT: Scoring against Barcelona in the Champions League in 2005 and making enemies with Elen's Barca family!

ABOVE: JT and I celebrate being named in the FIFPro Team of the Year 2005.

LEFT: JT shows he's as accurate with champagne as with headers, spraying my eyes and missing my mouth.

LEFT: Me and my mentor salute the fans – two winners celebrate victory.

BELOW: The Chelsea family celebrate winning the league. JT, Roman's son Arkady, Roman, me and Eidur. One of my favourite images.

FAR LEFT: At the World Player of the Year gala in Zurich, 2005. Proudest moment of my football life to be named in the top three with Ronaldinho and Samuel Eto'o.

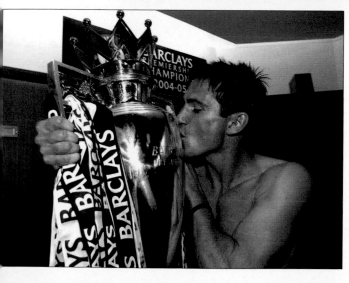

LEFT: Come here you! Planting a smacker on the Premiership trophy. I will never forget that feeling.

Portrait taken to celebrate the top 50 players going to the World Cup finals in 2006.
I had just played my 161st consecutive Premiership match at Portsmouth

didn't always play the way I wanted. When there is no consistency in selection then it will tell in the performance and
the fact that we finished sixth in the league but made the FA
Cup Final just about sums it up.

I had once again played on the wing at Old Trafford but
things looked up and I moved into the middle and we beat
Liverpool 4–0. The transformation was immediate. I scored
my first league goal against Bolton and I can honestly say that
it wasn't until that moment that I felt completely comfortable
in a Chelsea shirt.

It had nothing to do with the fans. After what I had been
through at West Ham I was relieved and pleased at the way I
had been received. I know what London is like. Some of them
must have been worried. People go for a drink with their
mates who are Hammers' fans who would have been saying,
'Eleven million, thanks very much. We didn't want him
anyway.' I had a lot of feedback at the time that people were
saying that kind of thing and it would have been understand-
able if some supporters started to wonder about me given
they saw me playing out of position – especially when they've
got people in their ear telling them I'm not worth the money.

On 20 January, I got my chance to silence them. After the
crap I had taken at Upton Park, West Ham arrived at the
Bridge and we gave them a hell of a tanking, 5–1 to be
precise, and it felt beautiful. Eidur and Jimmy got a couple
each and we murdered them. The away fans had started the
game giving me the usual abuse but shut up after about ten
minutes. I remember we were three up after an hour and they
didn't score until very late and I just spent the last twenty
minutes shooting from every angle I could to try and get a
goal against them. JT came up to me and was laughing.

'Desperate for a goal, Lampsy?' he grinned. 'Come on. Try a bit harder, will ya?'

He was taking the piss and so was I. He knew how much it meant to me. He saw it in my eyes and had heard enough about it in the changing room at training the week leading up to the game. Every time I got near the away section I smiled a broad smile just to let them know as well.

Thankfully Chelsea fans are more generous with their patience. They were good with me and as soon as I moved into the middle they were on side. I wondered where and how we would finish in the league. I thought that we could still make Champions League qualification but as the season progressed that dream slipped away as well. Maybe I wasn't being ambitious enough but I was pretty content to be playing every week knowing that we had the potential to make the top three. I had finished in fifth place once with West Ham but that was unusual rather than expected.

I looked around me though and felt that I was at a club which was going places. Franco Zola was an incredible player for Chelsea but he didn't get as much playing time that season because Jimmy and Eidur were amazing. They scored fifty-one goals between them and it was probably the best strike partnership I have ever played with. I wonder if I will ever see a better one in the Premier League. Everything about them was ruthless and magical at the same time: touch, passing, link up, and shooting. There were times in that year when nine of us were playing okay and those two won the game for us. I wasn't gutted that we didn't win the league and it was partly because I had guys like that around me who I knew were capable of lifting the club to claim silverware. I felt my own game was improving and I had stepped up in my career.

There were, of course, moments when I was reminded that we still had a long way to go. The League Cup semi-final second leg against Spurs was one of those. We were 2–1 up from the home game and on the verge of reaching my first final and we got pumped 5–1. It was horrible, especially as it was the first time in about ten years that they had beaten Chelsea. You learn from those defeats, though, and I learned quickly because we drew them in the FA Cup a few weeks later which by that time was a real pressure game for us.

We were well out of the top spots and this was the last chance of winning something. We had begun the campaign a bit shaky with a draw away at Norwich but then cruised through the replay at home. I was delighted to play West Ham in the fourth round though again we drew the first game at home and had to go to Upton Park to decide the tie. Jermain Defoe scored a couple for them and twice we had to pull it back before JT popped up in the last minute to clinch it. Nice one. He was emerging as a very important player for us. I went mad because I had taken the usual stick through the game and would have been distraught if we'd gone out to them.

The FA Cup run saved our season. Even though we lost the final to Arsenal, if it had gone the other way then people would have said that it was a really good year for Chelsea. We qualified for the UEFA Cup in sixth place and reached the League Cup semi-final. It's nowhere near the ambitions we have now but at the time it wasn't too bad. Personally I was pleased with the way it had gone and my performances had got better and better after Christmas and I had scored a few goals. I enjoyed the quarter-final at Spurs because we won 4–0 and got our revenge for the game a few weeks before. We had to play Fulham in the semi-final at Villa Park and once again it was JT who was on target to get us to the final in Cardiff.

I was buzzing the morning of the game. I had slept a bit but not much. I was desperate to play. The FA Cup Final was always something we had all got round the telly to watch every year when I was growing up, no matter who was playing. My Dad had played in two and this was my turn. Our preparation had been good, all except for Jimmy. He had been struggling with a calf injury and only flew in from Leeds the night before the game having seen a specialist. I was surprised when I found out he would start but both he and JT had undergone fitness tests a few hours before kick-off. JT had woken up feeling dizzy and had lost his balance and fallen out of bed. He went immediately to see the doctor and the doc went to see Ranieri. John had recovered by the time we had the team meeting but the manager had already decided to play Gallas in the middle in his place.

John was distraught. Like me, this was a competition he had grown up with and we both would have walked over broken glass to make the team. He was ready to play and had passed the test the same as Jimmy but the gaffer decided that only one would play. I didn't think that much of Jimmy's selection because when a player is passed fit you expect him to be just that but the warm-up in the changing room raised doubts. We stood in a circle to do some stretches and some running on the spot for five or ten minutes. Jimmy was there doing it but he had a Tens machine strapped to his calf to try and improve it and ease the pain. I had every faith in Jimmy but if he was doing that an hour before the biggest game of our season there had to be a question mark about whether he was able to play. Jimmy at 70 or 80 per cent is better than a lot of other players but the options were limited for the manager.

Jimmy is very ambitious and was desperate to play but unfortunately, after ten minutes of the game it was obvious he wasn't up to it. He tried and failed very early and Ranieri should have changed it earlier than he did. We had a decent first half – there was no score and we were holding our own and doing okay. We had a lot of possession but no cutting edge and I was pleased with how I was battling with Patrick Vieira.

In the end, it took the manager sixty-eight minutes to bring Franco on for Jimmy and by seventy we were a goal down. Ray Parlour scored before Freddie Ljungberg killed it ten minutes later. There was a perception that Jimmy was a favourite with Ranieri but I don't think that was true. Jimmy is one of the best strikers I have ever played with and one of the best I have ever seen. When he played it was usually because he deserved to. People forget that even in Roman Abramovich's first season at the club, when Jimmy would often be the one who was subbed for Hernan Crespo or Adrian Mutu, he still finished as top scorer.

Maybe Ranieri's decision in Cardiff was out of respect for what Jimmy had given to Chelsea. He deserved the chance to show if he was fit or not and Ranieri's error was perhaps that he didn't see how badly he was struggling earlier in the contest. On that occasion, the man famed for his tinkering didn't tinker enough.

The season wasn't quite over yet – or so I hoped. The squad for the World Cup finals was due to be announced the following week. We had played a few friendlies in the build-up and I managed a whole five minutes against Paraguay at Anfield in March. There was the usual speculation in the papers about who would go to Japan and who wouldn't and I seemed to flit between the departure lounge and sitting at home watching on the telly.

The vibe I was getting from Eriksson was always pretty good and I looked around at some of those who were in competition with me. I felt I was in a favourable position. I had played well against Vieira in the FA Cup Final and was optimistic, having finished the season well. The news broke that Eriksson was going to call those who were being left at home and I remember getting up late that particular morning without thinking about the fact that the squad was about to be announced.

My mobile rang. It was a withheld number. Despite being quite pessimistic by nature I still thought I would go. I heard his voice say: 'Hello Frank. It's Sven Eriksson.' I didn't have time to think and before he reached the end of his first sentence my heart had sunk.

'It was a difficult decision Frank, I assure you,' he said hoping to soothe the pain.

'You are a young player and there will be more opportunities for you to play in the World Cup.'

I was still trying to take all of this in. I was in shock. Even though I had never convinced myself I would be going to Japan, I had hoped, hoped deep within me, that I would be on that plane.

'Look,' said Eriksson. 'Go and enjoy a holiday this summer and come back well next season. I will be coming to watch you for Chelsea and will be looking to pick you for the Euro 2004 qualifiers.'

'Yes. Thanks. I will.'

I could barely squeeze the words out. My mouth was dry and the phone fell to the floor. I was dumbfounded. I walked around the flat. I wasn't going anywhere – not Japan, not anywhere. I finally sat down and wondered what I should do. I was too embarrassed to call anyone and talk about it.

I wondered if life could get much worse than this. It did – and quickly. Instinctively, I switched on the TV and the squad announcement was making the headlines on Sky. It turned out there was a reserve list as well as the actual selection. There I was half-thinking I would be on the plane and it turned out I wasn't even on the waiting list.

Not even on the f***ing wait list. I thought about what Eriksson had said to me, went over the conversation again and again in my mind. It was a horrible call to make but he did it the best way possible. When the shock subsided I got very angry – not with Eriksson but with myself.

What could I have done better to have forced my way in? Where could I have played better? Could I have scored more goals? Did I train hard enough? The third degree became a fourth and then a fifth and so on. I couldn't help but scrutinize every little moment of the season. It didn't help or solve anything.

So, I got angry with the situation, convinced myself that there was nothing I could do now and that I had to go through the feelings and then get on with it. When the emotions subsided, I decided the best thing for me was to get out of the country. I watched the World Cup on TV but I didn't enjoy it. My head was still buzzing with what might have been. The only thing on my mind was getting back into the England team.

CHAPTER 6

LOVE MATCH

SIX thousand and eighty-five miles – that's how much distance I put between myself and the misery of not making the World Cup squad. I prepared myself for the ordeal of dragging the rejection around for quite some time. I thought it would be impossible to escape the hurt of being left out. I was wrong.

I walked into Thomas Cook and booked a holiday to Mauritius. That was easy enough but what really helped me put the pain of missing out behind me was the woman who sat next to me on the plane: Elen Rivas. We had only known each other a few weeks but there was something about her which gave me balance even when it felt like my world had been turned upside down. I have never met anyone like Elen. She is intelligent, funny, intuitive, and has a beauty which stopped me in my tracks the first time I saw her. The circumstances were difficult. Trying to begin a conversation among the seething, noisy throng of a nightclub is not the ideal start to a relationship.

Talking to Elen, however, was an event I had to build myself up for. I was out with some mates having a laugh. We generally keep ourselves to ourselves for obvious reasons but another group of people we knew arrived at the bar. Elen was among them and the moment I saw her I was smitten. She was talking with her friends and so didn't notice me as I looked at her.

I drifted out of the conversation I was involved in and stared at her until she instinctively turned her head and glanced in my direction. Embarrassed that I'd been caught, I interrupted the chat which was continuing without me. I was flustered. I was trying to divert attention from myself but I needn't have bothered. She knew.

It was schoolboy stuff but I lacked confidence with girls. Even though I was used to the company of women it was a new experience to come across someone who had that instant effect. It's a fact of life that when you are a footballer you attract a certain amount of interest from females whenever you go to a bar or club. It's part of the culture now. People say football is the new rock 'n' roll and if you choose to get involved then there is plenty of opportunity to spend time with the groupies and admirers who hang around players. I had never had a serious relationship in my life. Actually, that's not true. I was married to football at a very young age.

After moving to Chelsea, however, I realized my celebrity status had increased. An £11 million transfer fee attracts its own notoriety. Most of the time it was laughable. I would spend ten minutes talking to some girl in a club and the next day we were an item according to the gossip columns. I never had a real girlfriend before Elen. The longest relationship I had experienced lasted about six months and was with a South African girl. We saw each other a couple of times a week but it wasn't full on. The whole thing fizzled out just as I signed for Chelsea and I never really gave it another thought until a couple of years later when I was on a beach in Miami with Elen, and Kutner called.

'Who the f*** is this girl?' he inquired with his usual subtlety.

'Who? I don't know what you're talking about,' I replied completely off guard.

'Well, she says she used to go out with you and that you dumped her in a bad way.'

'What? When?'

'In the *News of the World* this morning.'

The penny dropped. She had sold a story to the paper, saying she loved me and I had treated her badly by ending the relationship the way I did. It wasn't true. It was, however, a harsh lesson about the way fame can make people envious and bitter. In the months I saw her love had never been mentioned. We were not suited to each other and that was obvious from the way the friendship failed to develop. I had never been in love and didn't know what it meant or felt like. With Elen, I have never known anything else.

In the bar, I shuffled my way towards her trying to make it look like I was heading in that direction anyway. I said hello and introduced myself. That in itself can provoke a strange reaction in people. People who know who you are already just laugh nervously when you say 'Hi, I'm Frank.' I never assume anything though and with Elen that was just as well. She nodded her head and smiled but as she told me her name I began to panic. There was something about the way she spoke – an accent. Her English was great but she pronounced her words with a throaty purr that was very sexy but also threw me.

'Barcelona', she said when I asked the obvious question.

'Ah, good football team though they're a bit s*** at the moment,' I replied nervously.

She rolled her eyes a little. I wondered if I should just knock it on the head there and then. It was hard enough to have a conversation because of the music, throw in an Essex boy after a couple of beers and a stunning Catalan woman and it's all getting a bit silly.

I had to have another go. There was something about her that made me believe I had a chance. I couldn't quite put my finger on it. A kindness in her words and a look in her eyes said she was interested in me even though I was having the dating equivalent of a botched penalty kick. It was partly down to shock, not that I thought about it there and then. I just never imagined in a million years that I would date a Spanish girl. My mind was closed to other cultures back then. I was very much a home boy whose interests and tastes didn't venture much beyond the boundaries of London and where I grew up.

We talked for far too short a time before she left with her friends for another club. The company, it seemed, was not as good as I would have liked to think. I thought of her often even though my track record with girls suggested that I had been wasting my time in the first place.

A couple of weeks later I was sitting in Scalini with my cousin Mark and Billy Jenkins having lunch when a stunning girl flashed past the window. She wore a white fitted top and her face was partly hidden by a pair of large framed sunglasses which were very fashionable. As usual, the restaurant was buzzing with assorted people meeting and eating. We were still talking when I caught sight of the girl from the window take a seat at the next table. I looked at her for a few seconds and leaned into Mark. 'See her,' I said, trying to be as discreet as possible without pointing, 'I could marry her.'

I wasn't trying to be twee or trite. Mark nodded his approval.

We were finishing up when a conversation between our table and the one next door was struck up. I looked directly at the girl who had arrived last and realized it was Elen. She looked different. Her hair was tied back and I noticed how bright her eyes were every time she smiled. There was a little embarrassment that we hadn't recognized one another sooner but it quickly evaporated in the more relaxed atmosphere of my local eaterie. We got on really well and I discovered from her disarming and candid questions that she didn't have the slightest clue that I was a footballer or who I played for.

I have been with other footballers in these situations and most of them don't seem to think twice about cutting straight to the part where they get the girl's number. I am much more shy and it wasn't until we were making to leave that I finally plucked up enough courage to ask for hers. She smiled and wrote it down without hesitation.

'What you up to now then?' I said clutching the piece of paper tightly.

'Going to hang out for a bit and then we're going out later. You?' she replied coyly.

'Don't know. See what happens.'

We weren't even out of the restaurant before I told Billy that we were definitely going out that night. It was midweek – a time I would never normally go over the door. This was not a normal situation though and Billy and I went back to my flat to prepare.

Elen told me the place she was going and we arrived early – embarrassingly early. The music was echoing around the place due to a lack of people but I didn't want to risk missing her. Billy and I were perched at the bar trying to look as cool as possible in a half-empty room. She eventually arrived and

floated effortlessly in and then out again before I had anywhere near enough time to talk to her. It didn't matter, I had
her number and I was going to use it.

The following weekend I was in Birmingham for the FA
Cup semi-final against Fulham. The match was being played
at Villa Park on the Sunday and we were holed up in a hotel
outside the city. I stared at the numbers she had written on a
card and then at my mobile. I dialled.

'Hi Elen, it's Frank,' I said furtively.

'Fra-ank,' she repeated in her Spanish drawl which I now
know so well.

'Yeah, you remember. We met at Scalini and you gave
me . . . '

'Yes. I remember,' she cut my sentence off. 'Hey. Can I call
you back, I'm on the other line right now.'

'Yeah, sure,' and I put the phone down.

S***. She gave me the rubber ear. You know the moment
someone you barely know says they'll call you back, that
they'll be staging the Winter Olympics in Hell and you will
still be sitting by your phone. I couldn't believe it. I was
nervous enough about the game never mind getting the
brush-off from the girl I desperately wanted to go out with.

I lay on the bed and tried to get some sleep, without success.
After a couple of hours my mobile rang.

'Hi Frank, it's Elen,' came the voice. 'Sorry about before
but I was talking to my family in Spain and I didn't want to
cut them off. How are you?'

And that was it – as natural as the sunrise, she lit up my life
and has filled it with warmth and happiness ever since. We
agreed to have dinner back in London. Scalini, of course. It
was scheduled for the Monday night and I got my mate Tel to

come round to the flat before with a couple of beers. I needed to build up my courage.

I needn't have bothered. There was no bravery needed. All the nerves and worry disappeared within moments of sitting down. It's hard to explain, other than to say we just clicked – right from that very first moment we were alone together. There was no awkwardness or discomfort and very little small talk. I knew Elen was right for me – my heart was shouting it out.

We were inseparable after that. We had dinner every night or second night and then just started spending time with each other at our respective flats. Life was good. Life was great. It wasn't till I got the call from Sven-Goran Eriksson telling me that I hadn't made the World Cup squad that it nosedived. Even then, I consoled myself with the thought that I could spend a relaxing summer with my girlfriend.

Mauritius was just what I needed. Elen was just what I needed. When we got back I felt de-stressed and was already looking forward to next season. In a fit of madness a few weeks earlier, I had signed up to go on a lads trip to Las Vegas for a few days: me, Bill (McCulloch) Blood, and Banger. I didn't really enjoy it. We did the usual stuff. Played the tables in the casino and had a few beers and laughs. England were playing against Argentina in Sapporo and we had to stay up until four in the morning to watch it. I didn't particularly want to but felt almost as if I had to. It was painful – not because it was a bad match because from the national anthem through to the final whistle I wondered what it would be like to be playing.

Watching just isn't enough, neither is being there – only playing matters. Bill and Banger jumped out of their seats when the penalty was awarded but I stayed glued to mine. As David Beckham focused on what he had to do next so did I.

I briefly remembered how sick I had felt when I found out I wouldn't be going. I recalled Eriksson's words on the phone. 'I will be coming to watch you for Chelsea and will be looking to pick you for the Euro 2004 qualifiers.'

I had heard his words over and over since the conversation took place. Sometimes I let it go but at other times I imagined answering the England manager in a much different manner to the way I had. You always think of what you would have liked to say when the opportunity to do so has long gone. I wanted to tell him that I would be back next season, better, stronger, more determined than ever. I turned to Bill – someone I can confide in and who is a great sounding board for all the lads at Chelsea – and told him we needed to speak. 'All right geezer,' he said, and turned his head back to the screen.

The three of us jumped around when Beckham scored but I wasn't feeling much like celebrating. I was already planning my England future and besides, I was missing Elen. Bill has since told me that I was like a lovesick puppy for the entire trip. I believe him. I couldn't wait to get back.

I returned home with a renewed sense of purpose about my life and my career. Things between Elen and I moved very quickly and were helped along by the fact that I had to move out of the flat I had been renting during the first season with Chelsea and bought a new place near Old Brompton Road.

The timings didn't quite dovetail and I was intending on checking into the Chelsea Village Hotel for the weeks in between. I wasn't looking forward to it. Elen had a nice little flat in South Kensington and because we were getting on so well she said I should come and stay with her until my place was ready. I didn't need to be asked twice.

It was a fun time – partly because it was tiny space which

meant we were always together when we were at home. It was impossible not to be: the lounge was downstairs, the bedroom on the first floor, and you had to go through the bathroom to get there. We didn't care – it was cosy and we had a real laugh.

I came home from pre-season training and we'd curl up on the sofa with our dinner and watch *Big Brother* on TV. It took about two or three weeks to finalize everything in my new place but Elen and I were so natural together that I didn't hesitate about asking her to move in with me. I hadn't even imagined anything else and I wanted to be with her. It's funny, we might never have lived together so quickly had circumstances not conspired to give us a preview of what it would be like.

It was definitely a big step for me. I wasn't exactly a party animal, though I did like a night out with my mates, but after a taste of domesticity I just wanted to spend time with Elen. I still enjoy time out with my team-mates and friends and always will but when you fall in love your life changes. I certainly became more domesticated and within two months of living with each other we got a dog who we christened with a traditional Spanish name – Reggie.

Making commitments with Elen was easy. We were so comfortable with each other and we spent a lot of time at home. I enjoyed learning about the Spanish culture as well as the language. It was a natural progression for me. I had enjoyed the lifestyle of a young footballer – a lad's life and one which had given me experience both good and bad. I made some mistakes along the way about how to behave but I changed a lot after meeting Elen and nothing that was different about my life seemed strange to me.

Roccaporena was certainly familiar as we arrived there for

another pre-season. It was a shorter stint this time because we had already done a week at Harlington before going out and I was determined to improve on my first season at the club. Again I spent a bit of time with Bill Blood and we expanded the conversation I had started a few weeks earlier in Las Vegas.

'This year I'm going to take the bull by the horns and assert myself at Chelsea,' I said. 'I was too timid last season. I accepted being played out of position and I was too quiet around the training ground.

'I need to make my voice heard and my presence felt. It's a big season for me. I've had time to settle in and I now need to establish myself as one of the major players in the team.'

Bill's my mate and stuck up for me – even against myself! 'You're already quite influential Lamps,' he said.

I was on a roll though: 'You can't go around saying you're the main man if you're not doing it though. Look at Roy Keane and Patrick Vieira. They live and breathe it and no one doubts their influence. This is it Bill. This is my time.'

Bill has since reminded me of this conversation. He said there was a determination in my voice which he has heard again and again, at important times in the season – the day of a big Champions League game, the night before we won our first title. It's true. I felt differently that summer and I knew my life was changing for the better.

I had put enough space between myself and the World Cup to be able to analyse how I felt much more objectively. I had bottled up a lot of anger – I was sure I was good enough to make the squad and had been overcome by a lot of negative thoughts: about my game, myself, and the other players who had been picked.

'He's not better than me,' I would think. 'Maybe I could come on and change the game with a goal or a pass. I could do that better than him.' That's not being disrespectful to the lads who were in the squad. My Dad calls it 'professional jealousy' which is not being jealous of the person who may be playing in your position, but jealous of wanting to be better than you are. You should be gutted about not being good enough and find it hard to watch the games you're not involved in. For me, it was also part of the process of getting over it. I had been very depressed. It was a rejection which I had never experienced before on such a scale.

Not making it into Lilleshall was all I had to compare it with. Then, it was bad enough that my family and friends knew that I wasn't good enough to make the cut, but this was a very public humiliation and whatever people said to comfort me it did little to silence the nagging voice in my head which was telling me I wasn't good enough.

I was even embarrassed about telling Elen. I had warned her that the tournament was approaching and that the plan was to go to Dubai with the partners beforehand and would she want to come? I wondered what she'd think – we didn't know each other so well at the time and I was apprehensive that whatever I told her the reasons were, she might wonder if I was making excuses. Getting out of the country as I did meant extracting myself from the hype which had engulfed the nation.

I didn't want to hear how England got on in the warm-up games or receive the daily fitness bulletins. I didn't want to see the flags on the houses and in every second car on the streets of London. I am not unpatriotic. I love my country but I was in a stage of falling out with myself. It's the kind of experience which can make you retreat into yourself – like the world is against you.

The closest comparison I can make is with being dumped by someone you really want to spend time with. I went through the same anger, frustration, self-doubt and loathing as afflicts you when you are rejected by a girl. However, you can always call her and beg for another chance – that's not an option with the England manager. I felt utterly helpless. Some people choose to react in a positive way. It was my instinct to react without bitterness.

I resolved to become more assertive in every aspect of my career and when I saw Claudio Ranieri for the first time on coming back for training I looked him in the eye and felt a sense of dedication about the season ahead. I converted the frustration of not going to Japan into a burning ambition to succeed.

I had already started running on my own during the holidays and when we got started on the fitness training I just went for it. There is something in my nature that makes me feel invincible when I am in top physical condition – as if no one and nothing can touch me. It's not something I express openly – it's more of an innate feeling of well-being and self-confidence which apart from me, only my closest friends and family can detect.

It wasn't long before I had a tingle in my spine and a spring in every step I took. I had matured over the previous twelve months. I had left my first club, my home, and my family and made a new life around Chelsea. I was at the beginning of a serious relationship and I knew more than ever what direction I wanted my life to take. In short, I grew up. The progress I had already made with Chelsea gave me a platform to aim higher.

When I look back now I know without question that that summer was the pivotal period of my life. It was also the start of the most important phase in the history of Chelsea. I had changed for the better but at first I wasn't sure about how changes at the club would work out.

That close season, for the first time in years, Chelsea didn't spend big in the transfer market. In fact, they didn't spend anything at all. In previous times there seemed to be a revolving door ushering expensive footballing into and out of Stamford Bridge. The only two players to join in 2002 were on free transfers – Marco Ambrosio from Chievo Verona and Enrique De Lucas from Espanyol. The lack of activity was slightly confusing and only later in the season would the facts emerge about how badly the club was struggling financially. None the less, players tend to be pretty pragmatic and we viewed the fact that there were fewer comings and goings as an opportunity to let the team stabilize. There had been too much chopping and changing and I for one was happy that we would focus on the players we had, even if the truth was that we couldn't afford anyone.

Publicly, we set our sights on winning the Premier League though qualifying for the Champions League was more realistic. Ranieri, however, always put the emphasis on performance rather than results and ambitions. Even before individual games he would stress that it was the way we played that mattered most and not the result. Sometime he set targets but very limited ones, which puzzled me. For example, if we had finished sixth then he would call on us to move to fifth that season or if we got there in mid-season then he would perhaps say that we were able to improve a bit more and to go one better. Ranieri would never have said 'Right.

Let's win the league. Let's win every game.' Those were not phrases in his vocabulary. Caution was his style. He was keen on improvement by steps. It was a different way of working and he didn't want to heap too much pressure on the players or himself.

It wasn't my way, however, and I would often get frustrated. 'Why does he say that? Why doesn't he really challenge us to go out and win no matter what?' I found myself saying this to Eidur or JT a lot that season. We would lose a couple of games and be in another 'crisis meeting' and the boss would be talking about the importance of a good performance in the next game. I am not digging him out. We didn't have the players then that we had later and maybe Ranieri didn't believe we could take the title. It was his way of working but I could never imagine Mourinho preparing his team that way. In fact, there has been the odd occasion when Mourinho has said, 'F*** the performance, just get out there and get the result.' All that matters is the result.

Ranieri had other practices which I only now recognize were rather odd. For instance, he would compile a DVD of all of the strengths of the team we were playing next and show it to us while telling us where they might exploit our weaknesses. We would get frustrated by that especially when it would happen two hours before a game against the likes of Arsenal. It wasn't the best preparation – getting a preview of how they would destroy us over ninety minutes. Instead of telling us how we could undermine them, he showed us footage of Thierry Henry sprinting past five defenders and scoring a hat-trick. I appreciated that he came from the Italian school of coaching where avoiding defeat is the single most important factor, but when we are at home against the likes of Sunderland and Ranieri is warning us about what they might do to us, I think some of us saw it totally differently. We were the big club. They should have been worrying about us. The talk should have been about what we were going to do to them.

No one can take away what Ranieri did for Chelsea and I certainly don't deny what he did for me personally. I respect him greatly and it's only since discovering other coaching methods that I realize there are different ways of motivating players. At that moment, however, I was motivating myself for the most important season of my career. Whatever anyone else believed, I wanted to win the league but what none of us knew as we walked out of the tunnel at The Valley for our opening match against Charlton was that getting into the following season's Champions League was to be critical in determining the future of Chelsea Football Club.

If we had failed, then it's safe to assume that Roman Abramovich wouldn't have touched us in the following summer of 2003 when he was looking for a club to buy. The only thing in my mind on that August Saturday afternoon was how good I felt. We all did. Pre-season was hard but productive and the lads were fit and ready to explode out of the blocks. We were 2–0 down after half an hour.

I couldn't believe it. Everything had been positive all summer long and as soon as the real thing started it was falling apart. Richard Rufus scored after Paul Konchesky had already put them ahead and I thought, 'Here we go.'

Franco Zola then pulled one back before the break, and Carlton Cole came on in the second half and made a difference, scoring the equalizer with six minutes left. The game was in its dying minutes when the ball got deflected into my path.

I gave Dean Kiely an eye signal that I would hit the ball one way and then I steered it to the other side. It was the winner.

I ran to our fans to celebrate and it felt like it had all turned round in an hour. It was a great start and all of the optimism which I had taken into the game returned. So much can be said in football for getting the winning goal – it can cover up a multitude of things at times – but this was a great feeling and it made an impact and sent out the right signal.

After all of the things I had said to Bill Blood before it started it was more important to put it into practice. We played Man United next at home and drew 2–2, which was not the worst result before going away, to Southampton. This match was memorable because of a move which started in our half. I knocked the ball wide and kept running and Eidur returned the ball to me and I let it run just enough before dinking it over the keeper as he ran out at me. It's one of my favourite goals for Chelsea and complemented the one at Charlton. Two in three games was a boost for me but the fact was that we had only one win in that sequence put things in perspective.

That didn't change when Arsenal visited the Bridge. We were in the middle of a spell where no matter what we did we couldn't beat them. It had already been around eight years since Chelsea had claimed a league victory over them. We were a goal up and then Patrick Vieira got sent off. Kolo Touré, who had yet to establish himself, came on in place of Edu and ended up scoring the equalizer after an hour.

We got a couple more decent results and all in all it was a good start, if unspectacular. Europe beckoned once again as did more embarrassment. We played Norwegian side Viking Stavanger in the UEFA Cup with the memory of the previous season's fiasco against Hapoel Tel Aviv thrown in our face in almost every paper we read. That part of the build-up was inevitable. I was getting used to some people having a go and enjoying knocking us down. I had it at West Ham on a personal level but with Chelsea it seemed more to do with the club itself and to some extent the chairman, Ken Bates.

Ranieri told me on the day of the game that he was resting me. I was surprised and annoyed. In a game like that you want to put out your best team, bash them 4–0 at home and then you've nothing to worry about for the away leg. He did put me on at half-time and we were in control of the tie without playing brilliantly. A couple of goals to the good it looked pretty academic until we conceded one right on the final whistle. That shouldn't have been disastrous in itself but it made the lads more nervous than we should have been going into the away game. Memories of the previous season still haunted us and none of us wanted to put ourselves or the manager through that humiliation again.

We clearly carried some sense of apprehension onto the pitch in Norway because we were 2–0 down after half an hour. I pulled one back just before the break but we lost another on the hour. No one's head went down. We believed we had the beating of them and JT scored the goal which put us ahead just two minutes after them. We held out but not long enough. We were completely naive. We had allowed them to score in the dying moments of the first leg and, sure enough, Viking stunned us with a winner three minutes from the end. For the second season in a row we crashed out of Europe to a team we should have walked all over.

It was a disaster. We got back to the airport after the match and there were a lot of fans who had made the trip filing through security and waiting for their charter flights to leave. Understandably, they were not in the best mood and Ranieri took a bit of stick from some of them. It was a horrible feeling. There is nowhere to look in a situation like that and it's a bit unfair that the manager bore the brunt of the criticism. It was the players' fault first and foremost because we hadn't been clever enough and made it difficult for ourselves.

I had only had the slightest taste of European football at West Ham and one of the reasons for moving to Chelsea was to play on that stage and get more experience. If we thought the fans were harsh then the papers had a field day. Most of them decided that Chelsea were in crisis. It was an exaggeration, though by the time we lost at Liverpool the following weekend it was harder to deny – and it was still only September.

The England squad was now announced for the two European Championship qualifiers against Slovakia and Macedonia and I was included – which made a nice change. It was also an opportune time to get away from Chelsea and try to find some perspective again. I had not featured in the get-together at the very start of that season when Portugal had visited Villa Park but having missed the World Cup in the summer I wasn't so shocked at being left out. Even so, the words spoken to me on the phone the previous May entered my head and I wondered where I stood. Lee Bowyer played in that match and I began to wonder how far down the pecking order I was in Eriksson's eyes.

Not so far, was the answer. I was pleased to be included for the competitive games though I wasn't sure if I would make it on to the pitch. We travelled to Bratislava a couple of days before the game and despite the fact that it was the start of an important qualifying campaign, the game itself was very much overshadowed by events off the pitch. There were some incidents between rival sets of fans around the city in the build-up but that was nothing compared to the headlines being made by the manager.

The story broke about his relationship with Ulrika Jonsson two days before the game, and the media lay in wait for him to give his pre-match press conference on the Friday. I remember watching the pictures on TV as he walked up the stairs of the hotel where he was due to speak. Mr Eriksson rarely betrays emotion of any kind – in public at least. Even when he smiles it can seem like courtesy rather than a natural reaction. That's not to say he's disingenuous. He guards his privacy with conviction and given the scrutiny and intrusion which goes with being England manager, I don't blame him. He looked calm and prepared when he faced the reporters and cameras that day though he was noticeably flanked by senior officials from the Football Association which was not normal. Both Adam Crozier – who was then chief executive – and David Davies turned up in an overt show of unity with the coach.

I respected the FA's stance and thought they called it right. People expect the England manager to be completely devoted to the job and some would take that as far as not allowing him a personal life. We all suffer from time to time from unwanted attention in the media and in some cases it's also unfair or unwarranted.

None of the players had any doubts about the way he would handle it all. I certainly didn't and at that point I couldn't even claim to know him that well. I knew what he was like though – from the first time I met him I realized that he was a character who was very alien to football in England. I had been part of his first squad which played in a friendly against Spain in February of 2001. When I was introduced to him in the team hotel he was very polite, quite quiet, and had clearly done his homework on the players he had selected. It was a cordial introduction though I wouldn't say warm. He did not attempt to relate to the players the way we did with each other as some coaches do. Neither did he try to foster the type of relationship which most English players are familiar with – where the manager is an authority figure but more in a fatherly way than a head teacher. With Harry at West Ham, I was used to a boss who was very much part of our dressing room and the banter that goes with it, as well as knowing when not to cross the line that identified who was in charge. Ranieri and Mourinho have their own individual style but are similar in the way they get on with the players. Mr Eriksson, however, is quite unique in that respect. It's not that he is the cold fish that people often portray him as – in fact he is well liked and is held with much affection among the England team. At the same time, he has maintained a certain distance from us which clearly marks out the realm of his position.

None of us knew what to expect that first time but as the years have passed there is now very little that could surprise us about the England manager. Perhaps the best way to describe him is unflappable. We knew there wouldn't be any fireworks about what had appeared in the papers. Just because the man they described as 'The Iceman' had shown some passion, it didn't mean he would explode for their benefit. In fact, he was so unaffected by the whole episode that he never mentioned it to us as an issue in any way. That's very much his method and it didn't affect the players in any detrimental way. Some of them actually had a laugh about it. The dressing room remains a very macho environment and the fact that the manager had shown a side of his character which hadn't been seen before was a source of banter as well as a novelty.

Unfortunately for Mr Eriksson, that episode was the end of his honeymoon with the English media and I believe that the tide of opinion started to turn against him as far back as that September in 2002. The only response he could give that was unquestionable was actually down to the players – and they did respond, though not with my help.

It was a tiny ground in Bratislava. Even the dressing rooms were too small to accommodate the squad and coaching staff, and I found myself waiting outside in the corridor at the entrance. I was pissed off at not making the team while not even making it onto the bench made the whole episode seem pointless. I have rarely felt more of a spare part than I did that evening. There was a vending machine in the hall and we ended up eating bars of chocolate to pass the time before kick-off. The manager then appeared and started talking to me.

'How many goals have you got so far?' he asked.

'Two,' I replied.

'You look fit and well. How you feeling?'

I wanted to say, 'F***ing s*** actually, because I am standing in a corridor when I want to be getting ready to play.' Needless to say I bit my tongue.

'Yeah. Good, boss. Could do with some more games though!'

'Your time will come, Frank. Don't worry.'

The brief chat with him calmed me down, reassured me.

Standing around feeling out of it had dredged up a lot of the anxiety I had felt about the previous World Cup, but Mr Eriksson was able to allay some of that with just a short conversation. He has a way about him, a way of dealing with people which makes you feel important even if events suggest otherwise. It's one of his gifts as a coach.

Victory over Slovakia dampened the furore over the Ulrika affair and we returned to England to play Macedonia at St Mary's in Southampton. This time I turned up at the stadium to find my shirt out and my name among the subs. Oh well, progress I suppose. I stayed in the squad from then on until I made an impact at the end of that season in South Africa. I was playing pretty well but the team had a strong midfield of Beckham, Butt, Scholes, and Gerrard and it was up to me to fight my way in and I knew what I had to do.

When we got back to training with Chelsea the events of two weeks earlier against Liverpool seemed miles away. We had to play away at Manchester City which sticks out in my memory for reasons good and ugly. We won convincingly and I was really pleased with the way I played and even more so with the reaction from our fans. After the game they belted out my name and the song which they have made my signature: 'Super Frank Lampard'. It was the first time I had heard it and it was sung with so much passion that it really made me feel great. At West Ham that had never happened for me. There were only certain players who received individual adulation while others were ignored. There was no rhyme nor reason. I was buzzing with it at Chelsea though, but on this occasion it wasn't just the adrenalin from the win – I had also settled a score of a different kind.

I awoke early on the morning of the game full of nervous

energy. I had waited a long time for this day to come around. I knew what I was going to do and was determined to go through with it. I called Kutner.

'I'm going to let Berkovic know what I think of him today,' I told him.

'What?' he replied.

'I'm going to let him know he's in a game. I'm going to outplay him and let him know I'm angry.'

'What are you on about, Lamps?'

I was suddenly nervous and changed the subject. I am not a vindictive person nor am I a player who uses excessive force or dirty tactics. If I had told Kuts how angry I was then he would only have tried to talk me round. I was calm. I knew what I was doing. I was going to let Eyal Berkovic know that I was angry about the lies he had told about Dad and the hurt it had caused my family. No one was going to stop me.

I had no intention of causing him harm. I am not and never have been that kind of player. I am not capable of that kind of action as a person, never mind a footballer. I just wanted to let Berkovic know I wasn't happy, that in fact I was very upset with what he had said about Dad. I wanted to let him know I was there and that he should think carefully about making wrong and hurtful accusations about my family.

He had been quoted in the *News of the World* as labelling Dad a racist in his autobiography. He claimed that he'd been a victim of this during his time at West Ham and that it had been partly responsible for him leaving the club. It was a load of complete and absolute rubbish and it really offended me that he should say that and try to make that an excuse for his departure.

Berkovic left because of the incident in which John Hartson kicked him in the head during training. There was no racist element to that, just as there had been no ill treatment of him because of his nationality or religion. I saw Dad operate on a daily basis at the club and he never showed favouritism towards or prejudice against any player. He was well loved and respected by everyone at the club and never had any problems. Berkovic had also claimed that Dad would tell Harry to sub him (Berkovic) instead of me from midfield if someone was being taken off. And quite right too if he did – especially on a cold afternoon at the likes of Bolton when he was more concerned about keeping his hands warm instead of scrapping for a result like the rest of us. He is the opposite of JT and Jody – someone who is in it for himself and who would never stand side by side with you in a fight. I had nothing against Berkovic as a player – I enjoyed playing alongside him – but he caused me to feel extremely bitter when he tried to sully the reputation of Dad in such a cynical way.

I had considered other options. Talking to him wasn't really on – he'd always been a quite arrogant person who was always right in his own eyes. Denying the allegations was fine but it's the kind of thing which has so much stigma attached to it that even raising the subject presents its own problems. My mind was made up. I was going to teach him a lesson on the pitch.

Berkovic has always been a bit showy on the ball and I decided I would run him off a couple of times and make sure he knew what was going on. I had no experience of that kind of thing and relied on instinct to guide me. I didn't have long to wait. Berkovic likes to hold the ball when he's in space – he's always been a bit greedy – and I let him get comfortable enough on it before making my move. I went for the ball and my momentum carried me through the tackle and I hit him. Have that. There was no malice or violence, no studs – just enough to send him down. I tumbled clear towards the touchline and Marcel Desailly ran towards me and hauled me to my feet.

'What the f*** do you think you are doing?' he asked in a low, angry voice.

He had seen the whole thing from close range. He didn't know about my gripe with Berkovic but he had seen my eyes as I started my run at him. Marcel knew there was something going on but didn't understand what.

'You don't do that kind of thing. You don't,' he reminded me.

The referee brandished the inevitable yellow card. 'Fine,' I thought, 'I'll take it.' I was pleased that I had gone through with my plan. He wasn't injured but I had hurt him enough for him to know what was going on. It's not something I had done before or that I will repeat, as my disciplinary record shows – one red card in my entire career. I am no hooligan.

I put it behind me and it had no lasting affect on me as we tried to turn the victory at Maine Road into a habit else-where. Having got the whole Berkovic thing out of my system there was a sense of release. I felt I was maturing with every game that I played and even the smaller things in life seemed to give me a greater sense of self-belief. The promise I made to myself before the season started – that I would become a pivotal figure at the club – suddenly felt like a reality. Physically I felt sharper and stronger. I was also much more confident running with the ball and waiting for the right moment to make a pass.

That self-belief came through in my general play as well. In my first season I was nervous about demanding the ball partly because there were so many other great players around me. It wasn't conscious as such but I was very aware that I had the likes of Petit and Zola around me and I almost felt like I had no right to shout for possession in their company. Now I changed my attitude. I was facing the defenders and cajoling them to give me the ball.

Dad always said that I had to make things happen. To do that you need to have the ball at your feet. He was very forthright about my options when I signed for Chelsea. 'You can go there and play a bit of football and look good every couple of games son,' he said. 'Or you can shout for the ball every time you're near it and make things happen. Only then will people say that Frank Lampard won that game or this game for us.'

I knew he was right and I knew that is what I wanted to be. Even now, if I finish a game feeling that I haven't been as involved as I should, I will watch the TV highlights and read the reports to analyse my performance. If I haven't scored or provided an important pass then I feel I've let myself down. I lost all of the inhibitions which I had dragged to Stamford Bridge from my time at Upton Park. I was becoming the player I had always wanted to be even though I found this difficult to define to other people. There were players who I admired – like Keane and Vieira – but it was their spirit and talent which inspired me rather than their actual style of play.

I didn't want to be 'a goalscoring midfielder' in the mould of Robert Pires or Gus Poyet. I wanted to be a midfielder who scored goals – someone who was involved in all aspects of the play, from defending to making the final pass, as well as hitting the back of the net regularly. There weren't that many, if any, players to look up to who were capable of that. Keane did achieve it with double figures for a few years but he was more deep lying a lot of the time. Instead, I tried to take bits from everyone else and add them to my natural strengths.

Looking back, I think that combination of things is the main reason I played so many games in my first five years at Chelsea. If I were a manager I'd want a midfielder who could defend, who was at the heart of the engine of the team to drive it, as well as someone who could score and make goals. If you can demonstrate these qualities then you become indispensable. I would be happy to have a player like that.

At that time there was one more aspect I needed to perfect. I was just beginning to master the runs from midfield which have become my trademark. The extra training, the diet, and all of the aspects which had changed in my life since the transfer were coming together and making a difference. Ranieri had spent a lot of time coaching me about when I should break forward and when I should sit. It had been hard to start with, as my instinct was to attack whenever I could. I had scored forty goals from midfield at West Ham and saw Chelsea as a place where I could get more. Dad agreed, and it was his presence at home games especially which complicated my first few weeks at the club. He had just stopped being on the bench giving me instructions at West Ham and so it was still very much habit. At Stamford Bridge my parents sit in the East Stand on the first tier almost directly above the home dugout. At Chelsea, I would look to the bench and see Ranieri telling me to get closer to a man or press on. Dad would be above him gesticulating for me to make a forward run or tuck in behind or whatever. I would look at the bench for instructions out of habit and then catch a glimpse of Dad telling me to do something completely different. To his credit and despite years of habit, Dad quickly realized that he had to take second place to Ranieri. He has stopped sending overt signals but admits that in his mind he is still telling me what to do.

Some of the other lads had clocked this strange double-take phenomenon now and again and I took a bit of stick for it. Ranieri had a very personal way with his players and as I grew in importance in the team, he took me aside more and more and we talked about what he wanted me to do in a match. That kind of thing will always attract dressing room banter and the lads took to calling me son of Ranieri and referring to him as my Dad.

Whenever I got called to be given instructions by the manager, Eidur would say, 'Lamps, your Dad wants you.' Of course, when my real Dad turned up at games – as he does at every one – there would be two of them. That's how I became the man with two Dads. The joking around was all part of the team spirit which was building under Ranieri and an indication of the amount of respect and affection the players had for the him.

Ranieri was very passionate about his belief in me – indeed, almost like a parent – and it showed. It actually got to the stage where he was shouting 'Stay, stay' almost all of the time, even in training and practice matches. I would look over in disbelief. It hadn't clicked for me that most of my goals at West Ham had come from percentage running – making those runs all of the time though only one fifth might actually bring a goal.

What I learned was how to react to play in individual situations, to sense when I might best have the chance of a goal or not, and how to use the ball better when there was nothing else on. I have Ranieri to thank for that. He saw the potential in me when he bought me from West Ham and he made it real by curbing my naive urge to go forward regardless.

Things were looking up on the pitch as well. A run of games up until Christmas saw us beaten by Man United in the League Cup but on 21 December myself and Eidur scored and we went top of the Premiership with a victory over Aston Villa. It was a great feeling to get there and as a team we were on a high. I tend not to get carried away in situations like this, and I seemed on this occasion to have an innate sense that I shouldn't be over-optimistic.

I arrived for training on Monday and there was a real buzz. Jody, JT and Eidur were already there in our little 'English section' so called because of the way the old training ground was divided up into six mini-dressing rooms. There was an Italian room, a French room and the rest of the world. It was a terrible set-up for a football club and didn't help at all in building and promoting the team spirit. The spirit wasn't bad but the segregation made life more difficult. There was, however, compensation in the form of the relationship that developed with Eidur, Jody, and JT. We would chat a lot about games, the club, and where we thought we were headed. It was then that I first became good friends with the lads and out of that bond – Jody later left the club – the three core lieutenants of Mourinho's command got together. We three bridged the Ranieri era and the new one.

Eidur and I became good mates very quickly. He is a year younger than me which I still find remarkable as he has an old head on him, a sensible head. Eidur is very intelligent and inquisitive – he is always curious to know everything, whether it's how you are doing to what you think of a certain player or team. When you arrive at a new club only certain players will bother to ask about your personal life and family, and Eidur has always been very caring in that way. We both have kids now and I learned a lot from him about that side of life before Luna was even born. He is a very genuine person and we have become best friends over the years.

One of the reasons he is so appreciated at Chelsea is for his football brain. Eidur is one of the cleverest players I have ever come across – he knows exactly what to do and when to do it. Some players who have his talent to hold the ball and dribble will waste possession trying to beat men – not Eidur. He's far too cute and will always draw the man in to him and release the ball at the right moment. He's a joy to play with and if I lay the ball off to him and make a run I know that he is the one guy I can rely on to knock it straight back into my path. He is the quintessential link man, but his ability doesn't end there.

When I arrived at Chelsea I was blown away by Jimmy Floyd Hasselbaink. Anyone who ever got in the way of one of his shots will know what that means – literally. Jimmy is the most natural striker I have ever played with. He has the selfish streak which all great forwards have as well as the predator's instinct to make him successful. He and Eidur scored fifty-three goals between them the first season I was at the club but the following year only one of them got the chance to show he could do it again – Jimmy.

I felt very sorry for Eidur. Most of the goals Jimmy scored in 2001/02 Eidur either created or had a hand in but Ranieri decided that Zola would play a few games and then Eidur would get a few and it was very disjointed. There were times when he was playing really well and scored and he would be hauled off. I couldn't really understand it. Neither could he and I feel it held him back from making real progress, given the season he had enjoyed previously.

I understood Ranieri's predicament: Franco is very hard to drop, as is Jimmy, and maybe sometimes Eidur lost out because he was the easy option. The way we were playing didn't accommodate all three, so someone had to make way. Eidur and I would sit and chat about this in our 'private' dressing room and myself, JT, and Jody would offer support.

Elsewhere there were a number of formidable characters in the team – people like Zola, Desailly, and Petit all command respect for what they have achieved in their careers. Jimmy, on the other hand, would just demand the ball – all of the time. It took me a while to pluck up the courage but I knew that if I was to assert myself more at Chelsea I would have to stand up to him. It's not that Jimmy was a bully or anything like that – more that he was a very big personality who carried himself with a mountain of self-confidence. When I first started training and Jimmy shouted for the ball, I would pass it. That more or less went on for my first season. He was part of the hierarchy at the club and I was the new boy trying to fit in. My 'English' mates had all been there longer than me and made it easier for me, but it wasn't until I made the conscious decision to follow my instinct rather than someone else's instruction that I began to make my own way.

'Lamps! Lamps! Give it, give it!' It was Jimmy again, at training.

I held onto it and let go with a shot of my own which was saved by the keeper.

'Oi! I said give it here,' Jimmy shouted.

'F*** off, Jimmy.'

I could hardly believe what I had said. Neither could Jimmy. The training pitch went momentarily quiet while everyone waited for the explosion. Jimmy was well known for dealing with issues immediately. He walked towards me and I wondered if I was about to experience the Hasselbaink hairdryer. Maybe he would just kill me. He grinned – that wide, warm Jimmy grin which says everything is cool. And that was it. I was accepted. I ran back into the action and shouted for the ball more loudly than I had ever done. I was proud of myself and now I was going to prove I was right.

We were just at the beginning of the festive fixture list – a period where the championship often took a decisive turn in favour of one team or another. We went into it full of optimism. I was hopeful even though Chelsea traditionally did not stand up to this test and we had three games in six days in the league, two of them away. Ranieri called a meeting after training on Christmas Eve and mapped out his view on the coming week. We had Southampton at home on Boxing Day and then played Leeds at Elland Road before going to Highbury on New Year's Day. He said we had a squad of nineteen players and all of us would play over those first two games. I came in to training on Christmas Day and it was apparent I wasn't in the team for Southampton.

I went to his office to see him and he was obviously expecting me.

'Ah,' he said without surprise. 'I thought you might visit me.'

'What's going on boss?' I got straight to the point.

'I want to play and I am not being big headed but I think we should play our best team and win this game. Southampton at home is a great chance to get three points, even with a horrible trip to Leeds to come.

'If we get a win there then you never know. We've just gone top of the league.'

He listened to me but he had a look in his eyes which told me his mind was made up before he spoke.

'Frank. You must be patient,' he replied. 'You will play at Leeds and we will have six fresh players for that match.'

I started as sub against Southampton and only came on with five minutes to go, along with William Gallas. It was a crappy game which we drew and maybe that was fair enough. They were playing okay and Gordon Strachan had them well organized. We took it on the chin and went to Leeds two days later. We brought in the players that had been rested and lost 2–0. We were s***. It was a killer – having been top of the league a week earlier, we then couldn't capitalize and consolidate our position.

I can't be sure that we would have beaten Southampton if we had played our strongest team – that's an impossible call. But I have never come across a coach who said before a series of games that he was going to play this many players over the course of the matches. I am of the mentality that you play your strongest team and if they win then you play the same eleven as long as they are fit. We are professionals after all, and two games in three days should be manageable. You might be a bit tired but all teams have the same schedule at that time of year so you are up against players in the same boat. I know rotation was Ranieri's way but in retrospect it wasn't always the best way.

Roberto Sassi – Ranieri's fitness coach – had a big say in who was rotated and when. It was Sassi who conducted the blood tests and training measurements and he would advise the boss on who needed a rest. This rankled me and still does. Sassi wasn't a football man but he had a real influence and one which a lot of the players questioned.

To be fair, a few of us had a chat with Ranieri about a week later and he recognized that he had made a mistake. He was quite open about it and I respected him for admitting it. Sassi, though, would never admit he had made a mistake. Even if we had picked up three points from one of those two games we would still have been top and we might have pushed on a bit.

Worse was to come when we took on Arsenal, our direct rivals for the title, and lost 3–2. I don't blame the manager for that. He must take a lot of credit for the way I developed under his leadership and I will always be grateful for that. As a team, though, there was a chance we could have achieved more that season. Arsenal and Man United were not as dominant as they had been in the previous years and we showed we were capable of taking them on and challenging at the top. Crucially, what we lacked was their experience of what it takes to lead the pack and stay ahead of them, and that applies to Ranieri as well. You need to have that little bit extra mental toughness to win the championship – part of that comes from knowing what it is to claim the title, and part from knowing how painful it is to lose one.

Chelsea had not really been up there fighting it out with the big boys. The only team which had muscled Man United or Arsenal out of the top two places since Arsene Wenger arrived at Highbury were Liverpool – and that was a one off. This was all part of a learning curve for us and even though we were disappointed by how briefly we had been at the top we knew that we had to get on with the rest of the campaign and do the best we could. We still had a Champions League spot to claim and there was work to be done.

Unfortunately, sometimes it felt like we were being undermined by things that should have been in our favour. Take the Stamford Bridge pitch for instance. The winter period brings out the worst in it but that particular period saw it deteriorate to a virtual sandpit. Charlton came to play us in a match which became known as the 'battle of the beach'. It was bad but it's also true that it was the same for both teams. We were playing good football at the time and I would have thought that Charlton might have viewed 'the beach' as to their advantage, a chance to exploit Chelsea's supposed lack of stomach for a hard slog.

Scott Parker told me after he joined Chelsea a couple of years later that Alan Curbishley did actually tell his players to have a real go at us that day because of the state of the grass. They were told to stick their foot in and make it hard for us. It didn't work. We routed them 4–1 and ironically Charlton then lodged a complaint with the Premier League about the state of the pitch. Ironic, given their gameplan.

We weren't as soft as some people liked to think and I felt my confidence and physical strength build as the season went on. I was conscious of my ambition to make a real impact at the club and when we beat Leeds 3–2 at the end of January I felt as if I was getting there. I scored, Eidur got an overhead kick, and then Dominic Matteo got in the way of another shot which should have allowed me to claim my first double for Chelsea. I already believed that I had the ability to change games in short periods, but I wanted to be considered in the same class as Keane, Vieira and Steven Gerrard. They are regularly influential and dominate games and up until that time I wasn't considered in that bracket. These were the kind of games where you had to make the difference and I was beginning to state my case.

I was also desperate to make similar inroads with England. There was a friendly against Australia the following midweek and I took a knock on my ankle playing against Birmingham the Saturday before. Eriksson had rung Ranieri on the coach after the game because I had come off injured. The manager came and told me that Sven had been impressed with the way I had been playing and wanted me to start the England game. Was I fit? I was well pleased and said that I would be fine.

Despite the injury I was determined to play, especially as the game was at Upton Park. It wasn't my ideal venue because of the punters but I have always been immensely proud to play for my country and there was something appealing about doing it at the place where I had grown up in football. I strapped up the injury really heavily the day before in training and passed myself fit to play, though I wish I hadn't. I felt terrible in training and knew I wasn't right. I am not trying to make excuses because in the actual game I didn't feel too bad.

I started in the centre with Nicky Butt and we knew that the whole team was changing at half-time which became a nightmare in itself. We were two down by the break and the crowd were booing us off the park. It was typical of my early performances for the international team; I was playing but I didn't feel I was having much influence on the game.

It ended up 3–1 and was one of the worst defeats I have known as an England player. It was made worse by the fact that I was doing well for Chelsea and was so keen to carry that into the international scene. I felt I was going from strength to strength and even though I didn't have that much experience with the national side I could tell that this was not seen as an insignificant defeat. The press tore into us – some of it was justified and some not. One positive which came out of that night though was the international debut of a certain Wayne Rooney. Ironically, it was Franny Jeffers who scored our consolation but it was Everton's new teenage star who was set to become a sensation.

Our season continued to follow the familiar pattern of achieving most of what we set out to without ever really threatening to be spectacular. We lost at Manchester United which only served to confirm what we already knew: we wouldn't be champions. Ranieri kept us motivated in the league, though, and the prospect of getting into a Champions League place was more than enough to keep me going.

As it turned out, it was also what was required to keep the club going. I was becoming more concerned about the financial state of Chelsea and not just because of rumours and the stories in the papers. We were instructed not to swap shirts with opposing teams and the cutlery in the canteen at the training ground had been replaced with plastic knives and forks. There were cutbacks and we all felt the pressure mounting as the season drew to a climax.

We drew Arsenal in the FA Cup at Highbury and were more or less written off before the game. Another final appearance would, however, make a few quid for the club, so we went there determined to go through. We fought hard and I scored a sweet equalizer with ten minutes left, forcing a replay. We were confident we could beat them at home but they started the game like a hurricane and we were two down by half-time. We lost 3–1. All that was left to play for was third place in the league and the chance to make the Champions League.

Our rivals for qualification were Liverpool. As luck would have it, we were destined to meet each other on the final day of the season. With Manchester United winning the title, the media had latched on to the fact that the only race in town was for third and so the hype started early.

The run-in was nervy. We lost away at Villa and West Ham the week before the final match – particularly sore. By the time we were preparing for Liverpool's visit the contest had already been labelled 'The £10 million knockout' because of what was at stake. There was much more than that on the line, however, and we only found out the night before the game.

Ranieri decided to take the team to a hotel on the eve of the match. Normally, we would just go and stay at the Chelsea Village Hotel but for some reason we stayed in the Royal Lancaster. With the financial restrictions which affected us every day, we raised eyebrows but no one was particularly suspicious at the time. I thought maybe they just wanted to spoil us a bit in order to emphasize how much the game meant.

We had our team dinner as usual but afterwards Gary Staker told us we had to go to a room where someone was going to give us a talk. It was a bit strange and the lads wondered what was going on. We had never used a motivational speaker before, and some of the team were a bit sceptical. He was a big guy who introduced himself as a former American soldier and veteran of Vietnam. I was a bit confused. The lads were quiet and almost immediately this guy grabbed our attention.

He told a story of how he and his platoon found themselves at an impasse as they tried to reach a village to rescue some civilians. The Viet Cong had set up a gun post at a strategic point where they were well protected and could hit the Americans every time they tried to push forward. Several men had lost their lives trying to take the enemy position. The stand-off had lasted some time before one of his friends set off on a solo mission to destroy the enemy post.

He detailed every movement of this guy as well as every emotion that those he left behind had felt as they realized there was no chance he would survive. He threw himself on the gunner, having opened a grenade. He was killed instantly but gave his life so that others might live.

There was silence in the room. Some of the lads had tears welling up in their eyes.

Then, the soldier started shouting.

'You're gonna win tomorrow. You're gonna win or die tryin'.

'You're gonna die for your team-mate out there.'

He was stamping his feet and some of us were shouting with him. It was very moving and he clearly knew how to get people fired up. I was a little shocked from the experience but I felt good and everyone in the room was pumped up. If there had been any doubt within the camp about our ability to win, it was gone in that moment. Now, we knew we would win.

The atmosphere had calmed slightly when the chief executive, Trevor Birch, came into the room. It was quite unusual for him to see us altogether – especially the night before a game – and naturally everyone went silent.

'I need to tell you something very important,' said Birch.

'I'm not going to try to kid you or give you a picture which is more rosy than is real. The club is in severe financial difficulty. In fact, we have reached a point of financial crisis.'

There were a few gasps around the room – shock, but also morbid anticipation at what was coming next. We didn't have long to wait.

'In order to ensure that Chelsea FC will still exist next season you have to make the Champions League. In short, if you fail to beat Liverpool then the club will go out of business.'

I heard what he said but I wasn't sure I had understood properly. The whole evening had become surreal. Myself, JT, and Eidur started talking about it. We knew the club had money worries. The whole season had been dogged by talk of debts of £80–£100 million. As players you hear and read those things – and, of course, we felt the cutbacks – but in essence you try to get on with your job and win football matches. That's what we are paid to do. But Birch was a serious man who was also very earnest. We knew that this wasn't scare-mongering. To be honest, I am not sure that it was the right thing to do. We were very aware of the pressure on us to win that match and so it was a risk to lay the full load on the players' shoulders with regard to the future of the club.

I discovered retrospectively that when Birch had taken over at the start of that season he had reviewed all of the player contracts. He had looked at mine – which was considerable and then had four years left – and proposed that it might be better to offer to release me for nothing and save on my wages. Funny how the world changes.

Ranieri obviously knew what was going on behind the scenes but he didn't make any overt reference to it. As always, he wanted us to be completely focused on football. We were determined to get the win – for the club, the fans, the chair-man, Ranieri, and ourselves.

The atmosphere inside the Bridge was amazing when we took the pitch. It was essentially a cup final in the league – winner take all. Despite our resolve and what we knew the consequences of defeat would be, we went a goal down early on when Sami Hyppia scored with a header. It was the worst possible start. I allowed myself to contemplate what Birch had said the night before: lose, and no more Chelsea. I couldn't believe it would end like this. We couldn't allow it to.

I roared at everyone around me when we got the ball back to the centre spot.

'Come on! F***ing come on! You know what this means. Let's get back into this game.'

We started to get more of the ball – pass, pass, pressure, pressure. They opened up a bit at the back and we piled on top every time they got the ball. We forced a corner, a free kick, we came close, and finally we got level. It felt like it had taken an eternity – in fact it had been three minutes.

We celebrated but kept it short. A draw wasn't good enough; only victory would secure the club and we knew it. Our confidence grew until we were dominating every part of the field. The early nerves had disappeared and almost everything we tried came off.

Just before the half hour a loose ball fell for Jesper Gronkjaer and he belted a shot wide of Jerzy Dudek to put us in front. Everyone loved Jesper. He's a great bloke – very kind and funny. We all ran to celebrate with him in front of the fans, and I could feel the sense of relief around the stadium. We held on to the lead and deserved to win and could have done so more handsomely.

If only the 41,911 fans there that day had known what we did. The final whistle sounded at last. I was drained, physically and mentally. The supporters were going mad and we all joined up for a lap of honour. I enjoyed the moment. It had been a very testing season. I really felt like I had improved, scoring eight goals and coming second to Franco Zola as Player of the Year.

There was a party atmosphere; thousands of fans had stayed behind to sing and it felt like we had actually won a trophy. But I look back now and wonder what would have happened had we lost. I can't imagine. I don't dare to even think about it.

CHAPTER 7

ROMAN'S EMPIRE

I HAVE heard it said that revolutions don't start with a shout but with a whisper. Very few people knew of Roman Abramovich's plan to buy Chelsea and I first heard of it in a message on my mobile phone. Elen and I were on holiday in America and were lying by the pool of our Las Vegas hotel when I received an unexpected voicemail. It was Rio.

'A Russian billionaire is buying Chelsea mate. I'm tellin' you. This geezer is seriously rich and can afford any player in the world. There's gonna be big changes. I hope you're up for a fight 'cos you're gonna have one to stay in the team! Enjoy your hols!'

Cheers mate. Rio can never resist a wind up and in this case he had the chance of a lifetime. I wasn't sure what to make of it. There had been stories for months about different people investing in the club but I'd never heard of Roman Abramovich. I wondered about it for a while and then went for a swim. Probably just Rio having a laugh.

Two days later we were in Los Angeles and the story broke in England that Ken Bates had sold the club to a Russian oil tycoon. I called Dad and Kutner but there was very little hard information and a lot of wild speculation. The only thing for certain was that the new owner of Chelsea was rich – very rich.

Within days we were linked with the biggest names in the world; Thierry Henry, Ronaldinho, Andriy Shevchenko, Ronaldo – and they were just the strikers. In midfield we were supposed to be buying Emerson from Roma, Steven Gerrard from Liverpool, and David Beckham from Real Madrid. On top of that, Ranieri was to be replaced.

I called a few people for news and while everything I was being told sounded exciting for Chelsea I wasn't sure what it meant for me, but I've never been scared of competition for places in the team and never shirked a challenge. When I returned home I found that the place was already bulging with new signings. Glen Johnson, Adrian Mutu, Wayne Bridge, Damien Duff, Geremi, Hernan Crespo, and Alexei Smertin had joined and there was no sign of it stopping there. I looked at the intake: four midfielders already in, plus Claude Makelele, Juan Sebastian Veron, and Joe Cole still to arrive. Only the seven then. I thought about the situation and decided that I had two choices: I could leave Chelsea or I could become a better footballer. I decided to become a better footballer.

Mr Abramovich arrived at Harlington a couple of days after we had reported back for pre-season training. We got wind of the visit and everyone was there early (some of the younger players even washed their cars). There was a sense of nervousness around the place and uncertainty about what was about to happen. The man we met though was warm and seemed as anxious as any of us about meeting for the first time. He didn't speak any English but said hello politely to the players and staff. I watched him as he came towards me and was slightly surprised by his appearance. I suppose you imagine rich and powerful people to be very imposing characters but he seemed physically slight and quite shy.

With him was Eugene Tenenbaum who is his close friend and a director of the club, and a translator. Eugene speaks English as a first language but is fluent in Russian and has worked with Roman a long time. Ranieri was introducing everyone and trying to keep things as relaxed and casual as possible.

When Mr Abramovich came to shake my hand he smiled. I smiled and said hello as the manager told the new owner my name and position. As he listened he looked directly at me and very fleetingly I caught sight of the determination in his gaze which convinced me he wasn't here for a hobby. Mr Abramovich conducts business to be successful. He doesn't like to lose.

I also liked his style. He took one look at the rickety old set-up of the training ground with its partitioned changing rooms and grubby canteen and pronounced it to be 'really s***'. I don't know how to say that in Russian but he was absolutely right. He immediately instructed a search for a new site and for a purpose-built complex to be constructed.

I've been told he was in his helicopter helping to hunt for a suitable piece of land when they flew over Hyde Park.

'What about there?' he is supposed to have asked.

'You can't sir. The Queen owns it.'

'Won't she sell?'

The story has become a bit of an urban myth but the sentiment is accurate enough – Mr Abramovich will stop at almost nothing to get what he wants. There didn't seem to be any limit on the transfer budget and by the time we lined up for the first Premiership game of the season at Anfield there were six new faces in the squad, five of whom started the match. Everyone was feeling the pressure as we gathered in the Anfield tunnel. Ranieri didn't refer to the new owner in his team-talk, his focus remaining on the players and the club. He was trying to take our minds off the fact that we were now regarded as the richest club in the world and one which couldn't afford to fail.

It was a tough game, though. Veron put us in the lead in the first half and it looked for a long time that we would get the Abramovich revolution off to a winning start as the whole of planet football waited to see what would happen. Then disaster – Michael Owen equalized with a penalty and the day was deflated, until, that is, Jimmy netted with three minutes left. We ran to celebrate with him but the image which will live longest in my mind from that game was the one I saw later that evening on TV. The camera panned to the directors' box after the second goal went in and there was Roman Abramovich jumping out of his seat and exchanging high fives with the other club officials. I thought, 'He'll do for me.'

The second match of the campaign was just as memorable, though it was not for Chelsea. England met Croatia in a friendly at Ipswich on the following Wednesday night and I was fired up for it, not just because of the events of the previous weekend but mainly because I could sense a change in fortune in my international career. There had been a run of games over that summer which included friendlies against South Africa in May and then Serbia and Montenegro in June, followed by a Euro qualifier against Slovakia. Over that period I had managed to force my way into the reckoning with England, and in return, Eriksson had shown real confidence in me for the first time.

The trip itself was out of the ordinary. Travelling so far at the end of a long season for an exhibition match seemed strange, as was the opportunity to meet Nelson Mandela. It hadn't been on our schedule and didn't seem to be particularly well organized. We were sitting on the coach after training, two days before the match, and we were simply asked if we wanted to go. It meant getting up at 6 am to be on a flight from Durban to Johannesburg. I respect Mandela for what he has done and though he is not a particular hero of mine I felt I should go to represent England. The game was the next day and I would have preferred to prepare properly, and a lot of lads didn't go because of that. In the end I was glad that I went. Mandela came across as a very friendly man. It was a very humbling experience and it dawned on me that I was in the presence of someone who had made history by achieving amazing things for others. That's real celebrity. It was also quite an amusing occasion because Rio jumped to the front when we were being introduced, and in the photo I have he's sitting beside Mandela holding his hand. Rio was so excited, just like the big kid he can be.

As for the game against South Africa, I played the last half hour, made a goal, and generally did well despite seeing a St George's flag in the stand with 'WHU' (West Ham United) on it and a fat geezer caning me when I was warming up. Greeted by Nelson Mandela, international statesman, one day, slagged off by an ignorant football fan, the next – what a life. We won 2–1, and I realize now that my performance in South Africa was the turning point of my England career.

The midfield four which had played in the World Cup the year before was still going strong but the chance to prove myself came in the first match after the tournament. David

Beckham had broken his arm and wasn't fit and so I made my first start under Eriksson in the Serbia game. I played quite well but knew it wasn't enough and the question leading up to the Slovakia match in Middlesbrough was whether Jermaine Jenas or I would replace Beckham in the team. I got the nod but my happiness was tempered by the fact that I would start on the left of a midfield diamond. Anyone who plays on the left of midfield for England has to deal with the fact that no matter how well you play you will always be told that you're not the answer to the country's problems there. Despite what JT thought about my performances on the wing for Chelsea, I didn't really deserve the tag 'Giggsy'.

It was a big moment for me – starting a qualifying match. The manager had put his trust in me for an important game and I appreciated the responsibility. I was prepared for it and felt I was passing well in an open formation. Then we went a goal down. I walked from the pitch at half-time dreading the prospect of losing and everyone putting it down to the fact that Beckham didn't play and I did. Too much negative thinking – so I got my head down and spirits up and went out for the second half believing we would turn it round. Michael Owen scored twice, impressing on me what kind of player he is – someone special, someone with the ability to score goals when they're needed most.

Paul Scholes was another special talent. He was always the best trainer with England and one of the best players I have ever seen. He's razor sharp all of the time, passes the ball so quickly and accurately, and shoots with explosive power. In fact, he's possibly the best finisher in the business. As an attacking midfielder I looked at him and wondered if I would ever get to that level. There was a period when he didn't score for England and it was made into a big issue but what people overlooked in that scenario was that you make a rod for your own back when you have a habit of getting goals from midfield. I've suffered from it as well. People begin to expect it from you even though you don't get anywhere near the same number of opportunities as some strikers who might also be in a goal drought.

I've been called 'ineffective' because I didn't score in a particular match which can be annoying since it ignores everything else I may have contributed. In the England set-up, Scholesy was the forward point of the diamond which had Nicky Butt at the base and I remember while I was playing for the Under-21s, Peter Taylor taking me aside for a chat.

'I see you playing the holding role long-term, Frank,' he said.

'What are you talking about? I don't want to play there,' I replied. 'It goes against my instinct. I like to get forward and attack. It's the player I am.'

'No. I see you developing into a holding player and maybe going forward occasionally from deep. You've got to think about where you will best be able to flourish.'

I did, and I knew it was as an attacking midfielder. Maybe Peter Taylor was looking at Scholesy and thought I didn't have much chance of unseating him in the senior team and that changing tack was a better option for making the step up. But I had no interest in playing deep and was determined to make myself into the player I had always envisaged I could be.

I had three years between my first and second caps so I wasn't short of time to consider my options. Stevie Gerrard was relatively inexperienced then but in my eyes had already made himself a first-choice pick for England. Beckham was captain and playing very well and generally speaking the lads who were in the team were the biggest obstacles to me getting a chance. I appreciated that they were the best we had and to make an impact I would have to prove myself to be better. That didn't put me off, though I was becoming more aware all the time that international football could be even more fickle than playing for your club. Playing for England can be the best thing in football but it can also be the worst. There is little better feeling than representing your country and doing well. However, you're often pitted against smaller nations in potentially mundane games and if you are not completely aware and sharp then you can get punished.

We often play teams we are expected to thrash – like Macedonia, Slovakia or Liechtenstein – where you know very little about the opponents or the way they play. Technically they are often much better than the public perception of them. I can understand the public expectation because of the players England have, but international football is not as simple as big team beats little team. The crowd is edgy at those games right from the start – urging you to get forward, score goals, and play entertaining football – but the truth of the matter is that when you open yourself up naively like that you can get picked off and concede goals. Examples of this type of scenario are the Macedonia game at home – when we drew 2–2 – and then the Slovakia match at the Riverside.

It annoys me when people say or write that England should be convincingly beating this team or that because this ignores the reality of modern international football. I learned from playing under foreign coaches at Chelsea and playing with other internationals that you have to be sharper than your opponent. When I was at West Ham I would probably have agreed with the bulldog gung-ho spirit of 'up and at 'em' but that attitude will only get you so far against most teams and will see you torn apart by good ones like Brazil or Argentina.

You know what to expect of the big nations but my point about the smaller ones is illustrated by the example of players who look very good with their international sides but are less impressive when they join a Premiership club. That's because international football is slower and more technical by nature. You need to have the skill and the mentality to succeed in both.

I felt much more confident around the England scene as a result of the games that summer and by the time we got to the Croatia match I was buzzing. It told in my performance when I came on as sub for Nicky Butt and scored my first goal. The contest was unspectacular but there are few sweeter moments in football than when you let fly from twenty-five yards and know the ball is going in from the moment it leaves your boot. It is even sweeter when you're wearing the Three Lions. So what it wasn't a competitive match? I was off the mark for England and my self-belief was strengthened going into the game against Macedonia the following month.

For the Macedonia game I was asked to play at the front of the diamond in midfield, which can be a tough position to get right. You spend much of the time with your back to goal collecting the ball and trying to link players. Playing behind the strikers has traditionally been the domain of the skilful 'number 10' type – someone who is essentially a striker but whose ability is not limited to scoring goals. Diego Maradona is the finest example and for me the greatest player who ever lived. I am no Maradona (as Harry once pointed out) but what I have is something different – an ability to make play from deeper positions and then arrive at the right time around the box to have a crack at goal.

I felt slightly isolated at times in Skopje but I was doing all right. Obviously the manager felt differently. I was subbed at half-time. I hate being taken off at any stage in a match but this was just embarrassing. We were a goal down at the time and Eriksson felt he had to make changes. He brought on Rooney to play in the hole and the team went on to win 2–1. I was glad we won but gutted to be off the pitch. The manager subsequently said to the press that I had done well but he had to change it round to try and force a goal. This was a fair enough point but it wasn't much consolation for me. However, on the flight home I got a boost from the England captain.

I hadn't had much interaction with Becks until that point and when I first came into the squad I was a little in awe of him. I was still a young kid then and he was already a super-star. This sense of distance between us lasted for quite some time. But while I was sitting on the plane poring over the details of the game in my head and working out where I had gone right and wrong, Becks came and sat beside me.

'You all right Lamps?' he asked.

'Yeah. Okay. I'm pleased we won but a bit pissed off to be pulled at half-time,' I said.

'I know what you mean. You shouldn't be too down though, because you played well and you've been doing really well for England and Chelsea. People get dragged off much more easily in international football than at club level and it happens. Don't get too down on yourself, your moment will come.'

We chatted for a few minutes but it wasn't so much what he said but the fact that he made the effort which encouraged me. He was kind and supportive and I suppose playing the part of a good captain. It broke the ice between us because he is quite a shy person, like myself, and ever since then we have got on very well and I have felt much more involved. I was pleased for the support and finally began to feel a part of the England set-up rather than just 'a body'.

I played in the victory over Liechtenstein four days later when, unsurprisingly, we got some stick for only winning 2–0; but on the next occasion I met up with the squad I discovered what life with the national team was like when a firestorm breaks out off the pitch. It came like a bolt from the blue and had a significant impact.

On the morning I was due to meet up with the players for the match against Turkey news broke that Rio had missed a drugs test at Manchester United and had been kicked out the squad. I had no prior warning from Rio or anyone else, not even a rumour that something was wrong. I arrived at the team hotel and found that a meeting of the players had been called to discuss the situation. The United lads were obviously much better informed than most of us and Gary Neville was the most vociferous in his support of Rio, though the other United lads were very much behind him – backing up all that was said. The room was quiet and everyone was tense. None of us had ever known anything like it and while I would support Rio in every way possible, I genuinely didn't know what practical steps to take. Gary got on his feet and addressed the squad.

'Here are the facts,' he said. 'Rio missed a drugs test at Carrington [Manchester United's training ground] because he had already left, having forgotten that he'd been chosen to give a sample for testing. He remembered that afternoon and went back to take the test but was told that the officials had already left. The problem we face is that as a result of making an honest mistake he's been dropped from this squad and effectively found guilty of breaking the rules before any investigation has taken place.'

'F***ing hell, Rio, you stupid bastard.' I had a lot of sympathy for Rio but after the shock of reading about it in the morning, the possible consequences were now beginning to sink in. Rio could miss the Turkey match, but he could also miss the rest of the season – and Euro 2004.

Gary opened up the discussion and the lads agreed that there appeared to be a miscarriage of justice. We wanted to know what we could do about it. The United lads raised the idea that we should boycott the Turkey match in support of our team-mate. I wasn't so sure. I agreed that it was important to display unity but it was a very difficult situation since the 'enemy' we were fighting were the Football Association, who had decided on this course of action.

'The one thing we can do to let them know how strongly we feel about this is to go on strike,' Gary continued. 'We should all think about whether or not we go to play in Turkey.'

When I actually heard the words I was shocked. Yes, we had an opportunity to make an important statement about how we felt and take the stand we felt was appropriate. I looked around the room though and saw a lot of expressions which suggested surprise, apprehension, or just a lack of understanding of what all of this meant. I was behind the idea but I think most lads were simply swept along on a tide of high emotion. Gary had given a very passionate speech and had the support of the players in principle but I'm not sure any of us had really considered the implications of following through with the threat.

Nevertheless, the FA were made aware of developments and word came back that they were not prepared to negotiate. The delegation of four which makes up the players' committee met with the chief executive of the FA, Mark Palios, and returned very angry. The official response was that if we went on strike then they would pick another twenty players who were prepared to turn out against Turkey and scab on the rest of us. I didn't know Mark Palios very well but he always struck me as quite an arrogant person. I would have hoped that someone in his position would have tried harder to relate to the players and understand where we were coming from. Surely that's one of the most important aspects of his job. Instead, he preferred to swan around giving it the big 'I am' which irked me and most of the lads.

In fact, Mark Palios wasn't so very special, not special at all. The chief executive didn't have to make himself out to be the most important person at the FA. He could have gone about his business quietly and efficiently and left the manager and the players to get on with team affairs. He should've stuck to his own area of responsibility.

None of this helped the situation. Rio was out – end of story. Mr Eriksson called the players together later the same day, having spoken with some of us already. He knew what was being considered and to be fair he found himself in an impossible situation. He had always been steadfastly behind his players but on the other hand he had to try and put across the view of his employers – the FA.

'Look, I completely understand your point of view on this,' he said. 'And I think that you should support each other at all times. I admire that quality in you and I know that the team and me as your manager benefits from this unity. I think that the stance you are taking is morally correct but we have another problem and that is that we have to play a very important game against Turkey.

'If we don't, then all of the hard work we have put in so far will be in danger as will our chance to play at the European Championships. You must remember that is at stake as well as what you are fighting for.'

At this point a deadlock had been reached. Rio wasn't coming back into the squad and when some of the players started to talk amongst themselves about what might happen next there was a realization of what the consequences could be. We had been chosen to represent our country, to play for England in the match which would decide our fate in Euro 2004. And what about the fans, the ordinary people who supported us? We also had to consider the implications, both immediate and long-term, for all of us.

By this time the media were having a field day. Papers printed head shots of the players and branded us 'traitors'. It was all getting out of hand. I was pissed off at being so labelled by people who expected us to show strength and togetherness on the field – and I mean the FA and the media. And yet we were supposed to abandon a team-mate who was innocent? No chance.

We were due to fly to Istanbul on the Thursday before Saturday's game and the talk was of the flight being delayed while discussions went on. By the Wednesday evening I was convinced that there wouldn't be a strike. I understood the concept of using the strike as a threat, but I couldn't see it going beyond that. Even so, I'm sure there were some players who were prepared to go all the way. In the end, we got together and a consensus emerged that it was better to play the match, achieve the result which would see us qualify automatically, and then deal with the issue of Rio later. He would miss this game but we had a debt to him to make sure we got to Portugal so that he might at least have the chance to play there.

It was reported that Rio had sent a text asking us not to strike for his sake but to my knowledge that wasn't the case. I certainly didn't receive it or hear of it. He did send a text to some of the lads on the Thursday morning, when it had been decided we would go and play wishing us good luck and urging us to get a result. Rio was happy with the way the situation had been resolved partly because had we gone on strike he would have been the reason for a national scandal. No one wants that responsibility.

Everyone was predicting that the shambles which had characterized the preparation would have negative consequences on the pitch. In fact it had the opposite effect: the atmosphere at training the day before the match was intense; you could tell there was a sense of injustice felt by every player as the tackles flew in. The practice match was as competitive as I have ever seen it. F*** them. F*** them all, was the attitude we adapted. We would get a result to spite everyone who doubted us, everyone who slagged us off or questioned our loyalty to our country. Of course, against Turkey that is exactly the kind of fighting spirit which is going to make a difference. Their fans are hostile, their players adept at winding you up, but in our frame of mind we could match any such aggravation with a siege mentality that Jose Mourinho would have been proud of.

Becks missed a penalty but unlike his left foot, it didn't feel like anything had slipped away from us. JT came in for Rio and played brilliantly, blocking everything and anything in the way only John can. Emile Heskey got involved in a ruck going down the tunnel at half-time after being racially abused – I didn't see the fight but got there in time to be told that Emile had laid out one of the Turkey lads. Nice one.

I had never been involved in a team which qualified for the finals of a tournament and even though I only came on late as a sub, it was a fantastic feeling. All of the anger, anxiety, and bitterness which had built up over the previous days evaporated the moment the final whistle went. We'd won the group and were jubilant – we were going to Portugal. I wondered what Rio was doing at that moment and what he thought.

I have since spoken with him about all of this and he explained to me what happened the day he missed the test. I also know what he subsequently suffered through the months of the ban when he couldn't play. People don't know how hard that was for him, how lonely he was. It's the worst feeling in the world, training all week and knowing there will be no game at the weekend. I have only experienced this when coming back from injury and it's torture. Rio could have gone off on a world tour, or gone off the rails, or just gone off football. He deserves great credit for the way he trained so hard all those months and for the manner in which he returned to play. Rio has endured much scrutiny and expectation from a very young age because of his phenomenal talent and it has meant that every little aspect of his fitness, form, and the like is analysed as if it was some issue of national importance. That was the time of his greatest trouble and he survived – now he is prospering.

When I heard he had been hit with an eight-month ban I was angry. It was stated that a missed test is treated the same as a positive one but that is ridiculous. There was no proof to convict Rio of anything except being forgetful and I can vouch for his bad memory. When you consider that Mark Bosnich got fourteen months and Mutu ten months having admitted taking cocaine, Rio's treatment is a scandal by comparison. The rules say that people found guilty can be banned for life. If they are guilty then why are they not banned for life? I don't understand – surely drastic punishment is the only way to prevent more cases arising?

Then again, proper testing would help resolve the problem. I know how these drug tests are conducted and they can be a complete shambles. When I had tests at West Ham and in my early Chelsea days, you were nominated to give a sample after training, but when you go and have a shower it's entirely plausible that people could forget and leave without completing the task. The procedure has been tightened up a little now after Rio's case but I've heard stories about players missing a test on purpose, with their club or team-mates covering for them. No names were mentioned but the method was always the same. If these reports are true, it's clearly possible to miss a test on purpose and if so, then it's surely possible to miss one by accident. It's the responsibility of the people who conduct the test to make sure it's carried out – it's their job; ours is to play football.

Had Rio refused to take the test and left the training ground having made that clear then he would have been guilty of avoiding the test but that was not the case. From my experience the whole programme – not the tests carried out by individual clubs but the official ones done by the football authorities – is very unprofessional and often sloppy. The tests are not carried out frequently enough, nor is there any consistency. I appreciate that the element of surprise is necessary but the structure as it stands is ineffective in terms of properly policing the game. There is a randomness which borders on negligence – a player could be tested twice in one month or only once in three years. Surely every player should be tested at least once a month or even more? Also, the tests should be conducted with more regulation such as, for example, a player being taken to a specific area after training and only being allowed to leave after the sample has been produced. I would happily be tested every week or every day if it meant reassuring people that football is clean. It would also help prevent stupid stories and gossip spreading about players taking drugs.

One such episode involved me when some kid who played at Cardiff claimed that five Premiership players were using drugs. He predictably sold his story to a paper, which printed the allegations without naming the players, despite also claiming to be 'a friend' of those involved. After a couple of days rumours were rife that I was one of the footballers accused. This guy claimed that he had been on a night out with me and a few others and caught us doing drugs in the toilet. What utter bollocks. I rang one of the other players who was supposed to have been involved and he told me that the guy making the accusations was someone Rio knew from way back and who tagged along on a couple of nights out with us. I vaguely remembered the geezer but had never even spoken to him. What he had alleged wasn't just scandalous – it was potentially very damaging and totally fabricated. Since then there have been other rumours about me and other players doing drugs but the truth is that people just make this stuff up to try and make money or make themselves look important. I was even told that some website claimed I was gay. Elen will be shocked, not to mention Luna.

It's not just the individuals peddling this crap who are to blame. There comes a time when we have to examine ourselves and a society that encourages people to manufacture malicious stories about footballers or anyone else in the public eye in order to make money. There was a case when Cristiano Ronaldo was accused of rape in a newspaper and interrogated by police only for the story to be exposed as complete rubbish about a month later. An accusation of a sexual crime can be as damaging to someone's character as a conviction yet there was no evidence to suggest that in this case there had been any wrongdoing whatsoever. Ronaldo has to live with that accusation for life but what happened to the person who made up the story in the first place? Nothing except receiving money for telling lies.

Newspapers encourage this behaviour by offering money to people for 'kiss and tell' stories or even worse. I know that some stories published are true but others are just plain lies. I have always taken a keen interest in the media and how it works in all aspects. As a footballer, though, you develop a thick skin about some of the things that are written. It's flattering and satisfying to be praised in print but there are other articles which require a much more pragmatic approach. Personal criticism, team criticism and general gossip written about the club and the manager are all things which you learn to live with and mostly ignore. Some players do this by just not reading the papers at all. It's fair to say that I'm the opposite.

I regularly read a variety of newspapers, taking in what is of interest to me in both the front and back. At the start of the 2003/04 season, it seemed that Chelsea and Mr Abramovich were making an impressive takeover bid for column inches. Stories on transfers began to calm down to an average of around just five a day and the focus had shifted to the manager. We were used to this coverage by that time and Ranieri decided not to make a big deal of it. He made the odd joke in press conferences but had ignored the speculation in dealing with the players.

However, as the new season approached, more and more articles began to appear about the possibility of Sven-Goran Eriksson taking over at Chelsea. It was one story which refused to go away and, generally speaking, that alone seemed to give it a measure of credibility. I spoke about it a bit with JT, Eidur, and Jody but we were all long in the tooth enough to know that there was nothing we could do so just had to get our heads down and get on with it.

Things changed on the morning that pictures were published of Eriksson arriving at Mr Abramovich's house with the well-known agent Pini Zahavi. It had transpired that Zahavi had played a part in putting the Chelsea buy out deal together (he is also Rio's personal agent, hence the voicemail by the pool in Vegas) so now we knew there was substance to the Eriksson story. I arrived for training wondering what to expect.

Ranieri was already at Harlington and passed me at the entrance to the changing room. 'Good morning Frank!' The greeting was very normal though there was a slight quiver in his voice. I did my best to ignore it but I could sense the strange atmosphere around the place. We tried to carry on with training in the normal fashion and when it was concluded, Ranieri made sure that everyone would be upstairs for lunch after changing. I walked up the four flights of stairs with legs as heavy as if I had completed a ten-mile run. Once we were all seated Ranieri stood at the front of our tables and there was a sudden and eerie silence. This was it.

'I know what you are thinking,' he began. 'And I don't blame you after what you will have seen and read. All that I can tell you is that I have spoken with the owner and he has told me that I have a job here. He has told me that this is my team and what he expects of me and you this season.

'I am telling you that this is my job and you are my team. Let's ignore the things on the outside and concentrate on what we know and who we know. We are Chelsea – you and me, all of us. Let's remember that and do our jobs.'

I was half tempted to clap him but it didn't seem quite appropriate. They were brave words – words he would repeat throughout the season, not because he wanted to reassure us but because he felt he had to. Even after Eriksson was forced to admit the fact of the meeting with Abramovich and reaffirm his commitment to the England job, it did not remove the axe which hovered above Ranieri's head. He was, as he would very succinctly put it later on, 'a dead man walking'.

I had a lot of sympathy for Ranieri because of what he had helped me achieve in terms of my game and my career. I knew that a new owner of any business will naturally want to install his own man to run that concern but there was a bond between Ranieri and the players. I spoke to JT and Eidur about it and we agreed that we should continue to show the same loyalty to the manager that he had always shown us. Whenever we were asked in the media about Ranieri we supported him and reiterated our feeling that he was the right man to manage Chelsea. It's what we believed in our hearts and minds and I think that unity shone through that season.

We qualified for the group stage of the Champions League with ease but the experience had gone sour when we arrived in Prague to play Sparta in the opening match. The game itself was not the problem – it was what had happened well before kick-off in the team hotel. Ranieri announced the starting line-up and to my amazement, John, Eidur, and me were all on the bench. At first I thought there must have been a mistake or maybe it was a joke. For one of us to have been dropped would have been disappointing, two would have been serious, but three was surely taking the piss. Our places were taken by the new boys – the children of the revolution as it were – seven in all, as the old guard gave way.

I stormed out of the meeting room, closely followed by John and Eidur. 'F*** this,' I said, 'I worked my arse off last season to get this club into the Champions League – we all did – and I'm sure as hell not going to park it on the bench while the newcomers get to play. I was livid – as angry as I have ever been about a team selection. I went to my room and telephoned Elen.

'I've been dropped, babe,' I said, still seething.

'What?'

'I'm not kidding. I'm on the bench – and so are Eidur and John.'

'Calm down, Frank. What's going on?'

'I'll tell you what's going on – I could be leaving Chelsea because there's no way I'm spending a season on the bench to accommodate anyone else at the club.'

'Frank, calm down. Let's see what happens in the game and we'll talk when you get home.'

She was right but I was too steamed up to see it. I went to Eidur's room to try to find an answer, but the only one apparent was that the new players had been bought to replace us.

'I wish the f***ing revolution had never started,' I said, exasperated.

'I would happily take the old days now. At least we got a game,' replied Eidur.

Usually when you put me together with my mates Eidur and John, we'll share a joke and have a laugh but that night the bench was more like hell on earth – full of despair and loathing. On the pitch the team struggled, and I can't say I was disappointed. Ranieri told me to get stripped at the break and I came on for the second half, as we went on to achieve a 1–0 victory. John and Eidur remained on the bench.

We still talk about that night – although it proved to be a one-off – not because any of us believe we have a divine right to be in the team but because we had all worked so hard to get the club to that level of competition that we thought we had earned a chance to carry the team further.

We didn't encounter the same trauma in domestic competition where all of us played a major role in getting the team off to a good start in the Premiership with six wins and one draw in our first seven games. We then travelled to play a game in hand against Birmingham City knowing that a win would take us to the top of the league. It ended a draw but, ironically, we still went ahead on goal difference despite the fact we hadn't actually scored that night. I went for a warm-down feeling less elated than you might think given that we were leading the title race. I felt worse when I read Ranieri's feelings on the achievement.

'Top of the league is not important,' he told the papers. 'Maybe we can be a little bit pleased but not much.' It was typical Claudio – failing to accentuate the positive and praising performance rather than what was gleaned from it. That was his way and we were used to it but once again I wondered if this was the right way to go about winning a league title.

We played Arsenal the following weekend and while the lads were up for it the result went against us – again. We had enjoyed our lofty status for a whole four days and would not get to know the feeling again as Arsene Wenger's side embarked upon one of the most amazing feats in English football history in claiming the title without losing a match. We never gave up on the Premiership, though, and had other irons in the fire. Peter Kenyon had been poached from Manchester United to become chief executive and immediately warned us that we were expected to win at least one trophy. So far, we were going well in two, with the FA Cup still to come.

The Champions League was becoming something of an adventure for us. We were steely to beat Sparta Prague before everyone predicted more European embarrassment after Besiktas came to our place and scored twice. It was a warning we heeded. I scored home and away against Lazio and we found a rhythm in Europe which I had never known before. We qualified comfortably for the knockout round where we defeated VfB Stuttgart over two legs by scoring the only goal of the tie in Germany.

When we were on the pitch I could look around me and feel a genuine sense of optimism about the team. We had quality in every position and were delivering a level of consistency in results which we hadn't managed in my time at the club. Franco Zola was a joy to play with and we had a few big characters in the team who knew what it took to win major trophies. My only worry was that I remained to be convinced that we would. A lot of players had arrived and some had fitted in better than others but there still seemed to me to be a disparity about the squad which somehow didn't suggest that we could achieve something special. Chelsea had a reputation for recruiting players who were individual talents rather than building a cohesive team. Some people will blame the manager for that but I honestly don't think he was solely responsible. You can only sign the people you think will benefit the club as a whole and some of the players who arrived were only interested in themselves once they got there.

For all that, we were more together than I had ever known and when we discovered we would play Arsenal in the quarter-final of the Champions League the whole country went mad. They were, of course, still unbeaten and in fact had eliminated us from the FA Cup as well as inflicting another league defeat at the Bridge three weeks before we were due to meet in Europe. It was billed as 'The Battle of Britain' in the media and to us it was a contest we desperately wanted to win – for ourselves, for the manager, and for Chelsea. Britain could wait – this was about pride and the chance to get to a European Cup semi-final for the first time in our history.

It was also becoming a bit of a crusade on our behalf for Ranieri. Speculation about his position had intensified regardless of results and I could see it beginning to have an effect on his demeanor. I wasn't surprised. Given the immense pressure he'd been under it would have been hard for anyone to remain unchanged. Throughout that season he had periodically repeated his speech about his commitment to the job. When he sensed we needed reassurance he would kick in with a pledge that he was here to stay. He wasn't the only one under pressure but he always accepted responsibility for what happened on the pitch.

It seemed that ever since Roman Abramovich committed his first million to the club we had spent each day under the public microscope. Everything had been questioned: from our ability to what we earned, from our character to the record of our manager. We had answered some of the questions but now we had the chance to silence everyone, a chance to beat the invincibles.

The players were as pumped up as the fans for the match and Raneiri was as determined as any of us. Predictable stories of 'win or you're out' had appeared in the build-up and while he didn't feel the need to deny them, something fundamental shifted in his resistance. It was barely evident but certainly detectable – not so much what he said as the way he said it. His mood, and the vibe about what was going on, changed. He hadn't surrendered – no way – but he was more resigned than ever to the fact that every game in which he was in charge of Chelsea was one closer to the day he would leave. I asked Eidur and JT if they were sensing the same thing and we knew then that this would be our last big push for Claudio Ranieri.

The Bridge was alight with excitement as we kicked off against Arsenal but we couldn't deliver the victory we and the fans craved. Eidur put us ahead but the lead didn't last long when Robert Pires equalized. To add insult, Marcel was sent off in the closing minutes and suspended for the return leg. It was hardly a disaster but everyone outside of our team seemed to think that victory was now a formality for Arsenal at Highbury. Given how they had been playing, I suppose that was an easy conclusion to draw. Mr Abramovich paid his now customary visit to the dressing room after the game. He was very upbeat, told everyone how well they'd played, and that he knew we would do well in the second leg. I was grateful for his enthusiasm. We then thrashed Wolves and had a morale-boosting win over Spurs before the return Arsenal game and when the day of reckoning arrived we were more than ready.

Ranieri addressed us with an unprecedented degree of passion. He emphasized what we might achieve if we could put Arsenal out of the competition, that we had a chance to make history – a chance that doesn't come along too often. His Roman ancestors would have been proud of him because we walked into that arena like gladiators prepared to fight to the death.

It was just as well, since the tempo of the match would have caused some people to drop. It was as fierce a battle as I had known though we held our own in midfield and were a bit unlucky when Jose Antonio Reyes gave them the lead. Within six minutes we were level though I was so focused on victory, celebrating my goal wasn't a priority. Extra-time seemed a certainty but the manager had come to the touch-line and urged us to double up on the flanks and get in behind them. Arsenal had a habit of allowing their full-backs freedom to get forward and we had discussed negating that with runs of our own. With three minutes left, Wayne Bridge found himself running diagonally at the Arsenal goal. I was following on behind, hoping for a cut back. He left Lauren behind and ran towards the box. I could see a couple of blue shirts arriving in front of me. 'Pass it Bridgey, Pass it!' He didn't pass, nor did he cut it back to the edge of the area – he just drove it into the net all on his own. Bridgey, you beauty. We went wild – piled on top of each other with our new hotshot at the centre of it. When I looked round I saw the coaching staff embracing each other. We didn't have to wait too long to do the same.

I walked towards the tunnel feeling overjoyed and exhausted. Our fans were celebrating one of the most important wins in our history and you would have needed a surgeon to take the smile off my face. Then I saw Ranieri: he was on the pitch greeting us as we headed for the dressing room. He was laughing – I think – but the strain was showing more than ever. He hugged me.

'We did it Frank! We did it! Fantastic! Fantastic!' he said.

I drew back and looked him square in the face and that's when I knew for sure it was over. A single tear ran down his cheek as he held my arms. He was happy but he wasn't crying from joy. His tears were for a part of his life that was coming to an end, for the effort he had expended and the knowledge that no matter how hard he tried he would not be allowed to finish the job he started.

We went on to play AS Monaco in the semi-final. Rumours were rife that Kenyon had already met with Jose Mourinho and Didier Deschamps about replacing Ranieri the following season. Mourinho was also in the semi-final where his Porto side would play Deportivo La Coruna while Deschamps – a former Chelsea player – was in charge of our opponents. Our current coach deserved a lot of credit for the fastidious manner in which he kept on doing his job. No amount of pressure or gossip could distract him from guiding the club to a potentially historic climax that season.

We arrived in Monte Carlo for the first leg and during a walk along the marina we saw Mr Abramovich's boat which was moored in the harbour. Even by the standard of the 'monsters' worth millions which are a familiar sight in Monaco, his vessel was impressive. In fact, it made the others look like tugs compared to a luxury cruise ship. It was quite a sight and brought home to us just how powerful a man Mr Abramovich is. We were aware of the pressure mounting on Ranieri but whatever was to happen to the manager none of us looked at Roman as the bad guy – in fact he was Chelsea's saviour. We knew how close we had come to going bust and the truth is that without Roman Abramovich the club might not have been in existence, never mind competing in the semi-final of the European Cup. The new owner had inherited the players and the manager. He wasn't responsible for us being there but it was his prerogative as to what to do next. Hopefully, winning the Champions League might convince him we were worth our wages!

What happened the following night, however, left us all shocked and very much down and out. We started well and were pretty much in control of the match. Even when they scored Crespo pulled one back and we looked balanced and able to cope with whatever was thrown at us – everything, that is, from Monaco. The origin of our downfall was our own dressing room and it started at the break.

'Seba! Get stripped and warm up. You're going on,' Ranieri said to Veron.

'But boss. I'm not ready to play. I'm not fit enough,' came the reply.

Those of us who heard this exchange were dumbstruck. Veron had been carrying a slight injury but was fit enough for the bench and never made any complaint when he was named among the subs. It was a bit late, therefore, to be protesting.

'Seba! Get stripped. You're going on for Jesper.'

I turned to Eidur who looked at me in dismay. Jesper hadn't been amazing in the first half but he was having one of those games where he had the beating of his man. Besides, who would go wide left? Apparently Veron.

We returned to the pitch in a state of disarray. None of us could understand what was going on. We had been comfortable but now we had a man on the pitch who wasn't fit in his mind even if he was in body. It got better when Andreas Zikos was sent off but it quickly got worse again, shambolic actually. Jimmy was brought on for Mario Melchiot and Scotty Parker was sent to right-back. Jimmy jogged over to his position shrugging his shoulders as I asked him what was going on. A few minutes later, Scotty was dragged off for Robert Huth and I had a bad feeling that it was all going pear-shaped. I wasn't wrong.

We could have nailed that match. We were 1–1 – with an away goal – and they had only ten men. We were twenty minutes away from having one foot in the final. Instead we lost 3–1 and no one knew how. Apart from the boots being discarded, the dressing room was very quiet. I sat in a daze. Jimmy was the first to speak.

'What the f*** happened there?' he said.

No one spoke because we were all asking ourselves the same question. Perhaps Ranieri had an answer but if he did, he didn't volunteer it. He later confessed that it was his worst forty-five minutes in charge of Chelsea. That was obvious. He was known as the 'Tinker Man' but that was the most tinkering he had ever done while I was at the club.

It was also the most bizarre match I've ever played in and because it was so unusual people began to ask if the manager had deliberately sabotaged the team as some kind of advance revenge for his impending departure. I can't provide an explanation even now but I would hate to think that was the case. It was not in his character to be so devious or destructive with his own team. Claudio was also a man of great integrity who took pride in his work – the idea that he would undermine it was unthinkable.

The second leg became a formality. I don't think we had recovered from what happened in the first game and despite scoring twice we managed to concede two and Monaco went through to the final. The remaining couple of weeks of the season is a blur. Ranieri was given a hero's send-off at the Bridge on the last day and despite telling the fans he hoped to see them again he knew that when he did he would not be Chelsea manager. It would have been nice if he could have said goodbye to the players face to face but instead it ended with a phone call because the season had finished and most of us were already with international sides preparing for Euro 2004.

I am very grateful to Ranieri for what he did for me: for having the faith to spend £11 million to sign me; for taking me under his guidance and making me a better player; for taking Chelsea to the brink of success without actually tasting it himself. A few days after the final Premiership match I turned on the TV and watched the Champions League Final. I was curious. I am sure that we would have won it that year had we beaten Monaco but I was impressed with the way Porto destroyed the team which put us out.

At the end, I watched the players celebrate in front of delirious fans and saw Jose Mourinho accept his medal and then leave the pitch to allow his team to take the plaudits. He had just won the biggest prize in club football but he had the look of a man who was already hungry for more success.

CHAPTER 8

EURO 2004

ALL my life I have dreamt about football. When I was a child, I dreamt of playing for West Ham, of scoring the winning goal in the FA Cup Final. I have dreamt of games when everything I touched turned to gold. I have played in games which have turned into my worst nightmare.

Football and the dreams of those involved are bizarrely similar. Whether you are a player, manager or fan we all have fantasies about what might happen during a game. Occasionally, we are lucky enough to experience a moment in football which we thought was only likely to happen in sleep.

Mine happened on Sunday 13 June 2004. To be more precise, it came in the balmy evening heat of Lisbon's Estadio da Luz in the closing minutes of England's opening fixture of the European Championship finals. The image remains crystal clear in my mind despite the fact that it lasted only a few seconds.

There was a lull in play – a player down I think, though I can't be sure. Zinedine Zidane was shouting behind me in

French. I couldn't understand the words but I heard the panic in his voice when my attention was drawn to the huge scoreboard above the imposing stand on my right. And there it was – FRANCE 0 . . . ENGLAND 1 . . . Lampard 38 – my name in lights. Get in there! I allowed myself to absorb the moment, before the action resumed and I went about defending our lead with only two minutes left of my tournament debut for England. A few hours later I was lying in bed, struggling to come to terms with our defeat.

I kept replaying in my head the chances we had to finish it off, like some torture video: a couple of half chances I could have done better on, Rooney one-on-one with Fabien Barthez, Becks' missed penalty. Then came Zidane's free-kick to equalize, and Stevie G's pass back to the keeper when Thierry Henry bolted from nowhere to win the penalty that sealed our defeat. I rewound to the eighty-eighth minute and the scoreboard which said that I had scored the winning goal against France. At that moment I was a national hero. After what happened next, no one will even remember that I scored. I felt desperate – full of anger about the result mixed with self-pity that I'd been deprived of a little bit of glory. So much for the dream. I couldn't get to sleep for thinking about it.

The France game was the beginning of the adventure, though, not the end. It had been a hectic few weeks leading up to Euro 2004 and one question persisted in the press and for that matter in the minds of the public about the team which would start the championship: Lampard or Butt in midfield? The rest of the team was sorted, players picked, and names on shirts. The public perception, however, didn't actually match the reality.

While the nation debated the relative values of who was best placed to fill the second spot in the centre of the park, Sven-Goran Eriksson had taken me aside a few weeks earlier to clarify his thoughts.

'I know people will talk about whether you will start in Portugal or not,' he said. 'I am telling you now that you will play with Steven Gerrard. I think it's important that you prepare yourself for that.'

'Okay boss. I will, don't worry,' I replied before the information had in fact registered.

'Let people talk about it all they like but let's keep this conversation between us until we get to the tournament.'

It was good of him to volunteer it like that. He didn't have to but I was pleased he had. After the sickness and despair I felt when he called to tell me I wasn't in the World Cup squad two years before, I'd finally found the antidote. Along with the excitement I felt some sympathy for Butty. He was chosen as one of the best midfielders of the 2002 World Cup but on a positive note it was proof of just how far I had progressed in the interim. Having cleared the issue up, I could look forward to the finals and anticipate my first tournament with England, not that it would be exciting or anything – the opening match was only against France. I focused on that game as soon as the club season ended.

Some of the others were able to be much more relaxed during the week we had in Sardinia with our families before travelling to Portugal. It was a nice environment and it was the first time Elen and I had been involved in that kind of pro-longed get-together. But even when we were in the most laid-back situation – having a meal one evening with David and Victoria Beckham for example – I still found my mind was on what lay ahead. Maybe it was the fact that I genuinely didn't know what to expect. Playing in the Champions League and even the qualifying ties for the European Championships is a very different proposition to playing in the finals of a major tournament. This was confirmed the moment we stepped off the plane in Lisbon. We were greeted by an official party dressed in national costume with schoolkids excitedly singing and cheering. Everywhere I looked there were tournament logos and people dressed in the Euro 2004 uniform. For a few minutes the whole experience was slightly surreal and I almost had to pinch myself. There was a constant stream of people in football kit waving to us on the coach ride from the airport to the hotel. When I got to my room I instinctively turned on the TV. I found a UK news channel and saw the streets of every city in the England choked with cars flying flags and passing houses which were decked out in red and white. It struck me that this was it – this was what it was like to carry the hopes of the nation.

The atmosphere continued to build but rather than feel nervous I realized I was feeding off it. Training was hard in the sunshine but we were housed in the ornate surroundings of the old Stadium of Light which generated an atmosphere all of its own. As each day passed I felt more and more confident. This was where I wanted to be. This was where I belonged.

I couldn't have been in any better shape physically or mentally. Everyone knew what was expected and the fact that we were facing the defending champions in the first game made us keener. The only injury doubt was JT. He had picked up a thigh strain about a week before which had been niggling away at him. By Wednesday he was running out of time to be fit. That night we sat and spoke about what might happen.

John and I are very similar in that we always want to play, to train, to be involved. Even if we are injured or tired the instinct within both of us is always to get on the pitch if it's at all possible and even when it's probably not. It's a bit of standing joke at Chelsea with John. He'll limp in after training on a Thursday, clearly struggling for the weekend match.

'What's up JT?' someone will ask him anxiously.

'F*** it. My ankle's in bits,' comes the honest reply.

And he means it. Yet in spite of the pain he goes out and gives everything for ninety minutes two days later. That's JT for you. We had both come a long way that season – maybe not as far as we had wanted with Chelsea – but in three days' time we would play for England at Euro 2004. John was confident his leg would be okay.

'I can feel it a bit but with a bit more treatment I'll be fine,' he said.

'Yeah. I know you. You'd play on one leg if you had to.'

'Not sure if that'll work against Henry though, geezer.'

I was confident that a one-legged JT against France's best striker would be good enough. The next morning he was kicking the ball with both feet but was still unable to train fully. We both were aware of Eriksson's unwritten law that a player who can't train two days before a match won't be considered. By Thursday evening the muscle had seized up a bit. John called my room.

'I'm not going to make it for Sunday,' he said.

'What? You okay?'

'Yeah. I saw the doc and he said if I risk it now I could be out for the tournament. Ledley [King] is in I reckon.'

I was gutted for him. I knew this meant as much to him as it did to me. Ledley is a great player but with Rio missing because of his ban for the missed drugs test, this was JT's chance to show he was first choice for England.

Mr Eriksson called a team meeting and told us who would line up. Ledley was in sure enough and there was a tingle in my spine when I heard him say my name. Paul Scholes was to play on the left of midfield and Rooney and Owen up front. En route to the stadium I have never felt so nervous. I sat there smiling as the banter flew around but I was very aware that we were about to play arguably the best team at the tournament.

I visualized their line-up. Zidane had been my favourite player for five years or more but I had never had the opportunity to face him. Now was my chance, as well as having to deal with Vieira, Pires, Henry running in from the left. How would I cope? There was pressure on me because it was my first game in a finals. As usual, I decided to add some of my own pressure just for good measure. I wanted to repay the manager for having faith. When I ran out for the warm-up and heard the roar of thousands of supporters I thought about them as well. And then there was the fact that if I didn't perform there would be calls for Butt to be restored to the team for the next match. I wanted to prove to myself and everyone else that I was the right man to be there.

I was confident in myself and from the kick-off I felt comfortable – a comfort which extended right through the team as soon as Wayne Rooney – 'Wazza' to his team-mates – started to get on the ball. It was then I realized what an unbelievable talent he is. Immediately he was making play – laying the ball off, smashing passes diagonally across the field. I'd seen him do it in training, and in other matches where there was nowhere near the same pressure. But here? Against France? He was incredible as was his run when he left Mikael Silvestre for dead and won a penalty. But Rooney isn't just about pace – it's pace and raw power combined which make him so formidable. And then there's the talent. Looks can be deceptive and they certainly are in Wazza's case. With his build he looks a bit of a bruiser but he has the touch of an angel with a football. At 18, you wonder if a player can make all of those qualities work at once but it comes naturally to him. His awareness was as good then as any seasoned pro, and he's scared of nothing.

I remember before the game I was busy with my stretches and normal routine. No one was dressed. I looked up at Wayne and he was already in his full kit. He couldn't wait to pull on the jersey. He was flicking the ball around, banging it off the walls and having a laugh – no nerves, no fear.

He reminds me a bit of Teddy Sheringham in his ability to hold possession before dinking the cute pass in behind the defence. Almost every time I received a ball in a good position in that tournament it seemed to be from Wazz. He is incredible and even then there was a palpable sense that he was becoming a very important player for us.

I was ordinary by comparison. I was doing okay, nothing amazing, though as a team we were dominating possession and France had rarely caused us a problem. When the free-kick was given on the right flank after thirty-eight minutes I moved into position, hoping to latch on to a rebound or clearance. Dad always told me to go into the box on those occasions with a conviction that I was going to score. My experience told me I had a much better chance of a goal if I was actually taking the kick. My heading is not the best part of my game – it should be better but I see it as my weakest point. I held back from the line of players closest to the goal and waited for the delivery. In

2005, Chelsea recruited Thierry Laurent who is one of the physios with the French national team and he was on the bench that day in Lisbon. He has told me subsequently that Marcel Desailly – who was also on the bench – started shouting, 'Pick Lampard up, somebody run with Lampard,' as Barthez was organizing his defence. Marcel knew that I liked getting on the end of things but I'm sure he wasn't worried that I would head the ball into the top corner because that's something I never do – at least, not until then. I caught it well but lost sight of the ball momentarily until I hit the ground and saw it fly into the net. I don't remember much of what happened in the following couple of minutes except an elation which was new to me and which I would not experience again until the end of the following season when I scored the goals which clinched the Premiership for Chelsea at Bolton.

We got the break and we knew we were on top of the game. The manager acknowledged it and encouraged us to continue in the same way but warned us not to lose concentration – just keep the ball and feed it to Wazza and we would make more chances. He was right. What followed, however, was one of the classic 'if only' cases in recent English football history. I felt sorry for Beckham when he missed the penalty – especially as I am a penalty taker for club and country now. He caught it cleanly enough but Barthez went the right way. Maybe because they had played together for a few years at Manchester United he was able to guess right, but it was horrible for us. It's a daunting task and a huge responsibility to take on. The disappointment of missing is momentary though, because the demands of the game are so immediate.

However, in the context of the match at that point, I honestly didn't feel it made a huge difference. I looked around me and I saw a France team which had virtually given up. You can see it in players' eyes when they don't believe a game will turn – the resignation and desperation. It was obvious in their play as well. How often do France resort to hitting the ball long? Yet that's what they were doing for the last fifteen minutes of the game. We were dominating. Sol Campbell and Ledley King were clearing up everything and they weren't threatening us until the contest slipped into time added on and I saw Zidane standing over the free-kick. Trouble. Then Henry's run and the penalty. Zidane again. More trouble.

I got off the pitch as quickly as I could. There was a shocked silence in our dressing room which was only disturbed by the jubilant chanting coming from across the corridor: 'Allez les Bleus, Allez les Bleus.' Smug bastards. The only thing worse than losing is losing in the last minute. We didn't deserve the defeat, we really didn't. Steve McClaren and Sammy Lee were the first to speak. We had outplayed the champions for ninety minutes. There was nothing to be ashamed of. They were right, but the fact was we were now under pressure to qualify for the next stage. One game down, and we had to beat Switzerland and Croatia.

I woke up the next morning hardly having slept. The nausea from the defeat was still there in my stomach and at breakfast the coaching staff made a real effort to lift spirits. We had a 'warm-down' at the hotel, combining the gym, the jacuzzi, and then ice baths. In the afternoon we lay around in the sun with our families and the world began to look a bit brighter. Elen was very positive. She has learnt about football very quickly in the time we have been together and apart from her annoying habit of asking me why I'm not as good as Ronaldinho, she reads the game pretty well. She's developed a real bond with Alex Curran (Stevie Gerrard's partner) and Coleen McLoughlin (Wayne Rooney's fiancée) and some of the other girls, which began when they were out in Portugal. The friendship between the partners helps the whole spirit of the team though it also made our eventual elimination a bit harder as Elen was just as upset as I was because she wouldn't be spending another week in the sun with her new mates! She was even blaming me for not doing more to make sure we stayed in the tournament. Cheers darling.

We watched the France game on video and found grounds for optimism in the way we played. We put the defeat out of our mind and travelled to Coimbra for the match against Switzerland in good spirits. We were very aware that only victory would be enough to keep qualification in our own hands. However, the midfield had an added worry. In training we had been experimenting with a diamond formation now and again and it was something which Eriksson had mentioned as a possible variation. I was sceptical about it because I was positioned at the base, in front of the defence, with Gerrard and Beckham either side and Scholes at the opposite point. I felt strongly that it wasn't the best use of my skills and I knew the other lads – with the exception of Scholesy – were not wild about it either.

The day before the game we trained in the stadium. Eriksson always plays the team who will start the match against the 'reserves' in the final practice match and to our surprise he set us out in the diamond. At first I thought: 'Okay, there's obviously a good reason so let's just go with it.' After the first three goals went in against us and we were getting pumped in midfield I rapidly changed my mind. I was frustrated and could see I wasn't the only one. We were being passed around with ease. It wasn't working. The manager also spotted it: he must have. I'm not sure if Becks had a word with him privately after training but what happened that evening has since become infamous as the night 'player power' took over England. I have to say that what actually happened wasn't quite so dramatic.

After dinner Eriksson invited the four midfielders to a meeting with him. I was surprised, and wondered what was going on. We went to a private room and sat down.

'How do you see the diamond? Is it working?' he asked all of us at once.

I wasn't sure how to react. It felt like being back at school and sitting in front of the headmaster as he asked me to explain my picture in the paper when I had bunked off school to play for West Ham youths. I glanced either side of me at the lads who were more experienced. Our silence and shrugged shoulders said enough.

'Okay. Well, how do you want to play? What would make you feel more comfortable?'

I was astonished, as were the others. I could hardly believe that the England manager was asking us how we wanted to play in a game which could decide the team's fate in the competition. I respected Eriksson for it but this wasn't how I imagined it would be. Becks was first to speak.

'I think we would feel more comfortable with a flat four boss,' he said.

Stevie G agreed: 'I'm okay with the diamond but I'd prefer a flat four. I'm happy to play on the left side of it as well, if you think that'll work.'

I felt bold enough to add my voice. 'I would be happier in a flat four boss.'

Eriksson sat and listened. The whole conversation didn't last much more than fifteen minutes during which time we discussed the options. It's not as if we were novices in the game who didn't know any better. I have played in a diamond for club and country and it can work but when you have a player on each wing it adds a dimension to the game plan which is invaluable in both attack and defence – width. Furthermore, Rooney is not an out-and-out striker and his game often sees him drift in behind Owen where he would end up running into Scholes if he was playing at the point of a diamond. Apart from that, we didn't have a natural holding player for the base and that had the potential to cause confusion.

Scholesy was the only one who disagreed. He said he would prefer the diamond and we understood his argument but he didn't moan or argue about the prospect of reverting to a line of four. He wanted the best for the team as we all did and he agreed that if the rest of us would be more comfortable that way then so be it. Eriksson nodded his head and with that the formation changed.

The press predicted a diamond formation in the morning papers though word filtered out before the afternoon kick-off that we might have changed the shape. It seemed to cause a lot of controversy which I didn't think was justified. The manager was simply aware that the team might perform better with different tactics and so changed it in consultation with his players. I have been asked by Jose Mourinho about how I see a particular game and the way we should address it and I know he takes on board my thoughts before forming his plan. It's not as unusual as some people might think.

Ironically, this turned out to be my worst game in the tournament. There were a few times in the first half when I gave away possession but once Wazza knocked in his two goals it became easy enough. The performance saw the Rooney bandwagon go into overdrive and he fully deserved the credit. For someone so young he had an unusually strong influence in the squad and it wasn't just confined to the pitch.

Wazza was named after Gazza for good reason. He possesses similar God-given football talent and the ability to turn games all on his own, but he also has a personality which is able to relate to everyone with the same warmth and wicked humour. There were no cliques in that England squad but people by nature hang out with those they know best. For that reason the lads from each club would often sit around and chat or play pool. Wazza, however, would effortlessly glide from Chelsea to Liverpool and Arsenal and everywhere else in between. He got on brilliantly with everyone and became the focal point of each group he joined. He's also a bit like JT in that he's never content to put his feet up and relax. He always needs to be doing something, whether it's exercise, computer games or whatever. He was a bit like a little kid – constantly having a laugh, and even when you went to his room he would stand there playing keepy uppy while holding a conversation. I suppose what made all of this more amazing was the fact that in the eyes of the football world Wayne Rooney was making a name for himself as the most exciting young player on the planet. We were certainly aware of it but you wouldn't have known he was from his own demeanor – Wazza was just happy to be one of the lads.

There was a real sense of optimism before the Croatia game which was partly to do with the rise of Rooney but in fact the whole team was gathering momentum. We went into the match brimming with a confidence that not only would we win that game but that we could win the tournament. Of course, every time England take part in a major competition there is a belief that they can claim victory but I can only speak from experience and I wasn't the only one who had faith. JT had come back in against Switzerland which made me very happy. There's a certain comfort from taking club relationships into international matches and I always feel better knowing John is behind me. He's my mate but he's also the best centre-half I've ever played with.

We probably had our best game of the tournament against Croatia partly because we went a goal down. We were marking zonally at set pieces and were having some teething problems. Thankfully we weren't behind for long and I was pleased to put Owen through for the move which saw Scholesy equalize. Everything moved up a gear from there, with Wazza smashing in another couple while I scored with my left foot to round the match off and give ourselves a real boost going into the quarter-finals. We couldn't have asked for more. The level of performance was high and still climbing, and more than ever we allowed ourselves to think that we could go all the way.

Right through the team we were playing well but Owen was yet to score and for some reason attracting criticism. I watched a news slot on TV where someone was suggesting that he be dropped for the next game, and found myself shouting at the screen 'Are you mad?' Everyone in the squad was aware of Michael's 'duck', but far from seeing it as a negative we knew that it meant there was a goal coming very soon. He was born to score goals and no one will deny him his birthright.

We had to wait a day to discover our opponents for the quarter-final though we expected it would be the host nation.

We weren't disappointed – neither by the draw nor the way we chilled out immediately after qualifying. The partners and families came to visit again and on one of the days we were treated to McDonalds. It was a great shout by the FA. They laid on a whole table of Big Macs and chips and stuff and all of the lads tucked in like it was a feast cooked for a king – all that is, except Phil Neville. I remember diving into the unhealthy stuff and the boyish excitement among the players at getting to break the rules as a reward for doing well. Then I saw Phil on his own by the salad bar with a huge plate of lettuce and vegetables. It was amusing but not surprising. Phil is one of the most dedicated professionals I have ever played with. Even though in that squad he didn't get a lot of playing time, he always prepared himself in the proper way and would encourage all of the lads who were involved in the games. That was typical of the camaraderie in that group.

While life didn't seem like it could get any better, the pressure building up to the Portugal match hit harder than we had anticipated. Until that point we had done well but no better than expected and the tension around the quarter-final centred on the fact that we were now in the elimination phase – lose and you're out. There was no fear as such. I felt more confident about my game than I had ever done in my life and that self-belief ran right through the squad. We were aware of the expectations – we read the papers and saw the news from England and the thousands of people who shared our dream of making this our tournament, our time. In training, everywhere I looked I saw men I could rely on: John and Sol had formed a good partnership; Gary Neville and Ashley Cole were very solid; the midfield fluid; and up front we had the two best strikers at the finals. There was some debate about whether it was good or bad to be facing Portugal but if anything the pressure was more intense for them as host nation.

The Portuguese fans had been very sporting throughout – they had shown no hostility towards us or any other team and that didn't change on the day of the match. Everything was good natured on the way to the stadium and the only worrying aspect was the way I was feeling. I couldn't get out of first gear in the warm-up. It's extremely unusual for me, but some days it happens and there's no real reason for it. But did it have to happen that day of all days? 'I can get through it,' I thought, by forcing myself to sprint and lose the feeling of sluggishness. But it didn't work on this particular occasion. I looked around the vast arena which was already almost full. Both sets of fans were buzzing with expectation. Mum, Dad and Elen were all there, as was the new manager of Chelsea. Mourinho had been to watch England play in the tournament already but this was different. This time he was supporting the opposition, his own nation.

Nerves about the match were intensified by the fact that I didn't feel one hundred per cent, and when the game started I struggled a bit to keep up with the pace. I wasn't panicked, however – I knew that it would change as long as I stuck in there and kept going. My legs felt lighter after three minutes when Michael Owen did exactly what I thought he would – score an important goal. I felt stronger, we all felt stronger, and we managed to silence the very partisan home crowd and get our supporters going.

We never lost the impetus and even when Wazza went down under Jorge Andrade's tackle it didn't feel like it was the end of the world. It's not that I didn't realize what a big loss he would be, but in the heat of a match like that you don't have time to analyse. You have to get on with the game regardless and I was too occupied with trying to stop Portugal playing. Costinha was lying deep and it was hard to get close to him, while Maniche was spraying the ball around with real accuracy. But when I saw the stretcher come on, I realized the injury was serious. Some players go down, leave the pitch for a couple of minutes, and then return. Wayne is not one of them, so I knew pretty much straight away that if he was on a stretcher then he wasn't coming back. In retrospect, you appreciate that a particular moment was pivotal to the outcome of a game, but there was no time to think about it.

Portugal weren't hurting us with their possession but without Wazza our out-ball was less effective. He's great at running with it, stretching the play, and causing problems for the opposition which was exactly what had happened when he won the penalty against France. Without him, we were winning the ball but wasting possession and they were coming back at us much more quickly than we should have allowed.

There were some scary moments but overall we were coping. I was spending most of my time trying to close up space and my legs were getting heavy but we were in the semi-final at that point and I tried to focus on the positive. With a few minutes to go the ball went out and I looked up at the scoreboard and there it was: the dream all over again. Then came the nightmare – again. Helder Postiga headed in from a free-kick with ten minutes to go and the momentum swung back in Portugal's favour. Hold on. We had to hold on. We mustn't concede it like we did against France and as long as we reached extra-time, we still had a chance.

Extra-time was gruelling both physically and mentally. The way we allowed Rui Costa to run at us unchallenged before unleashing the shot that gave them the lead summed up the way we were all feeling. I couldn't believe it. There was a lull in the noise around the stadium which then turned to bedlam.

I wondered what to do. I wanted to scream in anger, to take the ball straight from the kick-off and score. I wanted to cry. One hundred and ten minutes of exhilarating and agonizing football, and it should end like this? I couldn't – and wouldn't – allow it to end like this. I'm no quitter and I knew this England team wouldn't give up.

There were still ten minutes left. We began to force some pressure without really threatening the goal. We won a corner and then another before Becks crossed the ball in and I saw it was going to reach JT. I had a split second to think. John had two options: he could go for goal and with his power had a good chance of scoring, but the box was crowded. He's also very accurate at laying the ball off and I sensed that might be the best option.

I shouted: 'LAMPS!'

John recognized the call and cushioned it across my path. My first touch had to be tight on my left foot otherwise I would have run into a tackle. In fact I had to almost stop it dead so I could swivel and get the shot away. I knew I would score after the first part came off perfectly. The second was sheer instinct and I caught it well.

I didn't see it go in but I heard the roar. It was just as I had imagined. I remember watching England play as a child on TV and seeing them score but it wasn't until you heard the crowd's reaction that you knew it really was a goal, as if we needed the joyful reaction to confirm what had just happened. Even now I watch the goal on video and it gives me goosebumps but only when I hear the roar of the crowd.

We kept up the pressure and when Sol headed a goal in the final minute we all thought we'd achieved the improbable. All, that is, except the referee. Urs Meier was very quick to stop us from celebrating. I think JT outjumped him and to this day he swears he didn't stop the Portugal keeper Ricardo from moving. I believe him – it's just a pity the referee didn't. That was a killer. I'm not sure if that had an effect on our momentum as we went into penalties. Some of the lads had ran to celebrate the goal that wasn't when Portugal were already taking the free-kick. That kind of thing drains you emotionally but the final whistle went and I knew what to expect. We had practised penalties a little before and we had a good idea of who would be stepping up to take the first five. I was number three.

There is no greater challenge to a footballer than to take a penalty in those circumstances. I have never been to a final and lost on penalty-kicks so maybe the pressure is more intense, but I doubt it. We joined up in the centre circle as Becks walked forward to take the first one. Despite the miss against France he was courageous and confident enough to step up to the mark. The home crowd had seen victory in extra-time snatched away by my equalizer so by the time Becks was preparing his run up their good nature had turned to a searing cacophony of jeers. He hit it over the bar. I gasped along with the rest of the lads. Becks looked down at the turf which seemed to have given way under his left foot. No one blamed him. It's not a blame game. We had to score the next one. If we didn't then it was almost certainly over – that was the reality.

Michael Owen scored and then Rui Costa missed to make it level. I had to score. As I was walking up I just blocked everything out. It's the only way I can handle it. It's a long walk and it's lonely but I felt confident that I would score. I intended to smash it down the middle but didn't catch it perfectly. Ricardo, however, went the other way and it went in.

It was a lovely feeling: to know I had done my bit and to feel all of the pent-up emotion released as the ball hit the net. Next up was JT and I have to admit I wasn't too sure about him. He never takes penalties at training and I admired his bottle to volunteer. He didn't seem too bothered as he ran towards the ball and then he slipped and for a split second it seemed our chance of winning had gone with his boot, but it was a goal. (At Chelsea, John will occasionally re-enact that kick, complete with the sliding foot – sometimes it goes in, sometimes not – but he is quick to remind people that he scored a penalty at Euro 2004.) Ashley scored and then Postiga took everyone's breath away by dinking his kick lightly down the middle. Cheeky bastard – he was either brilliant or stupid.

It went to sudden death and I began to feel that it was slipping away. Like the rest of the nation, I had seen England lose penalty shoot-outs in this kind of situation before – to Germany in Italia 90, Germany again in Euro 96, and Argentina in France 98 – and here we were again. I began to get more nervous. We had been a goal up until eighty minutes in a quarter-final and now we were facing defeat.

Darius Vassell was the unlucky player to miss and Ricardo beat David James to seal our fate. I walked around the pitch in the bleak aftermath in a complete daze. I was too emotional to actually feel anything. I knew we were out but in the confusion of the moment I was finding sights and sounds difficult to register properly, never mind thoughts on what had just happened.

We got back to the hotel where our partners and families were waiting. Elen put her arms around me and whispered in my ear, 'You were brilliant, darling. There was nothing more you could have done and you did incredibly well.'

I wasn't so sure. It's in my nature always to ask myself where I could have been better, how I might have managed to change the course of the game. Dinner was a sombre affair. We had a few beers to try and take the edge off but I was sinking lower and lower into a depression.

When I got to bed I couldn't relax. My body ached from the exertion of 120 minutes in the searing heat but it was my mind that was causing me most anguish. Was it fair for the ref to disallow Sol's effort? Could I have got closer to Rui Costa before he scored? I rolled these and every other permutation in my head over and over again without changing the outcome.

I awoke from a restless sleep and started to gather my things. I chucked my training gear into a bag disconsolately. Won't be needing that anymore. Boots, shin guards, kit. I paused to pick up my shirt from the first match. I thought of the header, the moment, the joy and then the abject disappointment.

This was what it's like to go out of a big tournament. A thousand memories and moments of wonder followed by a million ifs and buts. I grieved the loss of that game but as time passed I realized it was the loss of the opportunity to win Euro 2004 which upset me most. I genuinely believe that had we beaten Portugal then England would have gone on to claim the European Championship for the first time. Unfortunately that belief was scuppered by a penalty shoot-out but my dream lives on.

CHAPTER 9

THE SPECIAL ONE

IT'S not often you can say with conviction that someone has changed your life but I know it's true of Jose Mourinho. In fact, I knew very soon after I met him that he was unique – someone whose personality, ambition, and ability to instill belief in others made him inspirational. People mock him for claiming to be 'special' – I would advise against it. Look at what he has achieved already in his relatively short career in football.

I saw his introduction as Chelsea manager on television the same as everyone else. Myself, JT, Bridgey and Joe Cole were holed up in the England team hotel in Manchester preparing for Euro 2004 when Mourinho exploded into our lives. I watched his performance in the press conference at Stamford Bridge and thought he came across as arrogant and very confident but I don't have a problem with that when someone has the medals in their locker to back it up.

It wasn't his Champions League, UEFA Cup and Portuguese title wins which swayed me though. Once I met him I knew he was the real thing. I had two conversations with him that summer of 2004 which convinced me that I was dealing with a man who knew what he wanted and knew how to achieve it.

The unshakeable self-belief which is his trademark can have a very powerful effect on those he believes are of a similar mind. He can be intimidating but he also has a charm which is just as disarming. I began to understand him when we were in America on a pre-season tour that July. Training was varied and enjoyable and his likeable character made the lads comfortable. Nevertheless, I wasn't prepared for what happened after practice.

I was last in the shower and turning to leave when I was stopped in my tracks by the manager. There was a moment of silence as I waited for him to move but he looked me in the eye and I realized he had something to say.

'All right, boss?' I asked, wondering what I had done to invite an audience.

'You are the best player in the world,' he said without blinking.

I was slightly confused as well as completely naked. Talk about feeling vulnerable.

'You,' he said more forcefully, ' are the best player in the world.'

'Oh. Thanks, boss,' I replied cautiously. I was unsure if he was telling me this to boost my confidence. I knew that I wasn't the best player in the world and the only indication I had that he rated me was second hand or from the complimentary way he spoke to me in training sessions. He sensed a misunderstanding and made himself very clear.

'Listen. A year ago Deco was a fantastic player but now he is in line to win the European Footballer of the Year. Why do you think that is? I will tell you. A year ago he was the same player but now he has won the Champions League and the Portuguese title with Porto and he's proved he is one of the best.

'You are just as good as Zidane, Vieira or Deco and now all you have to do is win things. You are the best player in the world but now you need to prove it and win trophies. You understand?'

'Okay boss.'

I knew what he meant but I also felt a bit embarrassed. I wanted to get out of the shower and out of the conversation as quickly as I could. He had elevated me to a new level and I felt a massive surge in confidence. I was walking on air for the rest of that day and I called Mum to tell her what Mourinho had said.

'Yes,' she replied nonchalantly, 'I already knew you were the best in the world.'

I felt ten feet tall and trained harder than ever over the next couple of days. Everything I tried came off – passes, shots, even a couple of headers! We played Celtic in Seattle on the Saturday in our first game under the new boss. The city was experiencing its hottest summer for eighty-three years and it was more than 100°F when I jogged out as a second-half sub. That's all right, no problem to the best player in the world – except that I had an absolute stinker. I mis-hit passes, mis-timed tackles, and felt sluggish. I came off the pitch feeling a right mug. I couldn't face the manager. How could I? He had told me I was the best player in the world and I had just played forty-five minutes looking more Sunday league than Champions League. He didn't say a word – well, not until a whole year later when we were in New York the following pre-season. He came up to me during training.

'Lamps. Remember that game against Celtic in Seattle last summer?' he asked.

'Yeah. I was complete s*** wasn't I?'

'Yes, you were. You couldn't even pass three yards.'

We laughed and he put his hand on my shoulder. Togetherness and team spirit came easily and in abundance under Mourinho. If I had a pound for every time someone has asked me for the secret of his success then maybe I would have enough money to pay him to tell me. All I can say is that he has an intuitive understanding of the way people work, of their dreams and desires, and how to harness that energy and convert it into a winning formula. There is no one big thing he has done, no Mourinho magic which turns everything to gold; instead it's the little things that count – things like instigating a huddle in the changing room before we take the field for a game. JT came up to me the afternoon of that first match with Celtic and told me the plan.

'The gaffer said he wants me to get everyone round and I have to give a speech before the match,' John said. 'What am I going to say geezer?'

'I dunno,' I replied unhelpfully. 'I'm not sure I like the sound of that. It's embarrassing. Thank f*** you're up first.'

'Yeah, but you'll be next so we better work it out geez.'

'But it's only Celtic and pre-season. It doesn't matter. We're all just trying to get fit today.'

'That don't matter mate. I'm telling ya, he wants it to start today.'

All we could be sure about was that the 'speech' should conclude with the question 'Who are we?' and the shouted response 'Chelsea!' It still felt very strange when the time came to get into the huddle. JT was great. He set the tone with a real rant about winning, mixed with a lot of effing and blinding. My contributions have been a bit less boisterous but between us all we made it work in our favour and it was the beginning of a very special camaraderie which has got stronger.

Within a few weeks of entering our lives Mourinho had taken us from being a talented group with the potential to win major honours to a team which would settle for nothing less. I wasn't surprised. From the moment I saw him handle the media on his first day at Chelsea I knew that there was something which set him apart from everyone else.

That opinion was clearly not shared by the non-Chelsea lads at the England team hotel. I headed for the dining room and Mourinho's appearance on telly was the talk of the tables. His swaggering style had certainly made an impression and I learned immediately that I had a manager who grabbed people's attention. 'See your new gaffer on the telly?' I was asked a few times by some of the players. It was then followed by: 'Who the f*** does he think he is?'

I wasn't affected by this response. I understood their reaction – it was, after all, the same as that of the general public – but I'm drawn to individuals who have real character and I didn't feel threatened. My only concern at that stage was what he thought about me. Before Mourinho's appointment Didier Deschamps had been in the frame to succeed Ranieri and had been very complimentary about me which selfishly made me wonder if he might be the best candidate. By contrast, there had been only silence from Mourinho.

I had been preparing myself for his arrival though. A friend in the press called me a couple of days earlier and told me it was definitely him. Fine. He was articulate and well presented and, of course, he had just won the European Cup. Now I just had to wait to talk to him. The wait was short: Eriksson came to me after the meal and said that the new Chelsea manager was on his way to Manchester and wanted to meet me. 'Not you then, Sven,' I thought fleetingly.

JT, Coley, Bridgey, and I were shown to a room in the hotel and waited. We were all nervous. We had seen a stranger describe himself as the 'special one' and he was our new boss. What was I supposed to say to him? I had heard that he was very methodical and would call a team meeting to discuss the finest detail of planning for a match. My experience of that style of management before was with the England Under-21s when Howard Wilkinson was in charge. Wilkinson would call meetings about meetings about meetings – it was very boring and ultimately pointless. Being tactical and organized is something I believe is very important but there has to be balance.

The door opened and in came Peter Kenyon, Roman Abramovich, Eugene Tenenbaum and then Mourinho. I thought he would be very serious but he smiled and shook hands with us in a very friendly and informal way, putting us at ease. I noticed a twinkle in his eye which suggested he was excited about the adventure he had just signed up for. Kenyon spoke first, introducing Mourinho and saying a few words about how the club was going to go forward. I hardly heard him. His speech barely registered with me – my focus was on Mourinho who sat back in his chair looking extremely comfortable. I was on the edge of mine, literally.

'It's a pleasure to be here,' Mourinho began. 'I wanted to come and meet you because you are the English heart of Chelsea and a very important part of the team and I want you to be even more so for my team.

'This will be a very exciting time for all of us. We will bring in some new players but I wanted to come here to tell you myself that all of you will be major players next season. I have seen what you have done so far and think you are capable of more. With me as coach we will achieve that together.'

He then spoke to Coley directly. The rest of us were all established but Joe had been in and out of the team and had had a difficult first year at the club. I look back now and realize how perceptive Mourinho was – he realized that Coley was the one of the four who needed most encouragement.

'I know how I want to play you and how I can get the best out of you,' he said. 'I have good experience of making a skilful player work for the team. I did it at Porto and I'm sure we can do this together at Chelsea.'

We chatted for a few minutes and then Mourniho signalled that it was time to go. He had, however, one final point to make.

'I need to know that you are winners.'

It was a rhetorical question but the brief silence was followed by a nodding of heads and 'Yes boss' all round.

'Good. Because I am a winner and now so are you. We will win things together.'

And with that he stood up, shook us by the hand, and walked out of the room. Eugene and Roman smiled proudly. They knew they had the right man for the job – and so did we. I didn't see him again until after the European Championships though I know he came to watch all of England's games. I was relieved when he gave an interview during that period saying that he wanted to build the midfield around me. There had been a lot of chat about Porto's Portuguese players Costinha and Deco arriving at Chelsea, so this reassurance was welcome.

Harlington was a different place when I returned from holiday after Euro 2004. Mourinho had asked for huge nets to be installed behind the goals and we had ball boys around the practice pitch – previously I would have run to collect a ball myself – simple things but very effective. There was a rule book which he had distributed but he was careful to point out that the one rule he expected us all to adhere to more than any other was to behave as a professional footballer should.

John and I had been appointed as captain and vice-captain of the club while we were in the States and it became clear that I would have more interaction with Mourinho than I had been used to with any previous manager. Ranieri was never one to consult the players very much, but soon JT and I were being asked our opinion on possible transfer targets as well as the details of the training structure.

Before he signed a new centre-back he called us to see him and explained that he had identified four possible players: one was English, one Italian, a South American, and Ricardo Carvalho. John and I knew Carvalho from the European Championships and reckoned he was very good but Mourinho was tentative about bringing in too many Portuguese. We told him he should just buy the best.

At first I was wary about this level of involvement with management. I had been used to talking with Dad when he was assistant manager at West Ham and remember him coming home on a few occasions telling stories of players trying to tell him and Harry their job.

'We had that so-and-so in the office today,' he would say, 'telling us we should buy this player and that player. Who the f*** does he think he is?'

I seem to remember Paolo Di Canio's name being mentioned a lot in these conversations. This was a very different culture from what we were used to – maybe Paolo was accustomed to it but for John and me, being asked to give an opinion on everything was completely new.

Team food also changed. We had been accustomed to a strict diet of pasta, salad, fish, and chicken with nothing sweet or 'unhealthy' – now we had all of those things but also cookies for dessert and even Coca-Cola. Players appreciate being treated as adults, and Mourinho gives you the option: you can take the right route or the wrong route – but if you take the wrong route, he will know about it and there will be repercussions.

Some people chose to see how far they could push him. Hernan Crespo failed to turn up on time for the first day's training despite the fact Mourinho had called him to assure him that he was first-choice striker. A deal was quickly agreed to send him on loan to AC Milan. Everyone was well aware of what had happened. A line had been drawn and above it was an important message: Don't mess with the manager. Those who crossed the line found their career at Chelsea short-lived. Veron and Mutu were two other high-profile signings from the previous year who didn't survive. Seba went on loan to Inter Milan and never came back while Adrian was already well on his way to going off the rails.

Ironically, Mourinho had decided to get rid of him until Crespo pissed him off and so Mutu was granted a reprieve. He had arrived as part of the Abramovich revolution and seemed like a decent lad even though sometimes he had that 'can't be bothered' attitude about him. In the first few games of the 2003/04 season he looked very impressive, showing an ability to score goals with either foot. He had a bit of front about him as well, a cheek which came through in the presence of people he wanted to impress or get attention from. The most obvious was Mr Abramovich. When he came into the dressing room after games most players were respectful and friendly towards the owner of the club. Mutu behaved differently.

'Ah boss, boss!!' he would shout as soon as he saw him.

'How's that yacht sailing? I mean yachts,' and he would laugh loudly until he saw Mr Abramovich break into a smile. Quite often Mutu would usher Mr Abramovich into a corner where they would chat more quietly. I have no idea what they talked about but it seemed friendly enough. This was shortly after the buy out of the club and I think the new owner enjoyed being treated like one of the boys though I could tell from the way he looked at Mutu that he knew exactly what was going on. Quite often Mutu would bring up the subject of bonuses for the players and Roman would smile at him even though it was a bit embarassing.

I'm sure he had rarely come across anyone like Mutu before, or at least anyone like him that he directly employed. It was hardly the most subtle way to ask for a raise but to Mutu it was all part of a big act. He loved that – he was an extrovert who was rarely content if he wasn't the focus of attention. Despite his fooling around, Mutu was also a clever politician when it came to selecting the people he would befriend.

I didn't talk to him much but Mutu certainly made a point of singling out the players he felt had influence. Marcel, JT, and Franco were people I would often see him chatting with about the team, the way we were playing, and so on. He was cute that way. When he won Romania's Player of the Year there was a private plane to ferry him to Bucharest for the ceremony and he invited Marcel, JT, and Mario Melchiot along for the night out.

It was interesting to see him work the dressing room. We had a couple of team outings and Mutu would turn up in his urban terrorist gear wearing enough chains around his neck to give most gangsta rappers a run for their rhyme-gotten gains. It didn't stop there. He was happy to find a podium or posing post in the club where he could watch everyone around him watch him. I stayed near the relative sanity of the bar chatting with a few mates but before you knew it Mutu, smoking a big cigar, had taken over a table and was surrounded by women.

'Lamps! Lamps! Come to the table,' he shouted over.

I just thought, 'This lad knows how to live.' It's fair to say Adrian liked to party. I didn't think much of it then because he was still new at Chelsea and playing well. There was nothing to suggest he wouldn't be a valuable addition to the squad, but then his form dropped quite quickly and the goals dried up. Then he was injured and only appeared very irregularly in the team. During that time Mutu's social life began to get out of hand. He seemed drawn to excess – it was evident in the way he behaved around people – and the story of his two cars is a good illustration of his careless attitude when it came to his reputation.

He bought two Porsche 911s when he signed for the club – a blue one he used to come to training in during the week, and a black one which he preferred for weekends. Unfortunately, his apartment in Chelsea Harbour only came with one parking space and so he took to parking the one he wasn't using on a yellow line outside, knowing it would be impounded. At the end of the week, he would give one of the trainee pros the four hundred quid or so needed to get his car out of the pound and bring it back to Chelsea Harbour. This went on for a few weeks before someone at the club got wind of it and told Mutu to sort it out before it became a story for the tabloids. When a high-profile footballer is behaving like that it's only a matter of time before they will make the headlines. Mutu was a scandal waiting to happen.

Scott Parker lived near Mutu at Chelsea Harbour for a while. Scottie is the ultimate professional – never late and always well prepared – but on occasion he would travel to Harlington with Mutu. One morning he bumped into Mutu as he was coming out of the lift in their building. Mutu looked rough and had obviously enjoyed a good night – so good, he was just getting in. He begged Scottie to wait for him while he got changed into his training gear. Scottie agreed as long as he was straight back down and amazingly Mutu appeared and the two of them made it on time.

It wasn't the first time Mutu had come straight from a night out to the training ground. The lads started noticing that he would manage half a session or less and then complain that he felt a muscle strain or another minor injury. He'd head into the dressing room struggling from a lack of energy and nothing else.

I had seen it before with Mark Bosnich who had drifted out of the team and lost interest in training and playing. He started hanging around with a certain crowd in a particular social scene and had changed as a person. I had always got on well with Bozo but it got to the stage when I didn't recognize the one-time happy-go-lucky guy who used to give me a lift to training when I first signed. I never knew for sure that he was doing cocaine and never actually saw him take drugs, but when you come in from training and find your reserve goalie fast asleep on the massage table fully dressed you realize something is wrong. He wasn't knackered from exercise and it got so bad that I even remember having a conversation with Ranieri while Bozo snored in the background.

It was the same with Mutu in that I didn't know for sure he was using cocaine. I had heard a couple of rumours about it and noticed he was becoming more and more erratic. It was obvious that he was more interested in playing the field than playing on it. His mood became changeable – one day he would look very rough and blank you; the next he would be fine and as boisterous as ever.

When the story leaked that he had tested positive for cocaine I wasn't exactly shocked. I have no idea what the extent of his involvement with drugs was but what was clear to anyone was that his hectic social life was impacting on his ability to play football and I wasn't sorry to see him leave the club.

We didn't miss him. Mourinho had impressed on us from the beginning his decision to change the basic formation from 4–4–2 to 4–3–2–1. He wanted to break the lines up and make the team more fluid. It was actually more of a diamond to start with but the system evolved to the point where I moved from the front of the diamond to the left side of the midfield three.

The pressure built steadily leading up to the first league match of the season against Manchester United – even more than in the first season of Mr Abramovich's ownership. Now we had a 'special' manager and more new players and the expectation had increased in line with the spending. Seven new signings – Drogba, Carvalho, Ferreira, Kezman, Robben, Tiago, and Cech had arrived for a cool £82 million. Not bad for one summer.

Just for good measure the media had dubbed the contest a

managers' rematch because of the Champions League tie the previous season in which Mourinho's Porto had eliminated United at Old Trafford, causing something of a disagreement between our new boss and Sir Alex Ferguson.

Mourinho called a team meeting the day before the match. We had already discussed our tactics and were very well drilled on what to expect and what was expected from us. But the boss had a more important message to convey.

'You will read in the press and hear in the media me saying that I don't expect us to win the league in my first season,' he said. 'I want you to be very clear that I have said this only to keep the pressure off all of us. I also want you to know that I do expect us to win the Premiership this season. I know that we will. We are winners and winning is all that matters. I don't want to be second or third. We want to win this league and we will.'

I felt myself draw a sharp breath – no more of the Ranieri method of focus on performance and improve on last season. Winning was everything – new manager, new Chelsea. It was just what we needed. United came to the Bridge to take the wind from our sails but they didn't succeed. It wasn't pretty but we won the match thanks to a goal from Eidur. I didn't play particularly well and the diamond didn't function properly. We stayed strong though and defended sternly as a team and that was the direction Mourinho wanted us to take. We'd done a lot of work on defending as a unit and it paid off in that first game. He was cute enough to realize that he couldn't turn us into a fluid attacking unit in seven weeks so instead he made us hard to beat. In fact we had defeated one of our title rivals at the first time of asking. It was calculating and it was brilliant and that was the way we started the campaign until the fourth game when Coley came in and added a bit more flair.

Robben and Duff were both injured from pre-season and we would have to wait until November before we saw the new formation in full glorious flow. Until then we got a lot of stick in the press for being boring and defensive but the manager never remarked on it to us – he didn't care. I was concerned about my own form though. Mourinho had invested a lot of faith in me and I didn't feel I was justifying it over the first two games.

A couple of days after the victory at Crystal Palace in the third match he took me aside and told me that he liked the way I had run the midfield – the Prozone statistics had shown that I was involved in all four of the top passing partnerships in the match. That is what he wanted from me – industry and involvement. I scored my first goal in the next match against Southampton and we were undefeated until we went to Manchester City on 16 October.

People were already asking if we could emulate Arsenal and go the whole season unbeaten. The answer was no. Nicolas Anelka scored from a penalty and we lost the match by a single goal. That was it. The bubble had burst and now it would revert to same old Chelsea and collapse. Not a chance.

Losing was a new experience under Mourinho and I wondered what reaction it would provoke in him. The answer was simple: none. He told us straight after the game that we had done enough to win it twice, that we should not be downbeat. It was unrealistic to expect not to suffer one defeat. 'Just make sure it doesn't happen again.' He smiled as he said it and we understood.

Far from being the beginning of our demise defeat became

the catalyst for our most impressive spell of the campaign. The diamond had evolved to the more familiar 4–3–3 and Robben started to wreak havoc among opposition defences, having returned to the team after injury. Drogba was a powerful presence at the point of attack and I was running through from midfield to support and scoring more. We embarked on a goal spree which saw us score forty-seven times in our next twenty-one outings – not bad for a boring defensive team! Our momentum saw our points total soar and the manager sensed that he was now managing *his* team – he had won our hearts and minds.

A new confidence enveloped the squad and when Mourinho gave an instruction it was carried out as second nature. People began to notice that occasionally he would send a sub on with handwritten notes which would be given to me or John. There was no big secret – the note might contain instructions about who should be marked at corners or how better we could use our formation. Sometimes it would be much more blunt, carrying only the message: 'WIN.'

We knew what he wanted because we wanted the same. We were five points ahead of Arsenal when we travelled to Highbury on 12 December. They had been leading the Premiership at one stage but had their unbeaten run ended by Manchester United and then lost their way a bit. Mourinho cleverly transferred the pressure to them when he stated before the match that we needed only a draw. As always, we went there looking for victory.

Lads like JT, Eidur, and I who had been at Chelsea a while were sick of losing to Arsenal in the league. None of us had ever beaten them and Chelsea had failed to in fourteen years of trying. I was tired of feeling that we had been the best team in those derby matches but never had much to show for it. This contest would throw up little more joy for Chelsea in that respect as we were twice down at Highbury but came back to draw the match. Thierry Henry scored both though the second was a hotly disputed free-kick which he had taken quickly to beat Petr Cech who was still arranging our defence. JT and Eidur struck back for a 'moral victory' but more important was that for the first time we began to get the Premiership trophy in our sights. So too did the manager who from then on regularly pointed out how far ahead we would be if we won this game or that game. He used the building of a lead to motivate us to put more space between ourselves and our rivals.

We kept winning. In the past when we had to get a victory to stay ahead we would fail, but not now. Over the Christmas period, when we traditionally slipped up, we put together an impressive sequence of results: Portsmouth away, 2–0; Liverpool away, 1–0; Middlesbrough at home, 2–0. We were reaching perfection.

The Premiership was not the only competition where we were on a roll. January saw us take on Manchester United in the semi-final of the Carling Cup which people had mistakenly believed we would have been happy to sacrifice for other honours – not so with Mourinho in charge. The first leg at our place was high tempo and hard work. It ended goalless but the aftermath was not without incident as our manager told the press he had seen Sir Alex Ferguson berating referee Neale Barry in the tunnel at half-time. Mourinho then pointed out that the second half had been riddled with free-kicks (most of them in United's favour). 'It was whistle and whistle, fault and fault, cheat and cheat,' and not for the first time his words were scrutinized and inevitably used as a rod to beat him. He was charged with improper conduct by the FA and then fined £5,000.

The controversy merely fuelled our motivation in the return leg at Old Trafford but I had been aware for a while of the changing mood in the media towards Mourinho. I put it down to the fact that we kept winning games and some people were desperate to see us lose a few just to see how the manager would cope. But he kept his cool and ensured that none of the external pressure on him ever found its way into the dressing room.

We were still in the hunt for every competition we had entered and there had been a lot of headlines referring to a possible 'grand slam'. It wasn't something any of us had even considered. We hadn't secured our first trophy yet, never mind four of them, and that was the kind of distraction we could do without.

I never gave it a thought even after I collected Didier's lay-off at Old Trafford and swept a left-foot shot into the net to put us ahead in the Carling Cup return leg. After all of the furore surrounding the first game, it was a sweet moment for us. United, though, are still the benchmark for everyone in English football and there was no chance of them giving up. Ryan Giggs replied with a great finish to level it but we weren't finished yet. Duffa caused panic in their defence with five minutes left when he whipped in a free-kick and we may have been a little fortunate that it found the net. I couldn't have cared less – you can be the best team in the world but you won't win without a bit of luck. We were in the final – the first of the season, our first under Mourinho, and the first for Mr Abramovich. All we had to do now was beat Liverpool.

My previous experience of Cardiff's Millennium Stadium was very mixed. The FA Cup Final in 2002 in which we lost to Arsenal was a huge disappointment, though I took some satisfaction from the way I had battled with Vieira and the fact that we had made that stage in my first season with Chelsea. We checked in to the St David's Bay Hotel and John pointed out that it was the same one we had used for the match with Arsenal. He did this, of course, because he is superstitious.

A lot of players are afflicted by this strange condition and I am not totally immune though my good luck habits don't extend much beyond wearing the same watch for the next match after a victory. JT is different. In fact, he's unique when it comes to the lengths he will go to in order to re-create the exact conditions required to keep lady luck on his side – from keeping the same seats on the bus to using the same urinal in the dressing room at Stamford Bridge; from pre-match meals to counting lamp posts to parking spaces.

I dreaded the effect staying in the hotel might have on John, given that he had woken up with vertigo the morning of the 2002 FA Cup Final and only made the bench. I checked his balance first thing the next morning – perfect; a good omen already. It didn't last into the match though – within the first minute we were a goal down. We threw everything at Liverpool but nothing worked except a cruel twist of fate. Stevie Gerrard flicked the ball into his own net from a free-kick and the match went to extra-time.

Eidur played alongside Claude Makelele and me in mid-field and was excellent. People call him versatile but in fact he is just a very good footballer. He was the player who impressed me most when I first joined Chelsea. I was in awe of how natural he was with a ball at his feet and how sharply he turned thought into action on the pitch. He was outstanding in that final and when Didi poked a shot under Dudek to put us ahead I thought it was all over. However, there was more drama left, as they equalized and then Eidur's shot was spilled to Kezman who swept it home.

The memory of lifting the Carling Cup is sweet and my winner's medal is precious. We celebrated like you would expect for a team which had won their first trophy under a new manager though my favourite moment of the party was Roman lifting the Carling Cup at dinner to drink champagne from it. We all cheered and I don't think I've ever seen a broader smile on a man. I was content. I had left West Ham for Chelsea to win things and now after four years I had achieved my first and definitely not the last.

The Champions League was a competition which we felt very strongly about. For most of us, there was a nagging sense of unfinished business after the way we had lost to Monaco the year before. Barcelona was not the ideal draw for the first knockout stage and not just because they were the most exciting team in Europe. Ronaldinho's skills would be hard to contain though not as difficult to cope with as the demand for tickets in my house. All of Elen's relations are Barca fans and we were expecting a full house as well as a mini-family section at the Bridge for the second leg. The first match, however, produced a controversy the likes of which I have never been involved in.

It was as fierce a contest on the pitch as the build-up to it had suggested: bragging rights and the odd insult had been tossed back and forth and each side jostled for advantage. Once again we benefited from an own goal which saw us take a lead into half-time. Barcelona boss Frank Rijkaard seemed incensed by some of the refereeing and by the time I reached our dressing room there was clearly something very wrong.

Some of our coaching staff were shouting while others were pointing to the Barca dressing room accusingly. Mourinho ushered all of us inside and gave his summary of what we needed to do to stay ahead. It was calm enough when we left for the pitch but all hell broke loose when Didi was sent off within ten minutes of the re-start. He had already been wound up by the antics of Marquez and Puyol – big strong guys – who had been falling too easily in the first half and then protesting that he should be booked. Now it was the turn of their keeper to play up after Didi's innocuous challenge in a 50/50 situation. Barca players surrounded referee Anders Frisk and sure enough Didi was red carded. They scored twice to win 2–1. After the match I was told that some of our staff had seen Rijkaard approach Frisk in an area which was reserved for match officials only. Mourinho refused to speak at the post-match press conference and what ensued felt like a war waged on Chelsea by UEFA and the media.

The club protested that Rijkaard had attempted to influence the referee at half-time and pointed out that Didi had been sent off shortly after play resumed. UEFA were quick to deny the allegation though Frisk later admitted that he had to ask Rijkaard to leave a restricted area during the break, saying it was neither the place nor the moment to discuss the match. The situation spiralled out of control when Frisk then announced his retirement from refereeing, claiming he had received threats to himself and his family. UEFA's media chief William Gaillard popped up in the English media more times than Tony Blair as he slagged off Mourinho and Chelsea while another UEFA official, Volker Roth, labelled our manager 'an enemy of football'. It was a full-scale crusade against us. I was dumbfounded. I couldn't believe that people in positions of responsibility would wilfully inflame the situation in such an unnecessary way.

Just as damaging was the way the English media fanned the campaign. I could never imagine the press in Spain or Italy siding with UEFA against one of their major clubs. It would have been nice if people had defended us but no one was even prepared to entertain the idea that we had a genuine grievance.

To say we were fired up for the second game is an understatement. That simmering sense of injustice is one reason why we exploded out of the blocks and were three up after twenty-six minutes. After everything that had gone before, it felt like we were in dreamland. A minute later Ronaldinho brought us firmly back to earth with a penalty before reality kicked us even harder when he scored a magnificent second.

What had been billed as the most competitive meeting of the season was beginning to look like a free-for-all. For all our audacity though, scoring three against Barca meant nothing because we were out on away goals at that point. It took JT to stretch his full height and strength to head a dramatic winner in the final minutes to get us into the quarter-final and strike a blow for natural justice. We were delirious – well I was along with everyone at Chelsea though there were a few long Catalan faces around our house that night. Elen's wasn't one of them – she is Chelsea now and supports me ahead of her hometown club.

We had progressed but at a price. Mourinho was banned

from the technical area for the tie against Bayern Munich because of his comments about Rijkaard and Frisk but if UEFA's intention was to smack us back into line then they had another thing coming. We were more determined than ever to fly in the face of the establishment and Bayern were as much a part of the ruling classes as any club in Europe.

The match at the Bridge is one of the best I played that season. We were all fired up for it. The manager gave his pre-match talk the night before the game but he didn't use the situation to try to motivate us. He didn't need to. Speculation about where Mourinho would watch the action from threatened to turn our biggest game of the season into a circus of photographers balancing on the back of motorcycles. It degenerated further when a conspiracy theory was hatched shortly after kick-off that Rui Faria was concealing some kind of communication device under a woolly hat. Why not just go the whole hog and claim that Mourinho himself was hiding under there?

The truth is that the boss didn't need to be on the bench or even in the stand. When we are on the pitch he is always with us – in every move we make and every kick we take. We knew he was watching somewhere and hopefully he liked what he saw. We were a bit stuck at 1–1 and slightly concerned at having conceded an away goal. However, a chance fell slightly behind me but I managed to dig it out from twenty yards and beat Oliver Kahn to regain the lead. Nice one – but I wasn't finished yet.

Maka flighted a pass towards me and as I tracked the flight of the ball I realized it was a fraction too high to take on my chest. The angle wasn't great and I could sense a defender was closing me down. I had a choice: either I attempt an overhead kick or I allow it to drop over my shoulder and on to my left foot – probably two of the most difficult moves to execute in football though an easy way of making a complete tit of yourself. I opted for the second and caught the ball beautifully on the volley to smash it into the net – not bad for my 'weaker' foot. It's one of my favourite goals for Chelsea and though I don't normally keep boots I have reserved a special place at home for the pair I wore that night. The game finished 4–2 and we went on to battle to an aggregate victory in Munich to make the semi-final for the second year in a row.

It was quite an achievement. Even the media had begun to pay us some grudging respect though I have to say that the relationship between us and the press is not all bad. We stayed in Munich the night of the match and a couple of lads from the papers joined the players for a beer afterwards. They were buying. Cheers Dan.

Having been knocked out of the FA Cup at Newcastle in February meant we had a week to prepare to play Arsenal at home in the Premiership. Victory would put us fourteen points ahead with five games to play and while the title wouldn't be ours mathematically it would be a fitting way to celebrate its inevitability. It wasn't to be. A goalless draw left us needing six points and all of a sudden the manager could add astrology to his impressive list of talents. Earlier in the campaign he predicted that Chelsea would win the championship on 30 April when we would play away at Bolton. After we beat Fulham only Spurs could scupper his emerging rivalry with Russell Grant. Victory over Arsenal would hand us the title without kicking a ball and we all gathered in La Famiglia restaurant to watch their match.

The manager had decided we should spend the two nights

before the first leg of the Champions League semi-final against Liverpool in the Chelsea Village Hotel so it was a short hop on the Monday night. Roman brought some huge pots of the finest Russian caviar for us to eat. I love the stuff and was tucking in while most of the lads looked at me strangely. I reckon they were worth about five grand a pot and I was glad for the good food given how bland the game was. Arsenal were ahead for a while and then Robbie Keane had a header in the last few minutes. We all jumped up instinctively but I was quite relieved when it flashed past the post. I didn't want to win the league in a restaurant on the Kings Road. I had waited all of my life for that moment and no amount of Russia's finest caviar would have made up for missing out on being on the pitch and actually celebrating the victory as a football team.

I lay in bed thinking about what was ahead. In the next eight days we could clinch the Premiership and qualify for the Champions League final – again, not bad for a 'boring team' from west London! The first leg of the semi against Liverpool didn't quite match the ties against Barca and Bayern in terms of goals though the 'Battle of Britain' was thrilling as a contest. The return leg was no less enervating. The crowd at Anfield is so vocal and intense that it feels like they are directly above the pitch screaming on top of you rather than filling its sides. Maybe we got caught in the moment because we allowed our guard to slip early and conceded the now infamous goal that never was.

I have heard and read people say that Chelsea should stop whining about Garcia's effort. That it doesn't matter if the ball crossed the line or not because the referee gave a goal. Oh really? My reply is simple: If you had worked as hard as we had to reach that stage of the Champions League then you would feel a right to protest as well.

In fact, if we had scored that 'goal' and not Liverpool I wonder how their players would have reacted. No differently I suspect. We did everything to try and redeem the situation – piled on pressure, players up front and tried everything we knew to break them down.

When the ball fell to Eidur in the final minute within yards of the goal I thought we had them. One hit Eidur. One hit. His volley was true and it flashed across Dudek's goal and Jamie Carragher got a touch on it at the far post to make sure it didn't go in.

The whistle sounded and I felt a surge of anger well up in me. To get to one semi-final and lose to Monaco the year before was unlucky. To be involved in another the following season seemed unjust.

I tried to make sense of it. After all, they were struggling to qualify for the Champions League, while we were busy trying to wrap up Chelsea's first league championship in 50 years. We had beaten Liverpool twice in the Premiership so why couldn't we in Europe? No matter how hard I tried I couldn't work it out. All I was certain of was how low I felt at the result. I hate losing. I really hate it.

Conceding the title was not possible and in between the European matches we had a pressing date in Bolton and her name was destiny.

As we travelled north I remembered some of the things that had been said to me in the previous weeks about winning the league. It seemed that everywhere I went I ran into Chelsea fans, all of whom were eager to let me know what the title meant to them. It had been fifty years since Chelsea won the league – fifty long years – and even though I had only been with the club for a fraction of that time I felt the same pent-up frustration as the fans about waiting any longer. I knew what it meant to them because of what it meant to me.

We stayed at the Preston Marriott and the night before the game I threw the question out as I was sitting with John and Eidur chilling out: 'Imagine what it would be like to score the goal that wins the league?' We were silent as the thought drifted out there. I wasn't trying to pre-empt anything but it was something I had thought about, dreamt about, for much of my life and this was the first time I had been in a position where it was a possibility.

The journey from our hotel to the Reebok was full of nervous excitement. As always, I sat with JT, Eidur and Bill Blood and I blurted out the same question I had the night before. What would it be like? Come on! Come on! The adrenalin began to flow and when we arrived at the stadium we were all pumped and ready to go. You imagine you will be infallible in situations like that, that when the hand of fate beckons you towards glory, nothing can trip you up – that is until you go for the warm-up and find a pitch that looks like a cow field. Bolton are hard enough to play at home – a bad pitch in the freezing cold just complicates it.

They carved out their normal game and Kevin Nolan was flicking things on and they made a couple of half chances. We barely responded in the first half – we seemed to be seizing up in the bitter wind and allowing our grip on history to slip. The half-time team talk was designed to breathe some fire back into us. We were expecting a bollocking but the manager's anger was turned into a question.

'We are not playing well but we are not doing too badly,'

he said. 'Why? I don't understand. Keep it simple. Play the way you can and you will succeed. Before we had ninety minutes to win the league and now we have forty-five. Now go and do it!'

He was right. We hadn't worked this hard or come this far to let ourselves down. I felt renewed energy in my legs and a surge of confidence similar to when the manager had told me I was the best player in the world. I heard his voice in my head: 'You need to prove that and win trophies.' Now was my chance. Now was our chance to prove we were the best.

Didi cushioned the ball across to me but Vincent Candela blocked my sight of goal. I looked up for options but no one was in space. To hell with it, I'll have a go. I dropped my shoulder and got the half yard I needed for the angle to drive my shot past Jussi Jaaskelainen. Goal. Goal. Goal. Goal. Gooooaaaaaalllllll!!!!!!!!!

I spun away and ran shouting with every pace. I made a bolt for our fans at the other side of the box. Mum and Dad couldn't get tickets for the directors' area and somewhere in the blue bedlam they were celebrating the same as me. The lads smothered me with hugs and I had to fight them off to see some daylight. This was it. This was what it felt like to be a winner.

My heart was still pounding when minutes later I found myself in acres and acres of space. It was surreal – like a dream. I was just running – running like I would never get to the goal or the mass of blue and white who were standing on their toes behind it.

I could see Ricky pushing on beside me, shouting for a pass. I pretended not to hear. I was determined to finish it off. Dad was sitting behind the goal and when I got to the edge of the box he was shouting 'Shoot, shoot!' I couldn't hear him

Sunbathing with Elen in La Manga before going to South Africa for an England friendly in 2003.

At home with Mum. Always my number 1.

Me holding nephew Stanley while Claire holds Luna. Always family first.

On a family day out with Elen and little Luna.

In St Tropez with Elen and my mates! Eddie Jordan and Bono.

On Roman Abramovich's boat *Sussuro* with Elen and Mum and Dad giving it the big un! Not bad for a boy from Romford.

Me and my mate Tel – he's a top man.

ABOVE: Scoring the goal against
Poland that took us to the World Cup.
Come on Wazza!!

ABOVE: Leaving a nightclub with Kutner
– though a few drinks are no excuse for
his bad gear and dodgy hat.

LEFT: On the training ground with
England: 'Okay, Steve, I see what
you're saying…'

ABOVE: Have that!! Scoring in the blue.
Come on the Chels!!

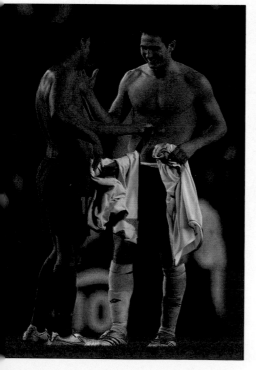

ABOVE: Scoring at Upton Park for
Chelsea, January 2006, and dedicating
the goal to my family in the stands.

LEFT: Exchanging shirts with the
best player in the world. I will
treasure that one for ever.

RIGHT: Celebrating a second Premiership title with my little girl on the pitch at Stamford Bridge. Just what I wanted.

BELOW: The 'Romario goal celebration' of rocking the baby after I scored against WBA at the Bridge the Saturday after Luna was born. Got another for Elen too!

BOTTOM: Me and JT with the lads in the trophy parade 2006. That's what Chelsea is all about – team spirit and a winning team.

Rio tries to make the
warm up interesting
with another tall tale!

A close shave against Trinidad
and Tobago in the group stage
at World Cup 2006.

Breaking from midfield
during our 2–2 draw with
Sweden at the finals.

Always trying. Firing in an effort from range against Portugal in the quarter-final.

The moment I'd rather forget. Ricardo saves my penalty in the shootout against Portugal.

Mr Eriksson and I show our appreciation for the magnificent support from the England fans.

because another voice in my head was telling me I should go round Jaaskelainen and roll it in – not my normal type of finish but stylish and if you're going to win the league then what better way to do it?

It took a few seconds for the rest of the lads to catch me up but they got there soon enough. It's hard to describe exactly what I felt just then – difficult because extreme emotions don't fit into words very comfortably. Elation is too temporary – this was more substantial and I can still feel it now when I close my eyes and re-live that moment.

Everything that came afterwards was fantastic. It was everything I imagined it to be and more. We soaked Roman with champagne then went back to the pitch and took him with us. There wasn't a lot of sensible conversation between us. He had lived every minute of that season and he deserved to take his share of the credit. He hadn't just pumped money in and sat back waiting for things to happen – he helped make it happen and he loved being out there with us.

I looked around for the manager and saw him sitting quietly in the dugout. He phoned his family, spoke to his wife and children, and was happy to have shared part of the moment with them while the rest of us carried on like loonies on the pitch. Outside the stadium John and I got our heads out of the top of the bus to sing with the hundreds of fans who had waited to see us. We were among them and that was a special moment. I knew how important it was and it meant at least as much to them and maybe more.

The celebration back at the hotel was very muted by comparison. We would play the second leg of the semi-final in the Champions League at Anfield on the Wednesday so we had a couple of beers with our dinner while it began to sink in that we were the Premiership champions. I was still buzzing with the adrenalin of the game and the goals but sat down with Eidur and we had a beer and watched the game on *Match of the Day*.

I could hardly believe what I was watching. I could see myself on the screen – me, Eidur, John, Coley, big Pete, Ricky, Geremi, Tiago, Maka, Didi. I scored one, then another. It was like watching a dream – your own dream, there for everyone to see, and it was perfect, absolutely perfect.

Losing to Liverpool three days later meant we failed by a whisker to make the European Cup Final for a second consecutive season. I hate losing. I really hate it. We had won two trophies though and in claiming the league we had proved ourselves to be the best team in England.

A couple of weeks later I picked up an individual prize when I was voted the Football Writers' Association Player of the Year. It was a great honour and the evening was made all the more special because I was able to share it with my family and friends – the people who mean most to me, those who have changed my life and helped me to get to the point in my career that I had yearned for more than anything else. Jose Mourinho is part of that special group though unlike him I would never tout myself as the best player in the world. Among the best in England, yes. I think I have proven that.

CHAPTER 10

EARNING RESPECT AT STAMFORD BRIDGE

THERE are many privileges which come with being a professional footballer and then there are those which are particular to playing for Chelsea. I don't take anything in my life for granted. Whether it's on the pitch or off, I appreciate the value of everything because I was brought up in a family where we were taught to equate good things with a reward for hard work.

I look back on the training regime Dad put me through from a very young age – the endless ball practice, my spikes, doggies, agility and stamina routines and with every exercise he reminded me that this was what I had to do if I wanted to become a professional footballer. Now, I don't need Dad to tell me what I need to practise (though he still does). I know myself.

Having won the league for the first time though, I found myself in unchartered territory. The elation of having achieved it quickly gave way to the question of how I could take myself and Chelsea to another level. I'm familiar with setting new targets but now I needed the experience of others to help me understand how to use success to ensure more. Thankfully, I could not have had better mentors than Jose Mourinho and Roman Abramovich.

Mourinho has become a very public figure but I understand Roman is and remains something of an enigma to most people. He's a very private man who doesn't give interviews and who is content to remain in the background at Chelsea. His relationships with people at the club, however, are very different. He is open, inquisitive and very visible with the manager and the players and I feel privileged to have got to know him and understand something of the man behind the myth.

The great thing about Roman is that he gets involved. Despite the fact that he has numerous and more pressing business interests which demand his attention all over the world he makes a point of being with us regularly. Whenever he's in London he comes to the training ground and makes a point of chatting with the lads – making sure everything is just right. Even when the rain is pouring down he turns up and watches us go through our routines. At games he will wish us luck beforehand and always comes to see us afterwards, regardless of the result. He shares our joy when we win and our disappointment in defeat.

When he first arrived most of us weren't quite sure what to make of him or how we should behave around him. Over the years, however, Roman has become an integral part of the club and has earned the respect of everyone for the way in which he has demonstrated his commitment to Chelsea and loyalty to those who are loyal to him.

Outside the manager, John and I have probably the closest relationship with Roman. We speak to him sometimes just minutes after a game to discuss how it went and at other times when he wants to gauge our view on specific subjects. I was nervous about voicing too strong an opinion at first. I grew up in a football environment where you listen to the people in charge – the manager, the chairman, your uncle and Dad. I didn't want to be seen to be putting my oar in where it wasn't required. I'm a footballer and I'm paid to play and win games.

But Roman has encouraged me to develop my voice on everything from the way we have played or can play to where the squad needs to be strengthened and how that should happen. I appreciate his candour and he listens to what I have to say. I would never cross the line though and that comes from the amount of respect I have for him and what he has achieved in his life and with Chelsea.

People perceive him to be a reclusive and distant man but my experience is very much the opposite. Elen and Roman's wife Irina get on very well and they are as normal as any couple despite the security which surrounds them and the fact that they have a few billion in the bank. Their lifestyle may differ greatly from most people's but the Abramoviches are very much like the rest of us. They laugh at the same jokes and relate with ease to people around them. I have rarely seen someone as excited as Roman was before the parade around west London after we won our first title, and when he celebrates a goal his reaction is as natural as any of the other 40,000 fans in the stadium. It's actually quite beautiful because it's so simple.

I have never had the relationship with a chairman that I

enjoy with him. I also have a lot of time for Ken Bates. He would take me out for dinner and we still have a good friendship but he was a different kind of owner. Roman, though, has made me feel that I am more than just a well paid and valued employee. He sees Chelsea as his family and John and I are senior members who have a part to play off the pitch as well as on it. I am not just his number 8: to Roman I am part of the Chelsea DNA.

I suppose it was partly because I'm comfortable around him that I felt I could push my luck a little when I had heard a whisper that the Chelsea Player of the Year would get to go on his boat. No one had confirmed the reward at the club but I was in the running to win the accolade and had done so the previous year. I spoke to Elen about it and she reckoned I had nothing to lose and might as well ask if it was true. Nothing ventured nothing gained and all that. Egged on by a curious girlfriend I got up the courage and gave it a shot.

'Boss, is it true that the Player of the Year gets to go on your boat?' I asked him one day at The Bridge. Roman laughed. Shit. I'd put my foot in it.

'No, no, I read somewhere that was going to happen.' I knew I shouldn't have brought it up. Eugene tried to take the edge off my embarrassment by intervening.

'Do you mean one of the dinghies, Frank? he said.

I laughed with them. I was digging myself in deeper and deeper here. I couldn't believe I'd brought it up now. Roman stopped laughing just as I was about to kill myself.

'Okay. Let's see what we can do,' Roman said.

'Oh. Okay, then. Cheers, boss.'

I never mentioned it again. I figured one humiliation in

front of your billionaire boss is enough to last a lifetime. Anyway, as it turned out I won the club accolade as well as the Football Writer's Player of the Year, while JT won the PFA award. A few days later I bumped into Roman and Eugene at the training ground. Eugene called me over.

'Find out how many days you want on the boat and we will arrange everything for you,' he said.

'Really? Ehm. Just a week would be great,' I stuttered.

'No. Just let us know how many days. It's fine,' he replied. At this point Roman was nodding his approval and smiling. F*** it, I thought. I'd got this far.

'All right, I'll have two weeks then!'

I rushed home to tell Elen and we looked at dates. Roman's secretary arranged everything else and sent through the details of the boat and where we should meet it. It all seemed too good to be true. Me? The lad who struggled to get into the West Ham team? Won the League and then voted Player of the Year and now about to holiday on *Susurro*, one of the most expensive private boats at sea? Are you sure?

Elen and I flew to Antibes and joined *Susurro* there. It was more like a floating palace. We walked from one spacious room to another. Everything was beautifully decorated and neatly appointed. We were offered some champagne and introduced to the crew – only the ten staff plus two chefs then.

We enjoyed that first day on our own and relaxed. There were five bedrooms – enough to invite the whole family and we wanted to share it with them. They would arrive the next day so we made the most of the solitude. We were woken the following morning by the low hum of the engines, looked out of the windows and saw we were pulling out of port. I wandered out on deck where one of the staff brought me fresh coffee and fruit. Yes. This is the life.

Mum rang: 'Where are you darlin'?' she asked. She and Dad had arrived at the port with my sisters and the children. They were looking for the boat.

'Don't worry,' I said. 'I'll send a tender to get you.' I couldn't quite believe I had just said the words 'I'll send a tender to get you.'

We went up on deck and waited for them to arrive and I'll never forget the look on their faces as they were helped aboard. All except Dad, that is, who played it cool with his sunglasses on and doing his best to pretend that staying on a £40 million yacht was an everyday occurrence in the life of Frank Lampard snr. Not bad for a boy from Romford!

We sailed to Cannes and then on to St Tropez. It's quite a tight little port there and we had to navigate our way in very slowly. As we did, a crowd gathered in the marina. Having clocked the size of the boat they were clearly expecting to catch a glimpse of royalty or at the very least a Hollywood film star. At first we slunk down on our chairs a bit embarrassed but in the end thought 'sod it'. We donned our shades and decided there was no escape. No one was expecting a family from Essex to disembark.

Thankfully Roman was in the vicinity on his main yacht *Pelorus* and invited us all for breakfast. He sent his tender to get us (I was getting used to the jargon by now) though the boat which picked us up was like a yacht itself. As we approached we could see a helicopter on the top as well as a mini-submarine.

Roman met us and we spent a couple of hours on board chatting about football, the season just passed, and what was to come. Dad is never shy of voicing his opinion and he enjoyed getting to speak one to one with the main man. Meanwhile, Milly and Mia were running around Roman's feet and nicking the food from the buffet while he joked with them. I smiled at the fact that my two little nieces had absolutely no idea who Roman was or that they were having a laugh with one of the most powerful men in the world.

It had only been a couple of days and I was trying hard to get used to the high life but every time I found my bearings something else unexpected happened – like Eddie Jordan, the Formula One tycoon, pulling up beside our boat and inviting the whole family over for drinks. Surreal, totally surreal. He's a really nice guy though and made us very welcome. We headed back to ours and had a barbecue when Eddie called.

'Frank. Have you and Elen got plans for tonight?' he said.

'No. Not in particular,' I replied.

'Good! Then your coming out with me. There's someone I'd like you to meet.'

'Who?'

'Bono.'

Oh, okay then. It was a great night, one I'll never forget. Thankfully I have some pictures to help convince me that it was actually real. I am not a huge music fan but Bono is a person who I'm in awe of for what he has achieved in his own profession but also because he has devoted so much time and energy to charitable causes with the desire to improve the lives of others. He's also a very down-to-earth and genuine guy. We talked football and had a laugh.

The next day we sailed on to Portofino and then Sardinia where Jamie and his wife Louise met us. We chilled out and I was very happy that I was able to share such a remarkable experience with my family. I guess people imagine that as a Premiership footballer my life is quite special and I would agree but those two weeks opened my eyes to another world.

John had a week after we left and enjoyed it just as much and though the whole episode started off a little clumsily with my question, I realize what a generous gesture it was by Roman. I think he wanted to show his appreciation for what John and I had given to Chelsea that season. More than that, he is generous of spirit – someone who enjoys sharing the benefits of his hard work – and I respect him all the more for that.

It would be impossible to know Roman, however, unless you understand the part which has driven him to be such a successful businessman. He is affable, charming and light-hearted but he is also determined, ambitious and ruthless – qualities I admire greatly. He hides that side well from most people but once you get to know him and he trusts you, windows begin to open which shed light on how he has achieved such remarkable success.

He is similar in that way to Mourinho. Both are clear on what they want and single minded in their pursuit of it. More than anything, they want to win. My experience of Roman reminds me of time spent with Jose. My relationship with the manager grew very quickly because of our football connection but I realize that it's the mutual recognition of what drives us as people which is the true bond. So it is with Roman.

I don't know the exact details of his background but from what I have read Mr Abramovich had a very humble start in life and has made his own luck. In his career there has been no second place and no room for failure so when we play a match I feel it's almost that we have to win because that's what he does. There's no option.

That's how Mourinho is and that's why he is very much Roman's commander-in-chief. If you play for Chelsea now you can't settle for being runner-up. If you want to coast or you can't be bothered pushing yourself to the limit then you will be found out. You must go the extra yard to ensure victory and if someone else takes your place in the team you fight to get it back like it's life or death. You have to be ruthless because that's the way Roman is.

I've had one-to-one conversations with him and in those moments I have looked in his eyes and seen only unyielding determination. I can sense that his hunger for success will never be satisfied and I appreciate that. It's how I am. Almost as soon as we won the first league title Roman asked me how we would win it again. He has asked me why we lost a certain game even though the result had no bearing on the outcome of the championship. He doesn't miss a single thing. He wants everything to be just right. Not almost perfect. Perfect.

It would be easy to say he doesn't really understand football and that you will always lose some games but this would be a simplistic reading of Abramovich. He may be relatively new to the game but he learns at a phenomenal rate and the reason he asks why we conceded a certain goal or why a certain player isn't doing as well as he should is because he wants to know everything. Knowledge is power, not money.

Abramovich is also very like Mourinho in his thirst to discover the reasons behind a certain event or result. We might have played poorly and still won 1–0 but he is not satisfied with that kind of victory. He wants to understand why we didn't perform better, and more importantly, what can be done to remedy the situation. I see the manager talk with Roman frequently after games and while their professional backgrounds may be very different there is clearly a meeting of minds and kindred spirits.

Together with Eugene, Peter Kenyon and the chairman Bruce Buck, Chelsea have a unity of purpose which is not typical of every football club. They share the same ambition and none of them hide the fact that they want the same thing and will do everything possible to attain it. That philosophy runs right from the owner through the officials and the players.

It's a great strength in people to ask questions about things they don't understand. It would be easy for Roman to rest on his laurels – take credit for what has been achieved and pretend he knows everything just because it happens to be working well. That is not his personality though. I have been too shy in the past to ask about things I don't fully understand for fear of looking stupid or incompetent whereas now I am inquisitive about any subject which I want to comprehend fully. Part of the reason I have become more confident in this respect is Roman's example. If he can sit and ask basic questions about football – he who is a billionaire and has made a huge success of his life – then why shouldn't I do so with others? Roman, and not just Mourinho, has been an inspiration to me.

Some people spend their life looking for problems but Roman is always seeking an answer. I know he talks at length with the manager about the team and the club and how we can improve and progress. When he comes to me and asks my opinion I feel a slight pressure because I know he will have discussed things with Mourinho first.

There have been conversations between us when he has asked how I think a particular player is performing. My reply was to say that he could improve a certain part of his technique at which point Roman's answer was very simple: 'So why don't you tell him?'

I was slightly taken aback by his directness and explained that I had done so during games but it hadn't had much effect. Roman came back again: 'Well you have to make him understand.'

He was right. I did need to take responsibility and at that moment I realized that one of his greatest qualities is that clinical ability to identify a problem and then a simple solution. He knew there was no point in him telling players how they should play (though of course they would listen) but that as vice-captain and one of the senior pros, I could.

I thought about it and knew then what he was really about. I saw the ruthless side of him – not quite nasty but I knew here is a man who will not take any shit or excuses. He wants to win. It amuses and annoys me when people attribute Chelsea's success to money. It's true that Roman has spent a lot on players but those who throw around accusations that Chelsea 'bought the title' are ignorant of the way the club and the people there work to achieve success.

True, Roman is very rich. However, he is also a very intelligent and clever manager of people and assets. He has proven that in his field of business and now he is proving it on the football field. Only those behind the scenes who work closely with him – the manager and the players – really know the secret of our success and if pressed to give a single answer I would put spirit ahead of everything else.

There is a sense of community at Chelsea which has Roman at its head followed by the manager, his staff and the players. We are all working for each other and towards the same goals. Anyone who doesn't subscribe to the common purpose is not welcome. Those who disagree with its methods don't last.

During the course of defending the title in 2005/06 there were a couple of periods when we weren't as good as we should have been. We had to have a look at ourselves and ask what was going wrong. We reminded each other of the strength we gained from everyone pulling in the same direction during the previous campaign. There were a few team meetings. Questions were asked. Are we as strong as we think we are? Why are we not competing in the same way?

Everyone needs that reminder now and again. When you go fifteen points clear of the pack so early in the season people can get carried away with themselves. It can happen easily. We needed to remind ourselves of our core values and what made us champions in the first place.

The manager asked us if we believed our standards had dropped below the level we had reached a few months previously. He asked if we thought that was acceptable. He asked if we thought Roman Abramovich would find that acceptable. He demanded that we put it right. We did.

To be fair to the manager, he more than anyone at the club had tried to guard against any complacency creeping in as we prepared for a second season in his charge. He wasted no time in preparing us for the challenge which was ahead. Nor did he try to soften the prospect of how difficult it would be to retain the championship. He called a team meeting on the first day of training and sat us down in front of a projector screen. A picture appeared of us celebrating with the Premiership trophy from the previous May. We resisted the temptation to cheer. We knew there would be a serious point.

'Last year, we were champions,' he said, but before we had time to acknowledge him he had flicked the screen on to a list of qualities which he explained we would need to possess to win a second title. He spoke of raising our own personal standards to reach another level; of being able to cope with the added incentive every team would have to beat us because of our status; of needing to guard against overconfidence and remain ambitious. The list went on – as did he – explaining each part in detail. The message was loud and clear. It would not be easy to win another championship and it would be an impossible ambition if any of us thought it was just a matter of showing up.

Mourinho was slightly more aloof than he had been the year before when he first joined the club. He came in then and built a relationship with the players quickly and easily. Now, as he spoke to us about the coming season there was a certain distance in his manner, likewise around the canteen and training ground. I asked John and Eidur if they had noticed anything. We wondered if he was all right, if there was something brewing under the surface waiting to blow up – trouble. I thought I'd learned to read his moods quite well after a year but there are times when the manager withdraws into himself and can seem introvert – unusual for a man who is normally so gregarious.

This atmosphere prevailed for five weeks – the whole of pre-season – until I realized what was going on. He had intentionally behaved more coolly towards us to keep us on our toes, to make us feel less comfortable and so make sure we never fell into a comfort zone. I could see his point. Had we come back having won the title and relaxed into the same old routine then perhaps – even subconsciously – some players might have felt that success would be just a matter of more of the same.

I've got to hand it to him – it worked. I found myself speculating that he wasn't happy with me as did everyone else. It made me want to do everything absolutely right – run faster, train harder. Like Roman, Mourinho has a steeliness about his character which he'll show whenever he thinks it's required.

He has other means of keeping us sharp as well, including strengthening the squad with players who will challenge for your place in the team. People probably thought that I was irreplaceable when the 2005/06 season started after what we had achieved in the previous campaign. I probably thought I was. Then I heard Stevie Gerrard was joining the club and my first reaction was to be really pleased. Stevie is one of the best midfielders in the world: he's dynamic, inspirational, and has the ability to score goals for fun – just what we need. Hang on. Just like me. The thing is, I reacted positively to that prospect and I hope I always will. Thankfully, I could be pretty certain in this case that the manager was pursuing

Stevie to play him alongside me. I had heard the rumours build up to the point where I was sure he was going to sign for Chelsea that summer.

It was a very exciting prospect. A midfield of Stevie, Maka and me would be hard to equal in England and Europe. I think Stevie thought he was joining because he put in a transfer request at Liverpool and you don't take that action without first putting a lot of thought into it. In the end he made a decision to stay at Anfield which I respect. I would have loved to have him play at Chelsea but I think he has basically committed himself to Liverpool for the rest of his career now. A lot was made of the situation in the press, saying it was a rejection, but I don't think too many players had turned down the chance to join the Chelsea revolution before that.

I realized that if there were to be midfielders coming in then departures must also be on the cards. That much was obvious from the fact that we had to have subs in practice games at training because there were so many outfield players. The excess of playing staff was quite uncomfortable and some midfielders even found themselves doing shooting practice on another pitch while the rest played a game because there was no room for them on the field.

In the end, Jiri Jarosik, Alexei Smertin and Tiago all left the club while Michael Essien and Shaun Wright-Phillips signed along with Asier Del Horno. Nevertheless, there was still an overload and it keeps you looking over your shoulder no matter who you are. It's just the way of Chelsea. It's also the way of Mourinho. I know him well enough now and I think he would admit that he loves a fight. He's a winner and he thrives on competition and there is no way he would be content to go through life coasting and being no better than mediocre. That mentality is passed on to the players whether it's having rivals for your position or taking pot shots at our rivals elsewhere.

Before the season started he called a team meeting where he had Arsenal's fixture list on a screen. He pointed out that after each of their Champions League games they were playing at home in the Premiership while we frequently seemed to be travelling to a difficult away game at the likes of Newcastle or Liverpool. His anger with that situation became a public debate when he famously referred to Arsenal as 'angels' while we were 'devils'. It caused a big row in the papers and people were taking the piss asking why he was moaning about something as mundane as the fixture list. Especially when it's all done randomly. Isn't it?

I think he had every right to make his point because we're a team and we don't want to be disrespected or have our season made harder by fixtures if others are getting an easier ride. Why should we just keep quiet and accept things like that? We knew that it would be harder the second season and here was an example before a ball had even been kicked. The fact that he made his point in a press conference which turned into a controversy made the players take notice. Our manager stood up and attacked a scenario he thought was unfair. He did it for us and for Chelsea even though he was potentially holding himself up to attack and ridicule.

At a team meeting he made the point that the fixtures were another example of what we were up against in our battle to defend the title. It made us more determined than ever to make sure we won it again. He is a shrewd and clever man and there are times when he will take that kind of action in a calculated way because he knows the kind of reaction it will provoke. It's not always the case that he's trying to manipulate a situation. It's simply in his personality to confront aggression and injustice head on.

I was there in Barcelona in 2005 when it all kicked off after our Champions League match in the Nou Camp and I know that a lot of the time he was fighting a just cause, yet he was portrayed as the villain and criticized for his actions and comments. Maybe his attitude is unconventional – he is very strong in his conviction and that might shock people but a man should not be condemned for holding to his principles. He was standing up for the players and for the club. I appreciate the unswerving loyalty he has shown to me, likewise the other players. He has the complete loyalty and commitment of the dressing room because he has earned it.

That's not to say that he shies away from criticizing us when it is justified and the opening match of the 2005/06 season is an example of when he did just that in order to get the right reaction. We had gone to newly promoted Wigan Athletic for the first test in our title defence but the end result didn't reflect the match. Crespo scored in time added on to take three points and afterwards the manager told the media that we didn't deserve to win. In fact, we barely deserved a draw. I didn't feel sharp enough and we looked sluggish all over the pitch. For all the talk beforehand about making sure we would be champions again, this game taught us a lesson about what the season would be like.

Wigan had been incredible and only a wonder goal had got us out of jail. Mourinho didn't mince his words in the dressing room afterwards though he didn't single out anyone in particular. He paid respect to Paul Jewell and his team for the way they had performed but made it clear that if we played as badly a week later against Arsenal then the season would turn into a long goodbye to the title rather than a glorious defence.

The boss was desperate to win but the rivalry with Arsenal took on a more personal twist because of the growing animosity between him and Arsene Wenger. I was aware of it, though mostly through what I read in the papers. Both managers were quite open in their hostility, which I put down to good old fashioned banter more than anything else. Of course people take things and run with them and they can get way out of control, yet when I look at Mourinho and Wenger I see very similar qualities.

They are both talented, highly motivated, and very passionate individuals. They both want to win and they're not scared to admit it so when things got a bit out of hand between them I wasn't overly surprised. The rivalry between the two clubs has always been fierce so given Mourinho is no shrinking violet it was probably only a matter of time before there would be fireworks.

Wenger had a habit of constantly referring to Chelsea's spending in the transfer market which I suppose stemmed from his frustration at being poor by comparison. Both Essien and Wright-Phillips were strongly linked with moves to Arsenal before we jumped in and bought them for a combined fee of £45 million. Relations had never been great – the Ashley Cole saga didn't help – and they reached an all-time low during that season when the two seemed to be trading blows like a couple of old-fashioned prize-fighters.

I don't have a problem with it. I think it's great that two managers can come out and have that kind of battle – it makes life and the game more interesting for all of us. There has been a calming down since and if they still harbour some ill feelings towards one another it's no more than any ordinary work environment is capable of throwing up. It's not possible for everyone to be friends especially when they are competing for the same trophies.

On the pitch, we felt there was unfinished business with Arsenal. We were champions and they came second but there had been a lot of crowing from their side about 'being the better team'. Bollocks. The best team wins the league and I didn't see Arsenal parading any silverware. Unfortunately we hadn't beaten them in the Premiership the season before so when we faced them at the Bridge in the second match the following August we had more points than three to prove.

It was a very tight game and in the end a lucky goal from Didi sealed it but it didn't mean any less to us. We were desperate to win, just as we had been in the Manchester United game the year before, because it was a statement of how determined we were to retain the title. Publicly Mourinho had declared that the championship would not rest on the result of a match so early in the season but in the dressing room he urged us to win and show Arsenal that we meant business.

From that successful if not so impressive start we began a sequence of games which had a bizarre result in terms of exacerbating the image of Chelsea as the most hated club in England. We beat West Brom 4–0 at home in a game which I will remember for the fact that Luna was born the previous Monday. I spent the night before the game sleeping on a squeaky camp bed in the hospital where Elen and our baby daughter were staying. I was a bit knackered from lack of sleep but the elation of seeing Luna safely into the world meant there was no shortage of adrenalin. I kissed my little girl before heading off to the Bridge and promised to celebrate her birth with a goal. The lads were brilliant with me when I turned up and John dragged me aside to say that if I scored we had to do the 'cradled baby' celebration made famous by Bebeto at the 1994 World Cup finals. As it turned out I got one for Luna and another for her Mum.

We recorded another three Premiership wins to make it six on the bounce without conceding a goal but our ability to take points and give nothing away seemed to provoke resentment rather than respect. 'How dare Chelsea continue to be the best team in the country?' appeared to be the attitude adopted by some sections of the media.

I went into training the week before the home match with Aston Villa and the lads were chatting about the fact that a reward of £10,000 had been offered by the *Sun* for the first player to score a goal against us. F***ing hell. I couldn't believe it. They wanted us to lose so much they were prepared to pay people to try and beat us. At first I was angry because it felt unjust for anyone other than your own club to offer incentive bonuses for specific matches. They got round that rule though and made it 'sweeter' by making the offer payable to a charity of the winning player's choice. As it turned out Luke Moore did get a goal against us that weekend and so the spell was broken. It did affect our concentration though.

We had enjoyed such a good start to the campaign that we began to relax too much at the beginning of games and it seemed to take losing a goal before we really started to play.

We had three home games on the spin in which we went 1–0 down. The manager called a few meetings about it because it got to the stage where though we were winning games 4–2 or 5–1 we weren't happy. Neither was he because we were waiting for something to happen in games before we kicked in. Those periods can be dangerous. Bad habits like that are not easy to pull back from. While there was no need to panic we did understand there was a problem. When we drew our match at Everton the talk was of staying unbeaten through the season; within a month a defeat at Manchester United dismissed that notion.

We lost by a single goal but the match was one which we had dominated and were very unlucky not to gain something from. I traipsed from the pitch very upset. Only a few months earlier I'd captained the team at Old Trafford as champions and we had been given a guard of honour by the United players as we took the pitch. Mourinho, however, salvaged the mood in the camp with his after-match analysis. 'You deserved to get victory or at least a draw from the game,' he said in the dressing room. 'Do not be downhearted for you fought like champions and if we continue in this way then no one will stop us from keeping our title.'

We needed that rallying cry. Everywhere we looked Chelsea were being caned and along with being accused of being unfairly rich and cheating, some people were saying that we were boring to watch as well. I was beginning to wonder if I was back at West Ham!

The 'boring' tag had started with Sir Alex Ferguson towards the end of the previous season and then resurfaced because we were twelve points clear. Boring for some maybe but not for us. Ferguson claimed we were too direct which was strange given that the OPTA stats for our season that year showed we had most goals, most shots on goal, most passes completed, and, critically, most points.

Some of the Liverpool boys then kicked off another round of banter baiting when they compared our style to the Wimbledon team of old. I found that one very amusing since Liverpool were the team who signed Peter Crouch, and if you do that you're clearly going to play to his strengths.

It was yet another episode in the rivalry between the teams flaring up in the face of competition. We had demolished them 4–1 at Anfield earlier in the league and so when we met again in February there was a lot of tension bubbling under the surface – some of it leftovers from the previous season's encounters.

We dominated the match and were two up and waiting for the whistle when a row erupted in the box between Arjen Robben and José Reina. Reina pushed Robbie in the face who then went down causing the usual spat of posturing between players. What ensued, however, was an unjust portrayal of Chelsea as the villains of the piece.

The first thing that should be considered is that Reina flattened Eidur at the corner flag. Then, when Robbie confronted him he lifted his hand. To me, those two actions taken together add up to a red card though players are often ordered off for lifting their hands alone. I know that I can't push someone in the face because I will be sent off, no matter what the provocation – and I've heard some interesting things said.

If someone in our team is sent off and we lose the game because of it then I will pull that player up for it. For that reason it actually doesn't matter if Robbie went down from

Reina's challenge or not – the moment he lifted his hand he risked being sent off. I don't argue that Robben didn't go down easily; I know I would never have gone down in the same manner in that situation. Players are different though. I have seen players do it in similar circumstances many times and I don't agree with it. I didn't feel angry with Robbie at the time and I defended him because he is my team-mate. Benitez chose to make an issue of it afterwards when he asked if Robben was in hospital. I would liked to have asked him if he had seen Reina nearly put Eidur in hospital seconds before with his wild lunge before he pushed Robbie in the face? If the Liverpool manager had said that his keeper also deserved to be sent off then fair enough – but he didn't. Furthermore, the incident happened in the final minute of the match which they had already lost so it made no difference. Benitez purposefully made a huge deal out of it because he wanted to shift focus away from a comprehensive defeat – a case of a lot of smoke bellowing from not much fire.

What pissed me off most though was that for weeks on end Robbie was labelled a cheat and a diver. I know he went down too easily in that match and I also know that he's not the strongest player in the world. If you touch him in training he can go down simply because he's so quick. A lot of it has to do with upsetting his balance on the run. It's a grey area in football and one that is difficult to judge correctly. If someone dives blatantly when there has been no contact then that is wrong. I don't want to see that in football and neither does any right minded person. It's even worse when it's done to win a penalty.

The Liverpool incident with Robbie sparked a general campaign to kick diving out of football but it seemed to me that a lot of the negativity was directed at Chelsea. It didn't help that Didier was frequently accused of diving during the season, capped by his comment on *Match of the Day* after a victory over Manchester City: 'Sometimes I dive, sometimes I don't.' That remark, however, was taken completely out of context – the context being that he used the word 'dive' when he meant to say 'go down'. He should also be given the benefit of the doubt in that he was speaking in a second language but more so because he was being honest about what happens in a match. What he was trying to explain is that when he is touched – with varying degrees of force – there are times when he will stay on his feet and others when he will fall. That is very different to admitting to being a diver, which is complete bollocks. Anyone in their right mind would never come out and say that on national TV and Didier is not stupid. But from that moment the question of diving spiralled into a massive issue which always seemed to have Chelsea at its centre.

I have seen and heard other managers accuse players from many clubs of diving when I know and have witnessed that some of their players have been guilty of exactly the same thing. So what? You forget those moments or you don't want to mention that player? That's not how it works. And then they jump on the bandwagon and have a go at Didi. It's a joke.

I watch Spanish and Italian football and there is a culture there of going down if you have passed a player but believe you haven't gained any advantage. People who have played abroad bring that culture with them and what is happening now is a reaction to the threat of this practice becoming more widespread.

Dad always told me to be careful when tackling in international football because if you get too close then an opponent will automatically go to ground. The truth is there is fault on both sides of that scenario. People argue that one player has gone down but on the other hand it's lazy defending to simply stick out a leg and put yourself and your team in jeopardy. It's harder to stay up and jockey than it is to just dive in.

I've been in games when one of our players has instigated a great piece of play to go past someone and is then caught but still manages to stay on his feet. I admit I have willed my team-mate to go down because I can see that he's not going to benefit from stumbling on after he has been fouled. I have also said it to them after the event. Ask yourself if you've ever seen a similar situation involving your team. Did you think the same as me? I bet you did. We all have.

The fact is that it's impossible to be objective about this if you are a player within a particular team for the simple reason that you have a vested interest in the outcome of an incident whether it be for or against you. We will all give partisan views based on allegiance and that's why the referee is the only one who can interpret and decide the consequences of a particular action.

There is a fierce debate about what's right and wrong in these scenarios and the conclusion I have come to is that anyone who dives where there has been no contact whatsoever is a cheat; I would say that of my own team-mate if one of them was guilty of doing so.

When contact has been made then the matter is not so cut and dried: each case has to be looked at on its own merits and in its own context before it can be adjudged to be against the law or spirit of the game. I will stand by my team-mates in situations like that because one of the greatest strengths we have is unity. I have to do that and my instinct is always to protect my team-mates - especially when it gets to the stage it did during the 2005/06 season where Didi was victimized by the media and some officials.

The 'diving' debate should also not be allowed to detract from other arguably more significant events in that season, notably the death of two Chelsea stalwarts. Peter Osgood and Tony Banks were highly regarded at the club for different reasons and I always found them to be generous with their time and very nice people. Ozzy was an absolute legend at Chelsea and for those of us who have tried to bring back the glory days to Stamford Bridge he will always be an inspiration. Tony Banks was a devoted fan who always had time for me and my family and who lived and breathed Chelsea. Like Ozzy, he will not be forgotten.

We moved to the Christmas period and went to Arsenal on 18 December for a match which had less significance in terms of the title race than it might once have had because they struggled through the first half of the season. It didn't make it any less satisfying to win well and we felt more comfortable than ever with our position. It wasn't until we turned up at Manchester City ten days later that something went very wrong.

I had surpassed the previous record for consecutive Premiership appearances at Portsmouth a month earlier. As the game drew nearer I had become more nervous that I might not make it. I had come that far and felt very proud that I had achieved something unique. The manager was also very supportive and put aside any thoughts of resting me because he wanted me to get the record. Never once did he ask me if I wanted to stop – he simply helped me through. After I played my 160th game, at Fratton Park, I immediately wanted to go on and make 200 or more. It's just the way I am. Then fate stepped in.

During the day of the match at Manchester City I had a viral flu and felt quite ill. When we got to the stadium I told the doctor who gave me a vitamin injection to try and quell the fever. Mourinho asked me if I was okay and I thought I was but after five minutes of the warm-up I knew I couldn't play. I sat in the stand while the game went on without me feeling physically sick with the virus and just as sick at missing the match and losing out on stretching the run a bit further. Understandably, people were coming up to me and asking me why I wasn't playing but I knew that there was no chance I could have. I would love to think I might get close to it again and I doubt an outfield player will break my record though I have a suspicion that a goalkeeper probably will.

I had a lot to feel proud of at that time apart from breaking the record. Having been recognized in England for my performances I was then voted runner-up in the European and World Player of the Year awards for 2005. I was pleased that my contribution as a player and goals in domestic and international football had pushed me on to a new level.

Ronaldinho beat me to first award in the Ballon D'or and he deserved the title. I went to Zurich for the World Player ceremony which I consider to be the ultimate accolade as it is voted for by the national coaches and captains of every country of FIFA. When the shortlist of Samuel Eto'o, Roni and me was announced a month earlier, I was content just to be considered alongside two such great players.

I arrived at the Opera House for the pre-ceremony press conference having heard a rumour that I was once again runner-up to Roni. I wouldn't have argued with that especially when I saw that the entire board of directors of Barcelona had turned up to support their men. No one from Chelsea had bothered to make the trip.

The official announcement was duly made and I was thrilled to be on the same podium as a player whom I regard to be the best on the planet and potentially the greatest who ever lived. Team awards are the ones which are most valuable but an award like that means a lot because it's one you can't bluff.

People can win the Golden Boot for being top scorer in a single season and then never be heard of again. Likewise, some players can win an award for an exceptional year and then slip into mediocrity. To be named in the top three in the world, though, you have first to get on people's radar by putting in the work and performances and after that move to a different level altogether to actually be nominated.

I have taken a real shine to Roni since we first met for the simple reason that is he is such a down to earth person. I was (and am) in awe of him and wasn't sure what to expect in person but he's so enthusiastic and friendly that you couldn't fail to like him. Previously Zidane was the player I idolized and saw as the ultimate footballer but Roni has taken that a step further again.

My all-time favourite player is Diego Maradona but Roni is still young and I wouldn't be surprised if he surpassed even the great El Diego by the time his career is over. At Barcelona he has single-handedly galvanized the team in the time he's been there and has been responsible, more than any other individual, for turning that great club around.

One of the reasons for that is his attitude. Football is as natural an expression for him as speaking is for the rest of us – maybe that's why he always plays with a smile on his face. I faced him two years in succession in the Champions League and he was devastating. People say of the best players – Thierry Henry is another – that when they are on their game there is nothing you can do to stop them. Roni is different again. He is goalscorer and creator; he's explosive and can deceive you with a trick from his boot or just a look in his eye. You're scared to tackle him because you know he can make one move and flick past you, leaving you for dead.

More important than any of this though is that so many times he plays the killer simple ball. Rooney is the same. He has all the skills and thrills to do whatever he wants with a ball but if there's a pass to be made which will get a goal then he plays it. Roni is no circus act. He's not there to please the crowd. He wants to win football matches and you cannot teach that; just like his God-given talent, it is pure instinct. I love watching him play and he has become the symbol of Barcelona in the time he has played there. Like the rest of Europe, I was eagerly awaiting the opportunity to play against Roni again when Chelsea were up against Barca in the first knockout phase of the Champions League.

We didn't go into the first leg on the best run of form. Losing 3–0 at Middlesbrough was the worst defeat to date in the Mourinho era, the only one where we deserved to get beaten because none of us played well. On other occasions we lost yet the manager has said we were the better team and at times I have agreed with him. Boro', however, was a hold your hands up job. We started badly and it got worse. I'd sensed the danger earlier in the season when we started to concede goals and then we shipped three in one match. Not the best preparation for facing, Roni, Eto'o and a certain Lionel Messi.

In addition, Barca returned to the Bridge having learned from the season before when we had ripped them apart in the opening twenty-six minutes. They were more compact in midfield and clever holding the ball. They created a couple of half chances before Asier Del Horno was sent off and once again controversy descended on the contest.

I immediately agreed with the referee's decision after Del's challenge on Messi, knowing how any physical tackle is viewed by a European official. When I looked at it on TV afterwards I thought it was more likely a yellow card. It certainly wasn't a good challenge – mistimed, resulting in Del falling into the Barca player – but maybe if the ref had taken a bit more time to decide it would have been different.

I felt like I had been in this movie before. Didi the season before and now Del. Barca are the last team in the world you want to play with ten men. We managed to get to half-time without conceding and in the second half with Eidur and I running the midfield, we were doing quite well. I whipped in a free-kick and John's presence was enough to cause chaos and the ball was flicked into the net.

Within minutes though I saw why if you get the chance to kill Barca off you must grab the dagger with both hands. Didi was through on goal but his shot was saved. Then from the corner they ran up the pitch and Eto'o scored an equalizer.

That's how quick they were: able to retaliate when you least expect it.

It had been a tough call for our manager. With ten men he may have been tempted to shut up shop and play for a goalless draw but Barca have so much talent that such a result is unlikely. I think he called it right and it was a lack of concentration on our part which cost us. Roni and Messi were on fire, blazing shots from all angles and threatening to blow us away.

They did just that with the second goal which once again was a sucker punch, delivered just when we thought we were getting a bit stronger. Going into the second leg 2–1 down was painful enough to contemplate but it was aggravated when I tore a small muscle in my hamstring while training with England. I missed the match against Uruguay and then that against West Brom in which Mourinho had the balls to stand up to Bryan Robson when the two had a row on the touchline. People said the pressure was showing. Oh really?

I trained in Barca on the Monday before the game and we were told that we would start with three wide men – Coley and Duff on the flanks while Robbie would play through the centre behind Didi. Mourinho's plan was to field three speedy attackers in the hope of over-running the defence with me and Maka behind them. Unfortunately our attack minded players didn't manage to do what the coach wanted of them partly because Barca read the match and did everything to stifle them.

Roni scored his customary goal and with a couple of minutes left I scored from a penalty but it was too little too late. We lost the tie in the first leg at home when we were down to ten men. A big deal was made of the fact that we didn't start in the Nou Camp with two strikers but I wasn't surprised by the selection. We couldn't afford to get exposed and go further behind and so the manager put out a team capable of attack and defence. Elimination was hard to take though not as bad as the previous two years when we had fallen at the semi-final stage to teams we felt we should have beaten. I felt Chelsea and Barca were the two teams in the competition capable of going all the way and so it proved to be.

After the game Roni came over to me and we swapped shirts and embraced. It was a mark of respect and friendship, then he smiled at me in this particular way and joked that one day he hoped we would be on the pitch together playing for the same team. There had been a lot of rumours about interest from Barca in signing me, and Roni had always been very generous about me in interviews. The Barca directors had also been very friendly towards me at the World Player of the Year event the previous December and I appreciated their courtesy.

Barca was the European team I was most interested in as a child in the days of Maradona, Romario and Ronaldo. I have always been intrigued by the stadium and when I got older I grew to love the city itself – now even more so since I have known Elen and we have visited her family there. People have tried to suggest that Elen's roots may be a reason for me wanting to leave Chelsea but the truth is that she has never tried to influence me in choosing one club over another, and is happy living wherever my career takes me.

Barca exude the majesty and glamour befitting one of the world's great clubs, and to have your name mentioned as a possible recruit is an honour in itself. If I ever did have an ambition to play abroad then Barca would be one of the clubs I would want to play for. I looked at Roni after he made his quip and thought about what he meant. We laughed and I wished him luck for the tournament. He didn't need it.

Even though we had lost, there was a part of me that realized how lucky I was to have the chance to pit myself against one of the greatest players in football. I have been fortunate in my experience so far to be able to include most of the best in the game among my opponents or colleagues and if Roni is the best attacking player there is then John Terry is certainly the best defender.

We are very lucky in England to have JT and Rio Ferdinand who are unmatched in the game. JT is unique in modern football for the way he is able to block any player by reading the game intuitively or through sheer physical force. He leads by example so no one can ever accuse him of asking them to do something JT hasn't done himself. He inspires as a captain and you know that you can rely on him 100 per cent every time you are on the pitch with him.

When you work so closely with someone it's a big advantage to be on the same page with regards to your approach to work. I didn't know him very well until I signed for Chelsea but almost immediately there was a synergy between us. We had grown up playing in the same league in east London and there is a mental fortitude about John which I know is one of my own strengths. We also share the hunger to win, a determination to succeed, and the motivation to play whenever possible.

Strangely enough, I got to know him a lot better through adversity rather than triumph. He went through a very difficult time after an incident outside the Wellington Club involving him, Jody, and a nightclub bouncer in September 2002. I turned up for training one Friday morning and neither of the lads were there – later that day we discovered that they had spent the night in a police cell. At that point football became irrelevant as I was very worried for both of them. We had an FA Cup tie at Norwich on the Saturday to which John travelled by car rather than in the team coach. He was on the bench and so was I. Spending the night in custody had clearly had a bad effect on him. The situation was made worse because he hadn't done anything wrong – as the court later confirmed. The whole situation became a long and drawn out process prior to the trial being heard, while all the time John became more and more concerned.

John and Jody are both very strong characters but Jody seemed better able to handle the pressure at that time. John by contrast became very emotional towards the end of the whole saga. I could understand why: he was just beginning to emerge as the one of the best footballers in England and though he was innocent of the charges laid against him it didn't mean he wasn't scared of what might happen should the situation get out of control.

We spoke about what was likely to happen and I tried to keep his attitude positive and his spirits up. I was concerned for him but I could barely imagine what he was putting himself through. He did come through it though, as a stronger person and was even identified as a suitable candidate for captain of the club.

When Mourinho arrived he assessed the character of John and myself and decided we were the perfect combination to lead the team and represent the club. We have grown as individuals since being awarded that responsibility but we have also become closer as friends. We even think alike when it comes to certain matters around the club. For example, I might notice something which I'm unhappy about only for John to raise it with me and ask my opinion. To a certain extent this is instinctive but it also reflects a shared desire to get things as close to perfect as possible.

We retain the same inner desire to continually improve ourselves. At 14 no one was touting John as the future best defender in England, never mind the world. Instead he was looked on as a stubby midfielder who couldn't run very well, yet he has taken his talent and made himself into the player he is. I can relate to this and appreciate what he has achieved in his life. Consequently when we see a young player who has ability but fails to apply himself, or just can't be bothered trying, we will get the hump with him in the same way.

We pick up on the same things and we want the club to keep moving forward which means making sure we take everyone else in the same direction. At training we work very hard and push on all the time even though as senior players people might think we have earned the right to take it easy now and then. We won't. It's not in my nature nor is it in his. We know how important it is to keep raising the bar at Chelsea. JT can lose at five-a-side and will be upset with himself all day. I'm the same. It might be a pissy little five-a-side which doesn't matter but it means a lot to John and I. The smallest details like that are important in building a winning mentality.

That's why I feel so comfortable around him both on and off the pitch. There's no one in the world I'd rather have in my defence than John. And he gets you about ten goals a season as well! Show me another defender who has a comparable scoring record. For me, John is the best central defender in the world and I'm proud to call him my team-mate and friend.

But it's not just me who feels that way. He plays a very important role as well in the way he brings all of the lads together and makes sure that the exceptional team spirit we have is maintained. He has all of the players' numbers in his phone and is the chief organizer of team days out to go-karting or golf. He set up one particular outing to Cheltenham races for the squad which was great fun except there was a dire shortage of winners among us and for the ridiculous newspaper stories about losing money which followed our trip. Gambling among footballers was already a hot topic of discussion in the media. Newspapers seemed to be particularly hysterical about it, which is odd given that betting is as much a part of British culture as football or fish and chips and has been a popular pastime across society. However, because of the ongoing obsession with the amount of money footballers earn it was suddenly deemed obscene that any of us should have a flutter. That denies the basic principle that gambling is relative to the amount of money you earn. The maths are quite simple: footballers are fortunate enough to earn more money than most professions and so can afford to bet more. Problems arise when people bet more than they can afford and suddenly find themselves in financial difficulty.

When I gamble – and I don't bet frequently – it is never very much and I always have a limit which I adhere to very strictly. If I reach that limit then I get very pissed off and stop automatically. I work hard to earn my salary and I prefer to think of myself as more cautious with money. Though I never gamble very much, I have been cited in some press stories as having lost x amount which is nonsense. I always bet well within my limit and much less than I could stake if I wanted to.

There are also those who claim that there is a massive betting culture in football that is addictive and out of control. I realize that gambling can be addictive but that kind of environment doesn't exist in my experience. As long as people do it responsibly then it's not causing any harm and shouldn't be the subject of scandal.

As a high-profile player you understand that everything you do will be scrutinized and analysed by the media but as far as gambling is concerned there's no wrong doing – it's not like taking drugs or drink driving. It only helps fan the flames when ex-pros like Tony Cascarino claim that a certain player has staked £200,000 on a football match – it's wrong that he makes that kind of accusation off the back of gossip. I know it's untrue and it also gives a very wrong impression of what people are actually betting. Of course, it only makes a story if the sums quoted are scandalous. It happened the day we went to Cheltenham and a tabloid ran a front page story the following day claiming that we had lost £500,000 between us in a single afternoon. Normally I would laugh but in this case it's not funny – it's completely untrue, not to mention pathetic. I can categorically deny that the amount staked was anywhere near that figure. It would have been difficult to approach the alleged sum given that some of the Portuguese lads were making outrageous bets of a whole tenner a time on one race!

Betting was simply the latest football issue for the papers. A couple of years previously it had been sex, then drink, and now gambling was focus of their moral crusade against football. If you took away those three things from the lives of most people they wouldn't have much enjoyment left so why should I or anyone else be persecuted simply because we are professional footballers? Such questions seemed fair enough to ask in return (though we never get the chance) but there were other more pressing concerns which needed to be attended to on the pitch.

We had gone through a patch in the season when our form, our ability and our reputation as champions was being questioned but it wasn't just the players who were under scrutiny.

The Fulham game in March 2006 was an example of the manager doing what he thought was right for the team. We were a goal down and not playing well so he decided to take off Wright-Phillips and Coley after around twenty-five minutes. After we lost the match, his decision was closely scutinized, with some people claiming that Mourinho had been impetuous. This is ignoring the fact that had we won then it would have been 'an inspired move'. It doesn't actually matter what other people think. If Jose Mourinho thinks the team is better off with different players on the pitch then I'm not going to argue with him. Why would I after what he has achieved in his two years at Chelsea? It was just another example of his ability to make a decision and act on his own conviction. I agree that it was a bad game for us to lose but I don't blame the manager for what was a poor performance by the players.

None the less, our lead was being cut down and Manchester United had had a game in hand on us for quite some time. There were drastic predictions of our demise, collapse, and general surrender. We reacted in the right way though. We drew at Birmingham three weeks later but apart from that we didn't drop any more points until the championship was won. I guess those who were looking at fixtures like West Ham, Bolton, and Everton and predicting a very sticky run-in for us were a bit disappointed.

We approached the home game against my former club in the knowledge that failure to win would allow Manchester United to get even closer. We were seven points ahead but we went a goal down to West Ham after eleven minutes, closely followed by the turning point of our entire season. I thought Maniche was a bit unlucky to be sent off for making contact with Lionel Scaloni in a 50/50 but there was no point in arguing. At that point I could almost hear the cheers of Man United supporters around the country as well as others who thought they saw the wheels falling off our title bid. Worse than any of that, though, was the sound of the away fans at the other end of the stadium dancing with joy as we tried to re-organize. I was waiting for the taunts and wasn't disappointed: 'Lampard, Lampard what's the score?' Yes, yes. I know. F***. Of all the teams in all the world to be caught up in this scenario with. F*** it. We'll just have to beat them with ten men.

I looked at the manager who signalled Crespo would drop deep and draw his marker while Didi would continue up front on his own. No need to change personnel. No panic. I liked that. It sent out the right signal. We were going to win. Within minutes Didi put us level from my pass and then Crespo and JT netted before half-time to put us in a winning position. Get in there. Willie Gallas scored a fourth and I could hardly believe it.

I'm not sure if any team has ever won a match in the

emphatic manner we did with only ten men. It was an amazing effort and mentally we knew then we had won the league. At the end we stayed on the pitch and celebrated with our fans. They knew how important that win had been and so did we. There were a few stray West Ham supporters left in the ground as I walked to the tunnel giving me some abuse. I smiled sweetly in their direction and held up a fist. Have some of that.

We went to Bolton the following week and I scored, before winning by three against Everton at home on Easter Monday. I netted my twentieth goal of the season against David Moyes' side which is a landmark total for a midfielder. People say that ten from midfield is a great return but having got nineteen the previous season as well, I would like to think that I've pushed my standards to another level.

Amusingly, Peter Kenyon had come up to me at the party in the Stamford Bridge gym the summer before, when we were celebrating the league title, and remarked on my feat.

'Congratulations on being top scorer,' he said. 'I bet you won't be next season.'

'I don't want to be,' I replied.

As it turned out I was top scorer, though I never did nail down what he bet me. I was especially pleased since there were spells in the season when I was playing alongside Maka while Eidur was ahead and so my options to run forward were limited. Scoring sixteen in the Premiership also meant that I beat the record for a midfielder held by Robert Pires and Paul Scholes who got fourteen.

The increase was in part due to changing my technique in hitting the ball. I used to strike it much more true, which is fine if you can direct the ball into the tightest corner of the goal at power. The modern football is lighter though, and if you hit across it you can make it move around in flight which makes it much harder for a keeper to save. Even big Petr in our team ends up palming a shot that is coming straight at him into the net if you catch it right and it suddenly changes direction.

With victory over Everton nothing could stop us on our course to another league win. We knew for a few weeks that the FA Cup was our only other chance of silverware and the opportunity of making history by becoming the first Chelsea side to win the 'Double' was an alluring one. Only one problem: we had to play Liverpool, again, and it was a semi-final.

I would be lying if I said that there wasn't an eerie sense of déjà vu about the whole scenario. Apart from the fact that this would be the tenth meeting between our two sides in two seasons, the pain of the Champions League defeat had not completely healed when we ran out at Old Trafford for another duel.

The situation was also strangely familiar in that we were well ahead in the league while their only chance of silverware was this last cup competition. I don't believe in fate as a rule but I began to wonder if something wasn't conspiring against us; a thought which occurred again after they took the lead.

Garcia then struck from range after the break before all of the pressure we had exerted finally paid off and Didi pulled a goal back with twenty minutes left. It seemed to be the longest twenty minutes of the entire season. Time and time again we pressed forward and wave after wave of attack ended in nothing. There is no more desperate feeling in football than chasing a lead in the dying minutes of a semi-final, more so the FA Cup which means an awful lot to me as an Englishman.

When the fourth official signalled five minutes added on, my mood lifted and I wondered if the omens had perhaps turned in our favour. We were getting closer and closer to an equalizer when Coley was put clear only seven yards out. I watched and was sure he would score. He must. He didn't. As the ball floated over the bar and into the crowd I knew our hopes of the Double went with it.

It wasn't Coley's fault. We had other chances – enough to win the game twice – but didn't take them. There was a sinking feeling, a sense of disappointment that the challenge of the season now boiled down to one game. But what a game. The stage was set for the title party when the invited guests were Manchester United. It could hardly have been more dramatic except for the fact that we were already comfortably ahead in the table.

There was still an air of great expectation around the game though. To most players and fans of my generation Manchester United are the team who have exerted the greatest influence on the English game; from the distinctive style of play to the incredible haul of trophies, they have proven themselves to be the dominant force in football in this country. To me they represent the yardstick by which all others must expect to be measured and having won one championship perhaps Chelsea came up to their knees – or maybe just the shins. The fact remained that no team other than United had successfully defended the Premiership title. I remembered sitting with Gary Neville in the England dressing room back at the beginning of the season and thinking about the fact that he has six league winner's medals – incredible. I wanted that. I also wanted Chelsea to be that good, that ruthless, and that successful.

The crowd sensed the significance of winning the championship against the most decorated club of the past twenty years and so did the players. We started with a real spark, going one up within minutes, that spread like a house fire as we scored two more to ensure there could be no doubt about who were the champions of England.

Coley scored a great goal which was well deserved, given the way he has made himself into an invaluable player under Mourinho – a status reflected in his importance to Chelsea and England. Joe is someone I have known for a very long time. I was a youth team player at West Ham when we were told to go out to the training pitch and watch a young boy play because he was so good. We were told he was the best prospect to come to the club in years and so with that build up we rushed him out. He was good all right: tricky on the ball, fast off it, and with an ability to beat players for fun. It was Joe Cole and he was ten years old. I felt a bit uneasy about the pressure he must have been under though; so much expectation surrounding someone so young.

That pressure only got worse as time went by. It was very unfair. Even Rooney hadn't had such a same burden because he exploded on to the scene at sixteen whereas Coley faced that build-up from the age of just eleven. Everyone could see he was exceptionally talented but the gap between talent and living up to other people's expectations can be very big indeed. When he came into the first team at seventeen he was tagged the 'new Maradona' and inevitably Joe started putting pressure on himself to add to the substantial pressure that already existed.

After I left West Ham he became a regular in the first team and was given the captaincy by Glenn Roeder, which I think was a mistake – not because Joe wasn't capable but because he already had enough to cope with. Why make him captain when that only added to the unrealistic expectations of the crowd? It was the season they were relegated and inevitably the captain takes a lot of the flack in that situation. Joe didn't need any more strain. Coley is passionate and can be quite volatile, and I know he took the captaincy on wanting nothing more than to save the club from going down. But the fact is that he was already the team's best player and so adding more stress to his load was not a good idea. It all got too much for him at Bolton in the relegation season and he was sent off.

When he came to Chelsea, Joe faced pressure of a different kind. In his first game he was desperate to show people what he could do and ended up very frustrated after having just a few minutes on the pitch. That was very much the story of his first season at the club. Since then Mourinho has treated him very differently. He has taken Joe aside and worked with him – honed his skill to help transform into a player who recognizes the importance of playing in particular patterns as well as being tactically disciplined. In short, he has converted an individual talent into a team asset. People think the manager has treated Coley harshly because he has spent time on the bench and on occasion been criticized by him despite scoring some important goals. I don't agree. Mourinho has done what was needed to make him a Chelsea player.

While the manager has been the guiding hand most of the credit for the transformation has to go to Joe himself. He would never have achieved what he has if he hadn't had the desire and the self-belief to make it. He has also found a new balance thanks to no longer heaping pressure on himself; now he knows he can impress people by releasing the ball at the right moment rather than beating a man for a second time. Things like that have made a huge difference to his game. He has developed and flourished as part of the team but it's wrong to accuse Mourinho of being too rigid and of discouraging flair players. The point is that there is a right time for that kind of thing and I don't think he is any different in his attitude than any other great coach.

The philosophy is simple enough. I get frustrated when a player does a trick and passes the ball a few seconds later than he might have. People will stand in awe of the skill and it's nice to watch but the most valuable players in football are those who are effective, who know when to do the right thing at the right time. There's no need for a step-over when there's a simple pass on.

The very best in the world know the difference. Ronaldinho is one of them – he doesn't waste time indulging himself when there are goals to be scored. There is an argument that skilful players should be given a free role in a team. This is a total fallacy. It's impossible to be a major influence in a team capable of winning the Champions League and play without responsibility. Maybe that worked fifteen years ago but modern football is a lot more demanding of every player on the field.

Every other week ex-players suggest that Joe needs to be 'set free' and I think 'Oh, I wonder why you aren't a manager? Maybe it's because you haven't got a clue.' Some claim that Joe needs to be given freedom to play as an old-fashioned wide player, but that shows a basic misreading of what's needed from a team to win the league.

Every player now has to have defensive duties and tactical awareness no matter how skilful they are, and you will only find someone who thinks he can get away with doing little of either in a middle-ranking team going nowhere fast. It takes dedication and practice to reach the very top level, and when I stay behind to work on my shooting or free-kicks Joe often joins me.

Few people have worked as hard on their finishing as he has and he is reaping the reward of that with the goals he's scoring. The fact that he was able to do it in the game which clinched the league was very fitting. I ran to celebrate with Joe and the rest of the lads when his shot hit the net and we were sure we had won our second title.

Unlike the season before, when it was impossible to predict my emotions after winning it, I had been in a way preparing myself for this moment for a while. I didn't enjoy it any less but the two experiences were a great contrast. The outpouring of joy which accompanied the win over United was for a season of extremely hard work and for the fact that we had proved good enough to retain the title. The difference a year earlier was that then we had experienced a communal release from fifty years of waiting, from half a century of frustration and anxiety. It was a feeling so special that I wonder if I will ever re-live it in my career.

After the United game, Elen and Luna joined me on the pitch along with some of the other lads' kids and partners. It felt amazing to hold my little girl and show her my medal. When we were presented with the Premiership trophy in 2005 Elen had been pregnant and I had said to her that we could look forward to sharing this moment with our new baby. I was very happy to be able to deliver another flag day. I have spent most of my life trying to make Mum and Dad proud but I realized that the person I most want to win trophies for now was huddled in my arms. And that's what keeps me going, keeps me fighting and wanting to get better.

I would like to think that deep down people do appreciate what we have done. The memories – and in some cases the scars – are still fresh and perhaps it will take a little more time for what Chelsea have achieved so far to sink in. We have taken the league by storm and because everyone outside of our club has allegiance elsewhere there is a degree of envy which Manchester United suffered from for years.

I hope that we have earned people's respect, though. However, many choose to focus on the money we have spent in an effort to take the shine off the trophies we have won. It's true that our transfer budget has been bigger than anyone else's over a short space of time but I doubt it's much more in relative terms than what Blackburn spent when they won the title or what Manchester United have spent over the last fifteen years. This issue annoys me because it's aimed at detracting from what our outstanding success. However, in some ways it motivates us to show people that it's not about the money. Yes, I enjoy being one of the best paid footballers in the world but I didn't get to where I am by luck. Everything I have I worked very hard for, and probably the most influential lesson Dad ever drilled into me was that you make your own luck.

I have grafted to get to where I am. I would love to say that I just woke up one day and found I could do anything with a football but that isn't the case. In a more general sense, the accusation that we have bought success also ignores the characters in the team, never mind their quality and the excellence of performance which has been achieved at the same time. For instance, John, Eidur, Carlo (Cudicini), Willie (Gallas), and I were all at Chelsea before the Abramovich revolution.

There's a lack of depth to the way people think of us at the moment. They prefer to skim what's on top and pick faults rather than see the true substance of what has made the club the best in the country. For that reason I believe that this Chelsea team will be better remembered in the future than we are appreciated right now.

If we didn't win another title and faded out then maybe this crop of players would receive some credit but if we dominate English football for ten years then the club will be regarded much more highly and we will not just be a winning team but the start of a dynasty at Stamford Bridge. Liverpool attained that status in the Seventies and Eighties and then Man United in the Nineties and maybe that's what people will say. Football is too emotional and our success is too fresh at the moment to be given much acknowledgement. People said that the great Liverpool team of the Seventies were boring and the Leeds team of the same era were a bunch of thugs but now there is a great nostalgia for both sides after years have passed and perspective been applied.

Longevity – to be part of a legend – is what I am fighting for as an individual and what everyone at Chelsea craves as a team. I don't think we can expect that level of respect after just two titles, and if I were to fade after just three or four good seasons as a player then I would be bitterly disappointed that I hadn't fulfilled my potential or destiny. All you can claim in two seasons is limelight not legend. Only a team which dominates for a sustained period of time can genuinely expect more. I believe that we have people at Chelsea who share that same ambition.

I know that Roman is determined to make the club bigger, better, and more successful. In the summer of 2006 he sanctioned a deal which brought Germany captain Michael Ballack to the club from Bayern Munich, a move which heralded a change in the recruitment policy of Mourinho. The emphasis before had generally been to sign excellent players who had yet to achieve significant success and who were hungry to do so. Four weeks later, the man widely regarded as the world's best striker, Andriy Shevchenko, also signed for a club record fee. Both players are at the very peak of their career and have a wealth of experience in club and international football. It's a development which some people questioned I would welcome given Ballack's position and ability to score goals from midfield. Those who did so don't know me at all.

I relish the opportunity to play with great players and to have them challenge me to up my game to a new level. With Ballack and Shevchenko, everyone at Chelsea has been served notice that the club is intent on achieving greater things. No one gets it easy at Chelsea, though, and I'm sure the manager has made the new lads aware of what is expected of them under his charge and working for Mr Abramovich. Already I can sense the sweep of change at Chelsea which is aimed at evolving the club, at pushing forward.

Any club which has achieved a measure of success cannot trade on its past but must plan for the future. At Chelsea we have the ability to develop and improve, utilizing all of the assets we already have at our disposal plus the ones we are able to acquire to help make that happen. I know Roman Abramovich and Jose Mourinho. I know John Terry and myself, and none of us are people who are content to sit back and admire what has been done. We need to move forward and make progress; win more titles and push ourselves and Chelsea to new limits.

If there is anyone who doubts that ambition then they don't know Chelsea. I have lived through one revolution at the club and prospered and I intend to be at the forefront of the next stage. It's like I have said: since I was a child I have tried to reach heights that seemed above me. Nothing has changed.

CHAPTER 11

GERMANY 2006

I LOOKED at John. The face I so often see smiling and joking was scarred with distress. There was little noise in the dressing room, some hushed words around the edges, boots discarded. Someone offered me water. I didn't need a drink; instead I poured it over my face hoping to wash away the nightmare.

I looked at John again. 'Don't cry,' I thought. There would have been little point in saying the words aloud. John was in tears and to his left Rio sobbed quietly, his head in his hands; friends who are a tower of strength, reduced to rubble. Everywhere I looked was a scene of emotional devastation. Grown men, men's men, weeping for what had happened, and what might have been.

'Don't cry.' It's what Dad always told me. When I was 11 I squandered a great chance to win a match for Heath Park. Late in the game I was through with only the keeper to beat. I missed and when the final whistle sounded I broke down.

'Don't cry son,' said Dad. 'Never show emotion in front of

your opponents. Even your team-mates. It's better to do that in private. Believe me. It's not the right thing to do in football. Don't cry.'

I never did cry again though all I wanted to do at that moment seventeen years later was burst into tears. I could feel the emotion welling up within me and I could barely swallow air for the lump in my throat but there were no tears. I couldn't do it. I wanted to grieve for the missed opportunity of making the World Cup semi-final. For the missed chance to become world champions. For the missed penalty.

I have never known a more desolate place than the England dressing room after we lost to Portugal in the World Cup. I've never felt more dejected but something within me wouldn't allow me to let go like the others. Maybe it's a strength to be able to bare your emotions like that – to embrace the pain and begin the process of leaving it behind.

Wayne Rooney wandered around trying to help where he could. I wondered how he felt now the contest was lost, wondered how hard it must have been for him to sit out the last stages of the biggest game of his life so far because of a red card. Someone said he'd stamped on Ricky [Carvalho] but all I'd seen was two Portugal players wrestling with him and then Cristiano Ronaldo rushing in and provoking the wrath of the whole of England.

'I didn't stamp on him,' Wazza replied when I asked him. Good enough for me. Wazza didn't say sorry to anyone after the match. He didn't need to. He's such a big personality within the group that everyone would respect him no matter what he said and no one on our side believed he should have been sent off.

I tried to take in what had happened. We lost and yet,

beforehand, I had looked at their team and there was nothing to fear. I was confident we would beat them. Without Deco to run their midfield and Costinha to lock up at the back I was sure we'd be too strong. We opened well and physically and mentally we got stronger as the game went on. I wasn't aware of Ronaldo trying to wind up Wazza before the game. Neither did I sense any build-up of tension between the teams as the contest raged on, so when I slipped a pass into Wazza there was no reason to suspect the explosion about to be unleashed. I saw Ricky get close on him but Wazza shrugged him off with typical determination. Someone else got involved and it looked to me like he was being fouled by both Portugal players for between five and ten seconds before the referee blew his whistle. Knowing how strong he is, I knew he would stay on his feet.

I didn't see his foot connect with Carvalho at the time. Momentum and the loss of balance can sometimes disorientate you in a situation like that and Wazza said he didn't stamp on him. Fair enough. Even the referee later insisted he was sent off because of the push on Ronaldo. That being the case, in my view it was a scandal. There is no other word to describe it. The way Ronaldo acted on the pitch was out of order. It sickens me to see players accosting referees with their arms in the air waving imaginary cards. I have never done it and never would but it happened time and again in the finals.

To make it worse, Wazza and Rio have always spoken of Ronaldo in a very positive way. They are mates at Manchester United. Mates? I can't understand why he would behave that way. If someone commits a bad tackle or an offence for which they know they risk being sent off then fine, you accept it. But to actively canvas for someone to be dismissed – especially a club team-mate – that's out of order.

Ronaldo is a great player and there was no need for him to behave that way. I was walking towards the incident when I saw him confront the referee – bleating for him to take action. I don't remember any Portugal player rushing at the referee when Luis Figo lashed his head into Mark van Bommel, in the second round match against Holland, demanding stern action. An offence for which he got a caution.

And yet Wayne Rooney shoves a hand in Ronaldo's shoulder from sheer frustration and is ordered off. Rough justice? When I saw the red card I thought, 'Here we go again.' A game we should win and now something's conspiring to take it from us. The memory of Wazza going off against Portugal at Euro 2004 came briefly to mind, a ghostly reminder of past misfortune. In that instant the flow of the contest changed from one in which we had the overwhelming potential to win, to one in which our best chance was to salvage something. I watched Wazza trail off the pitch and thought about how much more we would have to run being a man down. I didn't think Portugal would score before that point and, bizarrely, still felt the same.

THROUGHOUT the tournament we had suffered in the heat. Our second-half performances were invariably below the standard of the first period and at its worst – against Paraguay in Frankfurt – most of us could barely walk, never mind run, in the latter stages of the match. Gelsenkirchen felt different – cooler and less suffocating. We were also getting nearer the end, closer to the big performance we all knew was lurking inside.

I felt sharp. The build-up to the World Cup had been

gradual in the beginning. Jose Mourinho told me that I could get away for a break before the penultimate match of the season against Blackburn. The Premiership was won. John Terry was injured though and I felt a responsibility to the team to be there. Mourinho looked puzzled when I told him I would rather play.

He came to me again after the match at Ewood Park and stressed that there were five days until Newcastle. He convinced me to get away so Elen and I went to Antigua for a holiday where I trained every day. I supplemented running with work in the gym. It was fine, though I missed not having football-based training. Being fit is one thing but I like to be able to work with the ball. People look at the amount of games I play and think that I am fit and what I need is rest. I disagree. I know I need to top up my fitness to maintain the right level and when we went to Portugal with the England squad the week after the FA Cup Final it was confirmed to me why I need football-based training. We did the fitness stuff and I was fine but then we played five-a-side and my legs were really heavy. It's one thing running and getting a sweat up in Antigua but football demands a different kind of fitness.

There were times when I became frustrated – I know what I need to do to be sharp – because the manager gave us the day off when I would rather have been training. I prefer to keep pushing myself and increasing that sharpness. The Friday before we were due to return from Portugal we were told to take the day off so Rio and I did some work on our own.

The England squad returned to London and met up at The Grove Hotel where training began to get a bit more technical. We trained every day with a heart monitor strapped to us which gives the coaching staff a reading on how fit you are. Though I was told that I was the fittest player in the squad when we were in Portugal, I knew I was still a bit short of my optimum level; those measurements can be misleading. Cardiovascular exercise is not the same as playing football where the demands on the body are different to simply running round the pitch or doing aerobic exercise. Covering runners and sprinting between opponents to close down space is a whole different use of energy to regular, balanced running.

We had a couple of days off during the preparation and I knew that I wanted to train. Sometimes a manager needs to trust his players – especially the senior ones – to know what they need. I had a similar experience with Claudio Ranieri but I respect the manager's opinion – it's foolish to risk injury unnecessarily but everyone needs different things. In retrospect maybe I should have been a bit more forceful. I should have been practising more penalties as well.

Normally I would take around ten every day in training at Chelsea but I had been focusing on other things and had neglected the routine before the warm-up match against Hungary at Old Trafford. As soon as the kick was awarded the first thing I thought of was the fact that I hadn't been practising. It's one of those things. Like my spikes or shooting routines, if I have done them (and it's very rare that I haven't) then it would never have even entered my head that I might not be prepared. I panicked a little. To run up to a penalty with a trace of doubt is the worst thing. I didn't catch it the way I would have liked to and though it was a decent save I was disappointed with the situation and with myself. Afterwards I consoled myself with the thought that it was better to miss now than later. Little was I to know . . .

The next day I began a regime of practising every day. Other than the spot kick I felt that I played quite well in the game. Mr Eriksson explained to us before the match that he was going to play with Jamie Carragher in midfield and Stevie Gerrard as a second striker. I was pleased with the formation because it gave me licence to get forward and I felt sharp. Stevie scored, it went well and the team clicked. Just what you want.

Strangely, the media who had been crying out for that formation to be played then decided that we should change back to 4-4-2 with Crouchy playing up front and I realized that whatever the result there would always be another issue to be negative about. The spirit among the lads was good regardless. We had three days until the Jamaica match though personally I would have chosen a stronger team to test us in our final game before heading for Germany. With respect, the Trinidad and Tobago game was not one which we particularly needed to rehearse for. We're expected to beat Trinidad and Tobago anyway so setting up a practice match against a similar style of opposition would have limited benefit.

As it turned out I got a goal but more importantly Crouchy bagged three goals which was a real boost for him. He's a top lad and after the way he missed a penalty for his hat-trick it was a great strike which got him there in the end. At that stage we knew he would be an important player because of the injury situation we had. Michael was working hard to get fit and also scored that day while Wazza was busy focussing on his recovery. When the day came to leave for Germany it was quite a relief since the preparations had been turned into a circus in which one player's broken metatarsal took centre stage.

It had become the focal point of the media coverage and it wasn't a help. Will he be fit? We can't win it without him, can we? Wayne was quietly going about his business getting fit and the rest of us were focused on preparing for the finals. It's a sign of the times; football and the fact that we were in countdown mode for the biggest sporting event in the world take a back seat to the cult of celebrity. We saw it with David Beckham in 2002 and it was the same this time round with Wazza. It suits the media's agenda to turn a World Cup campaign into a sideshow about one player's fitness but in doing so they show a disrespect to the others in the squad. Is it right that England can only win the tournament if Rooney plays but they would be fine if Beckham, Gerrard, Terry, Ferdinand or any of the others were missing? I know Wazza doesn't think so and nor do I.

The sheer volume of coverage was bizarre, and slightly embarrassing for Wayne. He worked extremely hard to make sure he would play a part in Germany and when he sat on the bench for the first game against Paraguay he knew he was fit for the next and that he had already been passed to play. At that point it was only a matter of match sharpness and not health. All of us knew, though everyone else continued to guess. He was like a caged animal. In training he was working at full pelt and when he conducted an impromptu session on the pitch after the Paraguay match it was very much a public message of how good he felt.

When a player returns from injury there will always be little doubts that he might break down, but on the Tuesday he started playing practice matches and no one said that we shouldn't go near him in a tackle. I was tentative about it because I didn't want to be the one who put him out of the World Cup! He needed to take a couple of kicks though – when you have recovered from that kind of injury you need to feel secure in your mind that you are completely over it.

I had no doubt. He was flying into tackles, smashing the ball into the net and muscling people off the ball. Same old Wazza. His sheer enthusiasm for football is infectious and with his recovery the spirit of the squad lifted. I could hardly believe that just six weeks earlier I'd watched in horror as he writhed in pain on the pitch at the Bridge. It seemed like his World Cup had ended before it had begun but now he was on top of the world. Then came the bombshell.

There were rumours of a disagreement between Manchester United and the FA about Wazza being fit enough to take any part in the tournament. The two doctors who had passed his scan in Manchester were flown to Germany for consultation and all Wazza could do was wait.

He's not the most patient lad. He finds it difficult to sit still for two minutes never mind wait around on other people deciding whether or not he is allowed to do what comes most naturally to him. It was unbearable. He tried to stay positive while the wrangling went on and I couldn't imagine what must have been going through his head.

I spoke to him but he was never in any doubt. He wanted to play for England and couldn't have been more frustrated than to be put in this situation. Thankfully, common sense prevailed and he played his first part in the campaign only when medical opinion said he could.

Throughout, the lads had gathered round Wazza and supported him, which was no surprise – one of the great strengths of the squad is its sense of unity. No one player is more important than the team.

I have experienced a similar camaraderie at Chelsea and the spirit which bonds England can be traced back to the European Championships. Elimination hit us hard but we had to absorb a couple more hard knocks before we got back up on the big stage. We were beaten 4–1 by Denmark in August 2005 in a match in which we lost stupid goals and our shape. It was certainly one to learn from. We knew we had let ourselves down. We know the responsibility to do well every time we play for England. We got roasted by the press and, more surprisingly, by a host of ex-England players who said we had disgraced the jersey.

You expect to take stick for a performance like that and learn to become thick skinned. Criticism from outside is something you learn to live with and so it's rare to be shocked by it. When it comes from within, however, it can knock you off balance and I wasn't prepared for what happened after we beat Wales in Cardiff in a World Cup qualifier.

We hadn't played particularly well but managed to carve out a victory in a game made more difficult by the derby atmosphere. I had suffered from flu the week of the match and had seen the team doctor. I insisted I was fine to play and asked him not to let on to the manager. I trained at the Millennium Stadium the day before and felt sluggish but I would never put personal interest ahead of the good of the team. On Saturday morning I felt fine – I'm not offering illness as an excuse for anything.

I felt a bit leggy in the warm-up and it's hard to get out of that – harder because we didn't play well though we deserved to win. In the aftermath Mr Eriksson was given a grilling by the press and as part of his summary he said that I was 'a slow starter'. At first, I was annoyed. I have the greatest of respect for Sven and to be criticised by someone you hold in such esteem naturally hurts. Also, I didn't agree with him. The season before, I had scored a few goals early on, but this time round I'd managed two at home to West Brom. Even so, I didn't feel it was a valid comment. When a manager speaks about you in that way, it's embarrassing.

I was also a bit upset that it had been said in public. I would have preferred that he had come to me privately and asked me if there was a problem. If he had told me the same thing face to face I would have made my case and that would have been the end of it. I didn't respond at the time because I didn't feel I had to and I didn't want to get into a public disagreement with the England manager. In any event it didn't affect his confidence in me as I was picked to play against Northern Ireland in Belfast the following Wednesday. Just when I thought it couldn't get much worse, it did.

I wanted to respond positively but instead we recorded a result which was the worst in my time playing for England, a 1–0 defeat. It was a short flight back home but a long journey into a blaze of criticism. We knew what to expect and have never tried to bullshit our way out of a bad result. We hold our hands up. I have learned that playing for England means you have to be prepared to experience the greatest highs and the lowest of the lows. I think I am becoming acclimatized.

The result meant we couldn't afford to slip up against Austria and Poland at Old Trafford in October. I went into the international break determined to make amends for Belfast and with a lingering determination to cast off the doubts which had been raised about my game.

I'd netted another four goals for Chelsea by the time of the next international and, unexpectedly, penalty kicks once again became an issue in the run-up to the game. Becks had said to me after Euro 2004 that I should take spot kicks from then on after he had a bad run. It was a casual chat after training. You take them for Chelsea and you have a good record, he said. There was no huge moment but it broke in the press before the Austria match.

Since it had become public knowledge there was an inevitability about a penalty being awarded in the match. It only took half an hour. I wasn't sure how I would feel but I realized it was different from doing it for my club – more pressure, more scrutiny. I had to blank it out. I knew what to do; I converted comfortably and it turned out to be the winning goal. Nice one.

Not so good was Becks being suspended and Stevie pulling out of the Poland game. Ledley King was drafted into central midfield and we played well in a match which produced one of my favourite moments for England. Maciej Zurawski had pulled them level when Michael Owen flicked the ball on to me in the closing minutes.

I had no option but to take it high on the volley – difficult to keep down never mind steer in on your instep but I managed both. More important, we won the group and finishing top scorer in qualifying helped me put aside the disappointment of Belfast as well as improve my reputation in terms of starting a season.

The time between qualifying and the finals themselves was filled by the domestic season. The wait for the first match in Germany was more empty and taxing. It's an odd mixture of anticipation and sheer boredom. You are desperate to get started having worked for two years to make it that far, but besides training, the time in between passes slowly.

Sven got the balance right. He didn't show any change of character because it was his last tournament. He was focused and prepared. I found it frustrating to see him criticized for not showing emotion because I can understand why he is not demonstrative in public. He has his own way of working which is very tactical and involves all of his technical staff. I think this was his best tournament, though I only have Euro 2004 to measure it by. I noticed a step up and what is very clear is that the manager knows football inside out and his top-level experience came through.

People demand he show emotion but you can't start making passionate speeches three weeks before the start of a World Cup. Preparation is a very careful process and he did most things right. I wasn't particularly nervous before the Paraguay game. Instead I felt a real calm. I was ready. When the nerves kick in it is overcome by the desire to win. The opinion was that Paraguay were not a top team but it takes a bit of quality to finish fourth in South American qualifying.

We started the match brightly. Becks forced the own goal from a free-kick and we dominated most of the time. All of that changed after the break. We were completely gone. I came back into the heat and hoped I would be able to get through the half but after just a couple of minutes I was sluggish. I looked around and saw that everyone else was the same. It felt like all the blood in my legs had been replaced by lactic acid. I've never known anything like it.

The manager decided to take off Michael and put on Stewart Downing, leaving us with an extra man in midfield and Crouchy up front on his own. When the ball came to me

I should have scored but fatigue was a major factor and we didn't play through the midfield the way we should have done, conceding possession too easily.

Part of the reason was giving in to the temptation to knock the ball long to Crouchy. When he's there it's a natural instinct to hit the high ball. Dink it into him hoping he can bring it under control and hold it long enough for you to make up the ground. When you have a player of his stature it's natural to play to his strength.

At international level, however, if you hit a ball sixty yards then that's ground you have to cover to support him. The way we were struggling we could hardly cover twenty yards so you lose the ball and end up running around like idiots trying to win it back. It became a vicious circle of knocking it in and then chasing the game if it didn't work out.

The manager took a lot of criticism for the way we defended after we scored when in actual fact that attitude was down to the players on the pitch. There were plenty of chances to score more goals in the game but we didn't and so we had to be serious and concentrate just as much on not conceding.

The best teams in the tournament were winning games by a single goal. Argentina recorded one big win but that was the exception to the rule. It's not realistic to expect us to go all out and risk conceding goals and defeat. As time runs out and you are a goal ahead you naturally try to defend what you have.

Those who demand that we win games by three goals just to convince them that we are a good team lack a basic under-standing of how the game works at this level. I admit the per-formances against Paraguay, Trinidad and Tobago, and

Sweden were below par but its naïve to argue that if we go one-up then bringing on an attacking substitute like Aaron Lennon to kill the game off is the only way of ensuring victory. Football at World Cup level is as much a game of risk management as anything else and there is a reason why we set out the way we do. We're not crazy enough to try to win 5–0 every game just so people praise us as 'The Entertainers'. That's never going to happen. If you want to win the World Cup you have to be clever.

Predictably, we got murdered in the press so we were on a hiding to nothing for the next match regardless. A two-goal victory became another wake for English football even though Crouchy and Stevie scored good goals. After three goal attempts in the first match I should have opened my account in the second. One great chance missed and a couple of near misses set the questions running about my form. You accept it. You have to.

Assuming we avoided defeat against Sweden in our final group game, we had to consider the possibility that Germany might lose their final group match against Ecuador and so meet us in the next round. And there were three players on yellow cards including me, Stevie, and Crouchy. Two days before the game Sven told me that I would play but that the other two would not. The way the cautions were being dished out it wasn't worth the risk. We wanted to beat Sweden regardless of who we'd meet in the second round. The last thing we needed was an injury to Michael Owen. It happened only minutes into the game, and at first I didn't know he was so badly hurt. You fear the worst but it wasn't until I came in at half-time that I had the chance to speak to him and he said it was cruciate ligament damage.

I could scarcely believe it. He spends five months recovering from a broken metatarsal and then he has to go home early from and the World Cup and loses the rest of the year to a new injury. People are quick to judge footballers on how much they earn and how comfortable their lives are but it's harder to see the human side of football.

It's bad enough being unable to go to work and do your best and challenge yourself day by day to perform at the level you are used to. To miss out on a World Cup is even worse. Every man who pulls on a shirt to play for England does so for the honour of playing for his country. For the chance to make a difference for every England fan. For his family, his friends. That's the human side of football. Everyone is desperate to succeed and do well. Just as in any walk of life, it's important to gain satisfaction and rewards for your efforts that you can share with your family. Footballers are no different from anyone else in that respect.

With Michael out came more debate about Sven's squad selection. Questions had been asked about why we didn't have five strikers in the squad when two of our forwards went into the tournament trying to recover fitness. The inclusion of Theo Walcott had also been the subject of speculation.

Personally, I would have included Jermain Defoe as well. I played with him at West Ham and he is a natural goalscorer. Admittedly, a change in personnel wouldn't have altered the starting line-up in any of the five games. Crouch and Owen would still have begun the first, and the second would have gone the same way with Rooney introduced, and in the third Owen was fit to start.

At that point Crouchy came on and having scored his first goal in the Trinidad match that was obvious. In the fourth game you would play Rooney and the same against Portugal so in terms of the line-ups for each match I don't think they would have been affected.

I would have preferred some insurance though, and it would have given us more options. In that respect I would have taken Defoe. Though everyone would probably pick a different squad, it is likely that most people would come up with the same starting line-up – fitness permitting – but when you select 23 players it's a whole different matter.

Theo will be stronger and will benefit from having been part of the squad and that will have a positive effect for England in the future. As for the Sweden match, we defended set pieces badly and drew the match. It didn't matter: we won the group and my thoughts turned to more positive things.

I allowed myself to wonder how far we could go in the tournament. I looked at the games in our half of the draw and, the same as the fans, wondered who we might play in the quarter-final/semi-final. It's human nature. I wasn't afraid of anyone. Even when I saw Argentina win by six goals against Ukraine and string twenty-four passes together in scoring the best goal of the tournament to date, I wasn't scared of meeting them. I watched every team in the competition and was confident that we could overcome any of them.

I was pleased Argentina were peaking in the group stage. I remembered the reaction when we beat Croatia 4–2 in Portugal two years before – all of a sudden it was we could go all the way. I looked at how much we could still improve in this competition and how much more there was to come. Back at the hotel Sir Geoff Hurst said on TV that the team of 1966 were caned by the media for playing poorly before the semi-final. What a surprise.

I realized then that the secret to winning the tournament was not to bulldoze every team in sight by four or five goals but in fact to progress by hard work and stealth. We were more of a steamroller. We knew that we would be expected to flatten Ecuador and I was confident we would. I was shaken slightly when they went through one-on-one on our goal in the first ten minutes. My immediate thought was 'S***, please don't score because I don't want to go home with a paper bag on my head.' We had seen in the tournament that if you go one goal down just how hard it can be to come back. I had a good chance, which I put over the bar, that I know I should have scored. We won the game thanks to a free-kick from Becks – but it was still another victory.

The bandwagon trundled on to the quarter-final, though winning still wasn't good enough for some. The age-old question of Stevie Gerrard and I playing together in the middle of the park was raised again as a possible excuse as to why we weren't Brazil (who were also struggling). I hate that argument. It's so lazy. We put too much stress on systems. Uncle Harry used to say it was about the players who go out and play and not about the system. There was an obsession with whether Stevie and I can play together which is completely irrelevant. Maybe sometimes a holding player is added and others not. What team in the world would have two players who have achieved what Stevie and I have in the past couple of years at club level and doubt that we should be paired up? Brazil, Argentina, Italy? I don't think so.

I played with Carra, Michael Carrick, Owen Hargreaves and Stevie in the World Cup and I never felt anything but comfortable at all times. I find it strange when people question my own or Stevie's ability to defend or attack in midfield. Each of us have shown that we are capable of both, to a very high standard, and because of that people think that England will get double the player when the reality is that we work in tandem and each of us is not required to do everything all of the time.

Sometimes I play forward and he holds and at other times it's the reverse. It's a matter of playing with responsibility. People look at us as the dynamic individuals we are with our club sides and wonder why we don't appear to be the same with England. The answer is that we are but that it's impossible for us both to be that player at the same time.

If one of us is charging into a scoring position then the other must help protect the defence. Look at our scoring record for England and it tells you that we are converting chances with the same ratio as we do for Chelsea and Liverpool. I don't deny that we can improve as a partnership but I refute the suggestion that we aren't suited to one.

I have learned at Chelsea that the result is all that is important. For some people there always has to be another angle: it's the system; it's the players; it's the manager's lack of passion; it's the performance; it's the colour of our pants. Pants. That what it is.

The media in particular have got themselves in such a pickle about the England team that I wonder if they have lost sight of what is actually important. Here is a good example of how the press decide to pursue an issue and then perform a complete U-turn.

Before the finals began I attended a press conference where the subject turned to Owen Hargreaves. Owen is a good professional whose opportunities with England have so far been limited. However, having seen him play for Bayern Munich and having played with him in training, I realize what he has to offer. During the course of the conversation one particularly obnoxious journalist asked me, 'What is the point of Owen Hargreaves?' I was offended by the crassness of the question but I offered a sensible answer regardless. Three weeks later, Owen had a brilliant match against Portugal and that same journalist, along with many others who had written negative things about him, had changed their minds. Suddenly he had become a mainstay of the England team. Fickle? Judgmental? Or just uninformed?

I looked at the draw. Ecuador: we should beat them. Portugal or Holland? I fancied us against either, so it didn't bother me which of them won the match. France or Brazil? Well, if you get beaten by Brazil in the semi-final then you have probably lost to the champions.

In the end, part of the reason why I think we lost was bad fortune. Just as the team of 98 had when a 'goal' against Argentina was disallowed. Or in 2002 when Ronaldinho scored a freak winner. And then this time round we have Wayne Rooney sent off in the quarter-final in a climate where other fouls go completely unpunished. It seems to be the English way to lose in bizarre circumstances but it wears you down. It gets to the point where you want to tell Lady Luck to f*** off and take her bad sister with her.

It was a long week waiting for the quarter-final to come round. By Thursday we were training in formation, which was going very well, and I even scored a couple of goals!

We moved on to practise set-play patterns for a while and I jumped to meet a cross with Scott Carson. As I landed I heard my left ankle crunch. I thought that was it. I twisted my ankle a few times when I was younger and I'm familiar with the pain.

Great. That it should come to this. Two years of battling to qualify and several months of expectation wrecked by a freak fall in training.

Our physio Gary Lewin treated me all afternoon and by evening I was confident I would play even if I had to be strapped up. I went to bed and thought about the usual stuff; scoring a goal in the game, scoring a penalty, scoring in the final.

I did the same again the following afternoon only by now I was in the Gelsenkirchen Arena and we were preparing to meet Portugal. My ankle was fine and I asked Robbo to stay in goal while I practised some penalties. I took four. Only me. Four kicks, four goals. Right. Ready to play now.

When we got back I watched a DVD of the Portugal keeper Ricardo in action against penalties. I'd heard him boast that he does the same for the kickers so I decided it was time to even up the odds. I've taken a lot of spot kicks for Chelsea to the keeper's right side and scored. I figured his best guess would be that I would replicate that kick again.

I watched him in action. First he went right. Good. Then right again. Then left. And left and then saved one with his feet. I was confused. There was no rhyme or reason to his performance and I flirted with the idea of just blasting it down the middle. In practice I had placed the ball in all areas of the goal. Of the fifty kicks taken I never missed the target and on two occasions the ball was saved by the goalie. It's safe to say I felt confident about any situation which involved hitting a shot from twelve yards.

I did have one in the game though it wasn't a dead ball. It

came from a corner and I had time to bring it under control. I should have. Unfortunately, I had got to the stage where I'd missed a few and I got a bit edgy and snapped at it rather than remaining calm.

It wasn't the first. I became a victim of my ability to get into those positions. I analysed the stats after the Ecuador match, and against Paraguay I had three shots – all from distance and not the kind I would expect to go in as a matter of course. Against Trinidad from three good chances I should have scored one or two. Still, to be criticised for not scoring is hard to take. At least I was getting into positions to make chances. And where other players in my situation might have taken umbrage at the stick and lost confidence and even started to hide, I put myself right back in the firing line.

Against Sweden I had a header and one real chance but others were outside the box. I should have scored one against Ecuador. I looked and saw the statistic which said I had twenty-one attempts on goal – more than any other player in the tournament. No one was more disappointed than me that I didn't have two or three goals from that amount of chances.

I knew I should have scored but sometimes it goes for you and sometimes it doesn't. The margins which separate success and failure at this level are less than a hair's breadth. If I had played exactly the same and taken four of those chances then I would be competing for the golden boot and England would have made the semi-finals. It's a fine line and you have to walk that line in football.

The longest I went without scoring a goal last season was six games. I managed five in the World Cup which is an unlucky coincidence. My game is about getting into scoring positions. I have scored sixty-five goals in the last three years and I think a striker would be satisfied with that tally, so I am naturally judged on goals as well as midfield play. I know what's expected of me and I don't have any problem with it.

I felt confident that I would score at any time. I had been through this so many times in the past and it had always come right in the end. It can come off your studs, your arse or it can be a great strike. You don't care as long as it does.

Even after Wazza was sent off against Portugal I felt confident and comfortable that we would win through on extra-time and penalties. I think we all did. Not overconfident but he had an inner strength. We had practised penalties. Not just kicks but the walk from the halfway line. We knew what we were doing and some of us had been in an almost identical situation at Euro 2004.

It takes around 20–30 seconds to cover the ground between the centre circle and the penalty spot. It's amazing the amount of thought you can cram into such a short period when all you want to do is block out the world and feel the relief of the ball nestling in the back of the net.

Of course, the things you don't want to consider are the first to come to mind. The missed chance in the game. The saved penalty against Hungary before the tournament. I chased them and began to visualize my kick low to the keeper's left. There will always be an element of chance in this one-on-one battle but I figured that since most of the time I took penalties to the other corner Ricardo would hedge his bets and dive right.

I was wrong. Just before I started my run-up I allowed the slightest flicker of doubt to come to mind. It's human nature and there was nothing I could do to stop it. I didn't catch the ball cleanly. Ricardo guessed correctly and stooped to stop it.

The walk back to the centre circle felt like bare feet on broken glass. I'd failed to score from our first penalty in the shootout. Before the penalty I was aware that the hopes of every England fan lay square on my shoulders. Now I felt their anguish and disappointment. Among the very dark thoughts the only light was that there were still four spot kicks to come.

When Portugal missed twice I looked over to where my Dad was sitting and he stood with his thumbs up. It was a personal thing – not that we would definitely win but that hopefully I would get the chance to fight another day. When Stevie missed, I knew it was over.

I didn't need to see Ronaldo strut to the spot, see him kiss the ball as he placed it, and then smash it into the net. Some things are not meant to be and this felt like it was already over. A lot of people came up to me saying, 'Don't worry about it'.

I know it's well meant and I realize that people are desperate to comfort you in that situation but to be brutally honest there are no words to take away that feeling of complete desolation. I have seen people in similar situations and hoped I would never have to experience it, yet there I was.

In the dressing room the only one keeping it together was the manager. He was brilliant. He kept it brief. He comforted those who were most upset and kept saying that we deserved to win it. He told us that he wanted to get us all together back at our base hotel to chat to us properly.

When we got there I went straight to the bar. I was on my own for a while before the lads came in and we all had a drink. It was reflective and quite maudlin. Wazza was gutted and I felt sorry for him. There was no momentum for him in the competition. For all the obsessing about him he never even got the chance to show what we all know he is capable of. He was brought on late in the second game then played a couple without scoring and was sent off. Not ideal. It was over before he got started.

Of course he was angry about the sending off. I understood. He's a man's man and you do what your blood tells you – whatever that is – right or wrong. In this case he didn't do very much wrong.

We had a couple of beers and pored over the details of the match. Wazza was still furious about what had happened with Ronaldo and joked about what would happen when they saw each other for pre-season training. I'd like to be a fly on the wall at Carrington that day.

We were then asked to file into the meeting room where Sven wanted to talk to us. He welcomed us from the front, smiling and patting some of the lads on the back. He seemed very relaxed. He began by reiterating how disappointed he was for us that we had been eliminated and that we deserved to be in the semi-final against France.

Though his voice was warm and the words well chosen, he became very emotional – the only time I ever really saw behind the curtain. People criticize him for not showing his true feelings more but that's the man. When he came to England no one really knew anything about him. If you worked closely with him then you knew and understood him better.

He regularly takes the players aside individually and explains to them exactly what he wants from them. He encourages you and makes you believe that everything is within your capability. Several times in Germany he called

Stevie and I together and we talked in depth about movement off the ball and the pattern of play he wanted us to establish.

Sven's attention to detail is also very high. When he felt it necessary he called each of the departments of the team for a separate meeting to discuss the way we would approach the next match. In five games in Germany we won three, drew one and lost one on penalties. Okay it's not brilliant but it's not bad either.

I think the criticism of his tactical nous, and in particular his substitutions, is very unfair. For instance, his change of Michael for Stuart Downing against Paraguay was the right one for a team which was exhausted by the heat and needed fresh legs to help retain the ball and the lead. Against Ecuador he put in Michael Carrick because he correctly identified that the opposition's best ball players were on the flanks so we would get more time in the middle to pass.

And then there's Owen Hargreaves. Owen deserves credit for the way he played against Portugal but why doesn't the manager take some as well for having the balls to stick him in there when a lot of people were asking if he was even good enough for the squad?

Every coach has strengths and weaknesses and Sven has never claimed to be perfect, but his record in international and club management is better than most. I have a lot to be thankful to him for in terms of giving me a chance with England and encouraging me to kick on as an international footballer.

He finished his speech by thanking the players and staff for everything they had done during his time as England manager. For the good times and the not so good. As I had come to expect, he was respectful and in turn gained respect.

Becks replied on behalf of the players. He thanked Sven for his work and wished him well in the future. He didn't tell us of his intention to resign as captain, something that surprised me when it was announced.

Steve McClaren then stood up and said what a hard act Sven would be to follow but we should look to the future. It didn't feel odd to have McClaren there all the time until that last night when he addressed us. It was a lot of change to take in at one go.

Steve has always been an influence on coaching while Sven took a less hands on approach to that side. During the World Cup I got a glimpse of the changes he is likely to make. His approach is very scientific and he has very strong ideas about how to handle certain situations. Sven was always more pragmatic and willing to change things but that moment was the first time it hit home that the coach was changing.

Steve has done well to find the limits of when to speak without encroaching on Sven's authority. Eriksson gave him that licence – others wouldn't tolerate it. McClaren is a manager who makes sense when he speaks, whether it's about training or tactics, and that's something which players very much appreciate.

I have also seen him be more authoritative. Maybe he's moved up a level since he was given the England job and I look forward to seeing that develop. He respects the need to have a close relationship with the players, but not too close, and I can see him bridging the gap between being a strong figure of authority but retaining the confidence of his players.

Eriksson was criticized for being too loyal to some players but I never felt like my place was guaranteed with him. You feel secure but you also know that you are two or three games away from being under pressure. It's the nature of the game that there will always be someone coming through who will play well and could replace you.

Becks' relationship with Sven was another cause of conjecture and criticism for both men but I think it's very important for the manager to have a good relationship with his captain. I don't see anyone criticising Mourinho for having a close relationship with John Terry. People can say that JT plays every week for Chelsea and that it's different for an international manager but that's to oversimplify. Others claimed Becks has not performed and should have lost his place but there has to be a degree of loyalty. If there's not then the whole structure of the team is undermined.

If I were captain of England then I would expect the manager to respect me and retain a certain amount of loyalty. Becoming skipper of the national team is not something I have thought about a lot but if I was called on to lead the national team I know I would do a good job.

I have had the privilege of captaining Chelsea on a few occasions in JT's absence and have enjoyed it and I would love to do the same for England at some point in my career. It's not a role that is restricted to football, however, because as England captain you have to conduct yourself in a manner which accepts the responsibility that goes with the job all of the time – a bit like England manager.

You can't just expect to adopt that role on the field. There's a responsibility which comes with it of handling yourself in public, in the press, and you have to have a settled and stable life. Look at the greatest captain ever – Bobby Moore. Everyone looks at him with respect not just for what he achieved on the pitch but the way he behaved at all times. It's more difficult than ever to be captain of England with the kind of press scrutiny that exists at all levels. Everyone has an opinion about you and your life but I know I could handle that. JT has the ability to be England captain as does Stevie Gerrard.

Just because we did not win the World Cup this time does not make us a bad team. I hold my hands up and admit that I didn't perform to the level that I can. I am bitterly, bitterly disappointed by that. This was my first experience of the World Cup finals and I was desperate to do well. I was desperate to score. I know myself well and when I get a goal my confidence rises and my whole game lifts. Which player's doesn't?

I reckon I played okay in Germany but I was not at my best and that was partly to do with a lack of goals. That's where I let myself down and there are three or four missed chances which will haunt me for the rest of my life. When people ask why England didn't win the World Cup in 2006 I take my share of the responsibility for the fact that we didn't manage to give a big performance.

The players knew that we were not at our best in the first four matches though I regard the way we played and battled against Portugal and the circumstances we found ourselves in as a titanic effort. I knew that we had a great game in us. Maybe it's easy to say that in retrospect but analyse some of the other sides and ask the same questions.

Before the tournament everyone said Brazil were the best team – quarter-final exit. After the group stage Argentina were the team to beat – quarter-final exit. Even the finalists had their moments. France had to beat Togo by two goals just to survive the first round while Italy couldn't beat nine-man

USA and it took a fortunate penalty to see off Australia.

My point is this: the World Cup is a very difficult tournament to win and the margins which separate success and failure are very fine. For England, it came down to three missed penalties after 120 minutes against Portugal. I will forever wonder at what might have been for us because I am sure we could have beaten France in the semi-final and I had no fear of Italy. Our campaign looks worse than it was because as a group we failed to turn in the kind of performance which we know we are capable of.

Germany was a tournament which threw up as many surprises as disappointments. Who would have thought that Italy could overcome the scandal caused by the match-fixing trials at home to conquer everyone and claim the championship? Or that Zinedine Zidane would bow out of a glorious career in such controversial and ignominious fashion?

It was a frustrating tournament and I know England can improve but we have to get a sense of perspective about it. What we have already is a very good team with young players who will be better prepared come the World Cup in South Africa in 2010, and others, like me, who will be just as desperate to succeed.

The tournament may be over for another four years but the game isn't up for England or Frank Lampard. Giving up on a challenge, no matter how bitter the disappointment may be in trying, is not in my nature. Nor will it ever be.

TEENAGE CANCER TRUST

THERE is much in my life for which I am thankful. I realise that I'm fortunate to have been blessed with a strong family, loving fiancée and a beautiful little girl as well as a great career. I am also aware, however, that others have not been as lucky with their life experience.

I first heard of Lucy Hilton when Chelsea told me that they had received a request from her to meet me as part of the Make a Wish Foundation. I read her letter and we set a date when she would come to the training ground for lunch. A few days later, I was asked if it could be brought forward as Lucy's condition had worsened.

The call made me realise just what she was dealing with and we arranged for her to come the following day. I was nervous about the meeting, mainly because I was unsure of what to say. I needn't have been. Lucy arrived and it was she who put me at ease with her bright and bubbly personality. Right away she was joking with me and some of the other lads and by the end of lunch she was joining in the banter. She was clearly quite a character.

Before she left I asked her if she and her family would like to come to a match and that I would like to keep in touch. She took up the invite to come to Stamford Bridge and I got to meet her family and also got to know her a lot better. She would send me good luck text messages before games, and though she was shy on the phone at first I would ring her when I was at away matches and she became more confident. More than anything we had a laugh. She was an infectious person and fun to be around. She didn't look unwell. Far from it, and there were times when I wanted to ask her Mum, Nicola, if she was sure that Lucy wasn't going to be okay. I knew she was suffering from a brain tumour but she looked so healthy.

We saw each other and spoke regularly but towards the end of the 2004/05 season her health deteriorated. I would be joking with her one minute and the next she was having a faint moment. I could see the health draining from her. I was up north preparing for the match at Bolton in which we could win the Premiership. As normal, I called Lucy from the hotel.

'How are you, Lucy?

'Good. Good. How about you?' she replied.

'Yeah. I'm good. A bit nervous about the match. I've never played a game where we could win the league before.'

'You'll be all right,' she laughed. 'Hey, if you score will you say something for me on telly?'

'Of course. You wait and see.'

The next day I scored two goals and we won the Premiership. Afterwards, I kissed the camera and said, 'That was for you, Lucy.' When I finally got round to turning on my phone during a lull in the celebrations there was a text message from her: 'Well done, champion. Thank you.' It was lovely.

I called her later and she was chuffed that I remembered to say hi. Two weeks later we were to receive the Premiership trophy after our final match of the season against Charlton. I asked Lucy if she wanted to come out on the pitch with Elen and her Mum after the game to join the celebration.

She was more unwell than I had ever seen her but she insisted on walking with the aid of crutches to come out and meet the team. I realised how ill she was when I gave her a cuddle but I squeezed her too hard and she winced. Afterwards, there was a party in the Chelsea gym and she and her family came along.

Though she was in a wheelchair and was struggling with her speech, she made the most of joining in the celebrations, to be normal. I looked in her eyes as she spoke and I could see that she was getting weaker. I felt myself choke with emotion. I walked away from the group to a recess in the gym and burst into tears.

I wasn't really sure why. I just felt myself lose control. My sisters Claire and Natalie came over to where I was. Claire put her arm around my shoulder. Lucy's Mum had noticed my absence and came to talk to me.

'You've made her so happy,' she said. 'Please don't be upset. These have been the best few weeks of her life and there's no need to cry. When she dies she will be very happy that she has met you.'

I pulled myself together. I didn't want Lucy to see me like that. What did I have to cry about? As I said goodbye to her, though, tears welled up in her eyes and she broke down saying she didn't want me to go. I kissed her forehead and promised we would speak the following day.

The next evening my phone rang and it was Lucy's number.

'Hey, you! How you doing?' I answered.

'Frank, it's Lucy's Mum,' came the quiet reply.

My heart sank. Nicola didn't need to say anything but she explained that Lucy had used up all of her energy to come to the match and be part of my big day. I was devastated. Even when you know to expect someone's death it doesn't make it any easier to deal with. She was 11 years old.

Elen and I attended the memorial service a few days later and I began to question whether I should allow myself to get close to any kids in a similar situation. Inevitably, some die of their illness and I felt so cut up about Lucy that I questioned what I might do in the future.

I talked to Steve Kutner about becoming involved in a charity so that I might be able to make some kind of difference. Somehow. I was meeting more and more kids who suffered like Lucy. I was very touched by the way they handled themselves and even more so by their courage.

Kuts and I agreed that rather than reply to every request from a charity that I should focus my attention on just one and that way perhaps I could be of significant help. That is how I became a patron of the Teenage Cancer Trust. Kuts has worked in the music industry as well as football for many years and TCT already had some connections with people like Roger Daltrey of The Who and Bill Curbishley, brother of Alan, who managed the band.

At that time TCT were excited to become involved in the sport side of things and I hoped I could be involved as much as possible and have a positive effect. It was arranged for me to visit kids in two different hospitals – one old style ward and another which TCT had funded specifically for kids.

I was very tentative at first and went to UCL Middlesex Hospital. I was extremely nervous about the whole experience. What do you say to someone who has been through so much pain and had to endure the debilitating effects of treatment with strong drugs and chemotherapy? Some of whom have had to deal with the threat of dying and others who are actually waiting for their lives to end? Children who should have their whole life ahead of them.

I was afraid to say the wrong thing but I shouldn't have been. Once the ice was broken it was the kids who made me comfortable. I was able to make friends with them and I will never forget the feeling of knowing straight away that I wanted to try and help in whatever way I could.

One of the nurses sent a message the following day saying that the kids were still excited that I had dropped in and that others had managed to get up and about for the first time in a while. We started to arrange a fundraising dinner with the aim of raising awareness.

I was panicked about the whole thing. Very nervous that people wouldn't turn up – players, managers, friends, family. I was overwhelmed by the response though and most of the credit has to go to Kuts, Karen Millen and Debbie Pezzani for the organisation. We raised around £700,000 and I went home feeling very proud that I had been part of such a successful event.

The greatest task facing TCT is the construction of those special wards for kids where they can feel comfortable and where their treatment and recovery can take place in the best possible environment. Here they will be with other people their own age who they can relate to; a place where they can feel at home even though they are in hospital, where they can pursue their interests and have their music and stuff around them. I could relate to that need straight away. I'm sure most people can.

Unfortunately for Lucy, there was nothing that could be done but there is still much more that can be achieved to help other children who are suffering from similar illnesses.

More details on the Teenage Cancer Trust can be found at
www.teenagecancertrust.org

CAREER RECORD

Compiled by Mark Baber of the
Association of Football Statisticians up to 01/07/2006

PERSONAL SUMMARY

Full name: Frank James Lampard
Place and Date of Birth: Romford, 20/06/1978
Position: Midfielder
Height: 6ft 0in/183cm
Weight: 12st 6lb/79kg
Fiancee: Elen Rivas
Daughter: Luna Coco Patricia (born 23/08/2005)

Frank is the nephew of Portsmouth manager Harry Redknapp and cousin of former England international Jamie Redknapp.

EARLY CAREER

- Frank is one of the few current British footballers to have been educated at a private school. He attended the independent Brentwood School in Essex.
- His football career began at West Ham United at a time when his father was the assistant manager and uncle Harry

was the manager. He became a trainee at Upton Park in July 1994 before signing his first professional contract on 1 July 1995.

- The captain of a Hammers team that won their championship and reached the FA Youth Cup Final in 1996, it was at Swansea City in the Second Division of the Football League where Frank gained his first experience of senior football. He enjoyed a nine-game month's loan spell with the Swans in October 1995.

- Frank returned to West Ham to make his Premiership debut on 31 January 1996 when he came on as a substitute for John Moncur in a 3–2 win against Coventry City at Upton Park. He also came off the bench for the final game of the season against Sheffield Wednesday.

- A month earlier, Frank made his debut for the England Under-18 team against Scotland and retained his place in the squad for the UEFA Under-18 championships held in France in July 1996.

- England finished the tournament in third place and Frank played in all four games alongside the likes of Rio Ferdinand, Emile Heskey and Michael Owen who were later to become team-mates in England's senior international squad.

NOTABLE MOMENTS

20 June 1978	Born in Romford. Father is Frank Snr – a former West Ham United and England footballer.
14 September 1993	Makes his debut in youth football for West Ham United, against Cambridge United.
24 October 1994	Makes his debut in reserve team foot-

ball for West Ham United, at Queens Park Rangers.

7 October 1995 — Makes his debut in senior football on loan at Swansea City, versus Bradford City.

31 October 1995 — Scores his first senior goal for Swansea City, in a 2–0 win at Brighton & Hove Albion.

31 January 1996 — Makes his debut for West Ham United, as a sub against Coventry City.

23 April 1996 — On St George's Day, makes his debut for England Under-18, versus Scotland.

31 July 1996 — On the 30th anniversary of England's World Cup Final win, plays in the 3rd/4th Play-Off Final as England beat Belguim in the UEFA Under-18 Championship.

17 August 1996 — Makes his full debut for West Ham United, at Arsenal.

9 August 1997 — Scores his first goal for West Ham United, at Barnsley.

13 November 1997 — Makes his debut for England Under-21, in Greece.

19 November 1997 — Scores his first senior hat-trick, against Walsall in the Coca-Cola League Cup.

3 January 1998 — Scores his first goal in the FA Cup, against Emley.

4 September 1998 — Scores his first goal for England Under-21 against Sweden.

8 May 1999 — Makes his 100th appearance for West Ham United.

17 July 1999	Plays his first game in European competition, an InterToto Cup game against FC Jokerit.
24 August 1999	West Ham United win InterToto Cup beating Metz in the Final.
16 September 1999	Scores on his UEFA Cup debut, against Osijek.
10 October 1999	Makes his full international debut for England, against Belgium at Sunderland.
6 December 1999	Makes his 100th Premiership appearance.
1 June 2000	Makes his final appearance for England Under-21, against Slovakia.
16 April 2001	Scores his 37th and last goal for West Ham United, at Newcastle United.
21 April 2001	Makes his 187th and final appearance for West Ham United.
3 July 2001	Joins Chelsea for a fee of £11 million.
26 July 2001	Makes debut for Chelsea, in a pre-season friendly at Leyton Orient.
19 August 2001	Makes competitive debut for Chelsea, against Newcastle United in the Premiership.
16 September 2001	Sent-off for the first time in his career (against Tottenham Hotspur).
20 September 2001	Makes European debut and scores for Chelsea, in UEFA Cup against Levski Sofia.
23 December 2001	Scores first Premiership goal for Chelsea, versus Bolton Wanderers.
4 May 2002	Plays in FA Cup Final, against Arsenal.

11 June 2003	Plays first game for England in a competitive match – a Euro 2004 qualifier.
13 August 2003	Makes Champions League debut, for Chelsea at MSK Zilinia.
20 August 2003	Scores first goal for England, against Croatia at Middlesbrough.
22 October 2003	Scores first goal in the Champions League, for Chelsea against Lazio.
April 2004	Chelsea reach Champions League semi-final.
June 2004	Scores three of the goals as England reach quarter-finals of Euro 2004 Championships.
July 2004	Named Chelsea vice-captain as Jose Mourinho becomes manager at Stamford Bridge.
December 2004	Voted England Player of the Year.
27 February 2005	Chelsea win Carling Cup Final against Liverpool.
April 2005	Chelsea reach Champions League semi-final.
30 April 2005	Scores both the goals as Chelsea clinch Premiership title and are champions of England for the first time in 50 years with a 2–0 win at Bolton Wanderers.
June 2005	Voted Footballer of the Year by the Football Writers' Association.
November 2005	Voted runner-up to Ronaldinho as European Footballer of the Year by France Football.

26 November 2005	Makes his 160th consecutive Premiership appearance – a new competition record.
December 2005	Voted runner-up to Ronaldinho as FIFA Player of the Year.
April 2006	Chelsea reach FA Cup semi-final.
19 April 2006	Chelsea retain Premiership crown with 3–0 win against Manchester United at Stamford Bridge.
June 2006	Member of England World Cup squad in Germany.

CAREER BREAKDOWN

Totals by Competition

Competition	Starts	On as Sub	Goals	Yellows	Reds
Premiership	314	20	73	28	1
FA Cup	33	4	7	3	
Champions League	33	1	10	4	
Football League Cup	25	6	10	2	
UEFA Cup	8	1	3		
Division 2	8	1	1		
Intertoto Cup	6		3	1	
World Cup	8		2		
Auto Windscreens Shield	1	1			
FA Community Shield	1			1	

HONOURS
Individual
Barclaycard Player of the Month for September 2003.
PFA Supporters' Player of the Month for October 2003.
Chelsea Supporters' Player of the Season for 2003–04.
England Supporters' Player of the Year for 2004.
PFA Supporters' Player of Year for 2005.
Football Writer's Association Footballer of the Year for 2005.
Barclays Premiership Player of the Month for April 2005.
Barclays Premiership Player of the Season for 2004–05.
Chelsea Supporters' Player of the Season for 2004–05.
Selected for FIFPro World XI for 2005.
PFA Supporters' Player of the Month for October 2005
Barclays Award for first player to score ten Premiership goals in season 2005–06.
Barclays Special Merit Award in November 2005 for breaking consecutive Premiership appearances record.
Runner-up in 2005 European Footballer of the Year awards.
Runner up in 2005 FIFA World Player of the Year awards.
England Supporters' Player of the Year for 2005.

Club Honours
WITH WEST HAM UNITED:
InterToto Cup winners in 1999.

WITH CHELSEA:
FA Premier Asia Cup winners in 2003.
Football League Cup winners in 2005.
FA Premiership champions in 2004–05.
FA Community Shield winners in 2005.
FA Premiership champions in 2005–06.

SEASON-BE-SEASON BREAKDOWN

Season	Competition	Club	Starting Apps
1995-96	Premiership	West Ham United	
1995-96	Division 2	Swansea City	8
1995-96	Auto Windscreens Shield	Swansea City	1
1996-97	Coca-Cola League Cup	West Ham United	1
1996-97	FA Cup	West Ham United	1
1996-97	Premiership	West Ham United	3
1997-98	Premiership	West Ham United	27
1997-98	Coca-Cola League Cup	West Ham United	5
1997-98	FA Cup	West Ham United	6
1998-99	Premiership	West Ham United	38
1998-99	Worthington Cup	West Ham United	2
1998-99	FA Cup	West Ham United	1
1999-00	Premiership	West Ham United	34
1999-00	UEFA Cup	West Ham United	3
1999-00	FA Cup	West Ham United	1
1999-00	Intertoto Cup	West Ham United	6
1999-00	Worthington Cup	West Ham United	3
2000-01	Premiership	West Ham United	30
2000-01	Worthington Cup	West Ham United	3
2000-01	FA Cup	West Ham United	4
2001-02	UEFA Cup	Chelsea	4
2001-02	Premiership	Chelsea	34
2001-02	FA Cup	Chelsea	7
2001-02	Worthington Cup	Chelsea	4
2002-03	Worthington Cup	Chelsea	3
2002-03	UEFA Cup	Chelsea	1
2002-03	Premiership	Chelsea	37
2002-03	FA Cup	Chelsea	5
2003-04	Premiership	Chelsea	38
2003-04	Champions League	Chelsea	13
2003-04	Carling Cup	Chelsea	1
2003-04	FA Cup	Chelsea	4
2004-05	Premiership	Chelsea	38
2004-05	FA Cup	Chelsea	
2004-05	Champions League	Chelsea	12
2004-05	Carling Cup	Chelsea	3
2005-06	Champions League	Chelsea	8
2005-06	Premiership	Chelsea	35
2005-06	Carling Cup	Chelsea	
2005-06	FA Community Shield	Chelsea	1
2005-06	FA Cup	Chelsea	4
TOTAL			**438**

On as Sub	Goals	Yellow	Red
2			
1	1		
1			
1			
10		1	
4	4		
	4		
	1	1	
	5	3	
	1		
	7	4	
	1		
	3	1	
	2	1	
	7	3	
	1		
	1		
	1		
3	5	1	1
1	1	2	
1	1		
1	6	3	
	1		
	10	3	
1	4	1	
1			
	1		
	13	6	
2			
	4	1	
3	2	1	
	2	2	
	16	4	
1			
		1	
1	2		
34	110	39	1

NOTE Frank also played for West Ham United in a Worthington Cup tie against Aston Villa on 15 December 1999. However, due to West Ham fielding an ineligible player, the Football League ordered the tie to be replayed and the original result was expunged from the record.

CLUB GOALS

SWANSEA CITY

Date	Competition	Round
31/10/1995	Division 2	

Total Goals for Swansea: 1

WEST HAM UNITED

09/08/1997	Premiership	
15/10/1997	Coca-Cola League Cup	3rd Round
19/11/1997	Coca-Cola League Cup	4th Round
19/11/1997	Coca-Cola League Cup	4th Round
19/11/1997	Coca-Cola League Cup	4th Round
23/11/1997	Premiership	
03/01/1998	FA Cup	3rd Round
10/01/1998	Premiership	
10/05/1998	Premiership	
22/09/1998	Worthington Cup	2nd Round 2nd Leg
14/11/1998	Premiership	
10/01/1999	Premiership	
13/02/1999	Premiership	
20/02/1999	Premiership	
16/05/1999	Premiership	
24/07/1999	Intertoto Cup	3rd Round 2nd Leg
28/07/1999	Intertoto Cup	Semi Final 1st Leg
07/08/1999	Premiership	
24/08/1999	Intertoto Cup	Final 2nd Leg
16/09/1999	UEFA Cup	1st Round 1st Leg
13/10/1999	Worthington Cup	3rd Round
21/11/1999	Premiership	
26/12/1999	Premiership	
03/01/2000	Premiership	
11/01/2000	Worthington Cup	Quarter Final
05/02/2000	Premiership	
12/02/2000	Premiership	
11/03/2000	Premiership	
23/09/2000	Premiership	
29/11/2000	Worthington Cup	4th Round
26/12/2000	Premiership	
06/01/2001	FA Cup	3rd Round
24/02/2001	Premiership	
24/02/2001	Premiership	
07/04/2001	Premiership	
14/04/2001	Premiership	
16/04/2001	Premiership	

TOTAL Goals for West Ham United: 37

Home Team	Away Team	Time	Pen
Brighton and Hove Albion	Swansea City	57	
Barnsley	West Ham United	76	
West Ham United	Aston Villa	17	
West Ham United	Walsall	15	
West Ham United	Walsall	73	
West Ham United	Walsall	74	
Leeds United	West Ham United	65	
West Ham United	Emley	4	
West Ham United	Barnsley	5	
West Ham United	Leicester City	15	
West Ham United	Northampton Town	90	
West Ham United	Leicester City	76	
Manchester United	West Ham United	89	
West Ham United	Nottingham Forest	39	
Liverpool	West Ham United	24	pen
West Ham United	Middlesbrough	4	
FC Jokerit	West Ham United	70	
West Ham United	Heerenveen	7	
West Ham United	Tottenham Hotspur	45	
Metz	West Ham United	43	
West Ham United	NK Osijek	58	
West Ham United	AFC Bournemouth	77	
West Ham United	Sheffield Wednesday	76	
Wimbledon	West Ham United	81	
Newcastle United	West Ham United	84	
West Ham United	Aston Villa	47	
Southampton	West Ham United	65	
West Ham United	Bradford City	83	
Sheffield Wednesday	West Ham United	10	
Coventry City	West Ham United	69	
West Ham United	Sheffield Wednesday	72	
West Ham United	Charlton Athletic	45	
Walsall	West Ham United	6	
Bradford City	West Ham United	18	
Bradford City	West Ham United	75	
Aston Villa	West Ham United	87	
West Ham United	Derby County	7	
Newcastle United	West Ham United	80	pen

CHELSEA

Date	Competition	Round
20/09/2001	UEFA Cup	1st Round 1st Leg
23/12/2001	Premiership	
26/12/2001	Premiership	
16/01/2002	FA Cup	3rd Round Replay
09/02/2002	Premiership	
02/03/2002	Premiership	
13/03/2002	Premiership	
17/08/2002	Premiership	
28/08/2002	Premiership	
03/10/2002	UEFA Cup	1st Round 2nd Leg
21/12/2002	Premiership	
28/01/2003	Premiership	
01/03/2003	Premiership	
08/03/2003	FA Cup	Quarter Final
22/03/2003	Premiership	
13/09/2003	Premiership	
20/09/2003	Premiership	
22/10/2003	Champions League	Group G
04/11/2003	Champions League	Group G
09/11/2003	Premiership	
30/11/2003	Premiership	
28/12/2003	Premiership	
03/01/2004	FA Cup	3rd Round
01/02/2004	Premiership	
01/02/2004	Premiership	
27/03/2004	Premiership	
06/04/2004	Champions League	Quarter Final 2nd Leg
01/05/2004	Premiership	
01/05/2004	Premiership	
05/05/2004	Champions League	Semi Final 2nd Leg
28/08/2004	Premiership	
30/10/2004	Premiership	
13/11/2004	Premiership	
30/11/2004	Carling Cup	5th Round
04/12/2004	Premiership	
18/12/2004	Premiership	

Home Team	Away Team	Time	Pen
Chelsea	Levski Sofia	90	
Chelsea	Bolton Wanderers	87	
Arsenal	Chelsea	31	
Chelsea	Norwich City	56	
Aston Villa	Chelsea	64	
Charlton Athletic	Chelsea	85	
Chelsea	Tottenham Hotspur	90	
Charlton Athletic	Chelsea	89	
Southampton	Chelsea	80	
Viking Stavanger	Chelsea	45	
Chelsea	Aston Villa	57	
Chelsea	Leeds United	80	
Newcastle United	Chelsea	37	
Arsenal	Chelsea	84	
Chelsea	Manchester City	69	
Chelsea	Tottenham Hotspur	35	
Wolverhampton Wanderers	Chelsea	17	
Chelsea	Lazio	57	
Lazio	Chelsea	80	
Chelsea	Newcastle United	42	pen
Chelsea	Manchester United	30	pen
Chelsea	Portsmouth	73	
Watford	Chelsea	41	
Blackburn Rovers	Chelsea	25	
Blackburn Rovers	Chelsea	35	
Chelsea	Wolverhampton Wanderers	70	
Arsenal	Chelsea	51	
Chelsea	Southampton	75	
Chelsea	Southampton	83	
Chelsea	AS Monaco	44	
Chelsea	Southampton	41	pen
West Bromwich Albion	Chelsea	81	
Fulham	Chelsea	33	
Fulham	Chelsea	88	
Chelsea	Newcastle United	63	
Chelsea	Norwich City	34	

CHELSEA cont'd

Date	Competition	Round
15/01/2005	Premiership	
15/01/2005	Premiership	
26/01/2005	Carling Cup	Semi Final 2nd Leg
08/03/2005	Champions League	Round Of 16 2nd Leg
19/03/2005	Premiership	
02/04/2005	Premiership	
06/04/2005	Champions League	Quarter Final 1st Leg
06/04/2005	Champions League	Quarter Final 1st Leg
12/04/2005	Champions League	Quarter Final 2nd Leg
23/04/2005	Premiership	
30/04/2005	Premiership	
30/04/2005	Premiership	
15/05/2005	Premiership	
24/08/2005	Premiership	
24/08/2005	Premiership	
13/09/2005	Champions League	Group G
24/09/2005	Premiership	
24/09/2005	Premiership	
02/10/2005	Premiership	
15/10/2005	Premiership	
15/10/2005	Premiership	
23/10/2005	Premiership	
29/10/2005	Premiership	
29/10/2005	Premiership	
26/11/2005	Premiership	
26/12/2005	Premiership	
02/01/2006	Premiership	
28/01/2006	FA Cup	4th Round
08/02/2006	FA Cup	4th Round Replay
25/02/2006	Premiership	
07/03/2006	Champions League	Round Of 16 2nd Leg
15/04/2006	Premiership	
17/04/2006	Premiership	

TOTAL Goals for Chelsea: 69

Tottenham Hotspur	Chelsea	39	pen
Tottenham Hotspur	Chelsea	90	
Manchester United	Chelsea	29	
Chelsea	Barcelona	17	
Chelsea	Crystal Palace	29	
Southampton	Chelsea	22	
Chelsea	Bayern München	60	
Chelsea	Bayern München	70	
Bayern München	Chelsea	30	
Chelsea	Fulham	64	
Bolton Wanderers	Chelsea	60	
Bolton Wanderers	Chelsea	76	
Newcastle United	Chelsea	35	pen
Chelsea	West Bromwich Albion	23	
Chelsea	West Bromwich Albion	80	
Chelsea	Anderlecht	19	
Chelsea	Aston Villa	45	
Chelsea	Aston Villa	75	pen
Liverpool	Chelsea	26	pen
Chelsea	Bolton Wanderers	55	
Chelsea	Bolton Wanderers	59	
Everton	Chelsea	50	
Chelsea	Blackburn Rovers	14	pen
Chelsea	Blackburn Rovers	62	
Portsmouth	Chelsea	67	pen
Chelsea	Fulham	24	
West Ham United	Chelsea	25	
Everton	Chelsea	73	
Chelsea	Everton	36	pen
Chelsea	Portsmouth	65	
Barcelona	Chelsea	90	pen
Bolton Wanderers	Chelsea	59	
Chelsea	Everton	28	

PREMIERSHIP APPEARANCES AND GOALS

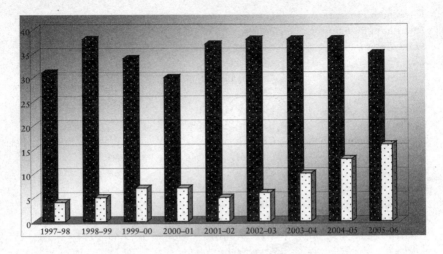

Season	Apps	Goals	Team
1997–98	31	4	West Ham United
1998–99	38	5	West Ham United
1999–00	34	7	West Ham United
2000–01	30	7	West Ham United
2001–02	37	5	Chelsea
2002–03	38	6	Chelsea
2003–04	38	10	Chelsea
2004–05	38	13	Chelsea
2005–06	35	16	Chelsea

CHELSEA PREMIERSHIP SCORERS 2003–04

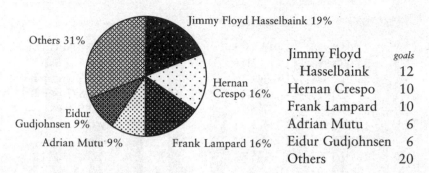

	goals
Jimmy Floyd Hasselbaink	12
Hernan Crespo	10
Frank Lampard	10
Adrian Mutu	6
Eidur Gudjohnsen	6
Others	20

CHELSEA PREMIERSHIP SCORERS 2004–05

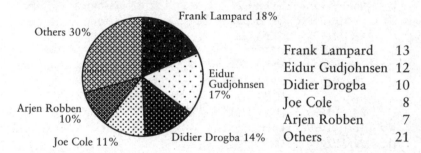

Frank Lampard	13
Eidur Gudjohnsen	12
Didier Drogba	10
Joe Cole	8
Arjen Robben	7
Others	21

CHELSEA PREMIERSHIP SCORERS 2005–06

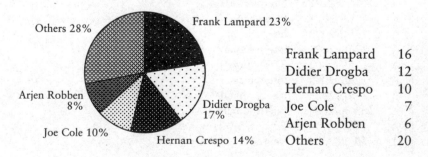

Frank Lampard	16
Didier Drogba	12
Hernan Crespo	10
Joe Cole	7
Arjen Robben	6
Others	20

FULL ENGLAND PLAYING RECORD

Cat	Date	Competition	Round
Y	23/04/1996	UEFA U18	2nd Round Group 6
Y	23/07/1996	UEFA U18	FINALS Group B
Y	25/07/1996	UEFA U18	FINALS Group B
Y	27/07/1996	UEFA U18	FINALS Group B
Y	31/07/1996	UEFA U18	FINALS 3-4
U	13/11/1997	UEFA U21	Play Off
U	17/12/1997	UEFA U21	Group
B	10/02/1998	B INTER	
U	24/03/1998	U21	
U	14/05/1998	TOULON U21	Group A
U	16/05/1998	TOULON U21	Group A
U	18/05/1998	TOULON U21	Group A
U	04/09/1998	UEFA U21	Group 5
U	09/10/1998	UEFA U21	Group 5
U	13/10/1998	UEFA U21	Group 5
U	17/11/1998	U21	
U	09/02/1999	U21	
U	26/03/1999	UEFA U21	Group 5
U	04/06/1999	UEFA U21	Group 5
U	03/09/1999	UEFA U21	Group 5
A	10/10/1999	International	
U	22/02/2000	U21	
U	29/03/2000	UEFA U21	Play offs 1st Leg
U	27/05/2000	UEFA U21	Final Round Group B
U	29/05/2000	UEFA U21	Final Round Group B
U	01/06/2000	UEFA U21	Final Round Group B
A	28/02/2001	International	
A	15/08/2001	International	
A	10/11/2001	International	
A	13/02/2002	International	
A	27/03/2002	International	
A	17/04/2002	International	
A	12/02/2003	International	
A	22/05/2003	International	
A	03/06/2003	International	
A	11/06/2003	European Championship	Group 7
A	20/08/2003	International	

Home Team	Away Team	Home Score	Away Score	Pens	Goal Times
England	Scotland	3	0		
England	Spain	0	0		
Italy	England	1	1		
England	Republic of Ireland	1	0		
England	Belgium	3	2		
Greece	England	2	0		
England	Greece	4	2		
England	Chile	1	2		
Switzerland	England	2	0		
France	England	1	1		
England	South Africa	3	1		37
Argentina	England	2	0		
Sweden	England	0	2		86
England	Bulgaria	1	0		62
Luxembourg	England	0	5		50
England	Czech Republic	0	1		
England	France	2	1		
England	Poland	5	0		54,59
England	Sweden	3	0		
England	Luxembourg	5	0		80
England	Belgium	2	1		
England	Argentina	1	0		
England	Yugoslavia	3	0		49
England	Italy	0	2		
England	Turkey	6	0		28
England	Slovakia	0	2		
England	Spain	3	0		
England	Holland	0	2		
England	Sweden	1	1		
Holland	England	1	1		
England	Italy	1	2		
England	Paraguay	4	0		
England	Australia	1	3		
South Africa	England	1	2		
England	Serbia and Montenegro	2	1		
England	Slovakia	2	1		
England	Croatia	3	1		80

FULL ENGLAND PLAYING RECORD contd

Cat	Date	Competition	Round
A	06/09/2003	European Championship	Group 7
A	10/09/2003	European Championship	Group 7
A	11/10/2003	European Championship	Group 7
A	16/11/2003	International	
A	18/02/2004	International	
A	01/06/2004	SUMMER TOURNAMENT	
A	05/06/2004	SUMMER TOURNAMENT	
A	13/06/2004	European Championship	FINALS Group B
A	17/06/2004	European Championship	FINALS Group B
A	21/06/2004	European Championship	FINALS Group B
A	24/06/2004	European Championship	Quarter Final
A	18/08/2004	International	
A	04/09/2004	World Cup	EUROPE Group 6
A	08/09/2004	World Cup	EUROPE Group 6
A	09/10/2004	World Cup	EUROPE Group 6
A	13/10/2004	World Cup	EUROPE Group 6
A	17/11/2004	International	
A	10/02/2005	International	
A	26/03/2005	World Cup	EUROPE Group 6
A	30/03/2005	World Cup	EUROPE Group 6
A	17/08/2005	International	
A	03/09/2005	World Cup	EUROPE
A	07/09/2005	World Cup	EUROPE
A	08/10/2005	World Cup	EUROPE
A	12/10/2005	World Cup	EUROPE
A	12/11/2005	International	
A	30/05/2006	International	
A	03/06/2006	International	
A	10/06/2006	World Cup	FINALS Group B
A	15/06/2006	World Cup	FINALS Group B
A	20/06/2006	World Cup	FINALS Group B
A	25/06/2006	World Cup	Round-of-16
A	01/07/2006	World Cup	Quarter-Final

TOTAL Number of England Goals as a full international: 11
TOTAL Number of England Caps: 45
England goal average: 1 goal every 4.1 games

Home Team	Away Team	Home Score	Away Score	Pens	Goal Times
FYR Macedonia	England	0	0		
England	Liechtenstein	2	0		
Turkey	England	0	0		
England	Denmark	2	3		
Portugal	England	1	1		
England	Japan	1	1		
England	Iceland	6	1		25
France	England	1	2		38
England	Switzerland	3	0		
Croatia	England	2	4		79
Portugal	England	2	2	(6–5)	115
England	Ukraine	3	0		
Austria	England	1	2		24
Poland	England	1	2		
England	Wales	2	0		4
Azerbaijan	England	0	1		
Spain	England	1	0		
England	Holland	0	0		
England	Northern Ireland	4	0		62
England	Azerbaijan	2	0		
Denmark	England	4	1		
Wales	England	0	1		
Northern Ireland	England	1	0		
England	Austria	1	0		24
England	Poland	2	1		81
Argentina	England	2	3		
England	Hungary	3	1		
England	Jamaica	6	0		11
England	Paraguay	1	0		
England	Trinidad and Tobago	2	0		
England	Sweden	2	2		
England	Ecuador	1	0		
England	Portugal	0	0	(3–1)	

INDEX

INDEX

INDEX

LIST OF ILLUSTRATIONS

463

Eidur cracks a joke (inset)
Reuters / Corbis

Page 13
Scoring opening goal against France
Mirrorpix / Ormesher Bradley

Extra-time equaliser
Empics / Mike Egerton

Saluting the fans
Rex Features / Jed Leicester

Page 14
Scoring against Barcelona
Rex Features / Olly Greenwood

JT spraying champagne
Empics / Mike Egerton

Page 15
Me and my mentor
Action Images / Reuters / Dylan
Martinez

Winning the league celebration
Rex Features / Darren Walsh

Premiership trophy
Rex Features / Darren Walsh

Page 16
Modelling shoot
Muir Vidler / Corbis Outline

Page 20
Scoring against Poland
Getty Images / Ross Kinnaird

Leaving a nightclub
Rex Features / Steve Dutton

On the training ground with
England
PA / Empics / Nick Potts

Page 21
Come on the Chels!!
Action Images / Reuters / Dylan
Martinez

Scoring at Upton Park
AFP / Getty Images / Adrian Dennis

Exchanging shirts
Getty Images / Phil Cole

Page 22
Celebrating with Luna
Action Images / Reuters / Daniel
Munoz

The 'Romario goal' celebration
Empics / Chelsea FC / Darren Walsh

The trophy parade
Empics / Chelsea FC / Darren Walsh

Page 23
Warming up with Rio
Action Images / Michael Regan
Livepic

Trinidad and Tobago 2006
AFP / Getty Images / Adrian Dennis

Breaking from midfield
Action Images / Tony O'Brien

Page 24
Shooting against Portugal in the
quarter-final
Action Images / Reuters / Shaun Best

Ricardo saves penalty
PA / Empics / Martin Rickett

With Mr Eriksson
Action Images / Reuters / Kai
Pfaffenbach

All other photographs supplied
courtesy of Frank Lampard.